Food in the
American Military

Food in the American Military

A History

JOHN C. FISHER *and*
CAROL FISHER

McFarland & Company, Inc., Publishers
Jefferson, North Carolina, and London

Photographs not otherwise credited are by the authors.

Library of Congress Cataloguing-in-Publication Data

Fisher, John C., 1949–
    Food in the American military : a history / John C. Fisher and
Carol Fisher.
        p.   cm.
    Includes bibliographical references and index.

    ISBN 978-0-7864-3417-6
    softcover : 50# alkaline paper ∞

    1. Operational rations (Military supplies)— United States— History.
2. Cooking for military personnel — United States— History.
I. Fisher, Carol, 1947–   II. Title.
UC713.F57   2011
355.8 — dc22   2010042004

British Library cataloguing data are available

Front cover images © 2011 Photos.com

Manufactured in the United States of America

*McFarland & Company, Inc., Publishers
    Box 611, Jefferson, North Carolina 28640
    www.mcfarlandpub.com*

To all who have served in the
American military

Acknowledgments

The undertaking of writing this book has been a journey, often times into unfamiliar territory as we explored obscure volumes and mined fragile manuscripts for the nuggets of information they held. When a traveler ventures into new environs, a competent guide is needed. We are indebted to many for their assistance in locating material, providing direction for our research, and making helpful suggestions. We also appreciate the understanding of friends and family from whom we have had to decline dinner invitations and other social engagements to devote more time to the completion of the project. Research involves travel and we are indebted to the Culinary Trust for the Linda D. Russo Travel Grant which made the travel necessary for the project less financially burdensome.

At the risk of unintentionally omitting some, we want to specifically mention the individuals and institutions that have been particularly helpful in our research. Luther Hanson, Curator of the U.S. Army Quartermaster Museum; Michael Crawford and Charles Brodine, historians at the Naval Historical Center; staffs of the library and the photographic section at the Naval Historical Center; the Marine Corps Historical Center staff; Stephen Allie, director of the Frontier Army Museum; Fort Scott National Historical Site rangers and staff; Jonathan Casey, archivist at the National World War One Museum; Charles Machon, historian at the Museum for Missouri Military History; Jan Longone, Phil Zaret, and staff members at the Clements Library, University of Michigan; David Moore and the staff at the Western Historical Manuscript Collection — Columbia, University of Missouri; South Carolina State Museum; University of Iowa Archives; Edward Ayres, historian at the Yorktown Victory Center; Stars and Stripes Museum; Greg Sitz, Greg Zonner, Joe Mathis, and Carl Skoglund at the Arkansas Inland Marine Museum; Dunklin County Library staff members especially Jonell Menton, Kathy Richardson, Norma Monroe, and Jewel Wayne DeVault; and finally military history authors Harry Spiller and Dennis Ringle. Some of our best insights were gleaned through formal interviews and casual conservations with numerous veterans and current service members. Those who have been especially helpful include Elmo (Mo) Baker, Maurice Barksdale, Bob Carter, Rick Carver, Frank Chambers, Everett Farmer, Ron Forbus, Paul Galanti, Michael Marmon, Bill Monroe, Mike Mowrer, Ray Nabors, Bill Orr, and First Sergeant Jeffery Johnson, 101st Airborne Division.

Table of Contents

Introduction

In this work we explore from the culinary and cookbook history perspective how America has fed its military. Previous journeys into cookbook history research exposed us to some early Army and Navy cooking manuals thus arousing our interest in the subject. Food is an intriguing topic — how is it obtained, how should it be prepared, and how can it be preserved? These questions have plagued humankind for as long as the earth has been populated. Food has been no less a challenging issue for the military. From Napoleon's revelation that "an army marches on its stomach" to Sanderson's recognition that "beans kill more than bullets" to Natick's goal of providing "warfighter recommended, warfighter tested, warfighter approved" food, military establishments have tried to keep their members well fed. Throughout America's history, feeding her military has presented at times a Herculean task for those responsible for this effort. The element of distance of transportation coupled with numbers has challenged the military feeding effort. Additionally, the food offered soldiers and sailors could be no better than the preservation and packaging technology at any given time.

American military food programs have progressed from simple campfire cooking to today's nutritionally sound, menu diverse, high tech, and ethnically correct feeding options. The company mess and ship's galley where nearly every item served was boiled have evolved into dining facilities and mess decks resembling food courts featuring multiple buffet lines. Lightweight MRE packages with flameless heaters have replaced the cold can of C ration corned beef hash for operational rations. First person food accounts harvested from diaries, letters, journals, and personal interviews yield insights into soldier, marine, airman, and sailor efforts to supplement the prescribed ration whenever possible and reveal the unchanging joy military personnel find in receiving the package from home.

Men and women entering military service today come with much higher food expectations than those in previous generations. Food is a morale builder in all of our lives but even to a greater extent in the military where long tours of duty take service members away from families, often placing them in dangerous situations. Because this is well understood by military leaders, the Department of Defense carries out extensive research to develop high quality food, but one of the highest priorities of this research is to offer foods that are well accepted by soldiers, sailors, and airmen.

1

Meals for the Revolutionary War

The flour was laid up on a flat rock and mixed up with cold water, then daubed upon a flat stone and scorched on one side, while the beef was broiling on a stick in the fire. That was the common way of cookery when on marches.
— Joseph Plumb Martin, Revolutionary War soldier

As the colonies moved toward their independence, on June 15, 1775, the Continental Congress resolved "that a General be appointed to command all the continental forces, raised, or to be raised, for the defence of American liberty."[1] A unanimous vote determined George Washington the choice for commander in chief of the army. On the following day, discussing plans for the army, members of the Congress ordered that "there be one commissary general of stores and provisions and one quarter master general for the grand army, and a deputy, under him, for the separate army."[2] A committee appointed to draft instructions to Washington delivered several requests in their report on June 20, one of which dealt with supplying the army with food. "You are to victual at the continental expence all such volunteers as have joined or shall join the united Army."[3]

The Journal of the Continental Congress reveals plans by the Congress to investigate the best way to provision the army in an action taken on September 21, 1775. "Resolved: That a committee of five be appointed to take into consideration the memorial of the Commissary general [Joseph Trumbull], and report their opinion on the best means of supplying the army with provisions." A note follows explaining that this action seems to have been taken relating to a letter from Washington dated September 7, 1775, which included an (unsigned) proposal by Trumbull.[4]

The first Ration of Provisions for the Army recorded in the Journal of the Continental Congress dated November 4, 1775, follows.

Resolved, That a ration consist of the following kind and quantity of provisions, viz;
1 lb. of beef, or ¾ lb. pork, or 1 lb. salt fish, per day.
1 lb. of bread or flour per day.
3 pints of pease, or beans per week, or vegetables equivalent, at one dollar per bushel for pease or beans.

1 pint of milk per man per day, or at the rate of 1/72 of a dollar.
1 half pint of Rice, or 1 pint of Indian meal per man per week.
1 quart of spruce beer or cider per man per day, or nine gallons of Molasses per company of 100 men per week.
3 lb. candles to 100 Men per week for guards.
24 lb. of soft or 8 lb. of hard soap for 100 men per week.[5]

Throughout the course of the war, Congress initiated and experimented with a variety of methods to administer the task of providing food for the army. A history of rations prepared by the Quartermaster School for the Quartermaster General in January 1949 details methods that were used to procure provisions during the Revolutionary War.

Under the first method, the commissary system, "The Commissary General appointed as his deputies and assistants successful merchants who were experienced in purchasing. These purchasing agents bought, stored, and transported food supplies and placed it finally in the hands of the Regimental Quartermaster, or any person who had been appointed to receive the rations."[6] A second method depended on the states to deliver specific food supplies to certain locations for the army. "In the spring of 1778, the Continental Army was 26,000 strong. The problems of feeding the troops became more and more difficult. The Commissary General, Joseph Trumbull, realizing the shortcomings of the supply system [commissary method], tried an entirely different method of providing food. He requisitioned provisions from each state, asking the state to appoint its own purchasing agent, who in turn would buy, store, and deliver certain quantities of food supplies at specified times." Regarding the success of this program, "This method proved to be even less effective, since transportation means were not always available at the right time."[7]

Congress made a decision in 1780 to try a third plan, one that used contracts for food procurement. "Under this system, a contract stated the price of the ration; the component parts were defined as to quantity and kind. The ration was to be delivered by the contractor, to the individual soldier, for the price fixed in the agreement. It proved that this method was better than the previous system for food procurement, but it was found not too reliable."[8] Special commissioners also worked to bring in food supplies. "The commanding officers of the various military installations were permitted to appoint certain special commissioners with responsibility to go and look for food supplies. They were able to pay for these provisions with money furnished by the United States Treasury, or with drafts or abstracts from the War Department."[9]

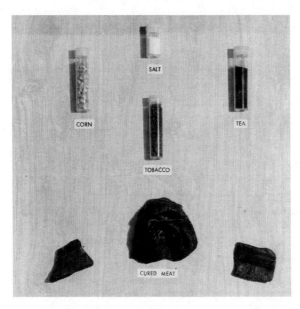

The army ration at the beginning of the Revolutionary War. Photograph courtesy Quartermaster Museum, Fort Lee, Virginia.

Also, the sutler system became a part of the provisioning process. Sutlers were to offer "so-called luxuries" for soldiers. "Vegetables, chocolate, coffee, and tobacco, except those supplied at hospital stores, were brought into camp by the sutlers." As well, "Usually, the sale of liquor to privates and to musicians was restricted, but these restrictions were seldom observed. While many sutlers must have taken advantage of the soldiers, they probably lost heavily when soldiers failed to pay their debts."[10] William Matthews and Dixon Wecter note problems with pricing by sutlers. "The sutlers were making such exorbitant profits that Washington was forced to fix their prices: peach brandy 7s. 6d. per quart, whisky and apple brandy 6 s., cider 1s.3d., strong beer 2s.6d., common beer 1 s., vinegar 2s.6d." They believe soldiers had little money to spend at the suttlers and at markets set up in the camp.[11]

Revolutionary War Rations

Although the paper version of the ration allowance does show some variety, not all items on the list found their way to the soldiers on a regular basis with some being delivered infrequently. Army historian Erna Risch believes "the Revolutionary soldier was largely subsisted on a bread and meat diet, and the Commissary Department was, for the most part, judged successful in its operations if it provided a sufficient quantity of flour and beef." She also points out that depending upon what was available, sometimes the rations issued varied from time to time.[12]

Two such examples occurred in July 1776 and in August 1780. Taking advantage of the summer gardening season, Washington offered a modification of the ration allowance ordering that "the Quarter Master of such Regiment requesting more vegetables be allowed to draw one quarter part of the usual Rations in Money to be laid out in Vegetables for his Regiment."[13] A second example occurred when Washington was concerned that because additional flour was being issued, "on account of failure of meat," the flour might run low.[14]

Without the conveniences of modern refrigeration, one might wonder how fresh beef could have been considered a viable option on the Revolutionary War ration list and furthermore, how it could be delivered to soldiers. The solution? Drive beef with the army and butcher on demand. When the army was in winter quarters and on the march, cattle were driven to them. Captain Simeon Thayer, who participated in the Quebec expedition early in the war, records an event when soldiers received much needed rations with the delivery of beef on the hoof while they were marching.

> We pushed on ... and after marching 2 Days and two nights without the least nourishment ... discover'd about 12 o'clock the 3rd Day some men and horses and cattle making towards us, at which sight Capt. Topham and myself shed tears of joy, in our happy delivery from the grasping hand of Death. The Driver was sent towards us by Col. Arnold, in order to kill them for our support.[15]

Providing fresh beef for 17,000 to 20,000 plus soldiers during the course of the war certainly brought with it a variety of challenges. First, cattle had to be located and purchased in quantities sufficient to meet ration requirements. Epaphroditus Champion reflects on his experiences as a deputy commissary of fresh provisions under his father, Col. Henry Champion, the chief purchasing agent for the Continental Army. His job was "to receive, provide for, and safely keep all the beef cattle, sheep, and livestock which were purchased for the army" and butcher animals and deliver meat as needed by the army.[16] Champion lists statistics that show how much meat he handled during the 542 days that he was with the army. He records that he "received alive and delivered slaughtered or dressed ... 3,019,554 pounds of beef, 40,275 pounds of mutton, 18,639 pounds of pork, 19,913 pounds of fat." He also "delivered alive 3,257 beef cattle, 657 fat sheep, and 35 fat hogs."[17]

Ephraim Blaine served as a deputy commissary and later became a commissary general of purchases. Blaine and his assistant, John Chaloner, worked directly with Washington's army during 1777 and 1778 at Valley Forge. The frustrations which came with the job of acquiring sufficient fresh beef for the army is evident in this purchase request. On May 30, 1778, Chaloner writes to Anthony Broderick: "You must immediately on Rect of this Collect a number of Beef Cattle sufficient to Issue Four days provision for 15,000 men and have them ready or near to your own house to answer the orders of Col Stewart or Jones they will be immediately wanted and we must not be disappointed."[18]

Steps had to be taken to assure cattle were kept out of reach of the enemy and also that they be positioned strategically for consumption when needed. Chaloner writes to Blaine: "Dunam of Kingwood has been here, he has three hundred head in Ulster County, which have ordered him to drive this way, but fear they have fell a prize to the Enemy, they having storm's and carried Fort Montgomery."[19] Washington explains how he would like the cattle supply placed for use of the moving soldiers. "It is absolutely Necessary that large Quantities should be kept in our Rear, to be killed or moved, as occasion may require."[20]

Commenting on the importance of salt in providing meals for soldiers, Risch states, "Salt was almost as essential in the Revolutionary War as gunpowder and almost as scarce. In the absence of refrigeration and canning processes, the colonists used salt as a preservative for pickling meat and fish."[21] Salted meat and fish made up an important part of the soldiers' food. Congress, Washington, and the commissaries all put forth efforts to this cause. When on the move, salted meat would be less likely to spoil.

Salt pork was one of the most commonly used meats during the Revolutionary War. Salting meat either in brine or packing in dry salt was the only means available of preservation at that time. Yorktown Victory Center.

Entries in Blaine's letter book provide insight into the process of salting pork and beef. "The Season is now arrived for the procuring of Pork for the army, the demand for which is and will be so great, that you cannot procure to much, You must by no means suffer a single fatt Hogg to escape you — The Scarcity of Beef will Require your utmost exertions ... and I flatter myself at the end of the season You will have safely cured 2,000 Barrels."[22] Blaine communicates with Joseph Hugg (October 18, 1777), assistant commissary of purchases based in Gloucester County,

New Jersey: "I do request you will apply to the commanding Officer for a party of Men, and proceed immediately to Egg-harbour, and Seize all the Salt you can find, forwarding the same to Pitts-town or some place of safety."[23]

Salted fish had its place on the ration list, offering additional variety from beef and pork. John Chaloner, writing to Nicholas Patterson, discusses the need to salt fish for the army: "The season for procuring shad is nearly arrived You must do your utmost endeavours to procure at least 1,000 Barrels & more if possible, you must do your endeavours to provide sufficient number of Barrels to cure them — & salt shall be timely ordered.[24]

Joseph Plumb Martin isn't impressed with all of the salted fish that he has been consuming for some time. "This fish, as salt as fire, and dry bread, without any kind of vegetables, was hard fare in such extreme hot weather as it was then." He tried to remove some of the salt by soaking the fish it in a brook. This didn't work. "We were quite sure to lose it, there being a great abundance of otters and minks in and about the water, four-legged and two-legges (but much the largest number of the latter), so that they would be quite sure to carry off the fish."[25]

Bread Options and Problems

Soldiers received their bread or flour allowance in one of three ways: soft bread, hard bread, or simply an allowance of flour. Military circumstances and availability of the item dictated how it would be issued to soldiers. When ovens were available or when assignments were made to bakers, soft bread became an option. Hard bread was generally used during marches, although, in some cases soldiers were simply issued flour in camp or for the march.

Risch explains the bread making system in place during the first two years of the war: "To obtain bread in camp, the commanding officer of a regiment would permit a soldier who was a baker by trade to go to a neighboring house to bake for the regiment" with the assistance of a couple of soldiers. "The flour of the regiment was pooled, and the bakers returned to the solder one pound of bread for each pound of flour received." She points out a problem inherent in this plan. "Since a pound of flour made much more that a pound of bread, the bakers were thereby able to make a profit for themselves of 30% in flour."[26]

Washington and Congress took several actions to provide soft and hard bread for the army during the course of the war. On May 3, 1777, Christopher Ludwick was appointed superintendent of bakers and director of baking in the Grand Army of the United States.[27] Risch points out that "he erected public ovens in suitable places in Pennsylvania and along the route of march in New Jersey" and "baked bread in the quantities required." Ludwick's use of public ovens wasn't a new plan of action. Risch shares the fact that Trumbull in 1776 "commandeered all available ovens in Hartford, Norwich, and other Connecticut towns to turn flour into hard bread for their use" when troops were marching to New York.[28]

References in printed sources during the war show soldiers simply being issued flour and being left to their own devices in camp or on the march to turn it into an edible form. Jeremiah Greenman in October 1775, serving in the Quebec Campaign with Col. Benedict Arnold, records this information in his diary: "Stopt by a Small Stream running in to Shedore pond ware we had delt out 4 or 5 oz. of pork 5 pints of luse flower."[29] A general order from Washington in September 1776 addressed this situation, possibly when complaints of this practice surfaced.

> If hard Bread cannot be had, Flour must be drawn, and the men must bake it to bread, or use it other wise in the most agreeable manner they can — They are to consider that all the last war in America [French and Indian War], No Soldier before (except those in Garrison) were ever furnished with bread ready baked, nor could they get Ovens on their march — the same must be done now.[30]

The result? The notorious fire cake so often associated with the Revolutionary War. Martin in his ever direct manner gives as detailed description of how fire cake was made during the Campaign of 1777. "And how was it cooked? Why, as it usually was when we had not cooking utensils with us, — that is, the flour was laid upon a flat rock and mixed up with cold water, then daubed upon a flat stone and scorched on one side, while the beef was broiling on a stick in the fire. This was the common way of cookery when on marches."[31]

Dr. Albigence Waldo, a surgeon at Valley Forge, records soldiers' response to a repeated diet of fire cake, a chant heard around the Valley Forge camp.

"What have you for your Dinners, Boys?"
"Nothing but Fire Cake and Water, Sir!"
"Gentlemen, the Supper is ready."
"What is your Supper, lads?"
"Fire Cake and Water, Sir."
"What have you got for Breakfast, lads?"
"Fire Cake and Water, Sir."[32]

Aware that this method of making bread wasn't ideal, in June 1777 Washington acknowledged that he preferred that soldiers have a means to bake their bread in a more palatable fashion. Therefore, he "recommends temporary ovens to each brigade, which, by men who understand it, can be erected in a few hours. Bread baked in these, will be much wholesomer than the sodden cakes which are but too commonly used.[33]

Beans and hard bread were common fare for Revolutionary War soldiers. Supply shortages and transportation problems often prevented provisions from reaching Washington's army. Yorktown Victory Center.

The acquisition of flour for the baking process had its own set of complications. The quantity alone necessary to feed the army created issues. The main army in a short three months at Valley Forge consumed 2,297,000 pounds of flour.[34] Risch indicates, using Trumbull's estimate, "that it would take 25,000 barrels of flour to support an army of 22,000 men for a seven month period."[35] Commissaries attempting to purchase flour sometimes ran into problems when speculating farmers and millers refrained from selling and milling their wheat. Washington has to address this problem in December 1776. He authorizes seizure of mills and grain to produce flour for his army.[36]

In an effort to keep flour and wheat from getting into the hands of the British, Washington gave orders to secure mills in areas through which the enemy might be passing. In one instance, he accomplished this by sending instructions "to remove the running Stones from the Mills in the Neighbourhood of Chester and Wilmington." Washington indicates that the parts taken from the mills "must be labeled with Tar and Grease" so that they "can be returned and made use of at a later date" and that they should be moved to such a distance that the enemy could not easily recover them. He adds that any flour in the mills should also be removed because he believes some was "intended for the Enemy."[37]

Even though bread and meat do seem to be the most sought after items on the list of provisions to be procured, recommendations and orders given to secure vegetables are documented in Revolutionary War documents and writings. Washington, on several occasions, expresses his concern that soldiers are not receiving enough vegetables in their rations. From Morris Town in May 1777, he sends this message to Brigadier General Alexander McDougall: "The health of the Army is certainly an object of the last moment; and ... it cannot be preserved, without a due portion of vegetable diet."[38] When transportation problems interfere with delivery of provisions, he complains to Trumbull: "Onions sent to Danbury, have laid there and perished, while the Troops have been destitute of every kind of Vegetabels, for the greatest part of the time since I took the command.[39]

Suggesting that wild greens could be a substitute for vegetables, Washington orders the regimental officer of the day to send soldiers to gather them each morning and distribute them among the men. "As there is a plenty of common and French sorrel; lamb's quarters, and water cresses, growing about camp; and as these vegetables are very conducive to health, and tend to prevent the scurvy and all putrid disorders—The General recommends to the soldiers the constant use of them, as they make an agreeable salad, and have the most salutary effect."[40] On another occasion, Washington, aware that soldiers may be out looking for wild greens to supplement their rations, issues this warning in June of 1778. "The Poke [a wild green commonly included in a pot of mixed wild greens] in this and in the succeeding Month begins to have a poisonous quality; the soldiers are therefore warned against the use of it."[41] Additionally, Washington allowed markets set up in camp by "inhabitants" [locals] in the vicinity of the army. "As nothing can be more comfortable and wholesome to the army than vegetables, every encouragement is to be given to the Country people, to bring them in; The least insult, or abuse to any of them coming to, or returning from market will be severely punished.[42]

The commissaries at Valley Forge pursue the purchase of peas, beans, and potatoes. Chaloner writes, "If you can purchase peas & any vegetables on Reasonable terms delivered here do it."[43] Blaine also writes that his usual purchases of "Pease" to be continued. In the same communication, he adds, "Cou'd Potatoes be forwarded by water without being Injured by frost would wish you to purchase some."[44]

The milk ration did not remain on the Revolutionary War official ration list. It seems that it was an "ideal ration" on the list when considering the task of providing milk for thousands of soldiers in a time when refrigeration and appropriate packaging was not an option in the storage of that kind of food. Communications do, however, show that efforts were made to purchase milk for the sick.[45]

Although references detailing the use of rice and Indian meal are less numerous than those referring to flour and bread, it is evident that these items were a part of the Revolutionary War soldier's diet. Congress empowered the commissary general "to import such quantities of rice from the southern states, as he shall think necessary for the use of the army."[46] In August 1778 Washington ordered a change in rations involving rice. "Half a Gill of Rice pr Ration is to be issued to the Army three times a Week in lieu of one quarter of a pound of flour which is on those days to be deducted from the usual Rations."[47] Indian meal and rice is included with other "hospital necessities" for soldiers in hospitals. An order in July 1778 explains, "A Hogshead of Rice will be delivered to each Brigade for the use of the sick."[48]

Food commonly requested for soldiers in hospitals included Indian meal, oatmeal, rice, barley, and molasses. As well, special subsistence items were requested "sometimes referred to as 'necessaries' and more often as 'hospital stores.'" Tea, coffee, sugar, chocolate, milk, raisins, barley, oatmeal, and wine were frequently on the hospital specialty list of provisions that were requested.[49] Smallpox, one of the most dreaded diseases of the time, plagued Revolutionary War soldiers. It is apparent that efforts were made on the part of commissaries to supply foods recommended by doctors for soldiers who would be inoculated. There is urgency in the language of the entries in Blaine's 1777 to 1778 letterbook as commissaries send out requests for supplying Washington's army with foods requested by the doctors. At Valley Forge Chaloner writes, "For Gods sake forward all the Indian meal you can the troops are inoculated and I fear will suffer for want of that article."[50]

Martin points out that not all were familiar with cooking methods using their rations of Indian meal and Indian corn flour during the campaign of 1780 when wheat flour was scarce.

> All the breadstuff we got was Indian corn meal and Indian corn flour. Our Connecticut Yankees were as ignorant of making this meal or flour into bread as a wild Indian would be of making pound cake. All we had any idea of doing with it was to make it into hasty pudding, and sometimes, thought very rarely, we would chance to get a little milk, or perhaps, a little cider, or some such thing to wash it down with: and when we could get nothing to qualify it, we ate it as it was. The Indian flour was much worse than the meal, being so fine it was as clammy as glue, and as insipid as starch. We were glad to get even this, for nothing else could be had.[51]

Washington makes references to the need for vinegar: "The Commissary General is to adopt every means in his power to provide Vinegar for the use of the army."[52] In making requests for certain food items, he combines requests for various foods, e.g., "Beer or Cyder, Vinegar and Vegetables," commenting that these items would "refresh the troops."[53] Revolutionary War historian John U. Rees notes that "soldiers commonly mixed their issues of alcohol or vinegar with water."[54]

The Use of "Spirits" During the War

A spirit ration did not appear as an *official* ration by action of Congress until 1785 when a gill (4 ounces) of rum per day was added. In 1790 the ration was reduced to "one half a gill of rum, brandy, or whiskey." Additionally, in 1794 the president was authorized to augment the ration "as he may judge necessary, not to exceed one-half a gill of rum or whiskey in addition to each ration."[55] However, during the Revolutionary War, requests and references to alcohol or liquor in various forms—rum, whiskey beer, wine, Jamaica spirits, West India spirits—frequently show up in the purchase requests of commissaries, orders from the commander in chief, and in soldiers' journals and letters. A ration modification ordered by Washington on April 16, 1778, demonstrates that he, as commander in chief, had the power to order ration modifications at that time. This new ration makes changes in quantities of items, shows omission of some items from the original ration list, and in this case delivers the addition of whiskey or spirits.[56]

Apparently, a variety of reasons resulted in the issuing of spirits if they were available. One reason seemed to be as a reward or payment for extra work or for a job well done: "The General is very well pleased with the Industry and dispatch of the 10th Massachusetts regiment in compleating the repairs of the works at Verplanks point, and orders that the regiment be served with an Extra Gill of rum Pr man."[57] Weather played a role in the issuing of spirits: "For this day and during the present spell of wet weather the whole army is to be supplied with full rations of rum."[58]

Celebrations called for a ration of rum. "Tomorrow being thanksgiving day a Gill of West India rum per man is to be delivered to the troops."[59] On July 3, 1782, Washington's general orders indicated, "Tomorrow being the Anniversary of the Declaration of the independence of the united States of America, the Commander in Chief is pleased to order that the rememberance of that auspicious Event shall be Celebrated by a Fue de joye. The Adjutant General will communicate the necessary Directions, the Army is to be served with an Extra gill of Rum per man on the Joyful Occasion."[60]

A general order from headquarters by Washington includes instructions and preparations for meeting the enemy with an order of rum: "Such Colonels of Regiments as have not sent for their Ammunition Carts, or drawn for Rum, for the refreshment of their men, in time of action, as per Order of the 9th. Instant, are to do it immediately, and the Quarter master must take care that it be used properly; the allowance is half a pint pr man.[61]

Currently, when bottled water offers a convenient option for satisfying soldier thirst, it makes the modern reader wonder just how water was supplied to thousands of soldiers while they were in camp and on the march during the Revolutionary War. Several orders from the commander in chief offer insight into this challenge. Concerns relative to supplying water for drinking and cooking purposes include locating water sources, protecting and maintaining them, and providing water when the soldiers were on the move.

Bodies of water, springs, creeks, brooks, rivers, and lakes in the vicinity of the army, served as sources of water used for drinking and cooking. The choice of campsite might be determined as to whether there was an adequate water supply. Springs were examined to see if they would provide sufficient water for the army, and measures were taken to protect and maintain water sources. Apparently, such bodies of water were not always kept in pristine condition. Private Elijah Fisher, a soldier in Reed's New Hampshire regiment, and at a later time a member of General Washington's bodyguard, writes his concern about the camp water supply: "The warter we had to Drink and to mix our flower with was out of a brook that run along by the Camps, and so many a dippin and washin in it, which maid it very Dirty and muddy."[62]

The hustle and bustle surrounding the army in preparation for a march involved not only matters related to strategic military maneuvers and ammunition but also arrangements for food for the soldiers for the next few days. Typically, orders were given to prepare or draw 2–4 days provisions, which sometimes meant that fresh beef had to be cooked prior to beginning the march. Another order: "Two days provisions to be cooked and ready this afternoon. Canteens are to be filled with water before the march begins, as no soldier will be allowed to quit his rank on that account."[63]

Blaine explains a plan to deal with an army on the move: "The Waggons I keep loaded for a moving Magazine, some loaded with Biscake [hard bread] and twelve Loaded with Rum: Should the Army keep at one place the supply would be much easier; am quite discouraged about our proceedings, God knows how it may end."[64]

Revolutionary War Cooks

Historian John U. Rees discusses two types of kettles used by the troops—those made of heavy cast iron and the other constructed of lighter weight tin or sheet metal. He believes the heavier version was primarily issued to a unit "assigned to a fort or serving in some other non-mobile situation." A second reason for issuing the cast-iron versions was if the lighter weight ones were not available. He notes that there is evidence of wooden bowls being issued to soldiers which were likely shared and concludes that "most soldiers likely found their own cups, spoons, knives, and perhaps forks." He points out that in some cases frying pans and skillets were issued although this was unusual. Discussing soldier created "makeshift cookware," he mentions "broilers fashioned from iron barrel hoops," examples of which have been excavated at Revolutionary camp sites, and "an iron spade converted into a pan, now in the collections of Morristown National Historical Park."[65]

Meat broiler. Soldiers sometimes fashioned devices from barrel hoops similar to this one on which to cook meat. Yorktown Victory Center.

In his study of the daily lives of the Revolutionary War soldiers through first person accounts and through military documents, Rees explains common methods of food preparation at that time. "Open fires, quickly built and often abandoned soon after they served their purpose, were the usual medium for meal preparation. When time and location allowed the army also employed large temporary kitchens (round or square) dug into the ground."[66] The Yorktown Victory Center in Yorktown, Virginia, celebrates October 19, 1781, as the decisive battle of the Revolutionary War which led to the British surrender under Cornwallis. One

Earth camp kitchen. Yorktown Victory Center.

of the features of the center is a re-created Continental Army encampment. There an earthen kitchen allows modern Revolutionary War enthusiasts to experience group cooking techniques used by soldiers at that time. During the process of creating an earthen kitchen a circular trench was dug. The dirt removed was mounded in the center of the circle. Fireplaces were dug into the inside wall of the circular trench. According to historians at the center, each mess of six (the number designated to a tent) was designated a fireplace with one from the mess assigned to do the cooking. In this particular camp kitchen re-creation, a camp kettle was suspended above the fire from either a piece of wood or an iron bar laid across the top of the fireplace. Rees also includes extensive historical research on camp kitchens at his website.[67]

Soldiers, because of varying circumstances, were sometimes left to their own devices when they lacked any sort of cooking equipment. Martin records the simple campfire method used for cooking: "We procured a day's ration of southern salt pork (three-fourths of a pound) and a pound of sea bread. We marched a little distance ... kindled some fires in the road, and some broiled their meat, as for myself, I ate mine raw."[68] After arriving at Valley Forge he explains how he cooked a pumpkin — all that he had to eat on that day. "I lay there two nights and one day and had not a morsel of anything to eat all the time, save half of a small pumpkin, which I cooked by placing it upon a rock, the skin side uppermost, and making a fire upon it. By the time it was heat through I devoured it with as keen an appetite as I should a pie made of it at some other time."[69]

Desiring to keep his soldiers as healthy as possible, several of Washington's orders focused on health concerns relating to soldiers' food. As mentioned earlier, he sought

One of the cooking areas in the earthen camp kitchen with a pot supported by an iron bar. Yorktown Victory Center.

variety in the soldiers' diet, demanded safe water, and was concerned that soldiers would know when to safely eat wild greens. Monitoring the soldiers' diet he ordered, "As nothing is more pernicious to the health of Soldiers, nor more certainly productive of the bloody-flux; than drinking New cider: The General in the most possitive manner commands, the entire disuse of the same, and orders the Quarter Master General this day, to publish Advertisements, to acquaint the Inhabitants of the surrounding districts, that such of them, as are detected bringing new Cyder into the camp, after Thursday, the last day of this month, may depend on having their casks stove."[70]

During the Revolutionary War, transportation situations, bad roads and problems with the acquisition of an adequate number of wagons seriously affected whether soldiers received their daily meals. When quartermasters were unable to acquire wagons, this in turn affected the commissaries' job of supplying food for the soldiers. Farmers in the area of the army were sometimes reluctant to allow the use of their wagons because they needed them for their farm work and were not sure when wagons would be returned. To Major General Nathanael Green, Washington indicated that he approved the seizure of wagons on a foraging expedition for the benefit of the Army: "If there is any good reason to believe that the inhabitants have Carriages and withhold them, make severe example of a few to deter other, our present want will justify any measure you can take."[71]

Additionally, containers to transport food items had to be constructed by coopers. Washington at times felt it was necessary to pull soldiers trained as coopers off the line to assist with construction of barrels so that his soldiers would have food transported to

Containers to transport supplies were important for the army and were sometimes in short supply. Yorktown Victory Center.

them. In October 1777 Dr. Isaac Senter, a surgeon, comments in his journal on problems related to transporting food during the march to Quebec: "We had now a number of teams employed in conveying the bateaus, provisions, camp equipage, &c., over this carrying place." He writes about problems with food containers: "A quantity of dry cod fish, by this time was received, as likewise a number of barrels of dry bread.... The bread casks not being water-proof, admitted the water in plenty, swelled the bread, burst the casks, as well as soured the whole bread. The same fate attended a number of peas."[72]

Campfire cooking during the Revolutionary War was primarily accomplished by men even though women were very much a part of the army, generally performing such duties as sewing and washing clothes. However, in some cases women did cook. In her intriguing study of Washington's main army, Holly A. Mayer discusses the roles of the camp followers and their contribution to the army as a community. For those who have the concept that the army of this time simply consisted of men armed and ready for battle, Mayer's book sheds quite a different light. "Soldiers alone do not make an army. They are the most fundamental part of that military force, but as hard as they work, and as much as they do, an army seldom marches out on their efforts alone." Mayer cites a British intelligence report from New York on August 11, 1778, which reported that of the 20,000 in the rebel army almost half were not actually in the army. She explains that "such women, wagoners, and others are camp followers: those people who live and work with the military and accept, willingly or not, its governance of their affairs." She continues, they "were male and female, young and old, and professed a variety of connections and occupations. They were people who were not officially in the army: they made no commissioning or enlistment vows. What kept them with the army was their desire to be near loved ones, to support themselves, and/or, in some cases, to share in the adventure."[73]

One such follower was Sarah Osborn, who was married to Aaron Osborn, a blacksmith and a veteran. Sarah's story and her work for the army is recorded in *The Revolution Remembered: Eyewitness Accounts of the War for Independence*. Editor John C. Dann selected Osborn's story from an extensive pool of applications for pension for service in the Revolutionary War. He believes that her story has significance. "The deposition that she submitted at age eighty-one to obtain her husband's pension is a narrative of her personal experiences as a cook and washerwoman with the continental army. It is in all likelihood the only autobiographical narrative of a woman traveling with the army, and it has been previously unknown to scholars."[74]

Sarah traveled with her husband who was a commissary sergeant with the Third New York Regiment. She discusses a march to Philadelphia where upon arrival, "Being out of bread, deponent was employed in baking the afternoon and the evening." There are 4 women in the group with whom she travels— the wives of two officers and a "colored woman by the name of Letta." She details an account of her cooking activities as the army moves toward Yorktown, the decisive battle of the war: "Deponent took her stand just back of the American tents ... and busied herself with washing, mending, and cooking for the soldiers, in which she was assisted by the other females [previously mentioned]." She indicates that she "heard the roar of the artillery for a number of days, and the last night the Americans threw up entrenchments ... and she afterwards saw and went into the entrenchments ... and ... cooked and carried in beef, and bread, and coffee (in a gallon pot) to the soldiers in the entrenchment."[75]

Osborn seemed to take the army environment in stride. One day when carrying provisions to the soldiers, "She met General Washington, who asked her if she 'was not afraid of the cannonballs?'" Her reply, "No, the bullets would not cheat the gallows, that it would not do for the men to fight and starve too." On the final day of the battle, she notices that "officers hurrahed and swung their hats" and she asked what was happening. After being informed that the British had surrendered, she continued doing her job, "having provisions ready, carried the same down to the entrenchments that morning, and four of the soldiers whom she was in the habit of cooking for ate their breakfasts."[76]

Opportunistic Meals

Matthews and Wecter comment on the ways that the common soldier supplemented his rations: "The company thief used to be almost as necessary to troops on the march as the quartermaster himself."[77] Ebenezer Fox shares a food story: "One afternoon some geese were discovered enjoying themselves in a pond near the road; and one of the soldiers, thinking that a little poultry would not be an unacceptable addition to our bill of fare, threw a stone among them and killed one of the largest of the flock." He then explains how the goose was eventually cooked. Before they were able to cook the goose, the head of a drum was removed and the goose placed inside it until they could get out of the area of the thievery. "When the camp fires were kindled at night, the goose was roasted, and our captain did not hesitate to eat a leg, wing, and a piece of the breast without troubling us with any questions respecting our right of possession."[78]

Soldiers participating in Colonel Benedict Arnold's Quebec Campaign at times desperately searched for supplementary food, cooking it, and in one instance preserving it for later consumption in order to survive when rations sometimes ran out or were reduced. John Joseph Henry delivers an account of locating and killing a "moose-deer" after traveling through an area that appeared to have little wild game: "A fire was kindled — the secondary guide cut off the nose and upper lip of the animal, instantly, and had it on the fire. What a feast! But we were prudent. We sat up all night, selecting the fat and tit-bits— frying, roasting, boiling and broiling."[79]

Henry also writes about a time when opportunity wasn't as kind to them when all of their provisions had been consumed. One of his companions came up with the ideas that "leather, though it had been manufactured, might be made palatable food, and would gratify the appetite." Consequently, "They washed their moose-skin moccasins" and then they were "brought to the kettle and boiled a considerable time." He writes, "The poor fellows chewed the leather."[80]

Also during the Quebec expedition, Dr. Isaac Senter recalls a "desperate situation ... in October 1775 while soldiers were waiting for provisions to arrive." Senter writes, "I found them almost destitute of any eatable whatever, except a few candles, which were used for supper, and breakfast the next morning, by boiling them in water gruel, &c."[81]

Captain Henry Dearborn, also on the Quebec Expedition, writes in November 1775, "This day Cap Goodrich's company Kill'd my dog, and another dog, and Eat them." Referring to the dog eating event, Caleb Haskell writes in his journal the following day, "Set out weak and faint, having nothing at all to eat; the ground covered with snow.... Eat part of the hind quarter of a dog for supper; we are in a pitiful condition."[82]

John Joseph Henry's diary includes an example of food bartering: "One of our party, exploring the country for deer, met with two white men who had come from a distance, mowing the wild grass of the meadow. An agreeable barter ensued: we gave salted pork, and they returned two fresh beaver tails, which, when boiled, renewed ideas, imbibed with the May-butter of our own country."[83]

Feeding the Continental Navy

The Captain is frequently to order the proper officers to inspect into the condition of the provisions, and if the bread proves damp, to have it aired upon the quarter deck or poop, and also examine the flesh casks, and if any of the pickle be leaked out, to have new made and put in, and the casks made tight and secure.
— From the rules and regulations of the "navy of the United Colonies of North-America," Congress, November 28, 1775

Recognizing the need to deal with the enemy on the sea as well as on land, Congress took action to establish a Continental Navy with the intent of disrupting enemy supply lines and harassing the British Navy. Samuel Barboo, in his study of the hygiene of shipboard food service in the Continental and United States Navy provides an overview of his subject: "Seamanship, ship construction methods, discipline, and life aboard ships of the Continental Navy and the early United States navy were closely patterned after the British Navy." He indicates that "the eighteenth century shipboard environment was characterized by a paucity of food, drinking water, and living space." As well, "The limited quantities of provisions, especially fresh water, restricted tactical planning by delimiting the length of sea deployment."[84]

Information in an article in *All Hands*, a naval personnel information bulletin, indicates that "prior to 1794 the rations served on navy vessels were probably the same as the ration allowance for the Army."[85] J.H. Skillman, in his historical account of navy food, agrees. "We find that the first armed vessels of the United Colonies were fitted out by General Washington and manned by Army personnel, so it is quite probable that the Army ration was the basis for subsistence prior to 1794."[86] Perhaps supporting this concept is an entry from Chaloner to John Ladd Howell, found in Ephraim Blaine's Letterbook of 1777 and 1778: "The Beef laid in for the Navy, should be sent on for the Army, if fit for use I wish to that the Stores in your Neighbourhood collected and not to remain in their present scattered condition."[87]

The birth of the United States Navy is documented at the Naval Historical Center website indicating that the Navy "traces its origins to the Continental Navy established by the Continental Congress on 13 October 1775 by authorizing the procurement, fitting out, manning, and dispatch of two armed vessels to cruise in search of munitions ships supplying the British Army in America."[88]

> Resolved, That a swift sailing vessel, to carry ten carriage guns, and a proportionable number of swivels, with eighty men, be fitted, with all possible dispatch, for a cruise of three months, and that the commander be instructed to cruise eastward, for intercepting such transports as may be laden with warlike stores and other supplies for our enemies, and for such other purposes as the Congress shall direct.
>
> That a Committee of three be appointed to prepare an estimate of the expence, and lay the same before the Congress, and to contract with proper persons to fit out the vessel.
>
> Resolved, That another vessel be fitted out for the same purposes, and that the said committee report their opinion of a proper vessel, and also an estimate of the expence.[89]

Information at the same website also notes that "the legislation also established a Naval Committee to supervise the work. All together, the Continental Navy numbered some fifty ships over the course of the war, with approximately twenty warships active at its maximum strength."[90]

Congress, on November 28, 1775, determined the rules and regulations of the "Navy of the United Colonies of North-America." Several rules pertained to the subject of food for sailors and marines. First, members of Congress indicated, "All ships furnished with fishing tackle ... the Captain is to employ some of the company in fishing; the fish to be distributed daily to such persons as are sick ... and the surplus, by turns amongst the messes of the officers and seamen ... without any deduction of their allowance of provisions on that account." Secondly, in the event of a shortage of provision on ships, commanders of squadrons and captains of single ships were given power to "shorten the allowance of rations." Those with this charge were instructed to take care "that the men be punctually paid for the same."[91]

Ration information applying to sailors and similar to instructions concerning soldiers' rations, came with directions for modifications when necessary: "If there shall be a want of pork, the Captain is to order three pounds of beef to be issued to the man, in lieu of two pounds of pork." It appears that there were also orders for a meatless day each week and also the addition of cheese and pudding, items not included on the Revolutionary War army ration list. "One day in every week shall be issued out a proportion of flour and suet, in lieu of beef, for the seaman, but this is not to extend beyond four months' victualling at one time, nor shall the purser receive any allowance for flour, or suet kept longer on board than that time, and there shall be supplied, once a year, a proportion of canvas for pudding-bags, after the rate of one ell for every sixteen men."[92]

The rules also addressed acquiring additional food in ports: "If any ships of the thirteen United Colonies, shall happen to come into port in want of provisions, the warrant of a Commander in chief shall be sufficient to the Agent or other instrument of the victualling, to supply the quantity wanted, and in urgent cases where delay may be hurtful, the warrant of the Captain of the ship shall be of equal effect." And finally, the captains of the ships received instructions for keeping the provisions in good order: "The Captain is frequently to order the proper officers to inspect into the condition of the provisions, and if the bread proves damp, to have it aired upon the quarter deck or poop, and also examine the flesh casks, and if any of the pickle be leaked out, to have new made and put in, and the casks made tight and secure."[93]

Congress gave the following daily ration in the form of a table indicating daily allowances scheduled per week.

Sunday, 1 lb. bread, 1 lb. beef, 1 lb. potatoes or turnips.
Monday, 1 lb. bread, 1 lb. pork, ½ pint peas, and four oz. cheese.
Tuesday, 1 lb bread, 1 lb beef, 1 lb. potatoes or turnips, and pudding.
Wednesday, 1 lb. bread, two oz. butter, four oz. cheese, and ½ pint of rice.
Thursday, 1 lb. bread, 1 lb. pork, and ½ pint of peas.
Friday, 1 lb. bread, 1 lb beef, 1 lb. potatoes or turnips, and pudding.
Saturday, 1 lb bread, 1 lb pork, ½ pint peas, and four oz. cheese.
Half pint of rum per man every day, and discretionary allowance of extra duty, and in time of engagement.
A pint and half of vinegar for six men per week.[94]

Understanding the importance of food in maintaining a positive morale on ships, Captain John Paul Jones, considered the Father of the Navy and one of the Revolutionary War's naval heroes, took special interest in supplying his men with food. In a biography of Jones, Samuel Eliot Morison includes the captain's list of provisions delivered to *Providence* in preparation for a cruise with 70 to 75 officers and men to be out for not over two months. Morrison believes the list gives an indication of what sailors on ships at this time ate and also that "Jones was treating his men far better than Navy regulation required." The list of provisions with Morison's explanations follows.

13 tierces [a cask holding 42 gallons] and 42 barrels salt beef and pork
10 tierces and 53 barrels ship's bread [hardtack] and 500 pounds "Bread Baked out of Ship's Flour"; 10 barrels flour
1 tierce and 7 hogsheads pease
2 barrels "Sous'd Heads" [probably pickled pigs' heads]
Two thirds of a cask of oatmeal
453 gallons "Continental Rum"; 130 gallons W.I. rum
170 pounds coffee [a surprising luxury for those days]
118 gallons molasses; 4 barrels vinegar

14 bushels onions; 10 of turnips and 50 of potatoes
179 pounds cheese; 600 pounds butter
440 pounds brown sugar
219 pounds candles.[95]

Samuel H. Barboo, in his study of navy food during the war, analyzes this list noting that "flour, molasses, and brown sugar were the basic ingredients used in preparation of plum duff," a popular pudding boiled in a bag, and that "butter and cheese are in excess" of rations set by the government. He surmises that "Jones recognized the value of food as a recruiting inducement in competition with the alluring prize money offered by the privateersmen."[96]

Morison points out an item of interest on the provision list that Captain Jones included when "fitting out *Ranger*," explaining that the captain "invested $199.66 in 'Live Stock &c. provided for the voyage to Europe, a part whereof' (the chickens) 'being destined for the use of the sicke on Board.'"[97] On another occasion, Captain Jones takes on "4018 gallons of fresh water, more bread and beef" and some time later "7710 pounds of hardtack, 82 barrels of salt beef and pork, and sundry other provisions including coffee, sugar and 'liquor.'"[98]

Barboo explains the berth deck messing process. He also notes that "a seaman chose his own mess, which was one of his few designated privileges" and explains that "the mess cooks prepared meals in the galley, under the direction of the ship's cook." Furthermore, "The daily allotment of uncooked food was issued by the purser's steward to the mess cooks elected by each of the messes." The mess cook's responsibilities also included delivering the food to his mess and then "stowing and cleaning the mess gear."[99] This type of messing would continue to be used for over one hundred years as sailors continued to man U.S. Navy vessels.

2

War of 1812 Food

I now devoured raw pork with greediness.
— Jarvis Hanks, drummer boy of the 11th United States Infantry

After major cutbacks in the army and total elimination of the navy at the end of the Revolutionary War, the intervening years between the Revolutionary War and the War of 1812 found soldiers and sailors in increasing numbers. The Quasi War (with France), the Barbary Wars (pirates), and conflicts with Tripoli defined the need for a stronger army and navy. Trade problems, impressment issues on the seas, problems possibly attributed to British influence, and for some Americans yet another opportunity to include Canada in the expansion process became reasons to go to war with England.

In June 1784 following the Revolutionary War, Congress debated the issue of the size of the peacetime military, reducing it to minimal status with troops "necessary for securing and protecting the northwestern frontiers of the United States, and their Indian friends and allies, and for garrisoning the posts soon to be evacuated by the troops of his Britannic Majesty." On the same day they determined how these soldiers were to be provisioned. They resolved "that the pay, subsistence and rations of the officers and men shall be the same as has been heretofore allowed to the troops of the United States."[1] Contractors continued to be used in subsisting limited numbers of soldiers sent to western forts in the years following the Revolutionary War, delivering primarily meat, flour and rum rations.

The following War of 1812 ration shows quantities and indicates that rum, vinegar, and salt were added — 20 oz. beef, 18 oz. flour, 1 gill rum, 1 gill vinegar, .64 oz. salt, .64 oz. soap, .24 oz. candle. Unfortunately, vegetables were missing. There is no mention of dried peas or beans, milk, rice, spruce beer or fresh vegetables. This limited ration "provided ample supplies of proteins, calcium, thiamin, and niacin, but was deficient in vitamins A, riboflavin, and vitamin C."[2]

The unpopularity of the contractor mode of provisioning during the War of 1812 spawned criticism and led to investigations. As an example, mortality in the troops sent to protect New Orleans raised questions about the quality of provisions being supplied by contractors in that area. Captain John Darrington gave this answer in response to a question concerned with the quality of provisions delivered by a contractor: "The flour was always bad, with the exception of one hundred barrels purchased by General Wilkinson. It was generally mouldy, sour, and frequently filled with bugs and worms. A small proportion of the pork was good; and also a small proportion of the fresh beef."[3] In the same report, commenting on the health of the soldiers and quality of provisions, Colonel Alexander Parker also responded to questions about provisions: "The troops generally arrived there in good health, but sickness soon commenced, and rapidly increased amongst them; their accommodations, as to barracks and quarters, were comfortable; their provisions, flour, pork and beef, were generally bad, of the meanest kind, and unfit for use."[4]

In the years following the Revolutionary War, the Quartermaster Department and the Subsistence Department were immediately discontinued. "Military supply was placed under civilian control in the post Revolutionary War years, and such control persisted until the outbreak of the War of 1812." Risch notes, "With the United States drifting into a war it was unprepared to conduct, Congress leisurely inaugurated a reformation of the supply agencies." She also indicates that in 1812 Congress once again established a Quartermaster's Department, "barely 3 months before the organization was to be tested by war."[5]

Contractor and Rations Problems

Provisions were not always of high quality and were not always delivered in adequate quantities and did not arrive at the time designated. Army historian Risch indicates that even though the Quartermaster Department had been brought back with the purpose of "receiving and transporting supplies" and the Commissary General of Purchases was to "procure and provide" supplies for the military, she believes that "Neither the War Department nor Congress had given any thought to the establishment of a Subsistence Department" since they had relegated that task to the contractors.[6]

By 1814 it was apparent that changes needed to be made in the methods used to get food to soldiers during wartime. Congressional records show objections to the system in place and suggested proposals for change. In the House of Representatives in November 1814, John C. Calhoun asked for an inquiry into the provisioning process. He bases this request upon a reliable source indicating that "the present mode of supplying the Army ... was frequently on great emergencies found wholly inefficient."[7] An inquiry led to a report delivered by James Monroe, at the time secretary of war. At the request of the Committee of Military Affairs, Monroe

War of 1812 ration. Courtesy Quartermaster Museum, Fort Lee, Virginia.

was asked to seek answers to several questions pertaining to the mode of subsisting, defects in the system, and possible alternative modes of subsistence. Monroe chose to use the words "officers of greatest excellence" who had been dealing with the provisioning process as military leaders.[8] He presented letters from Major General Winfield Scott, Major General Edmund P. Gains, and Col. John R. Fenwick. All three military experts agreed that the contract system failed in a mission to successfully feed the soldiers.

General Winfield Scott, in no uncertain terms, expressed his views of the contractor system after making this comment: "The movements of an army are necessarily subordinate to its means of subsistence, or, as Marshal Saxe expresses it, to considerations connected with the belly." He noted that contractors took advantage of certain situations. Scott believes that "the interests of the contractor are in precise opposition to those of the troops." He gives an example: "When the army is on a forced march, or is maneuvering in the face of the enemy.... The contractor avails himself of the hurry of the moment and issues provisions deficient in quantity and quality."[9]

Scott shares problems concerned with contractors issuing hard bread or flour. He seems to think that contractors provide the form of bread or flour on which they can gain the most profit instead of the form that would work the best in specific military instances. He also expresses concern about the delivery of vinegar and soap: "It is almost impossible for the General to compel the contractor to supply the troops regularly with soap and vinegar (component parts of the rations) because the trouble of procuring them generally exceeds the contract prices of these articles; and yet, nothing can be more essential to the cleanliness and health of troops."[10]

Major General Edmund P. Gaines writes about instances when contractors failed to provide required food for his soldiers. As examples, "The sub-contractor at Billingsport, New Jersey, as well as the one at Marcus Hook ... contrived to palm upon the troops the coarsest and cheapest provisions, and such are often damaged." His conclusion about the system of contracting rations: "If I were called before Heaven to answer, whether we have not lost more men by the badness of the provisions, than by the fire of the enemy, I should give it as my opinion that we had."[11]

Col. John R. Fenwick's statements express his negative opinions of the contractor system: "Contracts are never fulfilled to the letter, and never will be so long as avarice exists.... Bread half baked, sour flour, damaged meat, are amongst the many resources they employ; more than half the issues are made without the smaller parts of the rations; vinegar, soap, and candles, are retained under the most frivolous excuses." And he concludes, "There is not an officer or soldier in the army who would not petition you to do away this destructive system, and substitute commissaries, who would be actuated by feeling, honor, and the fear of disgrace."[12] As a footnote to this issue, in his book, *Desertion and the American Soldier, 1776–2006*, Robert Fantina investigated reasons for desertion. "Poor and/or insufficient food" was listed as one of the reasons for desertion during the War of 1812.[13]

Soldier Food

Donald Graves, editor of *Soldiers of 1814: American Enlisted Men's Memoirs of the Niagara Campaign*, in compiling the memoirs of three soldiers, shared the soldiers' experience of this time. Jarvis Hanks, drummer boy of the 11th United States Infantry, participated in "the hardest fought military operation of the War of 1812 — the Niagara campaign of 1814." Private Amasiah Ford of the 23rd Infantry and Alexander McMullen of Fenton's Regiment of Pennsylvania Volunteers also penned their experiences as soldiers during the war. Graves believes, "Taken as a whole, the memoirs of Hanks, Ford, and McMullen go a long way to putting a human face on the private soldiers of the United States Army during the War of 1812." In his discussion of the three soldiers, he comments on the importance of mealtime to the soldier: "In the army of the War of 1812, as in perhaps all armies, mealtimes were the high points of the soldiers' day."[14]

Commenting on the bland diet of beef or pork and bread or flour and an allowance of salt, Graves notes, "If they had the money, they could eke out this bland diet with items purchased from the sutler, a vendor authorized to sell to the troops. In their search for profit, these merchants took many risks — in August and September 1814, some braved British artillery fire and entered the lines at Fort Erie to hawk their wares. Naturally, their prices were exorbitant."[15]

General Orders from the 2nd U.S. Artillery Company orderly book kept at Fort Meigs on April 21, 1813, detail sutler pricing guidelines at that fort, the largest fort in Ohio during the War of 1812. The list includes the following items: "Coffee ... $ "62½, Refined loaf Sugar ... $" 62½, Imported Brown Sugar ... $" 50, Maple Country Sugar ... $" 37½, Tea — good Quality ... $3-00, Tobacco ... $" 50, Chocolate common ... $" 50, DO [Chocolate] first quality ... $" 62½, Maple & dissolved sugar Molasses ... $1-50, Molasses imported pr Galln ... $ 3-00." The list of items also included prices for pepper, butter, bacon, vinegar, brandy, sprits, and rum, and whiskey when sold by permission.[16]

In his memoir, Hanks writes about his first few months in the army including several of his food experiences. "Now was the first time I had ever slept on anything harder than feathers, neither had I eaten any kind of meat unless it was previously well cooked. I now devoured raw pork with greediness and was obliged to sleep, sometimes on hay in a barn, and sometimes the 'soft side of a pine board,' as we used to say." After being ordered to Sackets Harbor, a military post on Lake Ontario, he and his fellow soldiers traveled through several towns before stopping where locals offered food. "At a small town in Montgomery County, the people came with wagon loads of potatoes, milk, and other good things, which they presented to our officers to be served out to the soldiers, as a testimony of their hearty welcome they gave us, and of their disposition to forward us on towards the frontiers, where the enemy were daily expected." He writes of another time when rations were scarce. "I endured many privations and hardships ... often weary and exhausted with marches for weeks together; sometimes being so hungry and having so little to satisfy the demands of *appetite*, as to be willing, eagerly to devour turnip peelings, floating in dirty water of a ferry boat; and on one occasion to eat what was decided to be 'horse beef.'"[17]

Private Amasiah Ford describes a cold October evening meal: "Our stomach now began to crave for food for we had not anything to eat; but, at length our officer procured a beef. We killed it & every officer & soldier helped himself to what he needed & roasted it on the fire by means of a sharpened stick & ate it without any salt to season or bread to eat it with." The next morning they expanded their bill of fare by "roasting pumpkins in the fire & eating them with our beef" as a substitution for bread.[18]

Alexander McMullen, a private soldier in Colonel Fenton's regiment of Pennsylvania Volunteers, records opinions of his rations: "The Cumberland volunteers and the drafts from York and Adams arrived, and the regiment was organized into ten companies of one hundred men each. In a few days dissatisfaction began to appear in several companies, owing to the quality of the provisions. The flour was mouldy and the beef and pork unfit to be eaten."[19]

Captain Daniel Cushing's company orderly book and also his personal diary which covered his march to Fort Meigs and his time spent there from October 1812 through July 1813 delivers "an extremely interesting view of daily life at this major frontier post" according to historian Joseph M. Thatcher.[20] Fort Meigs was established by General William Henry Harrison "to serve as a temporary supply depot and staging area for an invasion of Canada."[21]

The orderly book of Cushing's company (2nd U.S. Artillery) records details about food and cooking at the fort. General Orders from headquarters at Camp Meigs on April 30, 1813, discuss the economy of fuel: "The commandants of Corps must see that no more is consumed than what is absolutely necessary for cooking — on no pretence whatever is a fire to be made for any other purpose and as soon as the cooking is finished the fires must be carefully extinguished — The Commandants respectfully will direct the Company Officers how many messes are to cook at one fire & will be held responsible that this order is punctually obeyed." Men, in the same orderly book, were given these instructions for supplementing their rations: "At Seven o'clock every morning four men from each Company will be permitted to pass the Centinels accompanied by a Commissioned officer to gather fruit & Sallad the men to goe out armed and return by 12 o'clock."[22]

An entry detailing an inspection of flour explains the process: "The flour now here belonging to the Contractor will be this day inspected. Lieut Col Butler is appointed on the part of the United States the Contractors Agent will appoint a person to be joined to Lieut Col Butler in the inspection by 12 OClock to day; at which time the inspection will commence. In case no person is appointed by the Contractor Capt Gratiot of the Engineers will join Lieut Col Butler in the execution of this duty. All flour unfit for use will be destroyed. Signed by Command A.L. Langham B.M.[23]

In his personal diary Captain Cushing also writes about the provisioning process. On January 23, he notes that "this evening came on to our camping ground four hundred and fifty pack horses laden with flour and salt for the Rapids." On January 27, 1813, he writes, "About 12 o'clock I arrived at Captain Vance's camp, who had charge of four thousand hogs. Brought a letter to him from General Harrison, ordering him to return to Upper Sandusky with the hogs, to have them butchered there." On March 2, 1813, Cushing records in his diary, "We have at this time 600,000 weight of pork salted, and will have as much more by the time they are done salting, and as much beef."[24]

With the coming of spring at Fort Meigs, Cushing indicates that he and his men took advantage of good fishing. On May 17, 1813, he records, "Fine weather this morning, my men in high spirits, fish plenty, no want of provisions, all that is wanting to have things complete is a little whisky. I took a sail in a small canoe this morning and caught 62 white bass that would weigh about one pound each: returned before dinner: caught them with a hook and a line baited with a red rag." He also notes that he has made a garden. And a few days later, "My men are well employed fishing. Two lieutenants caught 375 with hooks."[25]

Cushing writes about produce to be sold arriving at the fort. He mentions two men from Cleveland delivering and selling "a boat load of potatoes, 150 bushels ... in a few hours at $2.00 per bushel." On another day, "Mr. Asa Stoddard, Major Stafford and Major Farley arrived here with two boats from Cleveland laden with produce and dry goods; I got twenty four pounds of butter, a bag of pickles and a large cheese" and the following day he writes, "This day the gentlemen that arrived here yesterday with produce sold to the amount of $1,500."[26]

By the end of the war, with problems identified relating to soldier food, it appears that changes are being called for in the area of the process of subsistence. The contractor delivery system, along with items, or rather lack of items on the provision list came under scrutiny. Discussions and evaluations after the war would lead to changes in the way soldiers would be subsisted.

Feeding the Sailors in the Navy during the War of 1812 Era

Many of the seamen also furnished themselves with monkeys and young goats as pets ... when we sailed from thence, the ship bore no slight resemblance ... to Noah's ark.

— Captain David Porter aboard the *Essex*

Information at the Naval Historical Center explores the development of the United States Navy in the years following the Revolutionary War and prior to the War of 1812. "After the American War for Independence, Congress sold the surviving ships of the Continental navy and released the seamen and officers. However, the Constitution of the United States ratified in 1789, empowered Congress 'to provide and maintain a navy.' Acting on this authority, Congress ordered the construction and manning of six frigates in 1794, and the War Department administered naval affairs from that year until Congress established the Department of the Navy on 30 April 1798."[27] As well, under the Constitution, the Marine Corps was reestablished in an act on July 11, 1798.[28]

On March 27, 1794, Congress explained the decision to provide for naval armament: "Whereas the depredations committed by the Algerine corsairs on the commerce of the United States render it necessary that a naval force should be provided for its protections."[29] Congress in this act included the component parts the first official United States Navy ration. It also was organized like a daily bill of fare much like the ration allowance stated by Congress on November 28, 1775. Rules for the Regulations of the Navy of the United States line out the details.

"Sec. 8. *And be it further enacted,* That the rations shall consist of, as follows; Sunday, one pound of bread, one pound and a half of beef and half a pint of rice: — Monday, one pound of bread, one pound of pork, half a pint of peas or beans, and four ounces of cheese: — Tuesday, one pound of bread, one pound and a half of beef, and one pound of potatoes or turnips, and pudding: — Wednesday, one pound of bread, two ounces of butter, or in lieu thereof, six ounces of molasses, four ounces of cheese, and half a pint of rice: — Thursday, one pound of bread, one pound of pork, and half a pint of peas or beans: — Friday, one pound of bread, one pound of salt fish, two ounces of butter or one gill of oil, and one pound of potatoes: — Saturday, one pound of bread, one pound of pork, half a pint of peas or beans, and four ounces of cheese: — And there shall also be allowed one half pint of distilled spirits per day, or, in lieu thereof, one quart of beer per day, to each ration.[30]

Skillman notes that three years later "Congress reduced the daily allowances of pork and beef to 1 pound, increased the daily allowance of potatoes and turnips to 1 pound, added 4 ounces of cheese on Mondays and Saturdays, 1 pound of pudding on Tuesdays, increased the molasses allowance to 6 ounces, and ended up by adding 2 ounces of butter or 1 gill of oil on Fridays."[31]

Congress took additional steps concerning the provisioning process for the navy. The Naval Armament Act of 1794 determined that each of the new ships would have a purser who was a warrant officer responsible for feeding, paying for and selling clothing and small stores to the crew of the ship. In 1795 Congress established a Purveyor of Public Supplies, "thus instituting Navy procurement and supply ashore." The first Purveyors of Public Supplies, Tench Francis and Israel Whalen, acted as purchasing agents, procuring and providing naval stores as well as "generally all articles of supply requisite for the service of the United States."[32]

Early Navy Cooks

Thomas Truxtun supervised the construction of and later became captain of the *Constellation*, the first of the six frigates to go to war. "On September 7, 1797, *Constellation* was launched just in time as the United States entered its first naval war"—the Quasi War (1798 to 1801) with France.[33] In the same year, Truxtun wrote an account of the duties of the officers—"placed on the Books of the Navy, according to the British Regulations. Arranged with additions"—from an admiral to inferior officers, of ships of war. Among these descriptions of duties, he describes those of the cook.

> The cook of a ship of war (with his mate) is to receive, properly soak, and see finally delivered, such provisions as are served out, and put in charge to be cooked for the officers and ship's company. He is to be at all times careful of the fire, and attend particularly to the orders respecting fire; he is also to be very careful in putting by the slush [fat left from boiling meat], so that no grease is thrown about the decks, and that there is no want of that article for the uses of the service: and in the line of his business, he should be as accommodating and obliging to every one who has his kettle to boil, &c. as is consistent with his general duty.[34]

This job description, to use modern terminology, would be in place for decades to come.

The cook wasn't the only sailor who was involved with provision details. According to Truxtun, one of the duties of the quartermaster was to "assist the mates in their several duties; as stowing the ballast and provisions in the hold." He explains that the purser is "to receive, examine, and account for all provisions, &c. and to see that they are carefully distributed to the officers and crew, according to such instructions as he may receive for that purpose." The stewards and stewards' mates were to assist the purser in the distribution of provisions to the officers and crew. Coopers were in charge of "making and repairing water and other casks" and "overhauling the different sorts of provisions, water, and other stores."[35]

An article in the *Navy Supply Corps Newsletter* includes a significant event in naval history pertinent to delivering food to those on board ships: "'We met with the ketch INTREPID, carrying a cargo of fresh water, stock, and vegetables for the squadron' wrote Commodore Edward Preble in 1804, thus making the first record of an event which today has become commonplace — the supply of the fleet while at sea." The article continues, "The first underway replenishment altered the course of early American history, for it enabled Preble to remain at sea and enforce a blockade of the port of Tripoli, ending the war of the Barbary Pirates."[36]

Information at the Naval Historical Center website indicates that the Navy Regulations of 1814 were similar to the regulations in use by the navy as early as 1802. The 1814 document also addresses the duties of the ship's cook. In addition to having charge of the steep-tub and "anserable for the meat put therein," he was to see that the "meat was duly watered and that provisions were carefully and cleanly boiled, and delivered to the men." One additional duty: "In stormy weather he is to secure the steep-tub, that it may not be washed overboard; but if it should be inevitably lost, the captain must certify it, and he is to make oath to the number of pieces so lost, that it may be allowed in the purser's account."[37]

In some ways sailors may have been better off than soldiers in the army when it came to their supply of food because vessels were stocked before leaving port and also restocked at ports during the outward and return cruise. With soldiers on the move, obtaining and delivering subsistence at times became more of a challenge even though bread and meat were the primary items on the bill of fare. From a modern perspective, one might imagine and question the effect of the repetition and limitation of food choices in either branch of the military at that time.

In his article "Biscuits, Bugs, & Broadsides," historian Mark Hilliard gives his thoughts on the lack of variety in provisions during the War of 1812 era: "It should be remembered that in the 19th century, most Britons and North Americans, including African Americans, were generally used to and expected vastly less spice and variation in their foods than we do today." Regarding the quantity of provisions provided for the 1812 sailor, in Hilliard's opinion, "The Navy's official daily ration was more than adequate to fill a hungry working man's belly, as one can easily find by cooking and eating a supper of the issue provisions in issue amounts." He contends, "When properly cooked, an 1812 era military dinner of boiled salt beef or pork with mustard (issued to U.S. sailors during the 1812 War), and re-hydrated vegetables, followed by a ship's bread duff for dessert, can be downright delicious and nutritious, and with variation could probably keep even our jaded modern [palates] interested for weeks—before scurvy begins to set in."[38]

Including additional information on food for the sailors during the War of 1812, Hilliard discusses navy bread, certainly an important item on the sailor's bill of fare as well as with the soldier during these early military conflicts. In his discussion he points out that during the Revolutionary War and the War of 1812 the British and Americans used a variety of names for this provision: biscuit, sea biscuit, ship's bread, bread, and hard bread. Hilliard believes that "18th and early 19th century ship's biscuit was typically round, and much larger than commonly imagined." He explains that "original surviving examples in England and America are about ½ inch thick, and measure between 4¾ and 5¾ wide—a little larger than a CD." In his opinion they were made from whole-wheat flour and that this didn't change "until well into the 19th century, when white flour became more commonly used."[39]

Supplying and Stocking Ships

Of interest is the quantity of rations necessary to provision various vessels of the navy during the War of 1812. Documentation of ration estimates indicated for United

States Navy vessels of various sizes is recorded in the American State Papers with numbers of men on board to be fed ranging from 28 to 650 and rations estimates calculated for 1 year. An 1812 provision list for one vessel carrying 650 men included the following quantities of food items with the bill for this particular year tallying $53,972.20. Bread is at the top of the list and then salt beef and salt pork — the old stand-by meat duo of the Revolutionary War soldiers and sailors — still ever present on the nineteenth century navy menu. The provision estimate list reads: "207,594 pounds of bread, 592 barrels of beef, 507 barrels of pork, 170 barrels of flour, 16,900 pounds of suet, 14,828 gallons of spirits, 528 bushels of peas, 12, 675 pounds of cheese, 33,800 pounds of rice, 4,225 pounds of butter, 2,113 gallons of molasses, 2,113 gallons of vinegar."[40]

The process of stocking a ship with provisions basically involved contractors, navy agents, pursers and their assistants. The navy agent on shore worked with contractors to supply ships arranging for supplies and provisions to be delivered to a navy yard where ships were built, repaired, and supplied or re-supplied, or to some other specified place for transfer to a designated vessel. Barrels and containers of provisions were inspected when a contractor made his delivery at a designated location. They then had to be inspected again to see if they were packaged in an acceptable manner and if they were properly labeled once they were brought on board. The labeling process was essential to proper storage. It also provided documentation which would allow those in charge of provisions at the points of delivery to track the supplier if the provisions were found defective. Once the provisions were stored and the cruise was underway, the purser of the ship distributed stored provisions on the ship as needed.

Spirits in the Navy during the War of 1812

Charles A. Malin comments on the subject of spirits in the early navy at this time.

Rum or "grog," as it was more commonly called in those days, was issued to men from the beginning. In the early days of the U.S. Navy rum was a part of daily life and the grog ration was half-pint a day. During the days of *Constellation* there was a saying that showed the importance the men placed on their daily ration of grog. This saying — "Blow up the magazines; throw the bread over the side and sink the salt horse — but handle them spirits gentle like." In 1806 the Navy Department introduced whiskey to replace the rum ration, but rum was still generally preferred by the Sailors.[41]

Skillman cites a letter written as early as May 9, 1801, by Captain Thomas Truxton [Truxtun] to the secretary of the navy, expressing his concern about the use of rum on board ships: "The allowance of one-half pint of rum per day is too much for seamen, it requires great attention to prevent them being continually in a state of intoxication ... for they will in addition to their allowance find landsmen and boys who will privately barter their rum to them for butter, cheese, etc.... I am of the opinion that on account of health and other considerations it would have been better to have allowed the seamen but one gill of rum per day and in lieu of the other gill, molasses and tea, coffee and sugar."[42]

Restocking While on Cruises

Captain David Porter writes about the process of keeping his ship stocked during the cruise of the United States frigate *Essex* during the War of 1812. In October 1812, he, with 300 men on his vessel, sailed with instructions to "protect the American coast and to harass British shipping." Failing to rendezvous with a navy squadron in the Atlantic under the command of Commodore Bainbridge, he made a decision to sail "around the Horn, thus making the *Essex* the first U.S. naval vessel to carry the war into the Pacific. In his journal, he includes numerous discussions of matters relating to feeding his crew while on the cruise, which ended with the ship's capture by the British on March 28, 1814. His discussions of food situations aboard the *Essex* represent the governmental provisioning process for a ship and also the supplemental provisioning actions taken when stops were made at ports. As he departs from Delaware, he explains, "I took in as much provision as she could stow and provided ourselves with a doubly supply of clothing and fruit, vegetables, and lime juice as antiscorbutics."[43] Apparently the captain is aware to some degree of the relationship of lack of vegetables and fruits to scurvy.

Readers of his journal learn of the importance of maintaining an adequate water supply for the crew. In addition to explaining how their water supply was replenished, he writes about water conservation measures taken on board. Early in the cruise, when water was short, Captain Porter delivered an interesting water conservation measure: "Orders were given to lose no opportunity of catching rain water for the stock, of which we had a large quantity on board, every mess in the ship being supplied with pigs and poultry." When they needed water, they would stop, go ashore and refill the large wooden casks in which water was stored on board the ship. "We this day commenced watering but, after having to roll the casks about 500 yards, found great difficulty in getting them from the beach on account of the heavy surf. We were only able to get about 5,000 gallons." On one occasion, he makes this decision: "Finding that the large quantity of stock on board must necessarily consume a great deal of water or suffer, I directed that the seamen should kill all their Pigs."[44]

Sailors always looked forward to fresh provisions while in port. Porter records that they purchased fresh provisions while in port in Portugal: "The beef was very dear and very poor. A bullock weighing 300 weight cost $35. Sheep were $3, but very poor. Oranges cost 40 cents per 100, and other fruits in the same proportion and in the greatest abundance. The ship had on board not less than 100,000 oranges together with a large quantity of coconuts, plantains, lemons, limes, and casaba." He instructed the men to make their supply of fruit last as long as possible and aiding in that effort, he gave permission "to suspend it in the rigging and other airy parts of the ship, in nets made for the purpose, with a promise of severest punishment to such as should be detected in stealing from others."[45]

He also notes, "Every mess on board was also supplied with pigs, sheep, fowls, turkeys, goats, ... fowls at $3 per dozen and fine turkeys at $1 each." Reacting to the shopping spree, Porter reflects, "Many of the seamen also furnished themselves with monkeys and young goats as pets, and when we sailed from thence, the ship bore no slight resemblance, as respected the different animals on board her, to Noah's ark."[46] One must question what would become of the pets should a water shortage occur as it did with the stock previously mentioned.

Using a culinary trick, Porter came up with an interesting approach to dealing with "the pernicious vapors arising from the berth-deck" where men lived in close proximity. "What can be more dreadful than for 300 men to be confined, with their hammocks only 18 inches apart on the berth-deck of a small frigate, a space of 70 feet long, 35 feet wide,

Berth deck messing on a War of 1812 privateer. Engraving by Billings, from *The American Cruiser* by George Little. Courtesy Naval Historical Center, Washington, D.C.

and 5 feet high, in a hot climate?" His answer — after trying "fumigation with gunpowder and burning fires below, purifying by sprinkling vinegar, and ventilating by means of wind sails," he decided to bake bread in ovens on the berth deck the way the French did. Although the heat from the baking process was uncomfortable, it seemed to work. "While the ovens are heating, a constant current of air rushes toward the fire, the foul air is carried off, and fresh air rushes into supply its place."[47]

Along the way it appears that Porter found it necessary to adjust ration allowances in order to maintain a supply of food as he at times dealt with shortages and with deteriorating rations. As a precaution, "The crew had been on two thirds' allowance of salt provisions, generally on half allowance of bread and full allowance of rum." He noted that members of the crew were paid monthly for the provisions that they had not received. At one point they had a problem with weevils and worms in their bread "but they had only in a slight degree altered its qualities." He also mentioned that their supply of peas and beans also did not fare so well: "As the allowance of water enabled us to spare enough to permit boiling them, I directed them to be served. On opening the barrels, we found only a mass of chaff and worms." Compounding the food problem at the same time, they found that "the rats also, had found their way into our bread rooms."[48]

The overall provisioning plan in place for such a cruise involved purchasing additional provisions along the way since it would be impossible to stock enough provisions for the entire cruise. Porter's plan was to restock the quantity of wood and water consumed since the previous stop. On a two and a half day stop to take on water and wood, Porter reports in his journal: "The officers and men ... provided themselves with hogs, fowls, plantains, yams, and onions in considerable quantities from the boats alongside."

Locals along the shore brought items to sell to the sailors. Porter, as well, purchased provisions for the crew, this time jerked beef. In Santiago, Chile, in addition to again taking on a supply of wood and water, he purchased dry provisions, fresh beef, vegetables, bread, and fruit for the ship.[49]

At one point, Porter makes a decision to "double the Horn" and move into the Pacific Ocean to "annoy the enemy," a plan that had previously been approved by the secretary of the navy and by Commodore Bainbridge. With the assistance of the purser on board, he calculated his supply of provisions available for this two month leg of the cruise. According to the purser's report, he had the following stock of provisions: "184 barrels of beef, 114 barrels of pork, 21,763 pounds of bread, 1,741 gallons of sprits, 201 gallons of vinegar, 108 gallons of molasses, 10 boxes of spermaceti and 17 of tallow candles." Therefore, he calculated that "on two thirds allowance of beef and half allowance of bread, other articles in the same proportion as the beef, there was sufficient to serve as follows: beef, 36 weeks and 5 days; pork, 22 weeks and 5 days; bread, 22 weeks and 1 day; spirits, 13 weeks and 2 days; vinegar, 6 weeks and 4 days; molasses, 7 weeks and 5 days." Additionally, he was aware of a location where he could purchase jerked beef, fish, flour, and wine. Thus, with these evaluations concluded, Porter heads southward.[50]

A constant issue on board ships on long voyages was the problem of eating salted meats which led to a "desire for fresh meat." About this problem, Porter writes in his journal: "But since we left America, they had been deprived of almost every comfort to life. So great was their desire now for fresh meat that a rat was esteemed a dainty, and pet monkeys were sacrificed to appease their longings." Whenever possible, they stopped at ports in search of fresh meat ie. hogs, horse, turtles, and beef. Porter writes about a hunting expedition that he allowed: "As we had seen, with our spyglasses, several hogs and horses on shore, I permitted the officers and the most careful of the men to take muskets with them. In the course of a few hours, we had killed and got down to the boats ten hogs with some very young pigs." They also added a horse to their cache of fresh meat when a drove of horses passed the sailors during their hunting expedition. Writing of their "fresh mess for all hands," Porter notes, "The horsemeat ... was generally preferred to the hog it being much fatter and more tender."[51]

Passing through waters filled with whales, Porter and his crew were on the lookout for the tortoises of the Galápagos as well as for British whalers. Porter had previously learned about the tortoises as a source of meat. He described them as "extraordinary animals" that "weigh upward of 300 weight" and praised them as "a popular item on the ship's bill of fare" when they can be found. He describes the meat as "wholesome, luscious, and delicate" and furthermore, "After once tasting the Galápagos tortoises, every other animal food fell greatly in our estimation." Continuing to praise this culinary delight, he indicates that they were so fat that no oil or butter was required to cook them.[52] Porter and his crew are rewarded on both of their anticipated finds.

While in the area, they captured three British whalers estimated at a worth of half a million dollars. Porter notes, "The capture of these vessels relieved all our wants except one, to wit, the want of water." In addition to much needed supplies for the ship, "The vessels, when they sailed from England, were provided with provisions and stores for upward of three years and had not yet consumed half their stock." In addition the crew of the *Essex* helped themselves to "several delicious meals" prepared from tortoises of Galápagos that had been stored on the British vessels. The only regret was that they learned that the enemy had thrown several overboard "to lessen the vessel's weight in the battle." On a positive note, a few days later, the crew spotted about 50 tortoises floating in the water where they had been dumped by the British. They rescued them for later meals. As well, when they passed the island, they worked 4 days capturing "20 to 30 each day, averaging about 60 pounds each"—a total weight of 14 tons.[53]

The Navy Regulations, 1814

The 1814 Navy Regulations located at the Naval Historical Center website are "similar to the regulation in use by the Navy since 1802."[54] A perusal of the these regulations relating to sailor foods finds stores and provisions upon arrival at the ship being accounted for and inspected by the captain, the sailing master, and the purser. The captain also gets a weekly report on the state and condition of stores and provisions. He is to have storerooms examined frequently, aired out, and secured against rats. He is to make sure fires and candles are extinguished in the cook-room and to not allow any person to suttle or sell any sort of liquors to the ship's company.

Of interest are a few of the responsibilities of the sailing master which relate to sailor food. Not a small task, he is responsible for stowing the hold, meaning that he determines where and how the provisions and water and other ship supplies and stores are placed in the large lower storage area of the ship. This task is directly related to one of his other responsibilities, "to keep the ship in constant trim, and frequently to note her draught of water in the log-book." To keep a ship in trim has to do with how the boat is balanced fore and aft and her draught of water is concerned with how low the boat sets in the water. Therefore, how supplies and provisions are stowed will affect how the ship sits and performs in the water. According to these regulations, the sailing master also has to make sure that the oldest provisions are placed so that they can be used first. As well, he must keep track of and make reports as items are removed from and added to the hold area, for example, as salt beef and salt pork are brought up for use. Keeping this in mind, it is his responsibility to maintain a record and make a report of how much water is used daily and how much remains: "He is to observe the alterations made by taking in stores, water or ballast and how it affects the performance of the ship."

The section of the regulations dealing with provisioning the ship shows provisions "furnished upon the requisitions of the commanding officer, founded upon the purser's indents." The purser is responsible for expenditures and if he finds provisions unacceptable, a survey, an inspection by three officers, must be made of the supplies in question. The regulations address loss of provisions, shortened provisions, damaged provisions and substitution of beef for pork and vice versa. Regulations state the quantity of water allowed members of the crew and note proper care of casks. Ships are still supplied with seines for fishing and regulations indicate that the crew is to be "supplied with fresh provisions as it can conveniently be done."

Donald L. Canney overviews the status of the navy at the end of the war: "The end of the War of 1812 found the navy with seventy-five warships and 240 small craft." He points out that "two major developments in naval administration and long term growth came into play at this time." First, to assist the secretary of the navy, who up to this time "had sole responsibility" of the Department of the Navy, the Board of Naval Commissioners, consisting of three advisors, was created. The second development was the congressional Act for the Gradual Increase of the Navy of 1816. Canney indicates that at this time "the department consisted of the Secretary of the Navy (and clerk) and the constructors, clerks and naval agents at the yards and stations."[55]

Although the navy, following the war, was destined to experience growth and to establish a presence around the world, it would be early in the nineteenth century before the sailors who gathered on the berth deck for their meals would experiences major changes in their bill of fare. The navy food section in the following chapter discusses the role of the navy following the War of 1812, examines points of culinary interest in the 1818 Regulations of the Navy, discusses the part the navy played in the Mexican War, examines the changes that occurred in the navy in 1842, and then takes the reader on board four navy vessels for an examination of subsistence practices at this time through first person accounts. These individuals shared their experiences gleaned from months and sometimes years spent at sea during the nineteenth century following the War of 1812, some including the time of the Mexican War. Their accounts bring to life the culinary customs of the ordinary seamen and the customs of the officers of the navy brought about by traditions, rules, and regulations.

3

Post–War of 1812 and
Mexican War Military Subsistence

I boiled my pork for nearly two hours, and found it still so tough that it was harder
labor than I had been at all day to eat it.
— Pvt. William H. Richardson

Subsistence Department and Ration Changes

The difficulties in subsisting the army during the War of 1812 and the first Seminole War highlighted the need to develop a more efficient system of procuring and delivering rations to troops. Congress responded to the situation and Secretary of War John C. Calhoun's urging by passing on April 14, 1818, "An Act Regulating the Staff of the Army."[1] This act provided for the appointment by the president of a commissary-general to supervise the purchase of subsistence supplies for the army. Supplies were to be purchased through contractors, but they were now to be delivered in bulk to depots for inspection.[2] Responsibility for the transportation of these supplies to various posts fell to the Quartermaster Department. Both Congress and the army felt that this method would provide a more reliable stream of supplies. The act initially establishing the new commissariat system provided for it to be in place for five years, but in 1835 Congress made the change permanent after reauthorizing it five times. President James Monroe appointed Colonel George Gibson to the new position of commissary-general of subsistence April 18, 1818.

The secretary of war began to consider significant changes in army rations in 1819. A letter written by Surgeon General Joseph Lovell to Secretary Calhoun in 1818 outlined what he perceived to be deficits in the rations and his suggestions for improving them. Lovell believed that rations should consist as much as possible of foods with which the soldiers are familiar. The American Army ration included only flour, beef, pork, and whiskey. While he felt that meat was important for health, Lovell believed "the quantity required for this purpose has been exceedingly overrated." Lovell preferred corn meal to flour and believed that if flour was used it should be made into hard bread rather than soft bread and stated that "bacon ought to be furnished instead of salt beef and pork." He recommended that vegetables such as "peas, beans, and rice" be substituted for part of the meat ration explaining that this "would not only promote the health and comfort of the soldier, by approaching nearer to his accustomed food, but by enabling him to introduce frequent changes in his mode of preparing it."[3]

Lovell advocated other changes in the ration as well. He expressed concern over "the deleterious effects of ardent spirits" used by the troops, referring to the whiskey provided as part of the soldier's daily ration and suggested that perhaps "this troublesome poison should ... be altogether excluded, and the healthy drinks of molasses and water, or beer, substituted for it."[4] Finally, Lovell suggested the inclusion of pickles and vinegar in the ration, "[pickles] which, on account of the vegetable acid they contain, are both a pleasant and healthy stimulus to the stomach. Indeed, vinegar is of great use on many accounts."[5]

Section 8 of the act establishing the Subsistence Department also allowed changes to be made in army rations. In his report to Congress December 11, 1818, Secretary of War Calhoun outlined the changes.

> The vegetable part of the ration has been much increased. Twice a week, a half allowance of meat, with a suitable quantity of peas or beans, is directed to be issued. Fresh meat has also been substituted twice a week for salted. In the southern division, bacon and kiln-dried Indian corn meal has been to a certain extent substituted for pork and wheat flour.[6]

The substitution of corn meal for flour failed to be permanent. After a three year trial, it was discontinued because of a lack of acceptance by the troops.[7] Another significant action taken by the War Department relative to subsistence in 1818 was the direction given to all permanent posts to begin the cultivation of vegetables for use by the troops. More remote posts were ordered to also cultivate corn and to supply part of their meat ration.[8]

Sentiment to remove whiskey as part of the ration continued to be expressed in Congress and the War Department through the 1820s. Following Surgeon General Lovell's criticism of the whiskey ration in his 1818 letter to Secretary of War Calhoun, the army experimented with the elimination of it on a voluntary basis whereby soldiers would be paid the cost of the whiskey ration in cash instead of receiving the whiskey. This method proved ineffectual in curbing the use of alcohol. Efforts to curtail the use of alcohol in the military rations coincided with the rise of the temperance movement nationally. Not waiting for congressional action, President Andrew Jackson issued an executive

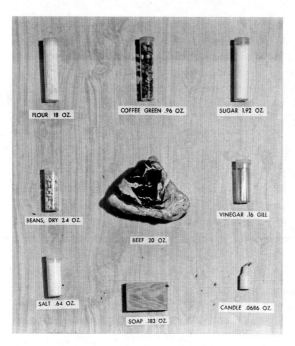

FLOUR 18 OZ.   COFFEE GREEN .96 OZ.   SUGAR 1.92 OZ.

BEANS, DRY 2.4 OZ.   BEEF 20 OZ.   VINEGAR .16 GILL

SALT .64 OZ.   SOAP .183 OZ.   CANDLE .0686 OZ.

The Mexican War Ration. Courtesy Quartermaster Museum, Fort Lee, Virginia.

order October 25, 1832, that replaced rum, whiskey, and brandy in the ration with coffee and sugar. Congress followed in 1838 with Section 17 of "An Act to Increase the Present Military Establishment of the United States." This act states

> that the allowance of sugar and coffee to the non-commissioned officers, musicians and privates in lieu of the spirit or whiskey component part of the army ration, now directed by regulation, shall be fixed at six pounds of coffee and twelve pounds of sugar to every one hundred rations, to be issued weekly when it can be done with convenience to the public service, and when not so issued, to be paid for in money.[9]

Supplying Troops in Mexico

The potential for war between Mexico and the United States remained high following Texas' independence from Mexico in 1836. Antislavery forces prevented the annexation of Texas for nearly ten years. Finally, in 1845 after James K. Polk's election to the presidency in 1844, Congress passed a resolution offering to annex Texas. Texas became a state December 29, 1845. The war officially began April 25, 1846, when the Mexican army crossed the Rio Grande from Matamoros and attacked a dragoon detachment commanded by Captain Seth B. Thornton.

The United States Army was woefully unprepared for war in two ways. First of all, the regular army numbered less than 8,000 and secondly the stockpile of supplies and the wagons to move them was much below what would be needed for war, and both the Quartermaster and Subsistence departments were understaffed, making procurement difficult. In addition congressional appropriation for procurement remained at the level for a peace-time army. Congress made a formal declaration of war May 13, 1846, authorizing up to 50,000 volunteers and appropriating 10,000,000 dollars to carry on the war.[10] The total number in service during the conflict reached 78,718.[11]

The Mexican War presented some supply challenges never faced before. It first of all involved garnering supplies and sustaining an operation outside of the United States and establishing a longer supply line than the Quartermaster Department had ever been called on to maintain. Secondly, this was the first war in which a major portion of the supplies were moved into place by water and in the final phase of the war an amphibious landing had to be supported. Historians sometimes refer to the Mexican War as "the first steamboat war."[12]

As volunteers swelled troop numbers, the need for rations and other supplies became critical. Quartermasters had difficulty in obtaining wagons as well as mules, horses, and oxen and drivers for the animals. Without sufficient transportation in place, troops could not advance. The organization and persistence of the quartermasters eventually put together enough wagons, draft animals and drivers so that troop movement could begin.

The Quartermaster Department utilized ships for the transportation of supplies and soldiers to a greater extent in the Mexican War than they ever had in the past. New Orleans served as the primary collection point for supplies and the embarkation point for volunteers headed to war.[13] Volunteers generally arrived at New Orleans via steamboats on the Ohio and Mississippi rivers. From New Orleans, transportation to Point Isabel at the mouth of the Rio Grande by steamer was arranged. Supplies arrived at New Orleans by a variety of ships either purchased or hired by the Quartermaster Department.[14]

The amphibious landing of Scott's forces at Vera Cruz presented a new challenge for the American military. This action required the use of surf boats, basically large row boats used to move men and supplies from ships onto the beach. The boats were made in three lengths, 40, 37, and 35 feet, and would carry about 50 men. Scott had 65 of these boats available for the landing.[15]

Travel aboard the vessels carrying troops and supplies was perhaps one of the most difficult aspects of the war. John R. Kenly wrote about some of his experiences traveling on the *Massachusetts* from Washington to Brazos Santiago near the mouth of the Rio Grande as first lieutenant with a group of volunteers from Maryland. Volunteers were expected to bring their rations with them shipboard, however, often there was no means of cooking and doing so risked damage to the ship as Kenly relates.

> Our ship has been twice on fire from the cooking arrangements of the men on deck, there having been no places provided for fires to cook with prior to leaving on our voyage, and those improvised being very insecure and a constant source of apprehension, and justly as it turned out to my mind.[16]

Sailing in the tropical heat of the Gulf of Mexico also made water supplies critical as Kenly reported, "We had a good deal of trouble about the allowance of water to the men." Soldiers found little space in the crowded conditions on the ships and conditions were generally unhealthy. "It is exceedingly hot, and the crowded state of our decks ... with the fear that our water will give out, — the men already fighting for their turns to obtain rations, — and the sick list swelling at a fearful rate, make us anxious and apprehensive."[17] Before arriving at their destinations, the small amount of water that remained was hardly in drinkable condition. "The little remaining water in our tanks smells worse than it is possible to imagine any fluid could smell, yet we wish there was more of it."[18]

The daily ration for troops during the Mexican War remained that which had been established in 1838 and consisted of the following: 20 oz. beef (fresh or most often salted), 18 oz. flour, 2.4 oz. dried beans, .16 gill vinegar, 1.92 oz. sugar, .64 oz. salt, .0686 oz. candle, .183 oz. soap, .96 oz. green coffee. The War Department's issuance of its General Regulations for the Army in 1841 made some slight modifications. The meat ration could include three-fourths pound of salt pork or bacon and instead of flour the ration could include 18 oz. of soft bread or 12 oz. of hard bread or one-fourth pound of cornmeal. Rice could also be included in lieu of dried peas or beans. Potatoes were used for their antiscorbutic properties, but difficulties with the potato crop in the 1840s prompted Commissary General Gibson to recommend dried apples.[19] Soldiers were not always assured of receiving all of these ration items. Transportation and supply problems often meant that not all items were included, making some meals not only meager in quantity but also poor in quality. Private Frank Scribner described one such meal following a day's march: "Our supper consisted of coffee and hard crackers filled with little black bugs." On another occasion he remarks about the condition of the hard bread and bacon but manages a bit of humor: "Imagine us trudging through a swamp, lugging our mouldy crackers and fat bacon, (for we are truly living on fat of the land)."[20] Private William H. Richardson with Doniphan's Missouri Volunteers describes one of his meals.

> It was composed of hard water crackers and mess pork, which would cut five inches through the ribs. I boiled my pork for nearly two hours, and found it still so tough that it was harder labor than I had been at all day to eat it.... I took it out, stewed and fried it. But it was yet spongy and stuck in my teeth.[21]

Cooking food in the field during the Mexican War. John Frost and William Croome, Illustrator, *Pictorial History of Mexico and the Mexican War*, Philadelphia: J. B. Lippincott & Co., 1871.

Soldiers cooked in messes of six to twelve or possibly more using camp kettles and mess pans. Limited availability of cookware made communal cooking necessary. One camp kettle holding four to five gallons was issued to every six soldiers. The camp kettles were used for boiling meat and vegetables to make soups, to carry water, and even for washing clothes. The Army also issued two mess pans for frying or baking to each six soldiers. Men were even provided with a few food preparation instructions in army regulations. For example, bread was not to be served while hot and soups had to be boiled at least five hours. Cooking equipment and rations were carried in supply wagons which followed troops on the march. Sometimes the troops moved faster than the supply wagons. Consequently, food did not always arrive at campsites at the same time as the troops.

To supply fresh beef, the army provided herds of cattle driven as part of the supply line. When the cattle had all been consumed, soldiers were most often subsisted on salt pork or bacon and flour or hard bread although rice and beans were a part of the ration. They generally felt satisfied with bacon and hard bread or flour as Frank Elliott reports from near Santa Fe: "Our rations small, but still, rations of flour and bacon have been received and we are now in the best of spirits, with well-filled stomachs."[22] Frank S. Edwards, also with Doniphan's regiment headed for Santa Fe, writes about their scarcity of rations when camped near Bent's Fort.

> General Kearney, in consequence of the scarcity of the provisions furnished for us, ordered that we should be put upon only half a pound of flour and 3/8ths pound of pork per day each man. This deprived us of coffee, sugar, salt, rice, etc. which had previously helped to make our provisions palatable.[23]

Soldiers were never happy when they lacked coffee. The coffee portion of the ration was issued as green coffee beans that had to be roasted and then ground. George C. Furber, a volunteer with the Tennessee Cavalry, wrote that a soldier roasted coffee in "his iron frying pan." Next the coffee had to be ground. Furber describes the process: "All the coffee was pounded in tin cups, with a stone, muzzle of a pistol or carbine."[24] Looking forward to their morning and evening coffee helped maintain spirits through difficult days.

When separated from the supply wagons carrying their cooking utensils, soldiers had to be resourceful in finding ways of preparing a meal. Richard Elliott shares how they managed to make bread without cooking pans.

> Our cooking utensils being all in the wagons behind us, all sorts of expedients to bake up our little dust of flour were resorted to; and many were surprised to find how well a roll of dough, coiled round a stick and stuck up before the fire, would, if turned occasionally, inevitably bake itself.[25]

William H. Richardson, with volunteers headed for Santa Fe from Fort Leavenworth, also mentions having fresh beef for supper after a day's march and that typically they only ate two meals a day.

> As usual, 8 o'clock found us ready to start. After a march of 14 miles, we encamped on Beaver Creek. We killed a beef and the soldiers busied themselves in cooking supper. Not having conveniences of home at hand, we dispensed with our dinner daily, and satisfied ourselves with eating morning and night.[26]

Foraging and Supplementing Rations

Soldiers during the Mexican War were resourceful in supplementing the rations supplied by the army through hunting game. Their accounts indicate that they utilized about any animals they could obtain. William Richardson recounts his hunting experience: "As yet we had not seen any game with the exception of two rabbits, caught by our men. They were of a novel species, almost white, with long black ears, and as large as a grey fox."[27] A few days later Richardson's unit encountered buffalo. "Herds of buffalo were seen scattered over the plains," he wrote. "The best hunters were picked out to secure as many as possible. The chase was a fine one, 13 were killed by the different companies."[28]

These soldiers were also creative in dishes they prepared with whatever they obtained. Richardson recounts, "A few of us entered upon the funny work of making soup out of pork, buffalo flesh, and fish, boiled up together. It was a rare mess, but we pronounced it first rate."[29] When crossing the Arkansas River some 362 miles from Fort Leavenworth Richardson reported "multitudes of fish in the river. We caught several varieties by spearing." He also reported that "a number of antelopes were killed here." Richardson thought that the antelope "tasted like mutton."[30]

The occasions when soldiers could obtain wild game or other food gave a much needed break from the monotony of regular rations. In spite of the frequent poor quality and small quantity of the rations, soldiers often endured the difficulties with a bit of humor. Richardson wrote in his journal of the bill of fare for one week: "Monday.— Bread, beef (tough as leather,) bean soup. Tuesday.— Tough beef, bread, and bean soup. Wednesday.— Bean soup, bread, tough beef — and so on to the end of the week."[31]

There were occasions when troops essentially had no supplies of food remaining. Richardson describes one such time.

> This evening we are without food, or nearly so. Martin Glaze, an old veteran, who has seen service, and belongs to my mess, got a few ears of corn and parched it in a pan, with a small piece of pork to make it greasy. When it was done, we all sat around the fire and at our supper of parched corn greased with fat pork.[32]

Even if soldiers had adequate rations, they often had to search to find fuel with which to prepare their meal. On both the plains and mountainous areas of the southwest, trees were few making wood for cooking scarce. At times they had to use an alternative fuel — buffalo chips. Although the chips made a good fire, they did little to enhance the flavor of food cooked with it. Frank Edwards describes the soldiers' cooking experience.

> There was plenty of it around our camp, and it had one advantage over wood, it requiring no chopping. It makes a good and hot fire without flame, but had a strong ammoniacal odor, which is imparted to everything cooked by it. Our buffalo meat, which we simply roasted on the live embers, of course partook largely of this flavor, supplying the want of pepper, which our mess was out of.[33]

Another challenge for troops during the Mexican War was obtaining adequate supplies of drinking water. Much of the region is extremely arid. Often troops had to carry water for long distances to their campsites. Camp kettles were pressed into service for this task. Frank Scribner describes how he and a fellow soldier made carrying them easier: "Another and myself set out with two iron camp-kettles swung upon a tent pole."[34]

While on the march, armies whenever possible would try to reach a river or spring before camping, and the soldiers took full advantage of good water. William Richardson notes in his journal, "This morning I filled my canteen with the refreshing water of Diamond Springs."[35] However, such good water was not always readily available. John Kenly describes the water they found after marching three days in the hot Mexican sun on their way to Camargo.

> At noon of the third day we reached a pond, in the water of which large numbers of cattle were standing to escape the heat of the noon-day, and the swarm of flies which annoyed them. For how many days these cattle had stood in this water we know not; but very few of us who drank it kept it *down* after it was swallowed, and the taste of that water was remembered for a long time with nausea and disgust.[36]

The Mexican War challenged the supply and transportation capabilities of the Quartermaster and Subsistence departments more than any previous engagement. The distance from supply centers meant that quartermasters had to purchase many of their supplies locally as the army moved forward. This was especially true with Scott's army following the landing at Vera Cruz and its movement toward Mexico City. Once beyond Jalapa, Scott obtained nearly all subsistence from the local countryside.[37]

While the army was ordered to pay for anything they obtained from the citizens of Mexico, there were sometimes difficulties in finding local sources of needed supplies and on occasion dishonesty on the part of those selling supplies to the Americans. Edwards, who served as a quartermaster for his company, was often sent to buy supplies. He recounts one monk who tried to cheat him on his corn purchase.

> I found a regular monastery; and making inquiries where I could buy corn, a jolly looking old monk in a cowl and rope told me he would be too happy to accommodate me.... After purchasing a sufficiency, which was measured in sacks, two of which are supposed to hold, when the corn is shelled out, a *fanega*, equal to two bushels and a quarter, I found the padre was trying hard to cheat me, both in measure and count; so, taking an opportunity to *accidentally* put out the light, I told the ten men who were with me to fill up their sacks which were larger than the measuring sack, and not to forget their pockets. When the light returned, every man had his full sack on his shoulder ready to carry off. The old fellow, evidently, noticed the fullness of the sacks, but knew it was not worth while to say anything — so after all; he did not make much out of me.[38]

The army quartermasters frequently purchased a variety of food from local Mexicans. Most often purchased would be flour, corn, cattle, and sheep. Soldiers also obtained extra items of food on their own in local markets. The army always seemed behind in paying the soldiers. Elliott records in his letters from Santa Fe, "The battalion has received no pay, although more than four months' pay is due."[39] This made obtaining food particularly difficult for officers since they did not draw rations as enlisted men did but were expected to purchase food from their ration allowance which amounted to twenty cents a day. Because the soldiers often lacked money, they resorted to barter. William Richardson found a way to obtain corn and onions: "Yesterday I traded off *two needles* to the Spanish girls for six ears of corm and some onions." Although not all ration items were available, the corn and onions improved his meal. "A breakfast of coffee without sugar, some very poor beef soup, and onions sliced up with parched corn, made a better meal for us to-day than we have had for some days past."[40] Some of the soldiers made items to trade for items of food. "A Mr. Hatfield was engaged in the manufacture of a *grindstone* to trade to the Spaniards for corn and beans."[41] Soldiers were apparently able to trade almost anything for corn: "Between meals ... we parch some corn, which we now and then procure of the natives in exchange for buttons, needles, or any little matter we can spare."[42]

In some parts of Mexico, soldiers found local markets filled with a variety of fruits and vegetables. In a letter written in 1847 from Jalapa, Lieutenant Theodore Laidly, with General Scott's forces, comments on the fruits available: "We find here a great variety of fruits here oranges, bananas, plantains, pine apples, etc. and it is quite a treat to get some fine fruit."[43] Elliott noted the quality of onions and grapes in Santa Fe: "Their onions merit an especial notice, as they seem to be the best production of the country. They are very large, and the flavor is much better than that of ours at home ... the grapes are their equal — in fact delicious."[44]

If they had the funds, soldiers could purchase items not supplied as part of their rations from sutlers. Incautious soldiers could incur substantial bills with the sutlers. For some, little would be left from their pay when sutler accounts were settled. Significant bills could accumulate because sutlers charged inflated prices for the items they sold, but they also incurred the risk of losing an entire shipment while enroute as well as the risk of not receiving payment for their goods. The Pay Department had jurisdiction over sutlers and gave them the right to stand beside the paymaster on payday and collect payment from soldiers owing them money.[45] Potatoes and onions were also among the items sold by sutlers—always at high prices. Although not always pleasing to the army, sutlers sold whiskey, which was popular with the less temperate soldiers since alcohol had been eliminated from the ration. Richardson reports a sutler selling whiskey "at 75 cents per pint." He further states that the result of the whiskey was a "scene among officers and men better imagined than described."[46]

In addition to whiskey, brandy, and wine sometimes sold by sutlers, soldiers serving in Mexico encountered some alcoholic beverages made by native residents with which they were not familiar. One quite common drink was pulque, made from the fermented juice of the maguey or agave plant. Pulque was popular with most residents of Mexico. The beverage originated with the Aztecs.

Soldiers found numerous eating establishments in Mexico which allowed experiencing foods new to their palates. Elliott writes about "taking my dinner of tortillas, boiled mutton and pepper sauce." He elaborates on the pepper sauce.

> Red pepper sauce, which is simply the peppers stewed, — or another dish, red peppers preserved in corn-stalk molasses, — do not go badly, when you get used to them, albeit, before you know exactly what they are, and dip a little too deeply into the dish, they prove somewhat calorific in the region of the thorax.[47]

Undoubtedly, they introduced some of these items to family and friends in the United States, perhaps helping popularize Mexican foods. Occasionally, some soldiers even had the opportunity to dine in the homes of local residents in small villages. William Richardson relates one such experience: "An old woman invited me in her house and set before me some tortillas and cornstalk-molasses which were quite a treat."[48] Some of the soldiers however were not immediately impressed with the hot peppers used in Mexican dishes. Richardson tells of his experience.

> When we arrived at Abique, an old man invited us to partake of his hospitality; an invitation we gladly accepted. We went in accordingly, and after all were seated on the floor in the posture of a tailor, a large earthen vessel was placed before us containing pepper sauce and soup; and a few tortillas, (a thin paste made of corn rubbed between flat stones) the sauce caused my mouth to burn to a blister.[49]

Writings of soldiers reflect frequent dissatisfaction with the kind and amount of rations they were receiving. In addition they show that at times soldiers were nearly without rations. Risch points out that "no official complaint of either the quality or the quantity of subsistence furnished to the armies was received by the Subsistence Department from any quarter."[50] It would appear that the army made a genuine effort to supply its troops with adequate food but that its efforts were constrained by the transportation, communication, and food preservation technologies that existed at that time. While mistakes were made and lessons learned, the efforts of the Quartermaster and Subsistence departments during the Mexican War demonstrated that an effective system of supply had been established.

Food for the Navy

*Princes do not sit down at their tables, groaning beneath a thousand delicacies ...
with a higher relish, than those with which the tempest-tossed, weather-beaten
sailor squats by the side of his greasy tarpaulin, and devours his humble dish of
lobscowse or duff.*
— E.C. Wines aboard the U.S. frigate *Constellation* from 1829 to 1831

Following the War of 1812, the focus of the Navy moved in the direction of gradual expansion. Donald L. Canney notes that Congress in 1816 made a decision to support an eight year plan to construct vessels. He considers the role of the navy at this time. With increased worldwide trade, "For the most part — the main exception being the Mexican War, American naval operations of this era were centered around the various squadrons." These squadrons were "concerned with showing the flag" and with "protection of trade and other interests in their particular segment of the world's oceans." He notes squadrons being formed in the Mediterranean, West India, the Pacific, Brazil, Africa and at home.[51]

He sums up the role that the navy played in the Mexican War. On the west coast the navy supported "revolutionaries in California," "American warships seized Monterey and San Francisco," and "naval and marine forces ... assisted in taking Los Angeles and San Diego." In the Gulf of Mexico, "the navy maintained an effective blockade"; at Vera Cruz "the navy organized and carried out its first major amphibious landing," and finally the Navy "bombarded the town of San Juan de Uloa" and "besieged the town of Vera Cruz." He also reminds that the Mexican War was "the first time in which steam warships played a significant role."[52]

Numerous regulations pertaining to provisions on board navy ships remain the same in the Navy Regulations of 1818 with the ship's master continuing to be responsible for the proper stowing of provisions and also keeping an eye on casks and their contents. An item in the regulations alludes to the problem of scurvy: "On Cruises of unusual duration and particularly in hot climates, ships are to be supplied with lemon acid, which is to be administered twice a week to the crew, in such quantities as the surgeon may deem proper."[53] The navy ration of 1818 continues to be formulated as a weekly bill of fare:

Sunday — ¼ lb suet, 1¼ lbs beef, ½ lb flour, 14 ounces bread, 1 ounce sugar, ½ pint spirit
Monday — 1 lb pork, 14 ounces bread, 1 ounce sugar, ½ pint peas, ½ pint spirit
Tuesday — 2 ounces cheese, 1 lb beef, 14 ounces bread, 1 ounce sugar, ½ pint spirit
Wednesday — 1 lb pork, 14 ounces bread, 1 ounce sugar, ½ pint spirit, ½ pint rice
Thursday — ¼ lb suet, 1¼ lbs beef, ½ lb flour, 14 ounces bread, 1 ounce sugar, ½ pint
     spirit — Tea 4 ounces per week, [also] Saturday 1 ounce sugar
Friday — 4 ounces cheese, 14 ounces bread, 2 ounces butter, ½ pint rice, ½ pint
     molasses, ½ pint spirit
Saturday — 1 lb pork, 14 ounces bread, ½ pint peas, ½ pint vinegar, ½ pint spirit[54]

The 1818 Rules and Regulations explain the plan for providing fresh provisions for two days a week when possible.

When in port, if it can be done conveniently, at a reasonable rate, the crew shall be supplied two days in each week with fresh meat, one day in lieu of salt beef, and the other in lieu of salt pork, and it is to be observed that one pound and a half fresh meat is considered equal to a pound of salt beef, or three quarters of a pound of salt pork, and the amount of the vegetables, greens, and thickening for the soup is to be equal to the amount of the articles which may, on the day of issue, be stopped in consequence of the serving out of fresh meat.[55]

The regulations also state, "In all cases when fresh meat is received on board, the commander is to see that it is good and wholesome; that it is fairly and equally distributed among the officers and crew; that no particular pieces are reserved for the officers or others; that a lieutenant, master's mate, or midshipman, attend the distribution in some convenient and public part of the ship, where it shall be pricked for in the customary manner."[56]

Prior to the Mexican War, the United States Navy's approach to mid-century brought several changes that affected navy provisions. The first dealt with the way pursers of the ship were paid. This change is evident in the Act of August 26, 1842, which stated "that all purchases of clothing, groceries, stores, and supplies of every description for the use of the navy, as well for vessels in commission as for yards and stations, shall be made with and out of the public moneys appropriated for the support of the navy." The same act determined that the purser would be paid accordingly dependent upon his job assignment, i.e., size of ship or work in naval yards or naval stations.[57] Consequently, "They [pursers] were forbidden to procure or dispose of supplies to the officers or crew for their own profit. Only the margin allowed by Congress could be charged, and with this legislation complaints of purser exploitation were finally laid to rest."[58]

Three days later, Congress re-worked the navy ration and listed its new component parts and a selection of substitutions, no doubt welcome when they were available.

One pound of salted pork, with half a pint of peas or beans; or one pound of salted beef, with half a pound of flour, and a quarter of a pound of raisins, dried apples, or other dried fruits; or one pound of salt beef with half a pound of rice, two ounces of butter, and two ounces of cheese; together with fourteen ounces of biscuit, one quarter of an ounce of tea, or ounce of coffee, or one ounce of cocoa; two ounces of sugar, and one gill of spirits; and of a weekly allowance of half a pound of pickles or cranberries, half a pint of molasses, and half a pint of vinegar.

Sec. 2. Fresh meat may be substituted for salted beef or pork, and vegetables or sour-crout for the other articles usually issued with the salted meats, allowing one and a quarter pounds of fresh meat for one pound of salted beef or pork and regulating the quantity of vegetables or sour-crout so as to equal the value of those articles for which they may be substituted.

Sec. 3. Should it be necessary to vary the above described daily allowance, it shall be lawful to substitute one pound of soft bread, or one pound of flour, or half a pound of rice, for fourteen ounces of biscuit; half a pint of wine for a gill of spirits; half a pound of rice for half a pint of beans or peas; half a pint of beans or peas for half a pound of rice. When it may be deemed expedient by the President of the United States, Secretary of the Navy, commander of a fleet or squadron, or of a single ship when not acting under the authority of another officer on foreign service, the articles of butter, cheese, raisins, dried apples or other dried fruits, pickles and molasses, may be substituted for each other and for spirits: *Provided,* The article substituted shall not exceed in value the article for which it may be issued, according to the scale of prices which is or may be established for the same.[59]

Section 5 of the same act dealt with a change in issuing spirits.

That no commissioned officer or midshipman, or any person under twenty-one years of age, shall be allowed to draw the spirit part of the daily ration, and all other persons shall be permitted to relinquish that part of their rations, under such restrictions as the President of the United States may authorize: and to every person who, by this section, is prohibited from drawing, or who may relinquish, the spirit part of his ration, there shall be paid in lieu thereof, the value of the same in money, according to the prices which are or may be established for the same.[60]

On August 31, 1842, Congress passed an act to repeal the act in 1815 that had created the Board of Commissioner to advise the secretary of the navy. Congress replaced it by creating five bureaus. The Bureau of Provisions and Clothing was responsible for feeding the sailors.[61] Information originating from a *Naval Supply Corps Newsletter* article detailing a history of the corps comments on the significance of this change: "Thus after 47 years of service, the supply organization of the Navy finally became an entity in its own right."[62]

Sailor Shipboard Food Experiences

Selections from the following first person book length accounts allow modern readers to go beyond lists of navy rules and regulations which guided the lives and eating habits of those aboard United States Navy vessels in the years following the War of 1812 and during the Mexican War. Descriptions and detailed accounts of food situations and food related activities provide a wealth of culinary information that pages of documents are unable to deliver. George Jones, *Sketches of Naval Life* (1829), speaking of himself as a "civilian," served as schoolmaster, teaching midshipmen, and as a captain's clerk on a Mediterranean cruise. His naval experience comes from the time he spent on the frigates *Brandywine* and *Constitution*. E.C. Wines, author of *Two Years and a Half in the Navy* (1832), developed a journal on a cruise in the Mediterranean and Levant on board the U.S. frigate *Constellation* from 1829 to 1831. Herman Melville wrote *White Jacket* (1859), based on an 1843 cruise in the navy spent as an ordinary seaman on the frigate USS *United States*. Signing up with the navy when he was thirteen, Chas. Nordhoff wrote *Man-of-War Life: A Boy's Experience in the United States Navy, During a Voyage around the World in a Ship of the Line.* It was published in 1855. These men describe galley areas and eating and drinking situations, tell how they supplemented their daily rations, and occasionally share a recipe.

George Jones describes the galley area on his ship: "Directly forward ... is the galley, a huge stove.... Each mess has a cook; and besides these, there is a ship's cook, who attends to the men's [ordinary seamen] food ... after it has been deposited in the coppers: when he thinks it sufficiently boiled; he carries a dish of soup and meat to the officer of the deck, who must taste and pronounce them fit to be served out, before it can be done." Jones explains that the officers' food is kept in the brig area and guarded by the sentry in charge. "The precincts of the brig are fitted up with ... festoons, and wreaths, and knots, of garlic, onions, celery, and sausages; among which, hang fowls, cabbages, cauliflowers, and perhaps a pig or two."[63]

He provides a lengthy discussion of the grog ration and how it is handed out. According to Jones, the grog tub makes an appearance twice each day, at dinner and at supper. He notes that he has heard of serving "half a gill, raw, in the morning, and evening; and a gill, diluted, at noon" on other ships and explains how the grog process is orchestrated on his ship at dinner and supper: "It [a small cask] is slipped to the starboard side of the main deck, and a large tub brought forward, into which its sparkling contents are poured; and equal quantity of water being also added. We use whiskey, in our navy: rum is the common beverage, in all others." He adds, "The men pass down to the gun deck.... A rope is drawn athwart ships, near the tub: each, as his name is called, crosses, and takes his allowance, which must be drunk on the spot.... The whole operation is superintended by the officer of this deck, who must watch them closely."[64]

Jones explains the difference between the rations of ordinary seamen and the officers' rations. The seamen's ration includes bread, water, vegetables, meat "in different proportions, through the week, according to a paper furnished by government. For tea and sugar, they keep a private mess account with the Purser: in port, fresh provisions are furnished about twice a week."[65] He then writes about the ration plan of the officers.

> The officers are treated differently: they receive from one to eight rations each, and draw it in money, each ration being valued at seven dollars and a half per month; and with this they furnish their table themselves; from the shore, if it is convenient; if not, from the ship, being charged by the purser with the articles they may draw. Each mess [officer's mess] has its caterer.... He provides for the table, presides at it, attends to the cook, steward and boys, and on him the comfort of his mess-mates very much depends.[66]

Jones explains the wardroom eating process where he eats: "In the wardroom, a servant is allotted to every two officers, except the first lieutenant, who has one to himself; besides this, they have a steward and cook." He thinks highly of their cook: "Our cook is an excellent one ... our dinner usually consists of soup, roast beef or mutton, or both, with fish, and a variety of vegetables, together with a dessert of three or four kinds of fruits; and for all this the bill is usually eight dollars per month, to each."[67]

Regarding shopping ashore, he explains the way it is accomplished: "The messes [officers' messes] usually get permission from the lieutenant to lay in fresh grub, and do it as largely as they can. Our gun deck is now covered with geese, turkies, chicken, sheep, pigs, and rabbits, each in their proper apartment: to these, add pet birds, a goat, a donkey, dogs, and pigeons cooing all around, and you will have some idea of the place."[68]

E.C. Wines doesn't appear to be very happy with his drinking water: "Our water was so bad both in taste and smell, that I generally held my breath till I had drunk off all I wanted, to avoid, as far as possible, the unpleasant sensations occasioned to the olfactory and gustatory nerves." Even though his water is bad, he keeps a somewhat positive attitude about his food. He concludes "never to despair as long as I could get beans or lobscowse" which he defines as "a dish composed of salt beef and potatoes hashed up together, and very *fashionable* when nothing better can be obtained." Wines explains that "the three standing dishes at sea are salt beef, pork and beans, and *duff,* a heavy indigestible species of plum pudding. In port fresh beef is substituted for salt.[69]

He discusses the eating arrangement of the ordinary seamen: "The men are divided into messes of from fifteen to twenty individuals each. Each of the members takes his regular turn of doing the duties of a berth deck cook a week at a time. The berth deck cook, so called to distinguish him from the galley cook, receives the daily supply of provisions when it is served out, prepares it for the coppers, and when cooked spreads the table and arranges it for the masticating process. When the meal is concluded, he gathers up the fragments and deposits them in the mess chest." Continuing his description of the ordinary seaman's table he writes, "The ships messes eat on the gun and berth decks. Their table is nothing more nor less than a square piece of tarred canvass, spread between two guns or mess chests, around which they seat themselves à la Turque. The whole of their table furniture consists of a large kid for the principal dish, a few tin cups and basins, and a spoon, knife and fork for each individual." Becoming somewhat philosophical about his observations of the ordinary seaman's table aboard the ship, he adds, "Yet, simple as all this is, princes do not sit down at their tables, groaning beneath a thousand delicacies, with greater contentment, or enjoy their luxurious viands with a higher relish, than those with which the tempest-tossed, weather-beaten sailor squats by the side of his greasy tarpaulin, and devours his humble dish of lobscowse or duff."[70]

Wines' account of a New Year's celebration shows quite a party on board his ship: "If to 'eat, drink and be merry' is any evidence of a grateful heart, then indeed our sailors were the most grateful beings in the world." He describes the cooking going on in the galley which "was scarcely sufficient for cooking their pigs, lambs and turkeys." He recalls, "About an hour after the second allowances of grog was served out, the thundering voice of the boatswain, echoed by his mates, was heard, 'all hands to splice the main brace, ahoy!'" This he interprets as, "All hands to take an extra cup of whiskey and water. Every man in the ship — stop-grogs and all — was at liberty to join in the libation."[71]

Herman Melville sees the responsibilities of the mess cooks, overall, a "little to do" job — except when dealing with duties relating to the issue of cheese and butter twice a week. He indicates that the mess cooks have "sole charge of these delicacies" and "the great difficulty consists in so catering for the mess ... as to satisfy all." The problem he sees with the distribution of the butter and the cheese is that each man has his own preference as to when he wants to receive his amount. Melville comments, "Some guzzlers are for devouring the butter at a meal, and finishing off with the cheese the same day; others contend for saving it up against *Banyan Day*, when there is nothing but beef and bread; and others, again, are for taking a very small bit of butter and cheese, by way of dessert, to each and every meal through the week. All this gives rise to endless disputes, debates, and alterations."[72]

It also fell to the mess cook to make the duff. Melville, determined to positively accomplish this task for his messmates, discusses various culinary strategies with fellow mess cooks. "Having well weighed them all," he decides to mold from his culinary research his own recipe and then moves forward with the task of making the duff. After mixing flour, raisins, beef fat (slush obtained from the ship's cook), and water, he proceeds to knead it and finally "decanted the semi-liquid dough into a canvas bag, secured the muzzle, tied on the talley, and delivered it to Rose-water [the assistant cook] who dropped the precious bag into the coppers, along with a score or two of others." The outcome? Unfortunately, as one might say today, his personally concocted recipe wasn't a "keeper." Upon removing it from its bag, his messmates were less than impressed, making him an unpopular cook.[73]

Because of the limited food choices, i.e., salt beef and salt pork, sailors adopted "contrivances in order to diversify their meals." Melville mentions several of these dishes — "Scouse, Lob-scouse, Soft-Tack, Soft-tommy, Skillagalee, Burgoo, Dough-boys, Lob-Dominion, Dog's Body, and lastly, and least known, Dunderfunk" — all variations made with limited ingredients on board the ship. According to Melville, "Dunderfunk is made of hard biscuit, hashed and pounded mixed with beef fat, molasses, and water, and baked brown in a pan." The cooking instructions? "Go to the ship's cook and bribe him to put it in the oven."[74]

Charles Nordhoff's time in the navy began with his enlistment at Philadelphia and placed him in California at the end of the Mexican War. Prior to boarding a U.S. Navy man-of-war, he and the other sailors recruited for the around the world cruise were placed on a receiving ship where they waited until enough sailors had been recruited for the cruise and until their vessel was ready for sea. He describes his first supper in this temporary home: "One of the sailors ... cut me a large slice of fat salt pork, gave it a dip in the vinegar pan, and laying it on a cake of bread, handed it to me ... but at sight of the raw meat which was being consumed on all sides of me, my appetite failed me, and I was content to eat a little bread and tea, and look on at the performance of the rest."[75]

He writes about the time when the seventy-four-gun ship was ready to be supplied and provisioned before leaving New York. He was surprised at the size of the ship he was about to board, and, consequently, impressed at the quantity of supplies and provisions (enough for 700 men for 6 months) that were being loaded. In addition to food, the loading included "powder and shot, spare clothing, sails, and rigging, to last the cruise of three years." He "joined a division of about a hundred, who were hoisting in barrels of beef and pork on deck from a lighter alongside." It took from four A.M. until six P.M. to load the ship "with intermission only for breakfast and dinner."[76]

Nordhoff explains where the different men on the ship eat. First, the captain's cabin and pantry is located on the main deck. Near the foremast, on the main deck, is the galley, or cooking range, for the commodore and captain. The next deck, the lower gun deck, is the wardroom, the "living room of the lieutenants, the surgeons, the purser, master, chaplain, and commodore's secretary." Continuing his tour of the eating areas, he notes, "The space between the guns on this deck is occupied by the 'mess-chests' and the mess-lockers, in which the pots, pans, and spoons used by the sailors, as well as the victuals, are kept." And then "immediately before the foremast is the ship's galley, where the cooks reign supreme. Here the food for the ship's company, as well as that of the lieutenants and midshipmen, is prepared."[77]

He notes that the next deck down is the orlop deck: "On the aftermost part of this deck, and reaching quite into the bottom of the vessel, is an enormously large space, tightly tinned throughout, which is used as a *breadroom*." According to Nordhoff, the midshipmen, purser, and ship's clerks messes are located on this deck. And finally, the hold is located below the orlop deck: "All the wet provisions, such as beef and pork are stored here" and "flour and other dry provisions." Also, this is the area where the spirit room is located and is "guarded by a sentinel."[78]

He includes information about water storage in this area of the ship: "Below the beams which support the tiers of the hold, are the water-tanks, large variously-shaped vessels of iron, made to fit nicely to the shape of the ship, throughout, and from which the water for daily consumption is pumped by means of a suction hose, which can be screwed into a hole left for that purpose in the lids or coverings of the tanks, thus enabling the master, who has that matter in charge, to take water from any tank he thinks proper." Nordhoff concludes his tour of the interior of the ship which he believes "will apply, with some slight variation, to all other ships of the line and frigates."[79]

Later in his diary, he comments on a typical day at sea.

On the second day out, we unbent the chain cables and stowed the anchors—a sign that we were fairly at sea. Our first port was to be Rio de Janeiro, and our course accordingly soon brought us into fine weather. And now commenced the regular routine of sea life; breakfast at eight, quarters at nine, dinner at twelve, supper at five, quarters at six—these were the landmarks which announced the passing of the day.[80]

At the stop in Rio de Janeiro, the men who worked in the hold took the tanks ashore to re-fill with water. He explains that even though the men and boys were not allowed to go on shore at this stop, they were allowed to shop aboard the bumboats. Before the shopping event took place, the contents of the boats had to be inspected by the assistant surgeons "to see that they contained nothing deleterious to health, and by the master-at-arms, to prevent the importation of anything obnoxious to sobriety."[81]

After the word was given that they could go aboard, he and his fellow sailors enthusiastically board the bumboat, anxious to see what items are for sale. Nordhoff indicates that he "determined to invest a portion of my capital in fruit." Fortunately, he "found there for sale, oranges, bananas, cocoanuts, fried fish, boiled eggs, soft tack (the ship name for soft bread)." As well he was introduced to Johnny Kacká, "a sticky preparation of guavas, wrapped up in plantain leaves, and tasting not unlike a mixture of three parts maple sugar, and one part clean sand." Evidently, this sweet treat was much in demand by the boys on the ship. After pricing the items for sale, he purchased "two dozen oranges, a bunch of bananas, and a small loaf of soft tack ... and a *chunk* of the much-prized *Johnny Kacká*." He is impressed with the fruit, especially the bananas, a kind of fruit that he had never tasted. Later in the cruise when they stopped in Hawaii, he sampled bread-fruit for the first time and probably the last because he was not impressed with its taste. He describes it as being "about as large as a man's head" and having a taste "which seemed to be a mixture of acid and sweet, but with a sickening flavor that makes it unpalatable." He remembers that supplies purchased for the crew in Japan included sweet potatoes, eggplants, carrots, pumpkins, small green apples and several hundred chickens.[82]

While in port in Rio de Janeiro, the crew enjoyed fresh provisions. Nordhoff writes, "The market-boats [sent from the ship], in the morning, had brought on board a day's allowance of fresh meat and vegetables for the crew—the fore and hind quarters of two large bullocks, and several hampers of sweet potatoes and other *greens*, and of this the ship's cook was now preparing a fragrant soup, the delicious odor of which pervaded the whole ship, causing us to long for the arrival of the dinner hour."[83]

Readers of Nordhoff's journal are able to understand how the re-supplying harbor stops worked. He explains, "Rio de Janeiro is head-quarters for the United States Brazil Squadron, and as it is a convenient harbor, and much used as a calling place of United States naval vessels bound to other stations our government has there a depot of provisions." The depot is "under the charge of a United States officer," and "it was from this store-house that we drew our provisions, to make up the deficit caused by the consumption on our outward passage."[84]

When explaining how food was prepared on his ship, Nordhoff described the coppers in which the food was prepared.

> The coppers, or kettles, in which the victuals for seven hundred men are prepared, are, as may be readily imagined, of no small size. On our ship there were three, one for tea or coffee, one for meat, and the other for rice or beans, or "duff." Each of these divisions are six feet deep by four feet wide, and between five and six long. In scouring them out, the

cook's assistants climb down into them, using sand and canvas to scrub them clean. When ready for inspection the doctor is called, and, standing on a ladder put down into each copper for the purpose, rubs his white-gloved hand along the surface and in every nook and corner.[85]

He adds that "the office of ship's cook is generally held by a colored man, they having best proved by experience to be the *handiest* or best suited for the place."[86]

Nordhoff and Melville also both discuss the drinking water situation on board their ships. Nordhoff writes about how the water was transported up to the drinking area and his concerns about the quality of the water: "I have seen *drinking water* pumped out of our tanks, into a *butt* on deck, which smelt so abominably as to make any approach to it utterly impossible, ere it had stood the open air an hour or two." He adds, "The gases arising from it, as it issued from the pump, would cover the paint all over the vessel with a copper-colored sediment, which it was almost impossible to get off."[87]

Melville includes a description of the scuttlebutt, where a controlled supply of water for various uses on the ship is served out.

The scuttle-butt is a goodly, round, painted cask, standing on end, and with its upper head removed, showing a narrow, circular shelf within, where rest a number of tin cups for the accommodation of drinkers. Central, within the scuttle-butt itself, stands an iron pump, which, connecting with the immense water-tanks in the hold, furnishes an unfailing supply of the much-admired Pale Ale [water].... The scuttle-butt is the only fountain in the ship; and here alone can you drink, unless at your meals. Night and day an armed sentry paces before it, bayonet in hand, to see that no water is taken away except according to law.[88]

Labeling the scuttlebutt the "town pump of the ship," he adds that "it is often surrounded by officer's servants drawing water for their master to wash; by the cooks of the range, who hither come to fill their coffee-pots; and by the cooks of the ship's messes to procure water for their *duffs*."[89]

4

Civil War Bill of Fare

I hain't got the box yet. The chicken won't be good for nothing. You ought not sent the chickens. I am afraid they will spoil the rest of the things.
— Henry Pippitt worries about his box from home

Supplying the United States Army

"The two sides, The United States of America and the Confederate States of America, readied themselves for battle in the spring of 1861." Before the war was over, "the United States put into the field some 1,556,000 men" and numbers serving in the Confederate Army indicate a probable estimate of "between 800,000 and 900,000 men."[1] During the following four years, members of the subsistence and quartermaster departments in the armies and purchasing agents and paymasters in the navy departments on both sides developed plans to feed soldiers and sailors. The ability to produce and acquire foodstuffs and the successful development and control of modes and avenues of transportation continued to be important factors as to whether those in the military had their appetites satisfied or went hungry. As well, the success and failure of battles and military and naval strategies during the war affected the supply of food.

The 1861 Revised Regulations

The 1861 Revised Regulations for the Army of the United States pertaining to rations are the same as the 1841 Army Regulations with the exception of the addition of desiccated vegetables, an increase in the amount of coffee from 6 to 10 pounds per 100 rations, and an increase of sugar from 12 to 15 pounds per 100 rations.[2]

A note as follows is attached to the ration regulations.

During the rebellion in the Southern States the ration is to be increased as follows: Twenty-two ounces of bread or flour, or one pound of hard bread, instead of the present issue; fresh beef shall be issued as often as the commanding officer of any detachment or regiment shall require it, when practicable, in place of salt meat; beans and rice shall be issued

52

in the same ration in the proportions now provided by the regulation, and one pound of potatoes per man shall be issued at least three times a week if practicable; and when these articles cannot be issued in these proportions, an equivalent in value shall be issued in some other proper food, and a ration of tea may be substituted for a ration of coffee upon the requisition of the proper officer.[3]

Eban Norton Horsford, known for his work in food chemistry at the time of the Civil War, includes information about desiccated vegetables, this new addition to the ration, in his publication, *The Army Ration of 1864.* He believes that "*the desiccated vegetables furnished by the Government are serviceable in arresting tendencies to scorbutic disease, and in promoting and preserving the general health.*" As well, he sees desiccated vegetables a better alternative to the problems associated with the decay of fresh vegetables during transportation.[4]

He also explains how vegetables are desiccated and packaged for the military. Vegetables are "thoroughly

A mobile oven baking bread for the army. Photograph from Francis Trevelyan Miller, ed., *The Photographic History of the Civil War.*

cleaned, sliced, dried in a current of heated air, weighed, seasoned, and pressed with the aid of a hydraulic press into compact forms, sealed in cases, and enclosed in wooden boxes. In this condition they are sent to the field. An ounce is a ration. A block one foot square and two inches thick weighs seven pounds, and contains vegetables for a single ration for 112 men."[5]

Supply Depots and Transportation of Supplies

During the war the army had a well organized system of depots classed in three categories: base depots, advance depots, and temporary depots to deliver rations. The base is "remote from the theatre of operations." The advance depots are "formed during offensive movement when an army proceeds so far from its base that it would waste time by drawing supplies directly from the base." Temporary depots "are small ones, sufficient to provide merely for the daily wants of the troops." Federal supply depots operated by the Quartermasters and Subsistence department were located in major cities "with the greater part of bread ... furnished from New York, Baltimore and St. Louis" and pork from Louisville.[6]

Beef continued to be delivered on hoof from different areas. A notable depot at Louisville accommodated "between 30,000 and 40,000 head" of cattle. "During the war the troops on the coast of the Carolinas and also the Gulf posts, including New Orleans, received their fresh beef by shipment of the animals from New York; and Louisville and Nashville were the supply points for the armies operating in that section."[7] A report from a commissary details information about the volume of beef distributed from the Washington site, "at the National Monument cattle yard in this city, where from 800 to 900 cattle are slaughtered and issued per month." These numbers from the same source shed additional light on the volume of beef (and mutton) handled: "March 1, 1864–July 31, 1865: 32,411 pound of mutton sold and issued to officers. March 1, 1864, to August 1, 1865 — 8,315, 590 pounds of fresh beef issued."[8]

Transportation of supplies, of which food for the soldiers was of major importance, was accomplished in three basic modes: railroads; steamers, sailing vessels, boats by sea, on rivers, lakes or canals; and wagons or pack animals on ordinary roads. Sharpe gives the advantages and disadvantages inherent in these modes. The advantage of water transportation was "limitless capacity." A disadvantage of railroad — "obstruction or destruction." An advantage of wagon transportation is that they can distribute what the other modes deliver.[9]

Soldiers were always concerned about the location of the supply train — how far it was from where they were located — because that was often how their meals were delivered and also how often items were delivered to be purchased at the sutler tent. Sharpe indicates that "the Train moves as follows: Wagons containing small-arm ammunition coming first, and then those containing the ordinance, subsistence, and forage, following after in the order named, and the sutlers' wagons bringing up the rear of the column."[10]

Supply train at City Point. Courtesy Quartermaster Museum, Fort Lee, Virginia.

Food for the Soldiers — Good and Bad

Immediately following the war, the War Department through the Office of the U.S. Commissary General sent out a questionnaire (mentioned above) to commissaries seeking information concerning the operation of the Subsistence Department during the Civil War. A compilation of the information received from the questionnaire resulted in the publication of *How to Feed an Army*. The use of desiccated vegetables, a new item on the ration list, brought in not so positive comments from commissaries in the field. C.L. Kilburn reports that "desiccated vegetables, desiccated potatoes, and peas will hardly be taken by the troops as a gift." From N.J. Sappington: "Desiccated vegetables ... are not much used by the soldier as they are generally only fit for making soup" C.C. Carpenter expresses concern about the use of the desiccated vegetable mix: "They do not know how to cook it properly ... will not touch [desiccated vegetable mix] in the field."[11]

Soldier accounts also discuss problems encountered with their food. Rations stated on paper were not necessarily delivered in full. Henry Pippitt complains, "I will have to bring my letter to a close now, for I want to eat my dinner. We have bean soup half made — and a piece of pork. You could not see a piece of lean if you had a spy glass."[12] George W. Barr, a surgeon, writes that some of the men are suffering from scurvy, "the latter clearly owing in the main to a lack of vegetable diet."[13]

Issues related to their rations of hardtack often surface in soldier accounts. Solomon Starbird shares a streak of good luck after actions have to be taken to get rid of bad hardtack. "Tonight we got nice fresh loaves.... The first since Washington about July 10 or 11.... Had no crackers. Had to burn heaps upon heaps of them to get rid of 'em so full of worms and bugs and mold. Had flour enough, but the flap jacks and bad heavy bread tore stomachs to pieces."[14]

It is difficult to find favorable comments in soldier writings in reference to salt beef. Thinking back to his not so pleasant memories of salt beef, better known in his memory as "salt horse," John D. Billings describes it as "penetrated with saltpeter ... often yellow-green with rust from having lain out of brine, and when boiled, was four times out of five if not nine times out of ten a stench in the nostrils." He also indicates that soldiers attempted to remove some of the salt by soaking it in a running brook at night.[15]

As in previous wars, the Civil War soldier was left to his own devices when supply trains arrived late, when rations were short, or when situations developed that interfered with the process of delivery. Consequently, soldiers turned to a variety of options to relieve their hunger and to satisfy their taste.

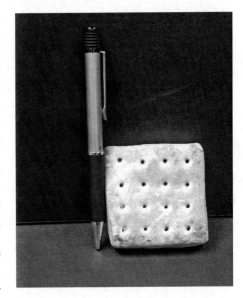

This is the type of hardtack eaten by Civil War soldiers of both sides although Confederate soldiers consumed more cornbread. An example displayed at the Museum of Missouri Military History, Jefferson City, Missouri.

Weighing the proper amount of bread to be issued for the ration. Photograph from Francis Trevelyan Miller, ed., *The Photographic History of the Civil War.*

According to the 1861 Revised Regulations, "Troops in campaign, on detachment, or on distant service, will be allowed Sutlers, at the rate of one for every regiment, corps, or separate detachment."[16] Bell Irvin Wiley writes that sutlers "helped relieve the scantiness and monotony of camp fare, but their cakes, pies, butter, cheese, apples and other delicacies were offered at prices which frequently placed them beyond the reach of the common soldier."[17] Billings sees sutlers as "both dry goods dealer and a grocer." He mentions a line of canned goods primarily sold for use in officers' messes because of high prices and also an item sold near the end of the war, self-raising flour, used by the soldiers to make fritters or pancakes.[18]

Soldiers delivered mixed messages when it came to sutlers. Philip Hacker chose not to do business with one sutler vowing, "We will be paid $58 next May, unless the cheating sutler gets a part of our wages."[19] H.G. Marshall takes his growling stomach to the sutler tent when he has a taste for something different and purchases two bowls of oyster stew at twenty cents per bowl.[20] Pippitt indicates that one time he was so hungry that he gave "4 stamps to the sutler for some ginger cakes."[21]

In addition to the option of purchasing from sutlers, the Civil War soldier continued the tradition of foraging to appease his hunger pangs. From one soldier: "After taking off our equipment, we charged on a lot of bee hives that were laying about town."[22] V.H. Moats said, "We have been living on sweet potatoes for some time past — plenty of fruit, melons, etc. Persimmons, grapes and nuts in abundance, but yet living is not very high."[23]

A soldier in the 118th Pennsylvania Volunteers Corn Exchange Regiment tells about a "movable feast" that he experienced: "Some hogs had broken their cover and were straggling through the woods seeking sustenance.... It required by a slight effort ... to treat such strolling beasts as wild.... Shots rang out ... and two well-rounded porkers fell victim to unerring aim. Pork boiled, fried and toasted 'ruled the roost,' and many ... gorged

Sutler tent. Sutlers sold items, not a part of the ration, to soldiers. These items were often overpriced. The sutler, however, did allow the soldier to have more food choices. Courtesy Quartermaster Museum, Fort Lee, Virginia.

themselves to restfulness with fresh pig before the evening shadows faded into the depths of night."[24]

Soldiers took advantage of local food sources. Edward P. Bridgeman writes, "Ford [a friend] and I fell out of ranks and took another road that led to a farm house to see if we could get a civilized square meal.... We got a New England farmer's dinner of roast beef, etc. ending with pie! What a good dinner for a quarter."[25] H.G. Marshall explains one of his local food sources: "We have had along back plenty of watermelon ... apples, peaches, pies and cakes, boiled sweet potatoes, etc. These we buy of the boys, men and women and girls who bring them round in baskets."[26] George Starbird writes about Negroes who come to camp carrying baskets of pies and cakes: "This morn on my relief between 7 and 9 o'clock I had one damson and one peach pie."[27]

Fields, woods, and rivers were likely foraging sites. When David McKinney went bear hunting, even though he didn't bag a bear, his kill was billed a success: "Wound up shooting several coons and some prairie chickens." At another time he writes, "Am living here now on bear meat, venison and wild pigeons— plenty in market, but very scarce when you try to hunt them."[28]

Soldier diaries and letters record appreciation and enthusiasm for packages sent from friends and family, and also the frustrations associated with the delivery process.

Packages were delivered by express companies, forerunners of modern day express companies. The Adams Express and the Southern Express were the leading express companies during the Civil War. Marshall J. Pixley in his brief history of the Adams Express company notes that "perhaps the most important service the company provided was the delivery and receipt of mail to and from the soldiers in the field." He adds, "Packages were shipped at half price to the men."[29]

William C. Jones first sends a request for a box from home via a letter. After he receives it, he reports on its delivery. "I received the two boxes this morning. The things came in good condition except the bottle of pickles which all went to smash, but fortunately nothing was injured by the vinegar. I have washed them thoroughly in water to get the glass out and have borrowed a new bottle and have put some clean vinegar on them and they are as good as ever. Tell Mary the doughnuts were almost as fresh as the day they were made and we expect to have a grand feast on them today.... Some of the vinegar got mixed with grandmother's candy and made it rather soft — but not enough to hurt the taste ... I shall make some lemonade today of the lemons and sugar.... Give my best love to Mary for her doughnuts."[30]

Knowing that there was a box on the way, Henry Pippett writes home worried about it: "I'm afraid I won't get the box, if I leave the fort. I will get the box, if we don't go to the front." In a second letter sent home he writes, "'Hain't got the box yet, but I expect it in a few days." A third letter expresses even more frustration: "I haint' got the box yet. The chicken won't be good for nothing. You ought not sent the chickens. I am afraid they will spoil the rest of the things."[31]

Northern Soldier Cooks

As men went off to war, they were faced with the problem of how to prepare their meals using a very short list of ingredients, minimal cooking equipment or in some cases, no cooking equipment. The concept of cooks trained by the military was yet to be an option at beginning of the Civil War. As well, mess manuals and military cookbooks had yet to make an appearance. That is until January 1862 with a limited publication by the Government Printing Office of *Camp Fires and Camp Cooking: or Culinary Hints for the Soldier* by Captain James M. Sanderson.

William C. Davis in his book *A Taste for War: The Culinary History of the Blue and the Gray* discusses the cookbook and includes information about the author. Sanderson, a New York hotel operator, became aware of cooking problems that the volunteer regiments were having in the early days of the war. He determines to do something about the problem, offering to teach soldiers how to prepare their simple campfire meals. At Sanderson's request, New York governor Edwin D. Morgan appropriated $200 for the project. It was donated through the U.S. Sanitary Commission, of which Sanderson was a member. They in turn "sent Sanderson and an experienced cook to Washington to the camps of the 12th New York." After Sanderson had two of the companies "doing remarkably better," he then received an invitation from the 15th New York to offer cooking instructions. "In six days he had the men cooking for themselves." There was also a "reduction in the cases of diarrhea from twenty a day to just five."[32]

At this point Sanderson recommended that representatives from each company

Typical mess kitchen used by troops of the Civil War era. Courtesy Quartermaster Museum, Fort Lee, Virginia.

should be trained to cook and also proposed "instituting formal military ratings and ranks for cooks." His proposal was turned down. However, Davis explains that Sanderson was given a commission by the War Department as a captain in the office of the commissary general of subsistence, and then wrote his culinary guide "during the balance of 1861," and it was "published in January of 1862." Davis comments on the significance of this small cookbook. "It was path breaking in its way, the first attempt at a cookbook for distribution to the military, though in this case specifically intended just for the Army of the Potomac."[33]

Sanderson opens his cookbook promising that his recipes "will produce the most savory and gratifying results." And this will be accomplished "using only camp fires, camp kettles, and soldiers' rations." He offers soldier cooks three ways to set up their cooking operation. Before moving on to his collection of recipes, he delivers his advice to the soldier cooks in "Sanderson's Cooks Creed."

> Cleanliness is next to Godliness, both in persons and kettles: be ever industrious, then, in scouring your pots. Much elbow grease, a few ashes, and a little water, are capital aids to the careful cook. Better wear out your pans with scouring than your stomachs with purging; and it is less dangerous to work your elbows than your comrade's bowels. Dirt and grease betray the poor cook, and destroy the poor soldier; whilst health, content, and good cheer should ever reward him who does his duty and keeps his kettle clean. In military life, punctuality is not only a duty, but a necessity, and the cook should always endeavor to be exact in time. Be sparing with sugar and salt, and a deficiency can be better remedied than an overplus.[34]

A concise rendition of his kitchen secrets follows: "Remember that beans, badly boiled, kill more than bullets; and fat is more fatal than powder. In cooking, more than in anything else in this world, always make haste slowly. One hour too much is vastly better than five minutes too little, with rare exceptions." And finally, "A big fire burns your face, scorches your soup, and crisps your temper. Skim, simmer, and scour, are the true secrets of good cooking."[35]

Soldiers generally prepared their meals with a minimum of cooking equipment — sometimes out of necessity, one of their own creation. Billings writes, "Men could be seen by scores frying the food in their tin plate, held in the jaws of a split stick, or fully as often an old canteen was unsoldered and its concave sides mustered in to active duty as fry-pans." He also describes mess kettles and mess pans of which he is familiar: "Mess pans ... are cylinders in shape, and made of heavy sheet iron ... thirteen to fifteen inches high ... in diameter from seven inches to a foot. A mess pan stands about six inches high, and is a foot in diameter at the top."[36]

Two soldiers try their hand at cooking. Edward P. Bridgeman, with "just a little flour ... to sustain the inner man," prepares a meal of slap jacks made of "simply flour and water ... without salt or a hoisting ingredient." He fries them in a "bright, span clean, new tin plate ... after he "anointed the plate, with a pork rind." He said it "would not turn worth a cent."[37] V.H. Moats writes home about a meal he helped cook. He seems to have a better cooking experience. "We just had our dinner. We cooked the rooster, got some flour and milk and made gravy and had a first class dinner, in fact I hurt myself eating and still we had enough for supper left."[38]

No stranger to the campfire, salt pork, in addition to being used for seasoning, was apparently the "fast food" or "grab and go" food item during the Civil War. Billings details how soldiers managed salt pork in their cooking efforts: "Company cooks boiled it." As well it was issued to soldiers raw. Instead of boiling it they "used it for frying purposes." He adds, "On the march it was broiled and eaten with hard bread" and "much of it was eaten raw, sandwiched between hardtack." He also reminds that it was used in stewing and baking beans.[39]

Company cooks prepared food in larger quantities. Starbird describes his company cook's area: "At the end of company, cook hangs his kettles on poles and boils the pre-pared coffee and the pork and beef, and cuts up the loaves from Washington ... men file past him and get their dippers filled with coffee and their plates (tin) with piece of meat and then each taking his presented knife, fork, spoon and bread (drawn at morn) from the haversack and seats self where he wishes to gobble down as much as he pleases."[40]

Food from Charitable Sources

Charitable agencies supplied food during the Civil War. Mary A. Livermore, an active member of the U.S. Sanitary Commission, headed the Northwestern Branch of this organization. She was instrumental in managing a successful Sanitary Fair held in Chicago, one of several held in major cities in the North. The fairs raised considerable sums of money to support the work of the commission in meeting the needs of the soldiers in the North. In her autobiography she discusses food contributions delivered by the Sanitary Commission: "It established a series of kettles on wheels, with small portable furnaces attached, in which soup was quickly made in the rear of battle-fields, for the faint and wounded, even while the battle was in progress." The commission "maintained forty

'Soldiers' Homes,' or 'Lodges,' scattered along the route of the army, and over the whole field of war, which were free hotels for destitute soldiers, separated from their regiments, or passing back and forth, with neither money, rations, nor transportation. Over eight hundred thousand soldiers were entertained in them, and four and a half million meals, and a million night's lodgings were gratuitously furnished."[41]

Livermore gives examples of supplies that were disbursed by the commission during one well known battle. After the Battle of Antietam, where ten thousand Union soldiers were wounded and left on the field, these food items were delivered by the commission: "3,188 pounds of farina; 2,620 pounds of condensed milk; 5,000 pounds of beef-stock and canned meats; 3,000 bottles of wine and cordials; several tons of lemons and other fruit; crackers, tea, and sugar."[42]

This shows the usual method of cooking in Civil War camps. Photograph from Francis Trevelyan Miller, ed., *The Photographic History of the Civil War.*

Following the war, Charles J. Stillé documented the work of the Sanitary Commission. As one of their projects, the commission worked to provide fresh vegetables for soldiers. When government sources indicated a need for fresh vegetables for the Army of the Cumberland in 1863, commission contacts were able to assist by delivering shipments of vegetables from Louisville. As well, fifteen thousand bushels of vegetables were sent from the depots in Cincinnati, Cleveland, Chicago, and Pittsburg to assist with the problem. The commission also managed gardens when a supply of vegetables could not be shipped. It furnished seeds, gardening tools, and about thirty thousand plants for the General Field Hospital at Murfreesboro. He adds that "the labor was performed by contrabands and convalescents, under the supervision of a practical gardener." Soldiers in the hospital enjoyed fresh garden vegetables in addition to "healthful exercise." The commission's depot near Vicksburg supplied large quantities of food to the Army of the Tennessee during the four months ending September 1, 1863, including some of the following items, to mention a few: "Butter—5,839 pounds; Eggs—2,476 dozen; Pickles—5,409 gallons; Sauer-Kraut—1,532 gallons; Potatoes—7,596 bushels; Ice—47,367 pounds; Crackers—25,517 pounds; Lemons—25,200; Dried Fruit—45,205 pounds; Dried Beef—1,496 pounds; Condensed Milk—11,282 cans."[43]

The United States Christian Commission was formed in November 1861 with the goal of promoting the spiritual and physical needs of the soldiers, sailors, and marines. For the purpose of this study, the focus is specifically on the commission's efforts and expenditures relating to special foods for "sick and disabled men." Commission historian Lemuel Moss points out that "those who were well and in active service could more

Opening procession of the Chicago Sanitary Fair. This popular group from Lake County, Illinois, brought one hundred wagons filled with garden and farm produce to be contributed to the soldiers through the Chicago Sanitary Fair. Money raised at the fair benefited the Northern soldiers. Photograph from Frank B. Goodrich, *The Tribute Book.*

comfortably subsist upon the ordinary rations. The enfeebled appetite of the sick and wounded needed something more delicate and attractive." Commission delegates who served on the battlegrounds carried with them "crackers and dried beef ... a bucket to carry water or coffee in, and a cup to serve it out to the wounded; stimulants, with beef tea in cakes, etc."[44]

The following partial list of the foods distributed by the U.S. Christian Commission during the months of May, June, and July 1864 in the armies operating against Richmond reveals the types and scope of contributions made in this one area.

Apples, Dried, pounds—3,955; Beef Tea, pounds—6,350; Cheese, pounds—5,950; Chocolate, pounds—2,472; Cocoa, pounds—3,083; Codfish, pounds—7,600; Fruits, assorted, cans—15,600; Jellies, cans—12,564; Milk, Condensed, cans—38,290; Peaches, cans—3,150; Sugar, pounds—18,127; Tomatoes, cans—18,178.[45]

At the City Point General Hospital, the commission manned a cooking tent where they prepared "beef tea, farina, corn starch, milk punch, lemonade." Even with this facility, Moss explains that an additional service was called for in these hospitals. This need was identified and addressed by Mrs. Annie Wittenmyer and led to the establishment of the Christian Commission Special Diet Kitchens. Their goal was "to facilitate the preparation of all kinds of hospital diet." Wittenmyer became the general superintendent of the Special Diet Kitchens. Moss writes that "in all, between fifty and sixty special diet kitchens were put in operation."[46]

Top: Soldiers' Home in Memphis, a home operated for sick and wounded northern soldiers. Photograph from Frank B. Goodrich, *The Tribute Book. Bottom:* The U.S. Christian Commission manned facilities to assist sick and wounded soldiers. They helped to provided special foods for these soldiers. Photograph from Lemuel Moss, *Annals of the United States Christian Commission.*

One of the few culinary works from the Civil War times was written by Wittenmyer: *Special Diet Kitchens in Military Hospitals*, a small collection of recipes used in the diet kitchens during this time. She designed the cookbook to enable managers and cooks to be able to prepare larger quantities of food and to show them how to substitute ingredients using what they have on hand in the kitchen. Recipes in the collection reflect a selection of lighter dishes although variety is evident in recipes in order to accommodate various medical problems.[47] Of interest is a concept that she put in place in her diet kitchens: "In this system, still used today, each patient had his own prescribed diet, organized by his own dietary slip."[48]

The Christian Commission responded aggressively and sometimes creatively to the needs of soldiers in the field. One action that was greatly appreciated by soldiers in the Army of the Potomac was a coffee wagon presented to the Christian Commission by R. Jacob Dunton, an inventor from Philadelphia. Moss includes a description of it: "It is constructed somewhat like a battery caisson. Each boiler will hold fourteen gallons, and it is estimated that in each one, on the march, ten gallons of tea, or coffee, or chocolate, could be made in twenty minutes, thus giving ninety gallons of nourishing drink every hour!" When it was time to deliver coffee to the soldiers at the hospital, after lighting fires, boiling water, and making coffee, the popular drink was ready to be distributed. "The vehicle [was] drawn by two powerful horses, and attended by half a score of willing laborers." Moss records some of the reactions by wounded soldiers. "I say, Bill, ain't that a bully machine?" "Yes, sir; it's the greatest institution I ever saw." "That's what you might call the Christian Light Artillery." "Good deal pleasanter ammunition in it than the Rebs sent us this morning."[49]

The coffee wagon invented by R. Jacob Dunton was presented to the Christian Commission for use with the Army of the Potomac. It could make 90 gallons of coffee or tea per hour. It was drawn by two horses to move it to serve coffee to the soldiers. Photograph from Lemuel Moss, *Annals of the United States Christian Commission.*

L.P. Brockett tells the story of Clara Barton's charitable work during the Civil War. Her work began when she was living in Washington as the Civil War opened. When the Sixth Massachusetts Militia arrived in Washington on April 20, 1861, "About thirty of them were placed in the Washington Infirmary." Brockett explains that "Miss Barton proceeded promptly to the spot to ascertain their condition and afford such voluntary relief as might be in her power. Hence, if she was not the first person in the country in this noble work, no one could have been more than a few hours before her."

On April 21 since no omnibuses ran because it was it was Sunday, "She hired five colored persons, loaded them with baskets of ready prepared food, and proceeded to the Capitol." As more troops arrived, more hospitals "were springing up and getting filled." She visited daily bringing "delicacies and comforts of her own procuring."[50]

Preferring to assist the soldiers where they fought, after appealing to Major Rucker, quartermaster of transportation, Barton was allowed to load railroad cars with supplies and travel to where wounded soldiers had been taken following battles. An effort in September 1862 found her "traveling with a loaded army wagon following the march of General McClellan." Along the way she bought as much bread as she could transport in the wagon. When she approached the line of battle, she learned that the army supply wagons had not yet arrived so she began "to distribute bread steeped in wine to the wounded and fainting." When the bread ran out, she mixed meal that the liquors had been packed in with flour and salt that she located at a farmhouse, making gruel "in large quantities which was carried in buckets and distributed along the line for miles." Barton assisted wounded soldiers through December 1864. In 1865 she was appointed "General Correspondent for the friends of Paroled prisoners" by President Lincoln.[51] Barton's early work with soldiers would eventually lead to her influence, in later years, of the establishment of the American Red Cross.

The Soldiers' Thanksgiving Dinner of November 1864

Frank B. Goodrich, in *The Tribute Book*, records the organizations and contributions that made the Soldiers' Thanksgiving Dinner of November 1864 event a huge success. For some time, Sara Josepha Hale, popular journalist and well known cookbook author during Civil War times, had been insisting that the country should have a declared national day of thanksgiving to be celebrated yearly. In agreement, on October 3, 1863, President Lincoln formally offered this declaration: "I do therefore invite my fellow-citizens in every part of the United States, and also those who are at sea and those who are sojourning in foreign lands, to set apart and observe the last Thursday of November next as a day of thanksgiving and praise to our beneficent Father who dwelleth in the heavens."[52]

In early November 1864, a gentleman in New York came up with the idea of a "grand Thanksgiving meal" for men serving in the military. He proposed "to supply the army and navy in Virginia with poultry and pies, or puddings, all cooked ready for use" to "show them they are remembered at home." He estimated that to fulfill this goal, "there will be about fifty thousand turkeys — say of eight pound each, and fifty thousand pies, or their equivalents, required to feed the soldiers and sailors on that day." He asked for volunteers "who can afford it" to have items "ready for shipment in this city from the 18th to the 20th of November," and adds that they will be sent to the army and navy of the Potomac so that they could be distributed the day before Thanksgiving.[53]

The final tally of foodstuffs delivered? "The committees received over $57,000 in money, and poultry and provisions valued at about $150,000 more. In addition to three hundred thousand pounds of poultry, the armies of the Potomac and the James received

The Thanksgiving Dinner of 1864 for soldiers and sailors was sponsored by citizens of the New York area. An estimated $250,000 (in money and food donations) was spent on the dinner. Photograph from Frank B. Goodrich, *The Tribute Book.*

"an enormous quantity of dough-nuts, pea-nuts, pickles, periodicals, apples, gingerbread, onions, tapioca, turnips, tracts, and other vegetables and viands." Summing up the grand foray, Goodrich writes that "the army Thanksgiving dinner of 1864 cost the people somewhat over a quarter of a million of dollars."[54]

Union Supply Depot at City Point

The Union supply depot at City Point deserves mention because of its importance in the final stages of the war. Captain Robert O. Zinnen calculates the quantity of rations available at City Point: "For planning purposes, the standard ration, three meals per day, during the siege of Petersburg was roughly three pounds consisting of the different food groups. The standard operating procedure required that 30 days of rations for personnel and 20 days of rations for the animals be on hand at City Point." He adds, "Consequently, at any time at City Point 10,800,000 meals or over 16,000 tons of food could have been found in the large commissary storage facilities." In order to supply the fresh meat ration, "City Point maintained two weeks rations or 2,500 head of cattle within its compound and another herd about the same size across the James River." As well, "The bakery section produced over 100,000 loaves of bread daily. Often, there bread was loaded straight onto the trains and reached the troops while still hot."[55]

The Cooper Shop Volunteer Refreshment Saloon was one of two facilities sponsored by philanthropic citizens of the Philadelphia area to receive and refresh passing troops by providing food and a place for bathing and rest. Photograph from Frank B. Goodrich, *The Tribute Book.* "A regiment consumes seven barrels of coffee, and as many gallons of tea."— Goodrich.

Provisioning the United States Navy

For many sailors the opportunity to eat three times a day became the highlight of the daily routine.

— Dennis Ringle, *Life in Mr. Lincoln's Navy*

At the beginning of the war, a decision by the Lincoln administration focused the United States Navy on its role in the war, the part it would play in the Anaconda Plan. Frank Allston discusses this role in his book, *Ready for Sea.* In the plan, "The Union Navy was to blockade the 3,500-mile coastline of the Confederate states and to cut the South in half by seizing control of the Mississippi River." Blockading vessels would take care of the coastal area and what would become the Mississippi Squadron would gain control of the rivers and inland waterways.[56]

In *The Blockade: Runners and Raiders*, the writers assess the state of the U.S. Navy at the beginning of the Civil War: "The Navy claimed only 90 warships and about 9,000 officers and enlisted sailors." However, numbers increased significantly during the war. According to the same source, "The wartime Navy would eventually boast 670 ships, 8,700 officers and 51,500 seamen." Secretary Welles and Assistant Secretary Gustavus Vasa Fox faced the task of not only purchasing, designing, modifying, and building a suffi-

The Union Volunteer Refreshment Saloon in Philadelphia functioned like the Cooper Shop Volunteer Refreshment Saloon. Photograph from Frank B. Goodrich, *The Tribute Book.* Food furnished at this and the Cooper Saloon included "beef cooked in every style, ham, pickles, excellent bread, sweet and common potatoes, tea and coffee, and often cake and pies." — Goodrich

cient number of vessels capable of navigating the 3000 plus miles of southern coastline, they also had to develop and execute plans to supply the blockading vessels.[57]

United States Navy Ration 1861

Crediting the new secretary of the navy for positive features of the Civil War ration, Norvelle E. Sharpe writes, "It was great food fortune when in 1861 Gideon Welles ... became Secretary of the Navy. He made strong recommendations to Congress for the first major ration reforms of naval vessels at sea; fresh meat, dried vegetables, and fruits."[58] Congress enacted the following ration for the navy in July 1861.

One pound of salt pork, with half a pint of beans or peas; or one pound of salt beef, with half a pound of flour, and two ounces of dried apples, or other dried fruit; or three quarters of a pound of preserved meat, with half a pound of rice, two ounces of butter, and one ounce of desiccated "mixed vegetables;" or three quarters of a pound of preserved meat, two ounces of butter, and two ounces of desiccated potato; together with fourteen ounces of biscuit, one quarter of an ounce of tea or one ounce of coffee, or cocoa, two

Wagons unloading supplies from transport ships at City Point, Virginia. Photograph from Francis Trevelyan Miller, editor, *The Photographic History of the Civil War.*

ounces of sugar, and a gill of spirits; and of a weekly allowance of half a pound of pickles, half a pint of molasses, and half a pint of vinegar.[59]

Additional sections of this legislation include features of the sailor's bill of fare. Section Two provided that "fresh or preserved meat may be substituted for salt beef or pork and vegetables for the other article usually issued with the salted meats; Allowing one and a quarter pound of fresh, or three quarters of a pound of preserved meat for one pound of salted beef or pork; and regulating the quantity of vegetables so as to equal the value of the articles for which they may be substituted." Section Three provided for additional substitutions in that "should it be necessary to vary the above described daily allowance, it shall be lawful to substitute one pound of soft bread, or one pound of flour, or half a pound of rice, for fourteen ounces of biscuit; half a pint of wine for a gill of spirits; half a pound of rice for half a pint of beans or peas; half a pint of bean or peas for half a pound of rice."[60] Section Four deals with diminished or varied rations and payment for these changes.

Section Five addresses the spirit ration.

That no commissioned or warrant officer, or any person under twenty-one years of age, shall be allowed to draw the spirit part of their daily ration; and all other persons shall be permitted to relinquish that part of their rations under such restriction as the President of the United States may authorize; and that the spirit portion of the daily ration may be suspended or stopped by the commanding officer, whenever, in his opinion, it shall be expedient, for cause of drunkenness; and to any person who, by this section, is prohibited from drawing, or who may relinquish the spirit part of his ration there shall be paid, in lieu thereof the sum of four cents per day.[61]

Congress, in Section Seven orders "that the Secretary of the Navy be authorized to procure the preserved meats, pickles, butter, and desiccated vegetables in such manner and under such restrictions and guarantees as in his opinion will best insure the good quality of said articles."[62] J.H. Skillman observes that "for some unknown reason, the item of cheese was abolished not to return until some 40 years later."[63]

About a year later, Congress passed an act to cease the spirit ration. This decision went into effect on September 1, 1862, causing many disappointed sailors: "The spirit ration in the navy of the United States shall forever cease, and thereafter no distilled spirituous liquors shall be admitted on board of vessels-of-war except as medical stores, and upon the order and under the control of the medical officers of such vessels, and to be used only for medical purposes." The same act of Congress raised the pay of anyone then entitled to the spirit ration by five cents per day.[64] Norvelle Sharpe notes in his historical survey of navy food that "after that, and for the next 45 year, there was little culinary change."[65]

Merrill in *The Rebel Shore: The Story of Union Sea Power in the Civil War* mentions several actions taken that made the supply effort of the blockade successful. The establishment of Port Royal as a naval station, once under northern control, allowed the South Atlantic Squadron to take advantage of "shore-based supplies and overhaul facilities." He mentions that Welles, when he didn't have enough supply vessels, "granted New England companies the right to send their schooners into the war zone" to deliver "stores and comforts to the squadrons." By July 1861 the Navy Department had steamers, converted for the purpose of supply, ready to begin their "beef-boat run to feed and coal the blockaders on duty with the Atlantic and Gulf squadrons." True to his commitment to fresh provisions for the sailors, Welles had the steamers "loaded with fresh meat and vegetables, clothing, small stores, ice, and candles."[66] Ringle explains how the ice necessary for packing fresh provisions on the supply ships would have been obtained: "The ice, when available, would have been brought down from the New York mountains to New York City. Ice when packed correctly, will last a long time. They usually packed the ice for shipment in straw or sawdust."[67]

Allston discusses the work during the Civil War of the Bureau of Provisions and Clothing under the direction of Chief Horatio Bridge. Bridge was instrumental in getting Congress to approve the way bread was supplied to the navy: "The old practice of purchasing bread from contractors frequently resulted in the Navy receiving poor-quality bread." Bridge's successful proposal created a system where the Navy "purchased flour and then supervised baking by contract bakers, resulting in higher-quality bread for the Fleet."[68]

Just as Civil War soldiers gathered around their campfires, enlisted sailors continued to eat their meals in small messes on the berth deck, officers in the designated wardroom area and the captain in his cabin. Enlisted sailors subsisted on the prescribed ration and officers purchased their food with portions of their wages. The ship's cook managed his part of the galley section with mess cooks picking up their prepared food in the galley and then delivering it to messmates located on the berth deck. In addition to the ship's cook, a cook prepared the captain's meals and another prepared the food for the officers who ate in the wardroom.

Cooking on the deck of the USS *Monitor* on July 9, 1862, in the James River. Courtesy Naval Historical Center, Washington, D.C.

Dennis Ringle explores what life was like for the U.S. sailor during the Civil War in his book, *Life in Mr. Lincoln's Navy*, including in it a discussion of sailor food: "Not only did the provisions provide nourishment for the men exposed to long hours of fatiguing work and standing watch, but meals also broke the monotony of blockade duty and contributed to the morale of the crew. For many sailors the opportunity to eat three times a day became the highlight of the daily routine." He notes that "the men patrolling the western rivers not only relied on supply vessels but frequently augmented their food by liberally foraging along the river, bartering with contraband, and purchasing from agents and loyal unionists living in the South."[69]

Ringle comments on positive features contributing to sailor food. He sees the use of canned goods bringing more variety to the sailors' diet. He points out culinary advantages that the navy had compared to the army indicating that the navy fared better when it came to cooks because the navy had the advantage of having cooks with the "express duty ... of preparing, cooking, and supervising all the meals served to the officers and men." When it came to their favorite nonalcoholic beverage, "One advantage steam powered-vessels had over sailing ships was the constant source of heat available to boil coffee." His assessment of the overall food picture gleaned from first person sailor accounts and from a review of numerous ships' logs shows "the navy's commitment toward a balanced diet." He concludes that supply ships, sutler schooners, foraging, fishing, and liberty enabled the sailor to obtain a variety of foods, and as well, while on shore, sailors also "enjoyed superb dinners prepared by local inhabitants trying to establish a livelihood."[70]

William Keeler served as a paymaster aboard a blockader, the USS *Florida*. Off the coast of Wilmington, N.C., in May 1863, he writes to his wife, sharing information about his duties concerned with purchasing food and also explaining how his letter will get to her.

> This, I suppose, will go by the *Massachusetts* on her return trip & will reach you via Philadelphia. This latter vessel is running for the express purpose of supplying the blockading vessels with fresh provisions & ice — no private speculation — vessel & stores belong to the government. She gets here on her downward trip once every three weeks & is gone about nine days when she stops on her return for mails &c.... To feed my *family* I usually get from her half a ton of beef & 12 or 15 barrels of potatoes. The ice she brings is as acceptable as warm weather can make it.[71]

Alva Folsom Hunter, at age sixteen, records his food experiences when he served for a year in the U.S. Navy in the blockaded area as a ship's boy on the monitor *Nahant*. His diary offers details about navy provisions and about the daily eating habits during the Civil War. He writes about assisting in taking supplies aboard, including canned items, and stowing them: "We boys were busy at what were to be our regular duties, and helping the steward unpack and stow upon the pantry shelves and in lockers scores of dozens of canned meats, fruits, vegetables and sauces, which were later to be served upon the wardroom table."[72]

At one point, when preparing for battle, Hunter mentions that the galley smokepipe was lowered and no cooking was allowed and explains that "the 'boys'" were called below to help prepare a lunch of sandwiches for the officers. Thinking it would be nice for the officers to have coffee with their sandwiches, he figures out a way to fulfill his wish. Determining to make the coffee "camp style," he asks the engineer if he could have " a shovelful of coal from one of the furnaces to make a pot of coffee on." The engineer gave permission and after grinding the coffee, Hunter returned to the fireroom to make it on his share of hot coals.[73]

Since they had no way of preserving their fresh meats and vegetables on this vessel, it was decided "to build a large ice box and place it on the main deck aft, where it would not interfere with the range of the guns. This ice box was eight feet long by four feet broad and deep, and when the supply steamer came in, we would buy and stow in it about half a ton of ice, which gave the cabin and wardroom tables cooled water for drinking and enabled us to keep fresh meats, etc. for a week or ten days. The ice was paid for out of the officers' mess fund." After they had received a new supply of fresh provisions, he writes, "The men greatly enjoyed having boiled beef and potatoes, or a hot, nourishing stew, for dinner, also a nice pan of beef and potato 'scouse' for breakfast, for several days after the coming in of the supply steamer."[74]

Symmes E. Browne, serving on a gunboat, USS *Forest Rose,* on the Mississippi River, writes about frequent foraging and trading experiences. He reports in a letter that at a plantation near Natchez, "We succeeded admirably, obtaining a good supply of vegetables and some poultry. The latter, however, were rather scarce, owing to the frequent drafts upon them made by our gunboats." A few days later, once again anchored a few miles from Natchez, he writes, "A party went ashore and killed a beef and brought aboard six sheep and about twenty bushels of sweet potatoes." He also indicates that locals from the area where they were anchored brought "various articles of food such as corn and apples, muscatines (grapes), sweet potatoes, quinces, &c,&c." He adds that they exchanged "tobacco, coffee & flour" for items brought on board that day. John D. Milligan, editor, notes the importance of provisions brought by friendly blacks to "a war craft such as the *Forest Rose*, whose companies subsisted largely by foraging."[75]

The Confederate Bill of Fare

The rebels are living on parched corn and peas. Their sick only have cornmeal and meat.

— William Speed, Northern soldier

Bell Irvin Wiley sums up the soldier food situation in the South: "One of the principal concerns of Johnny Rebs ... was food. In the early days of the war, rations were generally adequate, and some of the volunteers fared sumptuously. Government issues of beef, oven-baked bread, and vegetables were supplemented by all sorts of delicacies sent from home or brought in by patriotic citizens living near the camps." However, Wiley also contends that this was not long lasting as the war developed. He writes that the original government ration, the same as the ration for Union soldiers in place at the beginning of the war, was reduced in 1862 and again in 1863 and 1864. Supplies from home subsided "to a mere trickle," and "except in camps that were close to food-producing areas, full stomachs were the exception rather than the rule after 1862."[76]

Reflecting on his service as a private in the Army of North Virginia, Carlton McCarthy writes, "Sometimes there was an abundant issue of bread, and no meat; then meat in any quantity, and no flour or meal; sugar in abundance, and no coffee to be had for 'love or money'; and then coffee in plenty, without a grain of sugar; for months nothing but flour for bread, and nothing but meal (till all hands longed for a biscuit); or fresh meat until it was nauseating, and then salt-pork without intermission." And sometimes, they had no rations issued: "On one march, from Petersburg to Appomattox, no rations were issued to Cutshaw's battalion of artillery for one entire week, and the men subsisted on the corn intended for the battery horses, raw bacon captured from the enemy, and the water of springs, creeks, and rivers."[77]

About sutlers McCarthy writes, "The sutler's wagon, loaded with luxuries, which were so common in the Federal army, was unknown in the Army of Northern Virginia, for two reasons: the men had no money to buy sutlers' stores, and the country no men to spare for sutlers. The nearest approach to the sutler's wagon was the 'cider cart' of some old darkey, or a basket of pies and cakes displayed on the roadside for sale."[78]

Confederate Soldier Cooks

Like the Union soldiers, the Confederates had their share of cooking problems. J.F.J. Caldwell's history of McGowan's brigade records cooking practices and eating situations of the Confederate soldiers: "The chief causes that continued and increased disbase amongst us were ignorance of cooking and idleness about washing the clothes and the person." He recalls, "About midnight we were halted and lay in bivouac until late in the afternoon of the following day, occupied mainly in boiling fresh beef and baking tough biscuits."[79]

Two Confederate soldiers reviewed their cooking experiences. Randolph H. McKim writes about his cooking experiences while he served in Johnston's division of the Army of Northern Virginia. Their regiment was divided into messes of fifteen with two in each mess assigned to cooking, wood detail and delivering water. He notes that "in many of the Southern regiments there were negro cooks." However, the soldiers coming from Maryland had to learn to do their own cooking, "a slow and painful process." Cooking skills were at first limited to making "'slap-jacks'—composed of flour and water mixed, and floated in bacon-grease." With practice, their cooking skills seemed to improve. According to McKim, "By degrees we learned to make biscuits baked in the small oven, and to boil our beef (when we had any), and make soup at the same times."[80] About cooking on the march, Marcus B. Toney writes, "Our rations consisted of two small biscuits for breakfast and a like amount for supper. However, the country afforded some cattle as fine as I ever saw. We had also some fine blackberries.... One day I denied myself the usual two biscuits for breakfast, saved the dough, and had blackberry pies without any sugar for dinner."[81] On one occasion McKim suggests that he and his co-cook "create an apple pie" and invite the captain to eat with them. They had apples "the result of forage" but the question was "How on earth were we to make the pastry?" Thinking back to his childhood, McKim remembers "seeing our cook Josephine make pastry by "rolling out the dough thin and sticking little dabs of butter all over it—then folding it and rolling it again." He adds, "So we made some dough as if for biscuit, then rolled it with a bottle on the top of a barrel, and planted it thick with small pats, of butter—doubled it over and rolled it—and repeated the process until the butter was exhausted. The pie that resulted from all this culinary strategy *we* considered fit to set before a *general*, to say nothing of a mere captain."[82]

Confederate soldiers, like Union soldiers, learned to make do when cooking equipment or eating utensils weren't available. McKim remembers "making a loaf of bread about three feet long and one-eighth of an inch thick by wrapping the dough round my ramrod and setting it up before the fire to bake."[83] Dorothy and James Volo write that the government in Richmond "initially ignored the need for wide-scale provision of camp equipment" with a canteen being the only cooking equipment issued. They note the creativity of Confederate soldiers in designing make do skillets and coffee boilers.[84]

Caldwell explains how, in his experience, rations were prepared in the field. "Rations were cooked by details, at the wagon train, some two miles in our rear, and brought up to us. Corn bread and bacon were the usual issue, with a small quantity of coffee. We often ate the meat raw, and the bread was little more. The latter was generally sour on the second day, and gave heartburn of the most distressing character."[85]

Cornbread, Coosh, and Coffee

The Volos also examine the importance of cornmeal in the Confederate soldier's daily fare, writing, "At times the entire Southern army seemed to run on nothing but cornbread and hard tack." They explain that "cornmeal could be mixed with hot water to form mush, and was sometimes eaten with honey, molasses, or milk if any of these options were available." Additionally, "Some soldiers improvised a full dinner stew called confederate cush, or kush, of cornmeal mush cooked with meat, garlic, and bacon grease, ironically similar to a common preparation of plantation slaves." They also indicate that "cornmeal was also added to soups as a thickener." Even though sometimes "baked loaves of cornbread were available" to the soldier, most often they were simply issued cornmeal.[86]

McCarthy explains how the soldiers prepared their version of "slosh" or "coosh." with flour instead of cornmeal: "The meat is too little to cook alone, and the flour will scarcely make six biscuits. The result is that 'slosh' or 'coosh' must do. So the bacon is fried out till the pan is half full of boiling grease. The flour is mixed with water until it flows like milk, poured into the grease and rapidly stirred till the whole is a dirty brown mixture."[87]

Very important to the Confederate soldier, just like the Union soldier, was his coffee. Unfortunately this ration was often missing in the South because of the Union blockade put in place along the southern coastline that limited the South's ability to import coffee. A visit to a current website nets a collection of clippings from Civil War times found in southern newspapers. Readers at the time contributed directions for making coffee using a wide range of substitutes, some that the Confederate soldier would likely be able to access. Substitutes mentioned include the following: acorns, sweet potatoes, okra seeds, persimmon seeds, barley, rye, wheat, toasted corn meal, field peas, cotton seed, chickory, English garden peas and beets. Instructions for making coffee out of the above items generally involved a boiling or drying or roasting process before the substitute made it to the soldier's cup.[88]

Dwindling Rations and Searching for Food

Soldiers from the North and the South write about trading along the lines while on picket duty. Popular items, among others, for trade included coffee and sugar (from Union soldiers) for tobacco and sweet potatoes (from the Confederate soldiers). Starbird writes, "Rebels are on opposite side of creek. Officers exchange newspapers, coffee, tobacco, sweet potatoes, etc., pass also. This always by our officers disguised as privates."[89] Toney recalls an encounter with a Yankee picket: "I asked him how he was fixed for tobacco, and he said, 'Very short'; so we arranged on the morrow to get on duty again. I was to bring a plug of tobacco, and he a shot pouch of coffee ... so on the morrow we made the exchange, and I don't think that I ever enjoyed coffee as much as I did that, having been months without a taste of pure coffee."[90]

McCarthy also recalls that "the Confederate soldier relied greatly upon the abundant supplies of eatables which the enemy was kind enough to bring him, and he cheerfully risked his life for the accomplishment of the two fold purpose of whipping the enemy and getting what he called 'a square meal.'" As well he shares the feasting enjoyed by the Confederate soldiers after winning a battle.

> Imagine the feelings of men half famished when they rush into a camp at one side, while the enemy flees from the other, and find the coffee on the fire, sugar at hand ready to be dropped into the coffee, bread in the oven, crackers by the box, fine beef ready cooked, desiccated vegetables by the bushel, canned peaches, lobsters, tomatoes, milk, barrels of

ground and roasted coffee, soda, salt, and in short everything a hungry soldier craves. Then add the liquors, wines, cigars, and tobacco found in the tents of the officers and the wagons of the sutlers.[91]

McCarthy comments on the practice of Confederate soldiers eating in southern homes: "A large proportion of the eating of the army was done in the houses and at the tables of the people, not by the use of force, but by the wish and invitation of the people. It was at times necessary that whole towns should help to sustain the army of defense, and when this was the case, it was done voluntarily and cheerfully."[92]

The Confederate soldiers, like the Union soldiers, obtained food to supplement their rations by foraging. How much food soldiers were able to obtain through foraging was certainly dependent upon how many soldiers had come through ahead of them. In some areas armies on both sides had passed through agricultural areas leaving little to be found. In other cases, soldiers added easily to their bill of fare. As well, foraging efforts were affected by food items available during different seasons.

When rations were slim, soldiers continued to seek out food sources. On one occasion a country boy came back from a hunting expedition with a muskrat. He skinned it, cleaned it, and buried it for a day or two. After this, it was "disinterred, cooked, and eaten with great relish." A second story finds a private observing numerous rats in the corn-cribs in the area. He killed one, cooked it, and then "invited a friend to join him in eating a fine squirrel." The friend "ate heartily" until he was told what he had eaten. Even though it was "forthwith disgorged," he confessed that "up to the time when he was enlightened he had greatly enjoyed the meal." Sadly, he writes about "the most melancholy eating a soldier was ever forced to do." This, he explains, is when "pinched with hunger, cold, wet, and dejected, he wandered over the deserted field of battle and satisfied his cravings with the contents of the haversacks of the dead."[93]

Soldiers in McGowan's brigade, during the winter of 1864 and 1865, had a limited supply of food.

> Now we experienced a greater suffering for food and clothing than we had ever known before. The ration of food professed to be a pound of cornmeal and a third of a pound of bacon. But we received scarcely the full weight of the former, and the latter we had frequently to do without entirely. If I am not mistaken, we had no meat for a whole week, once. The most pitiful shifts were employed to procure us meat. Canned beef, imported from England (!) was issued a few times, and at other times, small bits of poor, blue beef were doled out. Sometimes we had coffee, and now and then a spoonful of sugar.[94]

Northern soldiers wrote about what they believed the food situation to be among the Confederates as the war progressed. Henry Pippitt writes, "The Johnny's keep coming over all the time when their 3 years is up, they just take and conscript them over. That's their reason they desert and not having enough to eat but corn cake. They have nothing to eat of any account at all."[95] William Speed writes, "The rebels are living on parched corn and peas. Their sick only have cornmeal and meat."[96]

Civilian Food Assistance in the Confederacy

J.L. Underwood, a captain and chaplain in the Confederate Army, writes about the worthwhile contributions of women of the South in *The Women of the Confederacy*:

"Throughout the South the women went to work from the first drum-beat. A great deal of it was done privately.... In nearly every neighborhood soldiers' aid societies, or relief associations, were organized and did systematic and efficient work throughout the four years. Supplies of every kind were constantly gathered and forwarded where most needed." He adds, "In all the railroad towns, hospitals and wayside houses were established for the benefit of the traveling soldier. These were maintained and managed almost exclusively by the women."[97]

After the Civil War, the United Daughters of the Confederacy, South Carolina Division, published *South Carolina Women in the Confederacy*. The editors state the purpose of the publication — to record that the women of this time were "a potent factor in furnishing food and clothing for the men on the battle line, and for the wounded and dying in the hospital." They contrast the efforts of the women of the South with those of the North: "No 'Sanitary' or 'Christian commission,' heavily endowed by leading capitalists or government funds, brought nourishing food and medicine to the wounded or fever-stricken Confederate. South of the Potomac, it was the mission of woman to attempt, and in hundreds of thousands of cases to successfully perform, this self-imposed and unprecedented task."[98] The section of this publication documenting the work of the Hospital and Soldiers' Relief Societies, includes an abundance of examples where food became the object of their contributions.

According to information in this project, Wayside Hospitals, sometimes referred to as Wayside homes or Soldier's Rests, were intended to be places where soldiers could receive food and wound care along their route. At some locations when stops were brief, women would board the trains with baskets of food and then the train would be on its way. Other locations had dining rooms and hospital rooms with the capability of boarding soldiers overnight.

Newspaper accounts reporting requests and needs as well as donations to Wayside Hospitals are included in the South Carolina publication. An article in the *Charleston Mercury* on January 4–7, 1862, notes that hungry soldiers will arrive needing "Refreshments ... immediately upon arrival." Another account indicates that donations of the following food items had been delivered to the Wayside Hospital: grits, lard, potatoes, pickles, brandy, coffee, tea, one pair turkeys, and a bag of meal. Also a large number of ladies are delivering "daily ... milk, soup, and refreshments of every kind." The article reads, "It is impossible to name the large number of ladies who daily provide milk, soup, and refreshments of every kind."[99] The *Columbia Southern Guardian* reported that the Ladies' Hospital Association, among numerous items, had contributed herbs, blackberry wine, catsup, lemon syrup, brandy cherries, crab-apple preserves, eggs, and a coop of chickens. The president of that organization announced that "chickens, butter, and milk are now the chief articles in demand at the hospital."[100]

The *Charleston Mercury* reported several beneficent actions by southern women. When a recipe for making portable soup was published in the paper, local ladies "made [it] in quantities and sent [it] on to Virginia." The item, similar to bullion cubes of today, could be melted down in water to make soup. In that same paper, a Dr. Bachman favorably reported that "at Greenwood, on the Greeneville road, the daily practice [of local women] is to set tables under the trees to give a meal to every soldier passing through."[101]

As the war was coming to a close, the ladies in Columbia combined their efforts in January 1865 to organize a grand bazaar at the old State House. In a time of sad events they transformed the location into a festive event, hoping to raise as much money as possible for supplies for their soldiers. All of the Confederate states were represented in booths. One woman donated a jar of "sliced peaches, beautiful, yellow peaches, the like of which had almost faded from the memory of Confederates." Each slice sold for $5.[102]

Women of the south worked in a variety of roles in their assistance of the soldiers. The southern cause, like the cause in the north, had individual women who devoted themselves on a full time basis to assisting soldiers. As an example, Phoebe Yates Pember served as one of the chief matrons at Chimborazo Hospital, one of the five large Confederate hospitals which were the result of the consolidation of several small hospitals in Richmond. She was given charge of the matron's kitchen and became responsible for the management of the diet of about three hundred men, preparing foods for the very sick during the war.[103]

Two books relating to soldier food surfaced in the south during the Civil War. *Directions for Cooking by Troops in Camp and Hospital*, a small 35 page cookbook, was printed in Richmond, Virginia, in 1861. Publication notes say that it was "prepared for the Army of Virginia, and published by order of the Surgeon General, with essays on 'taking food,' and 'what food' by Florence Nightingale." According to cookbook and food historian Jan Longone, Alexis Soyer is the source of most of the recipes in this publication. She explains the connection: "He was at the Reform Club in London and went off to the Crimea to help feed the soldiers. The recipes are from several of Soyer's books (no attribution except one title) BUT paraphrased and recipes changed in some cases (spices)."[104]

A second work, *A Manual of Military Surgery* by Dr. Julian John Chisolm, includes information about food for the Confederate soldier and as well a recipe collection in the appendix of his book. At the beginning of the Civil War, Chisolm received his medical training at the Medical College of the State of South Carolina and in France, wrote this manual for military surgery. It "quickly became a standard text for Southern army surgeons."[105] Considering the importance of food to the soldier, he writes in his preface, "I have incorporated chapters upon the food, clothing and hygiene of troops; with directions how the health of an army is to be preserved."[106] On the subject of food he writes, "Food of the soldier should be plain, nutritious fare, well cooked, which, with exercise as an appetizer, he will find no difficulty in enjoying, however monotonous his daily ration may be.... [T]he diet should be of a mixed character, and food should be of the variety easily cooked."[107]

Food for the Confederate Navy

Considering the severe shortages in much of the Confederacy for most of the war, the navy was notably successful in furnishing provisions and stores.
— Tom Henderson Wells

It was Secretary of the Navy Stephen R. Mallory's job to create a navy in the Confederacy. Regarding the process of feeding the sailors, Tom Henderson Wells, in his study of the organization of the Confederate Navy writes, "The Confederate navy adopted the United States Navy ration system but was compelled slowly to modify it." Wells indicates, "Many items, such as cheese, butter, and raisins, which appear on the ration list were never obtainable, and tea and coffee were procurable only through cruisers or at exorbitant rates from blockade runners." However, he also notes that "the navy was eating so well in April 1864 that Paymaster John De Bree was constrained, in the interest of interservice harmony, to recommend appointment of a board to review the navy ration and reduce it."[108]

He explains why the navy fared better: "The navy ate better than the army for several reasons." Exploring the situation he writes, "The ships (except for the James River Squadron) were far from the immense concentrations" of the armies. "The cruisers sometimes brought in coffee, tea, and sugar which were turned in to the naval hospitals, the general navy store, or bartered for other provisions." He also writes, "Cloth was also sometimes used for trading purposes." Finally, he believes that "the navy seems to have had an alert, efficient organization which was flexible enough to meet changing conditions."[109]

In his work he directs attention to communications archived in the Official Records of the Navy. The following letters, from that source, give a sense of the kinds and quantities of food that were being purchased, how and where they were stored, as well as issues that navy agents, paymasters and the secretary of the navy faced in dealing with foodstuffs. The navy agents appear to be aggressive and capable in its efforts to keep food stocked for the Confederate sailors.

This letter was written from Augusta, GA, in August 1863, by Navy Agent W.F. Howell to Paymaster DeBree, who was in charge of the Office of Provisions and Clothing. One of the first issues that surfaces is that it appears that army commissaries and naval agents collect ration items in the same locales. His letter seems to indicate that the two branches are working together without interference during the collection processes. Howell mentions that he has arranged for a miller in Augusta, Georgia, to grind wheat and that the same miller is also grinding for the army.[110] His letter addresses the effect that military movements have on his ability to meet his supply needs: "Alabama can not, I think, be depended on for supplies to any extent, as it is probable the products of the State will be principally consumed by General Johnston's army." He writes that has been sending his agents to purchase in Georgia and North and South Carolina.[111]

He mentions additional purchases. Just as salt was critical in the preservation process for both of the armies during the Civil War and in previous wars, so it was an important item on the navy agent's list. Fortunately, this agent has been successful in purchasing "150 sacks Turk's Island and all the Liverpool salt that will be required to pack pork and beef when the cold weather comes on." Additionally, he has also arranged "for distilling whisky and making all the vinegar the department will require after the 20th of October." Even though "sugar is very high and but little to be had, the Army having impressed it all," he was able to acquire "from 40,000 to 50,000 pounds while they were impressing the same." Howell writes that his agents have been instructed "to collect the new fruit crop and wheat, and in the course of 30 to 40 days I hope to be prepared for requisitions upon me."[112]

Navy agent Howell communicates to Paymaster De Bree that he has been unable to get the quantity of bacon that he needs for the navy so he "purchased hogs, which I purpose to kill and cure as soon as the weather will permit. I have on hand 200, and have contracted for 400 more." Additionally he explains, "The cow peas stored here were unfit for issue and I am issuing them together with corn to fatten the hogs."[113]

Paymaster De Bree communicates with Mallory discussing the effects of the blockade on food supply. He commends Howell and W.W.J. Kelley in the organization of "a packing establishment for curing beef and pork" in Albany, Georgia. In the same letter De Bree discusses an exchange system used to obtain supplies for the navy: "Exchanges of sugar, molasses, and flour for wheat, bacon, pork, dried fruit, etc., have proven very advantageous. Owing to the difficulty of small farmers and the poorer people off the lines of railroad obtaining a supply of sugar, molasses, and, in some sections, of flour for their family use, and to the danger of impressment if collected in large quantities, they are very willing to exchange their bacon, beef, pork, and vegetables for these articles."[114]

Of interest is a letter sent to Mallory on October 18, 1864, from Paymaster James A. Semple. It informs the secretary about the conditions of ration supply at this time. It seems that the work of the agents and paymaster have been quite successful in stocking food for the navy: "I have now to inform you I have now in the storehouse at Rocketts a supply of bread and flour for eight months; beef and pork, six months; rice and beans, six months; sugar and molasses, five months; and tea and coffee for eight months from the 1st of November next." He then mentions 500 barrels of flour at or in transit to a specific city. He believes the supply of wheat on hand "is sufficient to last until a new crop of wheat is made." He follows with an account of significant provisions stored at naval stations at Savannah, at Charleston, and at Wilmington. Additional stores are available at the general storehouse at Charlotte. On an interesting note, the report shows "in the general storehouse 100,000 pounds of coffee, 30,000 pounds of sugar, and 1,000 pounds of tea, with 50 barrels beans and other component parts of the ration" stored for the navy. He also mentions the success of "a flouring mill and bakery recently established" that is producing "5,000 to 6,000 pounds of hard bread daily, which can be increased by skillful workmen to probably 8,000 pounds per day, which will be sufficient for the Navy."[115]

Tom Henderson Wells arrives at these conclusions in his study about the Confederate Navy: "Considering the severe shortages in much of the Confederacy for most of the war, the navy was notably successful in furnishing provisions and stores." Wells credits this success to "its mobility, small size, and dispersed nature." He also mentions "its captures that helped ease the food problem for the navy." Finally he gives much credit to "the initiative and ingenuity of navy agents and paymasters."[116]

5

Army Food during
the Westward Expansion

Bought a dozen eggs. They turned out to be condensed chickens, but the sutler charged the small sum of one dollar and twenty-five cents for them just the same.
— A.M. Mulford, 7th U.S. Cavalry

The Frontier

The period of westward expansion occurred in two stages. First, immediately following the Mexican War, and second, the period after the Civil War. Following the Mexican War when so much new territory was added, the Regular Army troops took on the task of securing the region while volunteer units were being mustered out of the service. With the outbreak of the Civil War in 1861, most Regular troops were recalled to the East. Duties in the West were largely assumed by Volunteers. While they did achieve some successes against the Indians, the Volunteers, for the most part, were commanded by men much different in their approach than Regular officers.[1] According to Risch, "The task of reestablishing control and making the West safe for the emigrant awaited the end of the Civil War and the return of the Regulars."[2] The Volunteers' greatest success was in continuing the development of a system of forts begun by Regulars.[3]

The goal of manifest destiny, having the borders of the United States stretch from ocean to ocean, was achieved at the conclusion of the Mexican War. The army now had a greatly expanded amount of new territory to make secure for the fur trader, miner, rancher, and farmer rapidly pushing westward.[4] With post-war reductions in military expenditures, a small army was spread very thinly over a large area. Life in the frontier army was "dangerous and monotonous, comradely and isolated, professionally rewarding and stultifying."[5] Often they served at posts with no more than a company of infantry or cavalry. Food was a major source of the monotony for frontier soldiers. They obtained little variation in their diet from the ubiquitous bacon, hard bread, and coffee.

81

Supplying the Western Forts

The greatest challenge faced by the Quartermaster and Subsistence departments in supplying the western army was the distance supplies had to be transported. With many posts located long distances from inland waterways, nearly every item of supply had to be transported by wagon or pack mule. Lack of developed agriculture and manufacturing in the region meant local procurement of supplies was generally not an option.[6] Expeditions had to be outfitted with all supplies needed. This meant they would be accompanied by long wagon trains, slowing their movements. Transportation improved only after the Civil War with the building of more railroads.

During the Mexican War, the Quartermaster Department transported supplies with its own wagons. Difficulty in hiring experienced teamsters made Quartermaster General Jesup favor contract freight hauling. In May 1848 this method began to be used. The system expanded and by 1855 most overland freight was hauled by contractors. The firm of Russell, Majors and Waddell became the primary freight hauler for the army on the Santa Fe and Oregon trails.[7]

Elizabeth Custer, wife of the general, gave this description of the Conestoga type wagons used in the wagon train that they were a part of, leaving from Fort Leavenworth headed for Santa Fe.

> The journey from Fort Leavenworth to Santa Fe, New Mexico, then took six weeks. Everything was transported in the great army wagons called prairie-schooners. These were well named, as the two ends of the wagon inclined upward like the bow and stern of a fore-and-after. The blue wagon-beds, with white canvas covers rising up ever so high, disclosed, in the small circle where they were drawn together at the back, all kinds of material for the clothing and feeding of the army in the distant Territories.[8]

Individual wagon trains could be quite large, sometimes with as many as 500 wagons divided into 100 wagon divisions. On average, 100 wagons covered about a mile of road. Wagon trains generally moved two and half miles per hour, covering eighteen to twenty miles per day.[9] Percival Lowe with the 1st Dragoons in the 1850s at Fort Leavenworth describes assisting in the setting up of wagon trains. "By the first of June more than six hundred six-mule teams ... were organized into trains of about twenty-six wagons each, and about five hundred and fifty of them sent out with columns of troop en route to Utah."[10]

The Ration and Cooking

The ration established by the army regulations of 1841 was still in use with few changes until the Civil War.

> Three-fourths of a pound of pork or bacon or one and one-fourth pounds of fresh or salt beef; eighteen ounces of bread or flour or twelve ounces of hard bread, or one and one-fourth pounds cornmeal; and at the rate of four pounds of soap; one and a half pounds of candles; two quarts of salt; four quarts of vinegar; eight quarts of peas or beans, ten pounds of rice; six pounds of coffee and twelve pounds of sugar to the hundred rations. On a campaign, or on board of transports at sea and on the lakes, the ration of bread is one pound.[11]

Additionally, the regulations further provided information about how meals should be prepared.

> Bread and soup being the principal items of the soldiers' diet, care must be taken to have them well prepared. The bread must be thoroughly baked, and not eaten until it is cold. The soup must be boiled at least five hours, and the vegetables always cooked sufficiently to be perfectly soft and digestible.[12]

The official army ration remained unchanged until 1861 when desiccated potatoes and vegetables were added. The ration according to the 1861 Revised Regulations was as follows.

> Three-fourths of a pound of pork or bacon, or one and a fourth pound of fresh or salt beef; eighteen ounces of bread or flour, or twelve ounces of hard bread, or one and a fourth pound corn meal; and at the rate to one hundred rations, of eight quarts of beans, or in lieu thereof, ten pounds of rice, or in lieu thereof, twice per week, one hundred and fifty ounces of desiccated potatoes, and one hundred ounces of mixed vegetables; ten pounds of coffee, or in lieu thereof, one and one-half pound of tea; fifteen pounds of sugar; four quarts of vinegar; one pound of sperm candles, or one and one-fourth pound of adamantine candles, or one and one-half pounds of tallow candles; four pounds of soap, and two quarts of salt.[13]

Fresh beef was provided by the cattle herd that would be driven behind the wagon train on campaigns or kept at the post when troops were in garrison. The regulations stated that fresh beef if available should be provided at least twice a week.[14]

Officers drew rations from the subsistence stores but had to pay for them at the price they cost the commissary, not including transportation. Because of their better pay, officers were usually able to have a wider variety of food available for their meals purchased either from the commissary, sutler, or local markets. Additionally, officers often paid cooks to prepare their meals. The cooks may have been civilians who either came with the officer and his family to the post or were hired locally. Sometimes an enlisted soldier would work as a cook for an officer to earn extra pay. Soldiers doing this work were referred to by other soldiers as "strikers" or "dog robbers." There were other advantages for the striker. Martha Summerhayes, wife of an army officer in Arizona following the Civil War, hired a soldier named Bowen to cook for them for ten dollars a month. Summerhayes discusses some of the advantages for the striker:

> They liked the little addition to their pay, if they were of frugal mind; they had also their own quiet room to sleep in, and I often thought the family life, offering as it did a contrast to the bareness and desolation of the noisy barracks, appealed to the domestic instinct, so strong in some men's natures ... they sometimes remained for years with an officer's family.[15]

With the help of Bowen and canned goods from the sutler Mrs. Summerhayes is able to give dinner parties.

> One day, feeling particularly ambitious to have my dinner a success, I made a bold attempt at oyster patties. I took a can of Baltimore oysters, and did them up in a fashion that astonished myself, and ... each guest was served with a hot oyster patty.[16]

While on a campaign in 1867, General Custer writes to his wife about the food he and some other officers are having prepared by their soldier-cook.

Many of the subsistence supplies were shipped and stored in barrels such as these. Photograph made in restored quartermaster storehouse at Fort Scott National Historic Site.

> Really, he does remarkably well for a soldier. We have for dinner apple-fritters, tomatoes, fried eggs, broiled ham, cold biscuit and coffee. For breakfast we are to have fried onions, baked potatoes, fried eggs, mutton chops, apple-fritters, and some warm bread.[17]

Such fare is quite a contrast to what the enlisted soldiers usually had on marches: bacon, hard bread, and coffee.

Francis M.A. Roe, wife of a cavalry officer, comments on some of the variety of items the sutler made available around holidays.

> At holiday time, however, it seems that the post trader sends to St. Louis for turkeys, celery, canned oysters, and other things. We have no fresh vegetables here, except potatoes, and have to depend upon canned stores in the commissary for a variety, and our meat consists entirely of beef, except now and then, when we may have a treat to buffalo or antelope.[18]

Fort Gardens

Post gardens provided a means of supplementing soldier rations. While it appears that the government's primary interest was in the reduction of costs, soldiers did benefit from having access to fresh vegetables at least part of the year to provide some variety to a bland and monotonous diet. Nearly all forts attempted the growing of vegetables and other crops although success varied depending on the climate and availability of water for irrigation at any particular fort location.

Fort Snelling, established in 1819, near the present location of Minneapolis-St. Paul, Minnesota, grew vegetables for its own use from its beginning. Colonel Snelling, founder and fort commander, hoped to make it self-sufficient. The fort cultivated one hundred fifty acres each of corn and wheat in addition to garden vegetables.[19] In her book, *Feeding the Frontier Army*, Barbara Luecke provides lists of vegetable seeds ordered for the fort, compiled from fort records and letters written by Colonel Snelling. The list includes familiar garden vegetables, including onions, beets, turnips, lettuce, radishes carrots, parsnips, cucumbers, peas, bush beans, cabbage, squash, and watermelon.[20] Such a variety of vegetables would certainly have been a welcome addition to the soldiers' most common menu of bacon, beans, and hard bread. The inclusion of vegetables added nutritionally to the soldiers' diet as well. Extra produce was stored in the three root cellars at the fort.[21]

Colonel George Croghan was appointed inspector general of the army on December 21, 1825. In that capacity he made numerous inspection trips to forts on the frontier between 1826 and 1845 and wrote official reports of those inspections. These reports provide glimpses of efforts to grow food at the forts of that time period. Each company stationed at a fort usually grew its own garden as Croghan noted at Fort Howard in August 1834. "There is a separate garden belonging to each particular company."[22] About Fort Snelling in 1838 he wrote, "The government ration is sufficient of itself, and to it may be added the abundant supply of vegetables at all times to be had from the gardens of the several companies."[23]

Fort Leavenworth became one of the most important western forts. Its location on the Missouri River allowed it to become a supply depot for the outfitting of wagon trains carrying food and other supplies to forts throughout the west. Large scale agriculture developed on the fort's 1,332 acre farm where corn, wheat, oats, barley, buckwheat, and hay were grown. By 1851, the farm was operated by thirty farmhands instead of the troops.[24]

Despite this area devoted to growing food at Leavenworth, when Croghan visited there in August 1843 he found there had been some difficulty in growing food that year: "The fare is not so good now as it was last year, but only because there is not so abundant a supply of vegetables." In contrast, he found when visiting Fort Crawford later the same year that "few or none of the families in Prairie du Chien live as well as the soldiers of this garrison or can boast of so great a variety of vegetables."[25] Similarly in June 1844 he observed that at Fort Washita, "The post gardens furnish a variety and abundance of fine vegetables."[26]

In 1851, Secretary of War Charles Conrad emphasized growing food at forts, issuing General Order No. 1 requiring all posts to grow gardens. Conrad envisioned the forts growing sufficient vegetables to supply the troops and hospitals each year. He also ordered all western forts to grow forage and grain crops.[27] Many forts were already attempting gardens and many grew crops on a large scale while others ignored the order because military action against the Indians left them too short of manpower.

The Quartermaster General published in 1872 an *Outline Description of U.S. Military Posts and Stations* covering the year 1871. This report contains some interesting, brief comments about gardens at various forts. As is seen in the following excerpts from this report, some forts were quite successful in carrying out the secretary's order while others made no effort to grow food. In some cases the local conditions were not conducive to growing vegetables although attempts had been made. A sampling of garden projects follows.

> Fort Arbuckle, Indian Territory [Oklahoma]: "Fine gardens are made. Fort Dodge, Kansas: "Gardens are a failure." Fort Laramie, Wyoming: "No crops can be raised or gardens sustained but by constant irrigation." Omaha Barracks, Nebraska: "Every crop and species of grain or fruit known in the Middle, Northern, or Western States can be grown in great abundance. The gardens are of the finest description." Fort D. A. Russell, Wyoming: "Efforts have been made toward planting a garden, but without success." Fort Sanders, Wyoming: "Potatoes, turnips, beets, carrots, parsnips, peas, beans, etc. can be raised." Fort Sedgwick, Colorado: "First garden made this spring (1869) destroyed totally by hail storm; would succeed very well.[27]

As an integral part of the food supply at most forts, gardens were highly valued by those living on the post. To illustrate, a letter written by Frances M.A. Roe, wife of a cavalry lieutenant, in 1872 at Camp Supply, Indian Territory (Oklahoma) laments the destruction of the gardens by a group of Indians riding onto the post property.

> Last Monday, soon after luncheon, forty or fifty Indians came rushing down the drive in front of the officers' quarters, frightening some of us almost out of our senses. They rode past the houses like mad creatures, and on out to the company gardens, where they made their ponies trample and destroy every thing growing ... this season the gardeners had taken much pains with a crop of fine watermelons that were just beginning to ripen. But not one of these was spared.[28]

Historian Don Rickey suggests that gardening "often became competitive, with each unit at the post endeavoring to raise the prize vegetables."[29] Corporal E.A. Bode relates in his memoirs that companies not only grew gardens but sometimes raised livestock.

> When a company was stationed at a fort they usually had a small garden of from one to five acres where a couple of members of the company raised enough vegetables to keep their table well supplied for the summer. In our company at Fort Sill the gardeners had the care of a dozen or so hogs and fed them on garden produce and weeds, in addition to the slop from the company kitchen — which gave us a profitable addition to our mess in winter.[30]

Soldier Life in Garrison and Field

Life in garrison at the western forts consisted of routine daily tasks referred to as fatigue duties such as caring for livestock, gardening, cutting wood, hauling water, repairing buildings, and working in the kitchen or bakery in addition to regular military drills. Soldiers in mounted units had the added responsibility of taking care of their horses. Corporal Bode commented, "There is more laboring than soldiering in the U.S. Infantry."[31] The time for taking care of various tasks was regulated by bugle calls. There were specific calls for each task including time for meals and even different calls for each meal.

At the fort each company prepared their own meals. Cavalry companies consisted ideally of one hundred men but usually contained only seventy to eighty men. Infantry companies, on the other hand, were set at thirty-seven men. Service as company cook usually rotated within the company. Cooking was considered regular fatigue duty and assignment was made to two enlisted men to serve as cooks in each company for ten days. This frequent rotation of cooks meant that the quality of the meals could vary considerably. If a soldier desired, arrangements could be made for him to serve as a cook for a longer period of time or even permanently. During this time he would be relieved of other duties although he received no extra pay.[32]

Bode explains how rations were issued: "In charge of every kitchen was a corporal or sergeant who had to draw the rations every ten days for all the men in the company and supervised their proper cooking and division among the men."[33] Proper cooking for the most part meant boiling. Virtually all components of the ration including beef, vegetables, bacon, salt pork, and beans were boiled and turned into some sort of soup. This would be served with bread and occasionally cooked dried apples. The desiccated potatoes and vegetables added to the ration in 1861 were regularly used but never proved popular with the soldiers, in part because of inept methods of preparation.[34] Frances Carrington, wife of Col. Henry Carrington, describes her first experience in cooking the desiccated vegetables.

> I turned my attention to cooking "desiccated" vegetables, of all sorts, compressed into a large cake, thoroughly dried, requiring but a *small quantity* for a meal, but this item of knowledge was to come later. At my first experiment, I broke off a very generous piece and deposited it in a large pot, happy to achieve both cooked vegetables and soup. When the vegetables got down to business, boiling and swelling at every moment, the situation became alarming. I began to dip out, at intervals, depositing in other vessels, till I wondered what was going to happen.[35]

A.F. Mulford describes the range of food eaten during winter quarters at Fort Rice this way: "We had potatoes, soft bread, bacon, bean soup, baked beans, and beef stews for changes, and taken as a whole, we lived pretty well."[36]

It was not until 1898 that a permanent position of cook in the army was established by Congress while formal training for cooks and bakers did not begin until 1905.[37] However, cooks were not totally lacking instructions.

In addition to directions provided in the general army regulations, the government produced several manuals to help army cooks. The earliest was prepared by Captain James M. Sanderson and titled *Camp Fires and Camp Cooking* discussed in chapter four. In 1879, the Subsistence Department published its *Manual for Army Cooks*. This manual was reissued several times, in 1883, 1892, and 1896. These manuals describe methods of cooking, provide weekly menus, and recipes.

At mealtime the food was served in the company mess hall with the men sitting on long benches at wooden tables. Tableware consisted of tin cups and plates and iron utensils. In the late 1880s, white ironstone china replaced the tin tableware. At times, money from the company fund was used to purchase special tableware and even monogrammed silverware.[38]

Bread was a staple of the army ration whether in the form of slapjacks cooked in a mess pan in the field, hard bread carried on marches, or soft bread baked in a fort bakery. Nearly every fort had a bake house operating every day to supply the eighteen ounces of bread allotted per day to each soldier.[39] Service as a baker, like company cook, was considered fatigue duty and two soldiers were assigned bake house duty for a period of two weeks. Like the variation in meals because of the frequent change in cooks, the rotation of bakery duty resulted in a wide variation of the quality of the bread soldiers received. The army provided little instruction for its bakers until after the Civil War. In 1878, the Subsistence Department published *Practical Instructions in Bread Making*. It is

Restored bake house at Fort Scott National Historic Site. Although no standard bake house design existed, this is typical of the bake houses that would have been found at western forts.

unclear if this volume would have been available at all forts and as Ketchum observes regarding the instructions, "Few enlisted men would have been able to read them."[40]

Companies sometimes did not use all of the rations issued. These could be sold back to the commissary for cash which would be kept in what was known as the company fund. Money was also added to the fund by selling back flour in the bread ration. The ration called for eighteen ounces of bread or flour per day and the commissary issued that amount of flour to the bakery. However, it did not require eighteen ounces of flour to make that amount of bread, thus there was usually extra flour to be sold back. This fund was administered by the captain or sometimes a senior noncommissioned officer.[41] Money from this fund could be used to purchase nonissue food items or other items desired by the company. Decisions on use of the company funds were made by a company council made up of enlisted men. This council met periodically to decide how the funds would be spent. In 1866, the Commissary Department began supplying such items as canned fruits and canned butter for purchase. Other items purchased with company funds included pickles, fresh vegetables, turkeys, onions, potatoes, apples, butter, raisins, currants, and spices.[42]

Soldiers also used their own money, when available, to buy additional food and other items from the sutler. Some popular items included canned oysters, canned beef, and sardines. However, the high cost of transportation often made the price of such items prohibitively expensive for most soldiers.[43] Ami Frank Mulford, a trumpeter with the seventh cavalry in the 1870s relates one experience of purchasing eggs from a sutler. "Bought a dozen eggs. They turned out to be condensed chickens, but the sutler charged the small

Dough trough. Dough would be placed in a box like this one, at Fort Scott National Historic Site, to rise.

sum of one dollar and twenty-five cents for them just the same."[44] He further speculates as to why the soldiers buy from the sutler when his prices are so high.

> The question arises, "But why do soldiers buy of the sutler if he charges such excessive prices?" Well, we all admit that we ought to pass up the sutler, but if a man is sick and tired of tack and bacon, and has only short allowances of that part of the time, and has a chance to get anything different, even if it takes a whole month's salary to procure one square meal, he will make to venture.[45]

Martha Summerhayes notes that orders were taken for beef daily from the officers: "Towards evening, a soldier came for orders for beef, and I learned how to manage that. I was told that we bought our meats direct from the contractor; I had to state how much and what cuts I wished."[46] Wild game secured by hunting parties provided the only other alternative to fresh or salt beef, salt pork, or bacon for meat. The presence of Indians sometimes meant that it was not safe to send out hunting parties long distances from the fort. When it was possible for hunting parties to go they "were able to bring back enough deer for many tables."[47] At some locations buffalo, prairie chickens, ducks, and turkeys provided other meat choices.

In the field on long campaigns, soldiers faced the most difficulty in obtaining enough food. Before embarking, an army would be outfitted with a wagon train carrying supplies and often a cattle herd trailing behind the train to provide fresh beef. A.F. Mulford describes the wagon train that accompanied the Seventh Cavalry on one campaign.

> Ah, do not forget the wagon train, for on that depends the life of the regiment, horses and all! Here it comes! See the six-mule teams strain on the heavily loaded wagons. Sixty-eight

Bread pans. After its initial rise in the dough trough, the dough would be placed in pans to raise a second time before baking. Pans were placed on shelves like these to cool after removal from the oven.

wagons, and all loaded with hard-tack, beans, coffee, camp equipage, and oats and corn for the horses and mules. And then comes the cattle herd, that is our meat on foot, and it will all be welcome.[48]

Brevet Brigadier General George A. Forsyth describes the usual fare for the frontier army when on marches:

The men, each with his tin plate and cup, receives his evening meal. It is not an elaborate one, the bill of fare being the same as for breakfast — namely, coffee, bacon, and hard bread.[49]

When in the field, the soldiers had to learn how to prepare their meals. A.F. Mulford relates his first experience cooking hard-tack and bacon.

I was initiated into the mystery of frying hard-tack and also lost my first ration of bacon in the operation. The bacon was first fried, and then the *tack* was fried in the grease, after which the mess was placed in hot water, and then the tack becomes tender and nice. I got things rather mixed up, and set my bacon and tack on fire, and so had to skirmish for supper.[50]

Occasionally regiments in the field even had the opportunity to trade with the Indians as Mulford describes when his unit was camped near Fort Stevenson, North Dakota.

A great many ... came to our camp with potatoes, onions, moccasins, and bead-work of different kinds, which they wanted to sell. They also had milk to sell, and our mess feasted on Mountain Stew, potatoes, and bacon, and were happy.[51]

Soldiers in the field were often able to supplement their regular rations with fish and wildlife from the area where they camped. A.F. Mulford describes a fishing experience, "We now find plenty of fish, and as soon as the camp duties are done, we grab a hunk of fat bacon for bait and go fishing. Cat fishes and suckers take to bacon readily, and a kind of chub was also our reward. We cook and eat a fish supper." Later on the same campaign Mulford writes about hunting antelope: "I got permission of the Captain to hunt along the line of march with Private Neeley. Antelope were very thick, but a little sly. I shot my first antelope on this hunt. Neeley shot five out of one herd." Sometimes the wildlife eaten tended toward the exotic, "We killed a large number of rattlesnakes in the camp, and *Crazy Jim* skinned, cooked, and ate one with as much relish as I ever saw a man eat a piece of eel. He said it tasted a good deal like an eel, only it was sweeter and not so tough."[52] Soldiers seemed to endure the monotony of their diet with good humor, as Mulford does while his Seventh Cavalry is camped near Fort Buford: "We now have a change of diet; hard-tack, bacon and coffee for breakfast; raw bacon and tack for dinner; fried bacon and hard bread for supper."[53]

Occasionally, however, soldiers ran out of rations and even encountered difficulty finding wild game and were forced to take extreme measures. Mulford explains, "Rations ran short, until we had nothing to eat but buffalo meat and bull-cherries. Finally we got where we could get neither buffalo meat nor bull-cherries. Then we butchered Indian ponies. The meat was good."[54]

The period of the Indian Wars in the western United States brought soldiers into close cultural contact with various Indian tribes, thus introducing soldiers to some new foods. One such food utilized by the Indians which helped them survive long, harsh winters was pemmican. At times soldiers traded with the Indians for this food. Augustus Meyers, serving in the infantry near Fort Pierre during the 1850s, describes his use of pemmican.

> When I needed a change from pork or bacon, I got some pemican [sic] from the Indians. Pemmican is buffalo meat cut in thin slices, without any fat, and dried in the sun without salting. It was nutritious, but hard to chew. It could be pounded into a kind of meal, and when mixed with pork-fat and fried in a pan, it was an acceptable dish. This and a piece of game when I could get it, made an agreeable change in diet.[55]

Meyers notes that he was invited to eat with the Indians and did so on several occasions "when they had cooked meat of some sort; but I excused myself when I saw any mysterious dish."[56] Meyers learned that one of the favorite meats of the Indians was roasted dog. Meyers writes that the "dog was roasted whole."[57] He didn't eat any of this Indian delicacy: "Although it was considered an honor, I declined." However, Meyers notes, "A few of the soldiers did eat some roasted dog, and declared it tasted good."[58]

Ration Component Quality and Nutrition

While the army made a genuine effort to keep its soldiers well fed during this period, several problems existed with the rations. One of the most prevalent problems was the condition of the rations when issued. Rancid bacon, hard bread and flour with weevils and mice refuse, and spoiled salt pork and beef were sometimes issued. For example, at Fort Berthold, Dakota Territory, in 1868 Colonel de Trobriand found "boxes of crackers more or less moldy, some hominy, and some barrels of salt pork more or less damaged. These provisions, condemned by a commission on sustenance, could not in consequence be given to the troops as rations."[59]

William Murphy with the 18th Infantry writes about the condition of bacon he saw at Fort Reno, Dakota Territory, in 1866.

> We loaded up some sacks of bacon. I do not know how old it was but the fat had commenced to sluff off from the lean, and it was from three to five inches thick. The bacon where the fat had commenced to sluff off from the lean was yellow with age and bitter as quinine. Some of the worst we shaved off, but we could not spare too much.[60]

Distance of transport for provisions hampered efforts to maintain fresh supplies at most forts and required that they keep several months or more rations on hand at any one time. The amount of subsistence supplies maintained at a post depended on the distance and difficulty of transport from the nearest supply depot. Fort Laramie, Wyoming, kept a six month supply on hand since the distance to the nearest depot, Camp Carling near Cheyenne, was eighty miles on the Union Pacific Railroad. This is contrasted with Camp Cooke in Montana Territory where "two years' supply is usually kept on hand." The nearest depot was more than two thousand miles away. The only practical supply route was the Missouri River, navigable part of the year, then by wagons from the river landing to the fort.[61] Poor storage conditions at the forts resulted in degradation of provisions, even if they were in good condition when received at the fort. In addition, simply keeping such items as flour and bacon for two years even in good storage conditions will result in spoilage. A.F. Mulford describes spoiled food sent to them while on patrol.

> A day later a wagon train arrived from Fort Peck, with rations. Instead of hard bread they brought flour, and salt pork that was spoiled. Each man was issued a quart of flour and a chunk of pork. We made flap-jacks. Taking a tin cup and partly filling it with wheat flour, we would add water and make a paste, and then add a piece of pork, and cook the mess. It was difficult to dig it out of the cup. It was worse than hard-tack and ancient bacon.[62]

The inadequacies of the rations sometimes led to diseases, particularly scurvy. Augustus Meyers writes about the problem at Fort Pierre, Dakota Territory.

> About mid-winter, scurvy made its appearance. We had been fed on a salt meat diet for nearly eight months and, with the exception of a few wild fruits, had had no vegetables. Those who were attacked became pale and listless. After awhile their gums began to bleed and their teeth loosened. Their joints swelled and the flesh became soft. If a finger was pressed hard into the fleshy part of the arm, it left a dent that remained for hours.[63]

Meyers goes on to explain the usual treatment at the forts for the condition.

> Little could be done for them, except to give them lime juice, which was among the medical stores. With great trouble some potatoes were obtained during the winter from the "States," as we called it. These were given to the sick, raw, scraped fine and mixed with vinegar and improved their condition very much.[64]

The army was hampered in fulfilling its obligations following the Civil War because of a cost-conscious Congress and public that wanted it to accomplish control of the Indians and security of the West "with a peacetime strength and on a peacetime budget."[65] The Subsistence Department generally felt that the ration was sufficient in quality and quantity and made few changes between the Civil War and the Spanish-American War.[66] While the army ration of this period was usually adequate in quantity and calories and was larger than that received by most other armies of the period, it continued to be lacking in vitamins, particularly vitamin C as evidenced by the periodic outbreaks of scurvy among the troops. Desiccated vegetables, which were never popular with the troops, and potatoes were added to the ration but were often not supplied in large enough quantities to meet soldiers' needs.

As knowledge of nutritional science increased, some within the army, such as Major T.A. McParlin in 1875, a surgeon at Fort Leavenworth, questioned the adequacy of the ration. McParlin felt that the ration was especially deficient in fresh vegetables and milk.[67] Gradually more items were added to the list of foods that could be substituted for those usually issued. In 1878, canned fresh or corned beef became part of the travel ration and later was added to the regular ration. Mutton or dried, pickled, or fresh fish could be substituted for fresh beef in 1879.[68] By 1890, pressure for more vegetables in the ration led to General Order No. 78, July 25, 1890, which directed that the Subsistence Department add one pound of vegetables to the ration in various combinations.

1. One hundred per cent in fresh potatoes; or
2. Eighty per cent in fresh potatoes and twenty per cent in fresh onions; or
3. Seventy per cent in fresh potatoes and thirty percent in canned tomatoes, or in such fresh vegetables as can be procured in the vicinity of the station, or which it may be practicable to furnish from a distance in wholesome condition; such as onions, cabbages, beets, turnips, carrots, and squash.[69]

By 1895, the Indian Wars were over with the Indians largely confined to reservations. The frontier was disappearing. Many small forts throughout the west were no longer needed and the army was deployed around the country at larger, permanent posts.[70]

6

Military Food
for a World Power

*I doubt if the war with Spain will be referred to in this generation without the odi-
ous hue and cry of the day of "rotten beef."*

— Russell A. Alger, secretary of war

Late Nineteenth Century Army

The Spanish-American War, the Philippine-American War, and the China Relief
Expedition were the three late nineteenth and early twentieth century conflicts that
brought the United States to center stage as a world power. Army numbers averaged
about 26,000, scattered around the country in battalion and company-size units.[1] Until
the late nineteenth century, the United States had been focused on development within
the country, particularly expansion across the continent from sea to sea. With the frontier gone, interest became focused on expanded trade, especially in the Pacific and
Caribbean areas.[2]

Public sympathy over Cuba's struggle for independence from Spain combined with
the sinking of the battleship *Maine* on February 15, 1898, in the Havana harbor brought
the country into war with Spain. Congress made a formal declaration of war against Spain
on April 25, 1898.

Preparations for War

The government moved quickly to expand the size of the Regular Army, reaching
59,000 by end of the war, and added to this number 216,000 volunteers from the states,
making a force of 275,000 soldiers to be supplied. The Quartermaster Department was
organizationally unprepared to meet the new challenges and also lacked sufficient field
transportation.[3] Railroads facilitated the shipment of supplies to camps set up to receive

94

new recruits. However, shipments were not coordinated and the lack of wagon transportation slowed the unloading of rail cars, creating congestion and fully loaded cars sitting for long periods of time on sidings. Conditions were especially congested at Tampa, the designated port of embarkation for troops headed to Cuba and Puerto Rico.

While the Subsistence Department made adequate procurements of food rations, distribution problems severely limited the amount of food soldiers in the field received, especially in Cuba. Subsistence supplies often remained at Cuban ports or even on ships. Roads were nearly impassable for wagon trains and were even difficult for mule pack trains to navigate when they were available for transportation. Such difficulties sometimes left soldiers critically short of rations. Charles Post, a private in Cuba, recounts a ration shortage: "For one week nothing came through, aside from ammunition, but hardtack. And we lived on it. Above all rode the persistent hunger; it was a ravenous longing for just the taste of food, real food."[4] Charles Gauvreau, who served with the 21st Infantry in both Cuba the Philippines, tells about supplies not being delivered to soldiers fighting in the field: "On arriving there [Siboney, Cuba] the first thing that attracted my attention was large quantities of bacon and other provisions piled near the shore." Yet within a few days his company finds that "we had no drinking water and nothing to eat."[5]

Ration Changes

Important changes in the army ration to expand the items included occurred in the late 1880s and 1890s. For troops in garrison, the meat ration could contain fresh beef, mutton, pork, bacon, salt beef, and pickled, dried, or fresh fish. The bread component was flour, soft bread, hard bread, or corn meal. Baking powder was issued when it was necessary for soldiers to bake their own bread. Vegetables in the ration included potatoes, onions, beans, peas, rice, hominy, canned tomatoes, and other fresh vegetables. Coffee, tea, sugar, molasses and cane syrup, vinegar, salt, and pepper were also on the ration list. The ration allowed for substitutions of the various components and the particular item issued depended on cost and availability.

The army also established a travel ration used when troops were transported by boat or train. These items included soft or hard bread, canned beef, canned baked beans, coffee, and sugar. After four consecutive days of using the travel ration, troops were to be issued canned tomatoes. In camps the ration list included pork, bacon, fresh beef, canned beef, fish, flour, hard bread,

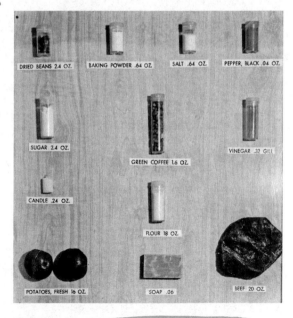

The Spanish–American War ration. Courtesy Quartermaster Museum, Fort Lee, Virginia.

beans, canned baked beans, peas, rice, hominy, potatoes, onions, tomatoes, coffee, tea, sugar, and vinegar. Since not all of these items would be available, the company commander could choose from the list when ordering. In addition, it was expected that company funds would be used to purchase from the commissary other items not included in the ration such as evaporated apples and peaches, cheese, pickles, prunes, syrup, and oatmeal.[6]

The publication of the 1896 *Manual for Army Cooks* gave the army cooks a complete guide to the preparation of food in both garrison and field situations. The book explains all parts of the ration and even provides a bill of fare covering four weeks but also indicates that these menus can be varied depending on the amount available to purchase additional items for the menu. Information explains in detail the kinds of cuts of meat and instructions for various cooking methods such as boiling, frying, baking, stewing, sautéing, and roasting. The book contains forty-four pages of recipes. These range from the common—fried eggs, vegetable soup, and baked potatoes—to the more exotic and unusual—Turkish Pillau, Crimean kabobs, and bombshells, a kind of meatball made in the size of artillery shells.

This manual also provides information about cooking in the field, describing how to build fires and how to use various types of portable field ovens. The oven most generally used during the Spanish-American War period was the Buzzacott Oven. The 1896 manual describes it this way:

> The Buzzacott oven is now generally used in the Army; it is an adaptation from the Dutch oven. It consists of a large rectangular box; the bottom is made of sheet iron or steel, with a top of similar material. It is compact and strong for transportation. The outfit includes all the necessary utensils for roasting, baking, frying, broiling, and stewing as well as many of the cooks' tools for the use of a full company of seventy-five men.[7]

The Buzzacott oven was used over an open fire for its heat source.

Food in Training Camps and Traveling by Train and Transport

While the ration list appears to have provided a variety of items, Spanish-American War soldiers received rather meager rations primarily as a result of transportation difficulties. New volunteers first encountered army rations either en route to or after arriving at one of the camps established to muster in volunteers.

Needom Freeman, a private in the Regular Army, comments on travel rations consumed while on the train from New Orleans to San Francisco, the port of embarkation for troops headed to the Philippines.

Cover of *Manual for Army Cooks*, 1896.

The rations issued to us on this journey consisted of hard tack, canned tomatoes, canned salmon, and last, but not least, nor more desirable, canned horse meat. [Freeman was referring to the generally despised canned beef portion of the travel ration.] To use a soldier's expression, such "grub" is almost enough to make a man sick to look at, but this made no difference, we had to eat it.[8]

Charles Post found his food acceptable once he arrived at a training camp in Lakeland, Florida: "That first evening in camp, we had a hot stew of fresh meat, bargained for at the Lakeland meat center. We had fresh bread, and stewed tomatoes with crumbled hardtack. It was good!"[9]

Troops and supplies were moved from the Tampa port to Cuba and Puerto Rico via transport ships chartered by the Quartermaster Department from private steamship companies. By early June, 17,000 men were in place to sail from Tampa to Cuba.[10] The haste with which preparations had to be made meant that most of these ships were not properly equipped for transporting troops. Quarters were uncomfortable and cramped, and the lower decks were poorly ventilated. In most cases, no provision was made to cook for the soldiers on board, forcing them to eat cold travel rations for the duration of the voyage. Ships carrying troops to the Philippines and China were generally equipped with galleys and more comfortable quarters.[11] However, soldier first-person accounts reveal little in improved conditions from the transports going to Cuba.

Conditions on transport ships to the Caribbean were difficult at best for soldiers. Herbert Ornando Kohr, a sergeant with the 7th Infantry Division, writes about conditions he encountered on the way to Cuba.

Cornbeef, beans, tomatoes, hardtack and coffee one meal; the next beans, tomatoes, hardtack, coffee and cornbeef; the next, tomatoes, hardtack, coffee, cornbeef and beans. This was our menu for the next twelve days, and this we received regularly three time each day, and of course we enjoyed it very much when we had begun to get used to it.[12]

Post's regiment boarded the *Vigilancia* for Cuba but found the accommodations and food poor.

Each company of the regiment cooked on little individual messes of their own. Cooking on the *Vigilancia* was simple. Dave Werdenschlag dumped the required number of cans of corned beef into a wash boiler, broke some hardtack into it, and then, on deck turned a steampipe from the engine room into it. It was not bad; the steam seemed to soften the hardtack, and perhaps it was the boiler scale from the fire room down below that gave a tang to the corned beef.[13]

Freeman describes the food served on the transport.

Our rations were very poor, scarcely fit for hogs to eat. They consisted of a stewed stuff of beef scraps, called by the men "slum;" prunes, hard tack and colored hot water for coffee. Once a week we had a change from this of salmon or cod fish. I believe those who shared this food stuff with me on this voyage will bear me out in the statement that it was tough fare.[14]

Food and Foraging in the Field

The war in Cuba left American troops in bad condition despite a quick and decisive victory. Poor food resulting from transportation problems combined with tropical diseases decimated American troops. Charles Gauvreau notes, "We had been without food and water for about twenty-eight hours."[15] He describes the arrival of rations.

> While we were away for water the food supplies arrived, and such as they were, seemed to be a godsend. Each soldier was allowed a small piece of bacon, three hardtacks, and a can of tomatoes to be divided among three. It was not very much for one who was hungry but I can assure you that it tasted mighty good to me.[16]

Gauvreau notes that the next rations they received included the infamous canned beef: "Later on we were given the famous canned roast beef that caused so much sickness, and from the eating of which many of the boys suffered fatally."[17] A soldier bivouacked ten miles north of Baiquiri at the end of June 1898 notes their use of local fruit: "Oranges, lemons and cocoanuts are plentiful and every trooper has his canteen full of lemonade all the time."[18]

With the surrender of Santiago, rations for Gauvreau's regiment improved somewhat: "We were then given fresh bread that had been made in Santiago by the bakers who were in the service, each man receiving half a loaf at each meal. Fresh meat was also given us, which was some change in the menu that we had had before."[19] Another soldier, Page Ligon, writing from Santiago August 6, 1898, feels they are receiving good rations: "We have fresh meat packed in ice shipped by the Armour Packing Company. Fried steak every morning, roast or stew for dinner and bacon for supper. We eat lightbread and not hardtack now."[20] Sometimes soldiers even had the opportunity to use their hardtack as an item for barter: "The Spanish soldiers whom we had taken prisoner of war would exchange cigarettes and cigars with us for our hardtack."[21]

The situation for food seems to have been somewhat better in both Puerto Rico and Cuba toward end of the war. In addition, individual soldiers seemed to have reacted differently to their food choices. James Burns with the Twenty-seventh Battery, Indiana Volunteers, at Guayama, Puerto Rico, in mid–August 1898, observes, "Every man cooks his own meals and we get plenty of good food, such as bacon, potatoes, beans, onions, hard-tack, canned corn beef, canned roast beef, canned tomatoes and the like." Burns also noted that "bananas and lemons are cheap, a lot of the latter fruit we partake plentifully."[22]

Charles Post describes the bacon — or as the soldiers not so affectionately labeled it, sowbelly — issued in Cuba.

> It comes about two to three inches in thickness, and the plastron of sowbelly is the full size intact of its original owner. On one side is the meat; on the other, the leather. Between three layers of leather is fat, pure, callous fat with a potential, under heat, of liquid lard. When we jacked sowbelly in the tropic sun down between Siboney and San Juan, we reached our battalion and company dripping from wool shirt to canvas leggings with melted lard. Later in the campaign, when hunger bested us, it was a nicely balanced question whether to fry our shirt or our sowbelly.[23]

Some soldiers serving in the Philippines felt their food was better than in Cuba. Charles Gauvreau noted, "We were given good food here compared to what we had in Cuba." He describes some of the food and its preparation: "We had good cooks who made very fine meals. Sweet potatoes and meat were very plentiful, and of course we had hardtack, coffee and some times cake. It is needless to say that there was no frosting on the cake."[24] Gauvreau discovered small stores in some areas: "Small stores had been started in Calamba where candies, bananas and oranges were sold and these were well patronized by the American soldiers."[25] The Commissary Department also made available canned food among other items that "soldiers were ... able to buy ... at reduced prices." Food crops were so abundant that Gauvreau observed, "Our transport took aboard a supply of vegetables and garden produce for our own use on the way back."[26]

Soldiers there also seem to have utilized foraging extensively as a means of supplementing their usual rations of bacon and canned beef. They found chickens, ducks, and hogs to be plentiful there and didn't hesitate to add these to their menu. Needom Freeman notes his company's success in supplementing rations.

> While awaiting orders on the river we consumed a great deal of time hunting chickens and ducks. These were very plentiful and easily caught. We fared well on these every day for a week. We also killed all the hogs that were necessary to supply our wants, and there were plenty of them.[27]

Not all meals were so liberally supplied as Freeman found on one expedition: "We returned to camp about ten o'clock that night. We had to cook our rations for supper after our return, but being rather a frugal meal of easy preparation but little time was required to prepare it; frying some bacon in mess kits composed all the cooking; hard tack and canned tomatoes composed the remainder of the meal."[28] At other times Freeman mentions that their meal consisted only of "canned beef and hardtack."[29]

Troops in service in countries outside the United States are exposed to the foods and customs of other cultures. Herbert Kohr noted the variety of food available in the local markets in the Philippines: "tropical fruits, bananas, plantain, cocoanuts, pineapples, oranges, limes, lemons, guavas, mangos, bread fruit, grape fruit, vegetables of all descriptions, sweet potatoes, onions, garlic, fish, shrimp." He is surprised to find they eat grasshoppers. "These are considered an extra dish in this country. In certain seasons of the year you can see people making large nets and gathering them in and selling them by the quart, or any quantity you wish to buy. The legs and wings are removed and they are fried or stewed." Kohr's company also took advantage of the abundance of hogs found in the Philippines, "We had fresh pork here, having come across several large porkers which had been fattened on rice."[30]

> Soldiers had to be wary of unfamiliar food such as wild nuts his company found. Here were large quantities of nuts resembling hickory nuts; of course everyone was soon busy helping themselves. A German corporal of our company filled his haversack with these nuts. They are very delicious, but contain a large amount of oil. It was not very long until everyone became sick, quite a number sitting along the roadside, pale and miserable, looking as if they had been deserted by all friends. Fritz Otto, our corporal sat there, rolling his eyes and groaning. We asked him what the trouble was he replied, "dem nuts, dem nuts." An entire regiment had eaten of these nuts and could not proceed any farther, being compelled to remain here in camp for the night, many of them vowing they would never eat another nut.[31]

Soldiers often drank cocoanut milk instead of water which likely prevented disease such as typhoid fever caused by contaminated water: "Here [Philippines] we seldom drank water, as the boys would chop down these trees and secure the green cocoanuts, cut the tops off with a sharp knife and drink the contents."[32] However, Charles Gauvreau notes that compared to Cuba, "The water was also much better."[33]

Another burden of supply was placed on the Quartermaster and Subsistence departments when in 1900 the United States sent troops to China to join a multinational force

Soldiers with Light Battery A, Missouri Volunteers, slicing bread in Puerto Rico, 1898. Courtesy Museum of Missouri Military History (Missouri National Guard), Jefferson City, Missouri.

there to protect foreigners and Chinese Christians from attacks by what was known in the west as the Boxer movement. The Quartermaster Department handled the placement and supply of troops in China with few problems even though it was still supplying combat troops in the Philippines.[34]

Items of food and drink encountered by soldiers in other cultures can prove detrimental as was the case of a drink native to the Philippines called "vino" or "beno." Numerous soldiers tried it and suffered deleterious effects when drinking it. Major Charles Lynch of the Medical Department explains the production and ingredients of beno in the 1903 Inspector-General's report.

> This is usually made from "tuba" which is the juice from the buds, unripe fruit of the nipa palm. "Tuba" contains a small proportion of alcohol, is not unwholesome and resembles somewhat the pulque of Mexico. Like that liquor, it rapidly undergoes an acid fermentation, and can only be drunk or utilized for the production of "vino" soon after collection. For this reason distilleries are established in districts where the nipa palm grows.[35]

The manner in which this juice was distilled resulted in the final product containing not only ethyl alcohol but also methyl alcohol and other alcohols harmful to the body.

The problem of soldiers consuming beno was exacerbated by the passage in February 1901 of what became known as the Anti-Canteen Act. With pressure from the Woman's Christian Temperance Union, Congress passed this legislation forbidding the sale of alcoholic beverages at army canteens. This forced soldiers wanting alcohol to frequent establishments away from their base which often sold poor quality and sometimes harmful drinks such as beno.

Post Exchange System

The method of supplying various nonfood items needed by soldiers and food items not included in the ration underwent several changes. After 1867 the sutler became known officially as the post trader. Post traders functioned much as sutlers although they could not take part of a soldier's pay for items bought on credit when pay was issued by the paymaster as sutlers could. They also were not required to make payments to the post fund. After 1870, appointment of post traders was made by the secretary of war rather than by officers at each post. The system was completely changed in 1895 with the issuance of War Department General Order No. 46 establishing the Post Exchange system. Post commanders were directed to establish an exchange which basically functioned as a general store. The exchanges supplied goods and services not normally supplied by the army. Canteens, operated by the Post Exchange, sold alcoholic beverages. The canteens became popular with soldiers as a social center.

Charitable Organizations

Following a trip to Europe, Clara Barton returned to the United States with a new purpose for her life — to get the United States to sign the Geneva Convention of 1864 which recognized the neutrality of those bearing a red cross on a white background aiding the wounded on the battlefield. She also promoted the establishment of a Red Cross organization in this country. She succeeded on both fronts. In 1881 the American Association of the Red Cross was incorporated in Washington, D.C., with Barton serving as its first president. In March 1882 President Arthur signed and the Senate later approved the Geneva Convention.

A group from the Red Cross including Barton visited Cuba shortly before the sinking of the *Maine* to see what could be done to relieve the suffering of the Cuban people, but before plans could be completed, the United States and Spain were at war. Barton returned home and chartered a ship, *The State of Texas*, to be loaded with supplies and return to Cuba. The Red Cross provided cots, blankets, and medicine as well as food. In addition to material supplies, they also staffed hospitals with nurses. A soldier with the Sixteenth Infantry, which was heavily involved in the battle for Santiago and was severely short of rations, writes about food from the Red Cross: "Day before yesterday Clara Barton sent each company twenty-five pounds of corn meal and seventeen pounds of rice. It was a blessing, I tell you. We all got a spoonful of mush, and it was the best thing I ever tasted in my life."[36]

Light Battery A, Missouri Volunteers, selling beer at their unit canteen. Courtesy Museum of Missouri Military History (Missouri National Guard), Jefferson City, Missouri.

In less than a year after the war began, Barton had in place seven hundred nurses for service in Cuba, Puerto Rico, and the Philippines. Scores of other workers were lined up to assist in these locations and at camps in the South and east and west coasts. Kitchen tents were set up near camps to provide home-cooked food for soldiers awaiting deployment.[37]

The Red Cross was particularly active at Camp Merritt in San Francisco where soldiers were stationed before leaving for the Philippines. Needom Freeman writes of enjoying a meal provided by the Red Cross while awaiting transport to the Philippines: "We found our regiment just ready to enjoy a grand banquet prepared by the Red Cross Society. It was prepared near the piers in a long stone building; long tables were piled full of all that a crowd of hungry soldiers could wish for."[38] The organization also saw to it that each unit enjoyed a good meal before departing. Freeman also describes extra food put on board the ship for use by the enlisted men en route to the Philippines. Unfortunately these provisions only benefited the officers.

The society, in addition to the dinner given to us, had several hundred dollars worth of provisions put on board our transport and all marked, "For enlisted men only on deck." The provisions put on board for us were well cared for — by officers, who took charge of them and guarded them so well that if an enlisted man got any of them, he had to steal them from under a guard.[39]

By the time the second expedition left for the Philippines the Red Cross had put together an extensive list of items for the troops on transport ships:

2 cases Phillips cocoa	4 dozen bottles lime juice
1 case condensed milk	6 large bottles of malted milk
1 case of alcohol	2 boxes unsweetened chocolate
20 pounds permanganate potash	500 pounds dried fruit
1 gallon Jamaica ginger	1 sack (501 pounds) farina
1 keg insect powder	2 cases whisky
1 case clam juice	3 bottles brandy
2 pails anchovies	1 case claret
10 pounds chipped beef	12 dozen towels
90 pounds steamed oatmeal	12 dozen handkerchiefs

Religious groups constituted the other charitable groups providing support for troops during the war. Those especially active included the YMCA, Christian Endeavor, and Catholic Truth Society. While their primary focus was the spiritual well-being of the men they also provided places for refreshment and entertainment.

Canned Roast Beef and "Embalmed Beef" Controversy

The Spanish-American War has become almost synonymous with bad beef products being issued to soldiers in the U.S. Army. As can be seen from first person accounts, soldiers often had to endure unpalatable rations. Russell A. Alger, secretary of war during the Spanish-American War, wrote in 1901, "I doubt if the war with Spain will ever be referred to in this generation without the odious hue and cry of the day of 'rotten beef.'"[40] The association of the Spanish-American War and bad beef persisted not only for Alger's generation but even today. During and immediately following the war serious allegations arose about the quality of both canned beef and fresh refrigerated beef provided as a part of the ration of soldiers. Notable too is the fact that this war was the first involving the army in which fresh beef was not supplied on hoof.[41]

President McKinley appointed the War Investigation Commission September 24, 1898, to investigate the conduct of the war, especially in Cuba and Puerto Rico. The commission was headed by General Grenville M. Dodge and thus became popularly known as the Dodge Commission. Major General Nelson A. Miles, commanding general of the army, appeared before the commission December 21, 1898, shocking the commission and the nation when he made allegations concerning the quality of canned and refrigerated beef supplied to troops in Cuba and Puerto Rico.

Miles charged that refrigerated beef issued to soldiers was preserved by the injection of chemical preservatives: "There was sent to Porto Rico 337 tons of what is known as so-called refrigerated beef, which you might call embalmed beef." Miles went on to state to the commission that he did not know that canned roast beef was part of the ration.[42]

In interviews following his testimony before the commission Miles elaborated further on both refrigerated and canned beef.

> I have overwhelming evidence that the embalmed beef was treated with chemicals in order to preserve it. I have affidavits from men who saw the beef undergoing treatment or embalming process. Now, as to the canned roast beef, that was different from the embalmed beef. The canned roast beef was the beef after the extract had been boiled out of it. You have seen the advertisements "Beef Extract, one pound contains the substance of from four to five pounds of prime beef." Well, this is the beef after the extract has been taken from it. They put this beef pulp in cans and labeled it "canned roast beef." The soldiers report that the canned beef was nauseating. If swallowed it could not be kept on the stomach.[43]

The testimony and public statements of General Miles greatly offended and angered Commissary-General Charles P. Eagan since they reflected directly on his competence and integrity. Eagan countered Miles' charges with such strong language that he was court-martialed for "conduct unbecoming an officer and a gentleman, and for conduct to the prejudice of good order and military discipline." He was found guilty and suspended from rank and duty for six years but was eventually reinstated and allowed to retire.[44]

However, the controversy did not end but resulted in further investigations. An Army Court of Inquiry consisting of officers of the Regular Army was convened by the War Department February 9, 1899, to investigate the charges made by General Miles in regards to the refrigerated beef and the canned roast beef products.

In its report, the court observed that both the refrigerated beef and the canned roast beef were common commercial products available to the public and also extensively used by the United States Navy without problems.[45] Armour and Swift were the primary suppliers of meat to the government at this time. While the fresh beef had long been a part of the army ration, canned beef first appeared as a ration item in 1878 and then only as a component of the travel ration. It was never intended to be used as the primary meat portion of the field ration for extended periods of time as turned out to be the case in some instances in Cuba.[46] The court came to the following conclusion.

> The court is of the opinion that the canned roast beef was not suitable as a travel ration on transports, considering the absence of cooking facilities, and the absence from that ration of fresh vegetables and condiments. For use on shore as a field ration, where the companies have their camp cooking equipment, and vegetables are available, canned roast beef is suitable for issue, say two days in ten, but not for two days in succession. In some organizations it seems to have constituted at least one-half of the meat ration.[47]

The court also found that inadequate care was taken of refrigerated beef during its transportation to units in the field. "The arrangements for issuing the beef and transporting it to the camps do not seem to have been either adequate or efficient.... As a consequence a considerable portion of the beef became tainted before it reached the regimental camps, and was either rejected altogether or trimmed down before being cooked."[48] The court learned that

> the wagons assigned to carry the beef were sometimes not clean, and often there was no protection from sun and rain; but the most serious mistake seems to have been due to a failure to arrange systematically for rapid conveyance and prompt delivery, so that the wagons could receive their brigade issues and return direct to camp, and so insure its speedy delivery for consumption.[49]

The court found that "the refrigerated beef is ... a suitable ration for troops when it can be issued to them in good condition."[50]

In its summary, the court concluded that "the refrigerated beef, furnished under contracts for the use of the armies, was not 'doctored' or treated with any other agent than cold air."[51] It also reiterated that the war with Spain was the first time canned roast beef had been used for anything other than the travel ration. The court further determined that no charges questioning the fitness of the refrigerated or canned beef had been made to the War Department before General Miles' appearance before the Dodge Commission.

While the army concluded military actions in Cuba, Puerto Rico, the Philippines, and China successfully, the mistakes made in supplying rations for troops, especially in Cuba and Puerto Rico made it clear that significant reorganization of the Quartermaster and Subsistence departments needed to be made. It also became evident that the climatic conditions in the region where troops were to be fed needed to be considered in choosing ration items. While there was not a shortage in the total number of rations purchased for the troops, inadequate planning and transportation resulted in long delays in getting supplies to troops on the frontline. Mishandling and improper storage caused rations reaching the troops to sometimes be in poor condition.[52]

Navy Food for a World Power

After the War with Spain ... tea and coffee were authorized to men at first "turning out." And so began our present practice of coffee at reveille.
— Commander J.H. Skillman (S.C.), U.S. Navy

The navy in the decades following the Civil War and moving toward the twentieth century experienced changes in administration and changes on board vessels. The practice of making purchases through civilian navy agents, established in 1776, was discontinued in 1865. This change placed more responsibility on the Pay Corps officers. Paymasters were then charged with the complete responsibility for supply of the navy ashore as well as afloat. Prior to 1886, each bureau maintained complete control over its own purchases and storage and issuance. This resulted in duplication and a navy inventory far in excess of the navy's needs.[53]

The solution to this problem came with the creation of the General Storehouse System in 1886. Stocks were consolidated under one general storekeeper at each navy yard and station. Aboard ship, stock was consolidated in a single supply department managed by a paymaster. A Navy Stock Fund was created with each bureau being charged for an item when it was issued. This fund was administered by the Pay Corps. In 1892 the officers of the Pay Corps became the accountants for the navy in much the same fashion as they had become its storekeepers. That same year the Bureau of Provisions and Clothing was renamed the Bureau of Supplies and Accounts.[54]

J.H. Skillman comments on subsistence of the navy in the final decades of the century following the Civil War: "Little of interest arose in connection with the subsistence of enlisted personnel until after the War with Spain, although in 1872 additional allowances of tea and coffee were authorized to men at first 'turning out.' And so began our present practice of coffee at reveille."[55]

USS *Powhatan* berth deck cooks during the 1870s or 1880s. Courtesy Naval Historical Center, Washington, D.C.

Frank J. Allston indicates that the Union had almost 700 ships at the end of the Civil War. However, with the war over, "Hundreds of vessels were decommissioned." He adds, "By 1880, the number of ships in the Fleet had dropped to 48 outmoded vessels" which found the U.S. Navy ranking twelfth in the lineup of world sea powers. However, he explains that changes were made to take the navy in a new direction when in 1881 "a Naval Advisor Board" was organized "to develop a comprehensive plan for a modern Navy." The addition of vessels with more modern construction and more modern technology moved the navy forward once again to its place as a world sea power.[56]

The Bureau of Provisions and Clothing also began the process of developing positive changes during the last decades of the century. In 1886 the bureau "sponsored an experiment in USS *Independence* [a receiving ship located at Mare Island Navy Yard] to eliminate berth-deck messing in favor of a consolidated general mess."[57] In a discussion of general messing eleven years after the project, Lieutenant-Commander Daniel Delehanty, the executive officer of USS *Independence* at the time of the experiment, indicates that he had for some time been of the belief that the "system in vogue for messing ... is faulty in the extreme." He details the success of the experiment.

> I had the honor to put in successful operation, the first consolidated mess. Like all innovations, it at first met with considerable opposition, but after a month or two the advantages were so manifest to the men in the better character of the food, its superior preparation, economy, cleanliness and adaptability, that all opposition ceased and the men willingly conceded that it was the only satisfactory way for them to mess on board ship, and the Independence mess is to-day operated exactly as it was ten years ago.[58]

Mess on board the USS *Olympia* in 1898. This photograph shows that the *Olympia* was using the consolidated mess at this time instead of berth deck messing. Courtesy Naval Historical Center, Washington, D.C.

A change in the method of procuring supplies was passed by Congress in 1890. Prior to this date, purchases were made by each bureau for its use. After this date supplies were purchased through centralized procurement with centralized accounting also put in place and the bureau was renamed the Bureau of Supplies and Accounts in 1892.[59]

A second consolidated mess, ten years after the USS *Independence* experiment, was initiated on the USS *Indiana* on May 1, 1896. Lieutenant Benton C. Decker discusses the project in an article in 1897. He opens with an explanation of the term "consolidated mess," indicating that it "comes from the fact that all the independent messes, with their cooks, caterers and mess funds, are consolidated in one general mess," and he follows with a description of how the mess was organized. The mess consisted of "about three hundred and eighty men, a ship's cook of the 1st class, two of the 2nd class, and four of the 3rd class, a commissary yeoman and a storeroom keeper." He adds, "Of all the ship's company only the chief petty officers and the officers' servants are excused from joining the mess." He notes, "Two of the cooks are stationed in the bakers, the others work the galley. In addition to the cooks there are messmen, taken from the landsmen, who receive the ration at the galley and serve it to the mess ... and are also responsible for the mess equipage."[60]

He explains how meals were served and also the advantages to the new system: "A spare coal bunker on the berth deck has been converted into a storeroom and serving-out stand. The consolidating of the messes renders the subdividing of the cold storage room unnecessary and causes it to serve the crew much more efficiently." He adds, "The centralization of the ration for the crew tends to make its distribution more economical. The services of a few trained, well paid cooks ensure the proper preparation of the ration and no waste from badly cooked food."[61]

The addition of the ship's store caused concern among officers "who feared a decline in discipline and efficiency." This new aspect of the ship "was inaugurated aboard the USS INDIANA in 1896, which at first sold only beer and used the profits to buy additional food for the mess." Apparently the success of the store later was attributed as much to the sale of "such personal articles as towels, soap, candy and tobacco" which had been added as to the sale of beer.[62] An advantage of the store was that the quality of the beer could be assured, the quantity consumed regulated, and a uniform price maintained. This allowed a reasonable profit. The profits could be saved in a reserve fund to be used for extra "sea stores" and for "extra occasions, such as Christmas" and for extra food.[63] He sums up the positive features, in his opinion, of the consolidated mess.

> The chief advantage of the system is thought to be that the men are constantly provided with a wholesome, steady diet. There will no longer be caterers running off with the mess money and the mess living on "hard bread and coffee." Mess money cannot be devoted to betting on boat races. Poor landsmen, in debt, are no longer seen at the mast begging for a few dollars to put in the mess. The indigestible messes served up by ignorant landsmen are no longer seen. The money paid cooks formerly is now saved to the men, the only cooks that are allowed extra compensation being the galley cooks; the chief cook receiving one ration and the others, each, half a ration. There is no longer the trouble between messes as to the stowing of sea stores and the finding of them in every stowhole.[64]

Decker includes a sample menu for a consolidated mess: "Breakfast: eggs, liver and bacon, coffee, bread and butter. Dinner: fresh corn beef and cabbage, potatoes, new onions and radishes, coffee, bread and butter. Supper: chicken stew, tea, bread and butter—condensed milk and sugar being supplied for the coffee and tea." He adds that during a landing drill sailors were "supplied with a substantial ration of sandwiches, sardines, and hot coffee, without any inconvenience." The usual Sunday dinner included roast pork, jelly, fresh green peas, new potatoes, and pie.[65]

Lieutenant W.F. Fullam, in written discussion section at the end of Decker's article, expresses his support of the general mess, offering his reasons for his support. He points out that on board a ship that has twenty messes "it takes twenty cooks and eight assistant cooks to run them. A sum of $400 is paid monthly by the messes to these men for cooking." In addition to this expense he calls attention to "the exorbitant prices charged by bumboats" as compared to the "groceryman ashore prices." He gives as examples "Potatoes, per 100 lbs—$1,60 vs. $0.85; Milk per quart—10 vs .05; Eggs (100)—1.32 vs .88; Milk, condensed—.20 vs. .25."[66]

Navy in the Spanish American War

Historian Charles Oscar Paullin writes about the involvement of the navy in the Philippines and in Cuba during the Spanish-American War in 1898. Rear Admiral George Dewey commanded the single Asiatic Squadron at Manila Bay and three fleets operated in the Atlantic around Cuba. Rear Admiral W.T. Sampson commanded the blockading squadron, Commodore W.S. Schley commanded the flying squadron, and Commodore J.A. Howell the northern patrol squadron. Paullin notes that "later, these three squadrons were united under the command of Sampson." Regarding the number of enlisted men serving in the navy during the war he indicates, "On August 15, when the enlisted force reached its maximum, it numbered 24,123 men," and "the marines were increased by some 2100 men."[67]

He discusses how the supply operation worked during the war: "The Bureau of Supplies and Accounts ... furnished 193 ships with naval stores." From a base at Key West and at several of the navy yards, "Large quantities of provisions, clothing and other articles were collected." Commenting on the arrangements made at these locations he writes, "The bureau maintained at Key West a three months' supply for 9000 men; and at Nor-

Engraving from *Harper's Weekly* February 12, 1876, of a ship headed to the arctic. Note sled dogs, casks of provisions, and sheep. Early sailing ships on long voyages sometimes carried livestock on board to provide fresh meat. Courtesy Naval Historical Center, Washington, D.C.

folk and Mare Island, each, a three months' supply for 4000 men." As well, "New York was the chief market for naval stores, and the New York navy yard was the chief receiving and distributing depot of the navy."[68]

Shortly before the war started, Dewey received orders "to fill his ships with stores and to buy a collier and supply ship, and within forty-eight hours after receiving his orders, he had purchased the *Nashan* and *Zafiro*." The first was filled with coal and the second with provisions. As well, "Early in May the *City of Pekin* was dispatched from San Francisco with three months' provisions for the Asiatic fleet and a large consignment of miscellaneous stores." Likewise, "In June a refrigerating ship, laden with 600,000 pounds of fresh meats and a like quantity of fresh vegetables, was sent from San Francisco to Manila." Also, according to Paullin, "Sampson's first refrigerating ship was the *Supply*, which on May 7 sailed for the fleet off Cuba loaded with fresh meats, vegetables, fruits,

Galley of the USS *Olympia* in 1899.

ice and other supplies." Additionally, "Two other ships, the *Celtic* and *Glacier*, were fitted out with refrigerators, and were used to carry supplies to the naval vessels in the West Indies."[69] Allston credits Edwin Stewart, chief of the Bureau of Supplies and Accounts and paymaster general at the time, who "pioneered the use of refrigerator ships in support of American Forces in the Cuban and Philippine theaters."[70]

A sampling of first person accounts documents the food experiences of navy men on board Spanish-American War era naval vessels. The first food account comes from a diary of a sailor, George W. Robinson, who served as a fireman in a boiler room. Information at The Spanish-American War Centennial website introduces the "quite rare" diary that "shows a side of the navy not frequently recorded — life in the boiler rooms deep in the bowels of the vessel." The introduction at the site explains what daily life would have been like in this area of the vessel: "The men who served in the boiler rooms, engine rooms and coal bunkers of naval vessels had the most unglamorous, and most difficult jobs in the navy."[71]

Robinson served on the USS *Oregon* when it made its fast trip starting in March 1898 from the West Coast around South America to Cuba to assist with the blockade. Overall, the opinions of his food experiences as an enlisted man seemed to be unsatisfactory. He unhappily compares the enlisted men's food to officer food. The transcriber of the diary notes that Robinson may have not been aware that officers purchased their food items out of their own money unlike enlisted men who were provided government rations.[72] It would seem that strenuous work in the boiler room would have contributed to the hunger that Robinson records in his diary. Unfortunately, it seems that his hunger oftentimes was not satisfied by his rations and sometimes even by food he was able to personally acquire from sources ashore.

When his ship stopped for coaling, Robinson writes, "Our boat had been sent ashore for fresh provisions and returned about non [noon] with sweet potatoes and some fruit, the only articles they were able to buy. The doctor condemned the fruit and we had to dump it over board but we had a good feed on Sweet potatoes. We were all pretty hungry, having lived ten days on pay masters stores which were not good."[73]

Robinson details the pros and cons of his rations and discusses additional on shore food purchases: "The canned meat is unfit to eat, the Salt meat has been in pickle so long that the bones are eat up and can be crushed in your hand. The coffee is ground and put up in 5 pound tins but has all molded and can not be used, the Sea biscuit is good as is also the Beans and some of the Rice, this is about what we have lived on for the last ten days." He and a few men were allowed to go ashore when off the coast of Peru. There they purchased "a few chickens at 6 cents apiece ... ordered beef ... a little bit tough and stringy but pretty good to men with our appetites." When coaling at another stop, they located more positive purchases. He writes, "Oh! What a feast we have today ... it was fun to see the men frying steaks over a scoop shovel in the furnaces."[74]

He continues to write about food issues: "We had an ice machine but the officers took all of the ice it made and left the crew without." He adds, "I have seen a ton of ice stacked up in the Ward Room to cool the atmosphere while the crew were drinking water right from the Evaporators, hotter than Coffee could be drank with comfort." After the *Oregon* reaches the blockading fleet, he writes that he is still hungry, and that they catch "a few fish over the side." His situation, the next day, doesn't seem to improve: "Up to 11:30 we had nothing to eat but after the fighting was over we fell back and had a sumptuous feast on hard tack and molasses—Oh ye Gods! And they tell us we are going to starve the Spaniards out."[75]

Bertram Willard Edwards served as an ordinary seaman on the USS *Oregon* also during the blockade of Cuba and at the Battle of Santiago. In his diary, Edwards, as a member of the Naval Reserve, records food experiences as he is being transported from Chicago to his assignment and his opinion of his food while serving in the blockade. His experiences are also preserved at the Spanish-American War Centennial website.[76]

On the train on the way to his destination, he and other naval reservists had "bags and boxes of things to eat." Later he recalls, "Oh, many and many a time, off Santiago, did I think of the good things in those boxes and the way we wasted the cake and cookies we couldn't eat." Edwards arrives one night after the *Oregon* arrived. He notices that "all hands were hard at work" and the ship is being coaled and supplied. Once on the ship, he recalls that he was assigned to mess No. 1. It appears that he isn't quite sure about how the messes work. After being assigned to his mess, he found out that the crew had already eaten so they "were given some canned corn beef and cocoa."[77]

He had his first introduction to how the mess worked the next morning. Waking up early he "saw one of the crew getting some bread out of a large chest." At first he thought the man was getting himself something to eat but then learned that it was a mess cook "starting to get breakfast." He found out that "there is no eating between meals on a man-of-war," and remembers from his short time in the navy that "nobody was allowed to lay a finger on anything until the pipe of the whistle."[78]

His overall opinions of his food experiences differ dramatically from Robinson's

A bugler gives the call for breakfast on the USS *Buffalo* in 1898. Courtesy Naval Historical Center, Washington, D.C.

experience, even though they were on the same vessel. Edwards writes, "There was always enough food to go around." He adds, "In all the time I was away I never had to complain about the food, although it was rather rough at times." His attitude of patience and acceptance of the food provided him may have been influenced by the brief time that he spent in active service and additionally, by the difference in his working condition and the working conditions of Robinson. Edwards left Chicago on May 14 and was discharged on September 12, as he writes, making his "term of service just a summer's vacation."[79]

According to James R. Reckner in an introduction to *A Sailor's Log*, Frederick T. Wilson enlisted in the navy in 1895 and by 1898 had become a chief petty officer. "Wilson was an engineer.... By the time he began his log, he had risen rapidly through the ranks of the engineering force from coal passer to fireman second class, to fireman first class, then directly to water-tender, a rating that carried the rank of petty officer, first class."[80] Wilson records a variety of food experiences in a log kept while he was on Asiatic Station from 1899 to 1901. It was not until after Wilson's Asiatic cruise that the berth deck messing system for enlisted men that had been in effect since the beginning of the navy would be replaced across the navy by the general mess.

In his log while serving on the USS *New Orleans*, Wilson, like Robinson, writes about the contrasts between the eating and drinking practices evident in the messing of the enlisted men and the officers. While officers have a supply of various types of alcohol, the enlisted man, not allowed this item on his ration list, sometimes took extreme measures to satisfy his thirst. Wilson shares one example.

> But Jack can drink anything he can lay his hand on if he is a tank, from alcohol to red ink. See 'em stand by to swipe a pot of shellac and carry it to some convenient spot pour water in it and stir it with a stick until the shellac forms in a ball. Then pour the alcohol off and strain it thro' a thin rag of some kind. The rest is easy. The sugar, condensed milk and water and they can mix a shellac cocktail with a squirt of Venetian red in it for a flavor, or whatever coloring they have in the pot of shellac.[81]

Wilson writes about a Thanksgiving meal and also gives his opinion of the general quality of the food he is experiencing: "Thanksgiving has past whilst in Colombo. We got in there on that day. Our Thanksgiving dinner was composed of bad bread, canned 'willie' of course was the piece de resistance, as usual. Slops, called coffee."[82] He delivers his opinion of the general quality of the food on the ship.

> Several of the men are suffering with abscesses and boils caused by bad food. I have never had occasion to eat such bad food before. In our mess, we have had five or six cooks, and none of 'em know their business, and the way food is prepared and served to us would kill a dyspeptic in a week. I haven't had a piece of well-baked bread since leaving New York, except what we had in port from bakers ashore, and everything else is on a par with the bread. Soggy potatoes, slops for tea & coffee, and "horse meat" or salt horse, and navy canned meats. I never could eat any of that stuff.[83]

Discussing the problem of bad cooks, he writes that "any young fellow can do all the 'cooking' that has to be done in a man-o-war. Only thing he must know is how to make bread. Everything else is of the simplest, mostly baked beans, beef stews, soup." He admits that "the acme of the cook art is making up 'canned willie' so as to disguise it and render it appetizing, whether in rope-yarn stew, cracker hash or blanket stew or sea pie, meaning a stew that [has] a cover on it."[84]

Fortunately, at ports along the way, Wilson is able to purchase extra food items to supplement his meals. He acquires "a good supply of oranges and pineapples before leaving Singapore." He writes, "Been living on them ... eat hardly anything at the mess table; hardly anything *to* eat." In Singapore he also laid in "a supply of fried eggs, meat hash, good bread, butter and tea."[85]

Wilson writes about "a most epicurean luncheon." He had hopes that there would be a duff because the cook was seen "trying to hunt up a 'duff bag'" the previous evening. He describes the bill of fare: "The spuds were black as tar when broken open, and the coffee was no coffee at all as far as taste went. But the meat!!! Salt horse of Revolutionary birth, and vintage of 1776. It made its presence known by its aroma." When he had seen the cooks carrying it to the galley prior to cooking, he noticed that "it was green in places." And the duff was missing. He learned later about its demise: "Turned a dark purple color on the cook's account, was spoilt, so he gave it a passage over the side. He [the cook] is young and no doubt will learn, but meantime, we grow thin."[86]

The crew celebrated Washington's birthday while they were in the North Pacific. Wilson indicates that the men had put in money to have a special dinner. But as luck would have it, they were at sea so the menu had to be adjusted. Instead of the "spread" they had planned, they had "'salt horse' vintage of '68 [1868], Minneapolis Creamery butter (put up especially for bluejackets' use), plum duff which was all right, as we had a good cook, stewed tomatoes, 'spuds,' and coffee which wasn't by any means bad, and we all managed to stow away quite a food 'feed.'"[87]

As the cruise continues, he has good and bad experiences with his food. In China he purchases from a bumboat "everything the bluejacket requires; apricots, English walnuts, sponge cakes, candy, eggs, beef steak." At one point he reports that his mess was "feeding very well indeed, having stuff lain in [in] abundance, and beside, having a good cook, a German, steady and to be relied upon." He indicates they are having "pumpkin pies, puddings, etc., at this time for dessert."[88]

Later, mess 15, his mess, has trouble getting food: "Some wag drew a picture of the menu provided for this mess. It was a sketch of three hardtack, labeled breakfast, dinner, and supper." Wilson relates that one old sailor complained about the beans they had for breakfast. He said, "We had a few beans for breakfast, and they were spoiled. When you can't get beans, beans cooked right, on a man-o-war, what are we going to do. Here was I, looking for a couple of days towards having my beans, only to find them spoiled."[89]

Reflecting on his food experiences Wilson reviews the problems he sees with the messing system. He admits that there were times when he was thankful to have enough "hard tack, canned William and coffee" and he is thankful for the fresh provisions served while in port because "That eases life up a bit." He takes issues with the aspect of the messing system that requires enlisted men to "put in the mess from three to five dollars per man, sometimes more, as there may be an 'assessment' caused by bad management of the mess affairs by the caterer or cook." He finally concludes this about sailor food: "We want good, plain, substantial food of good quality and quantity, food that God almighty intended that every human being should have that earned his living by the 'sweat of his brow,' whether on the 'vasty deep' in one of the big white ships, or whether following the plow upon a farm." He adds that he believes that the ration current at that time is obsolete, strongly suggesting a need for a change in provisioning the sailor.[90] For that sailor and others like him, change in the system of messing was just around the corner.

7

Military Subsistence "Over There"

Eating ripe tomatoes ... had 3 meals of them right in the front line, can you beat that.

—Pvt. Robert K. Brady

Army Organization

With the significant supply problems of the Spanish-American War still fresh in mind and two investigations of the problems completed, major reorganization of the War Department and army occurred between 1900 and America's entry into World War I. Unfortunately, in spite of reorganization the army was no more prepared for this war than any previous engagement. Two complicating factors were distance and scale. The distance to the Western Front taxed American shipping capabilities and the million-man armies fielded by European powers dwarfed the American army, which had a combined Regular Army and National Guard strength of 208,000 at the time of the declaration of war on Germany in April 1917.[1] To make up for the shortfall in size of the army, Congress passed the Selective Service Act May 18, 1917. The draft swelled the army's numbers to more than 3.7 million men by the end of World War I.[2]

To procure supplies for the increasing size of the army, the War Department moved to consolidate supply purchases. Food purchases before the war were divided among the thirteen depot quartermasters scattered around the country. Depot quartermasters, as Risch explains, "bought all subsistence ... from dealers in the immediate vicinity of the posts to be supplied."[3] In order to secure sufficient food supplies for the military while not unduly affecting civilian prices and to centralize purchasing, the Council of National Defense coordinated supply efforts with the National Canners' Association by making allotments to all U.S. canners for canned peas, corn, beans, tomatoes, and fruits.[4] President Wilson established the U.S. Food Administration by executive order August 10, 1917, under authority of the Lever Food and Fuel Control Act. With Herbert Hoover as its head, twenty food items necessary for the military were controlled by the Food Administration from production through processing and distribution. The primary kinds of foods controlled included meats, fats and oils, wheat, sugar, milk, and fruits and vegetables.[5]

A new procedure for quartermaster procurement of food supplies evolved under the Food Administration. Risch explains the process.

> The Quartermaster General obtained articles on the allocated purchase list by requesting the Food Administration to allocate the quantity required. The Food Administration allotted the amount to the producers of the commodity in question, dividing the business among them in proportion to their capacity. When informed that the allotment had been made, the Office of the Quartermaster General directed procurement through a proper general supply depot in whose area the designated industry was located, under terms and at prices decided upon by the Food Purchase Board. The Office procured under this control plan flour, sugar, all canned vegetables and evaporated fruits, salmon, sardines, canned milk, and fresh beef.[6]

Food procured through this procedure accounted for about 40 percent of all food obtained for the army. One goal of this procedure was to prevent supply disruptions and spot shortages: "The supply in no one locality is drawn upon so heavily as to cause a shortage."[7] The number of items purchased under this centralized, controlled system grew throughout the war, "until at the time of the armistice practically all items were included."[8]

Ration Development

Army rations came under scrutiny as a result of investigations following the Spanish-American War, particularly those rations suitable for tropical climates. The secretary of war appointed a board in 1899 to determine whether a different ration needed to be issued in tropical climates. They received letters and reports arguing for and against a different tropical ration, but no action resulted from the board's efforts.

In 1901, Congress authorized the president "to prescribe the kinds and quantities of the component articles of the Army ration, and to direct the issue of substitutive equivalent articles in place of any such components whenever, in his opinion, economy and due regard to the health and comfort of the troops may so require."[9] While the basic ration did not change at this time, under General Orders No. 56, April 23, 1901, a longer list of items that could be substituted within the ration was announced, allowing for greater flexibility. As had been done previously, there were several rations depending on the conditions of service. The garrison ration, the normal ration at a post or where cooking facilities were available, included the following items and their substitutes: meat components—fresh beef or fresh mutton, bacon, canned meat when impracticable to furnish fresh meat, dried fish, pickled fish, and canned fish; bread components—flour or soft bread, hard bread to be ordered issued only when impracticable to use flour or soft bread, and corn meal; vegetable components—beans or peas, rice, and hominy; potatoes or potatoes and onions, potatoes and other fresh vegetables (not canned) when available, and desiccated vegetables when impracticable to furnish fresh vegetables; fruit component—dried or evaporated fruits (prunes, apples, or peaches), with 30 percent of the issue to be in prunes when practicable; coffee and sugar components—coffee, green or roasted and ground coffee, and tea, black or green; seasoning components—vinegar or vinegar and cucumber pickles; salt; and pepper, black.[10]

The field ration was to be issued to troops in the field during active campaigns. It consisted of the following items and their substitutes: meat components—fresh beef or mutton, when procurable locally, or canned meat when fresh meat cannot be procured locally, or bacon; bread components—flour or soft bread or hard bread; baking powder, when ovens are not available or hops when ovens are available or dried or compressed yeast, when ovens are available; vegetable components—beans or rice, potatoes, when procurable locally or potatoes and onions when procurable locally or desiccated potatoes or desiccated potatoes and desiccated onions or desiccated potatoes and canned tomatoes; fruit component—jam, in cans; coffee and sugar components—coffee, roasted and ground or tea,

Hard bread used in the reserve and trench rations during World War I. Courtesy Quartermaster Museum, Fort Lee, Virginia.

black or green; sugar; seasoning components—vinegar or vinegar and cucumber pickles; salt; and pepper, black.[11]

The travel ration was issued "to troops traveling other than by marching or, when for short periods, they are separated from cooking facilities."[12] This ration was much simpler and consisted of soft bread or hard bread; canned corned beef, or corned beef hash; baked beans; canned tomatoes; coffee, roasted and ground; and sugar. In lieu of the coffee portion of the travel ration soldiers were allotted 21 cents per day to purchase liquid coffee.[13]

During this same period, the board examining rations struggled with finding an emergency ration to be carried by troops in the field and used only when regular field rations were unavailable. The board developed an emergency ration based in part on pinole, ground parched corn used by Indians and Mexicans in the southwest. Their efforts resulted in a ration consisting of three cakes made from parched wheat and powdered beef. Also part of this ration was three cakes made of chocolate and sugar.[14] Further modified and authorized to be produced in 1907, it became the emergency ration carried by soldiers of the American Expeditionary Force in World War I. The ration, often referred to as the Armour Emergency Ration because of the manufacturer, Armour & Co., was packed in oval metal cans and weighed twelve ounces.[15] Used in several ways, the meat cake could be eaten dry or boiled in three pints of water to make a soup. If boiled in one pint of water it becomes a thick porridge to be eaten hot or cold. When cold it could be sliced and fried. The chocolate could be eaten either as candy or turned into a drink by placing in hot water. Labeling on the cans instructed the soldiers that the emergency ration was not to opened except by order of an officer or when in an extreme emergency.[16]

By 1916 some further additions to the substitutive list had been made in the garrison ration. This included corned beef hash as a substitute for fresh beef when it was impracticable to furnish fresh meat, and for Thanksgiving and Christmas, turkey could be served when practicable. Jam was added as a substitute for up to 50 percent of the total issue of prunes. Some additional seasoning items added to the substitutive list were cloves, ginger, and nutmeg. Vanilla could be substituted for lemon flavoring extract.[17]

As the American Expeditionary Force prepared for combat in France, it became readily apparent that they were facing new combat situations including trench warfare and attacks of poisonous gas. These new combat conditions made it necessary to develop specialized rations to use when conditions made it impossible to prepare regular meals. In addition to the emergency ration, the Subsistence Division developed two other rations. The reserve ration, packed for the individual soldier to be carried and used when regular food could not be obtained, consisted of a one-pound can of meat, usually corned beef but it could be a slab of bacon, two 8-ounce tins of hard bread, 2.4 ounces of sugar, 1.12 ounces of roasted and ground coffee, and .16 ounces of salt. It contained 3300 calories, weighed 2.75 pounds, and was packed in a cylindrical can which was not practical to carry.[18]

Another special ration, the trench ration, was intended to feed men under the conditions of trench warfare. Each unit contained enough canned meats and canned hard bread to feed twenty-five men for one day. The meat items consisted of canned roast beef, corned beef, salmon, and sardines. Other components in the ration were salt, sugar, soluble coffee, solidified alcohol, and cigarettes. The items were packed in sealed, galvanized containers designed to prevent contamination from poisonous gas. Can openers were also included in the galvanized containers. The cans once sealed were buoyant enough to support two men in the sea.[19] Some disadvantages of this ration included its lack of balanced nutrition and its weight, making it difficult to handle.[20] While the quality of the canned meats issued to troops of the AEF was never officially questioned, they were not especially popular with the soldiers who disdainfully labeled canned corned beef as "canned willie." Soldiers also tired of the frequent supply of canned salmon which they referred to as "goldfish."

Large amounts of candy were made available for troops to purchase at canteens during the war. In December 1918 candy actually became part of the ration for troops overseas, giving each man a pound and a half a month. The first month of this system required 3,495,000 pounds of candy.[21] The ration included both chocolates and hard candy. Other ration adjustments late in the war included the substitution of prunes, figs, apples, and other dried fruit and jam in place of syrup. Cheese and macaroni and Vienna sausages were other additions to ration supplies. The milk allowance was increased from one-half to one ounce along with an increase of one-third in the soluble coffee allowance for front line troops.[22]

Schools and Manuals

Improvement in the preparation of food for the United States Army took a giant leap forward in 1905 with the establishment at Fort Riley of the first school to train military bakers and cooks. Such schools were a long recognized need, but the War Department and Congress had been slow to act. Commissary General Weston noted in his report for 1902, "I again reiterate the recommendation that has been made in seventeen annual reports by Commissaries-General since 1877 for the enlistment of bakers in the service.

I also renew my recommendation of last year for the establishment of one or more schools for the training of cooks and bakers for the service." Weston bolstered his argument for a school for cooks and bakers by noting that in 1899 the Medical Department started instructing some members of the hospital corps in cooking at Washington Barracks. Weston concluded, "A competent knowledge of the art of cooking is as necessary for those who cook for well men as for those who cook for the sick."[23]

In 1906, a year after the establishment of the first cooking school, the army published *Recipes Used in the Cooking Schools.* This thirty-four-page book contains recipes for soups, fish and oysters, sauces, gravies, meats, vegetables, bread, puddings, and desserts. The amount each recipe makes varies; some are for feeding twenty, some forty or eighty while others are for feeding one hundred. The first manual for use in the baking school, *The Army Baker*, was written by Captain Lucius R. Holbrook, a prolific writer of manuals and instruction materials for the school. Holbrook penned this volume in 1908.

The Subsistence Department published in 1910 *Manual for the Subsistence Department United States Army*; it contains all regulations pertaining to the subsistence department. It details specifications for components of the ration and provides guidance in selecting ration items to assure quality and purchasing procedures. It also outlines how records are to be kept and how ration values are computed. Post commissaries stocked a large number of items for purchase in addition to the stocks of ration items. These items could be purchased by soldiers and officers for their individual use and by cooks using mess funds derived from ration savings. This allowed for more variety in the bill of fare offered to soldiers. A few entries from the long list of the food items to be stocked as directed by General Order No. 172, August 11, 1909, and listed in the 1910 manual include: apples, apple butter, bacon, butter, chocolate candy, cabbage, cheese, cocoa, coffee, corn, crackers, eggs, flour, ginger ale, ham, jam, jelly, canned lobster, mustard, molasses, olives, oysters, pickles, sardines, Worcestershire sauce, pork sausage, shrimp, canned turkey, and walnuts.

Also appearing in 1910 was the *Manual for Army Cooks*. The 1910 manual has the distinction of introducing a recipe which in modified form remains a part of the army recipe collection to this day and became one of the most remembered if not most liked meals for generations of servicemen. That recipe is for chipped beef on toast which became better known among the soldiers as SOS. Luther Hanson, curator of the Quartermaster Museum at Fort Lee, Virginia, indicates that veterans groups often tour the museum and then eat at the base dining facility. Their most requested dish is SOS. The recipe has changed slightly from the original. Worcestershire sauce has replaced parsley as seasoning and it is now usually made from ground beef rather than chipped beef and is now officially called Creamed Ground Beef by the Armed Forces Recipe Card Service.

In 1916 the War Department published two new manuals: *Manual for Army Cooks*, a revision of the 1910 version, and *Manual for Army Bakers*. The *Manual for Army Bakers* describes the organization of bakery companies. During wartime, one bakery company is to be assigned to each division. These bakery companies consisted of sixty-one total personnel. In peacetime, the size is reduced to forty-eight. The companies were divided into units and sections which could be assigned to furnish bread for a smaller number of troops as needed. Using this manual bakers learn to bake garrison bread for use in garrison or permanent camps and field bread for use by troops more than a day's travel distance. Field bread was denser and had a thicker crust than garrison bread making it less susceptible to damage during transportation. Because of the longer baking time required, the manual instructs that "field bread should not be made except for instruction or in emergency to supply troops so distant that garrison bread can not be preserved." A company bakery usually produced 18,144 pounds of garrison bread per day when at war strength and 13,608 pounds at peace strength. Field bread could be produced at the rate of 9,072 pounds per day at peace strength and 12,096 pounds at war strength.[24]

This manual discusses the types of ovens used—continuous, which meant that the same fire could be used continuously to bake one batch of bread after another, and the intermittent oven in which the fire, usually wood or coal, was removed from the baking chamber before baking the bread. The fire had to be rebuilt and the oven heated before the next batch could be baked. The manual indicates that by the time of its publication only the continuous type was being installed at army posts. Field bakeries used primarily the portable No. 1 field oven. Bakers set up the oven over a trench dug in the ground in which a wood fire was built. The manual also instructs bakers in techniques for building an oven in a steep bank and for the construction of clay ovens using two sugar or salt barrels for a form.[25]

In preparing for the large influx of men into the army from the draft, the Quartermaster General realized there were not enough cooks in the army to prepare all the meals necessary.[26] The Quartermaster General received authority from the War Department to hire civilian cooks until enough army cooks and bakers could be trained. The Quartermaster General expected 687,000 men to arrive at sixteen different camps by September 1, 1917, and estimated the need for 12,000 cooks. The Hotel Keepers Association of America and the Chefs Association offered to assist in supplying some of the additional cooks needed. It was decided that these groups could provide at least 3,600 cooks.[27] "Civilian cooks were hired at the rate of one to each proposed kitchen in each cantonment."[28] To meet the ongoing need for cooks and bakers, the Quartermaster Corps organized schools and bakery companies at each of the sixteen National Army cantonments receiving draftees. Before July 1917, the army had four schools for cooks and bakers with each school having an average student capacity of one hundred.[29]

Inspections

Continuing concern over the quality of meat procured for troops as a result of the Spanish-American War embalmed beef investigations and new concerns in the public's mind over conditions in the meatpacking and other food industries stirred by such writings as Upton Sinclair's *The Jungle* led to passage in 1906 of the Meat Inspection Act and the Pure Food and Drug Act. The Meat Inspection Act established sanitation standards for slaughterhouses and placed federal inspectors in meat plants where the products were entering interstate commerce. Beginning in 1900, the Quartermaster Corps hired veterinarians to assist with meat inspections. The National Defense Act of June 3, 1916, established the Army Veterinary Corps within the Medical Department. In addition to its care of service animals, the Veterinary Corps provided inspection of meat and meat products, poultry and eggs, and fish and seafood. They also inspected locations where food was produced and processed. In 1917, the corps inspected over 1,000,000,000 pounds of meat.[30]

Top and bottom: Clay ovens, Camp Clark, Missouri. Courtesy Museum of Missouri Military History (Missouri National Guard), Jefferson City, Missouri.

Supplying the American Expeditionary Force

As commander of the American Expeditionary Force, Major General John J. Pershing sailed with his staff from New York on May 28, 1917, for France to make plans for the arrival of the AEF troops. Much had to be done quickly. In the words of Captain Shipley Thomas with the 26th Infantry, 1st Division, "Everything had to be organized not for the four divisions which would arrive in the fall of 1917, but for the two million men who would be in France before 1919."[31] In the area of subsistence, ports for receiving supplies had to be decided upon, storehouses either located or built, and refrigerating plants and bakeries constructed. The first troops, elements of the 1st Division, arrived in France June 26, 1917. The Ports of St. Nazaire, La Pallice, and Bassens became the principal ports for receiving American supply shipments.[32] A major task for the Quartermaster Corps was to establish depots for the storage of supplies. Three types of depots were established. Base depots received supplies first so ships could be unloaded quickly to prevent port congestion and allow ships to return to the United States to bring over even more supplies. Intermediate depots were located between the base depots and battle lines. Finally, Advance Section depots were located more to the interior, closer to lines of combat where supplies were being used.[33]

The small supply of fresh meat obtainable in Europe meant that the army would have to bring most of its meat from the United States. This necessitated refrigeration plants at ports, and at both intermediate and advance depots. A refrigerating plant built at Gievres ranked as one of the largest in the world. The facility also included an ice-making plant with a daily capacity of 500 tons.[34]

Closer to the front lines, the Quartermaster Corps established an Advance Section depot and mechanical bakery at Is-sur-Tille, one hundred sixty miles southeast of Paris. This bakery had a daily production capability of 800,000 pounds. Risch notes the important change in the manner of supplying bread for the army this bakery represented.

> The development marked an almost revolutionary change in the method of providing bread for the Army. In lieu of assigning bakery companies to operate field bakeries with the divisions of the Army, the Corps erected a large mechanical bakery in the rear of the regulating station, from which bread was supplied to the troops at the front.[35]

Mechanical bakeries required fewer men to operate compared with field bakeries. Seven companies of 101 men could produce as much bread as 27 companies in field bakeries.[36] The Quartermaster Corps and Engineers constructed mechanical bakeries having a capacity of 150,000 pounds per day at Brest and Bordeaux while one with a daily capacity of 120,000 pounds was constructed at St. Nazaire.[37]

One of the most difficult problems in supplying troops of the AEF was the "acute shortage of shipping in 1917."[38] There were not enough ships available to transport all the needed supplies plus the large number of troops headed for Europe. This required an initial dependence of the American forces on the local purchase of supplies. However with the critical food shortages throughout Europe not enough could be obtained in this manner. To save space on ships two new methods in handling food were introduced. One was the dehydrating of vegetables and the other was de-boning beef.

Fresh vegetables were difficult to ship great distances and required a large amount of ship tonnage. Benjamin Crowell, assistant secretary of war, notes that "to supply dehy-

World War I army supply wagon. Courtesy Quartermaster Museum, Fort Lee, Virginia.

drated vegetables meant the development of an industry." At the beginning of the war only three dehydrating plants existed in the United States. By the end of the war fifteen such plants were operating and had shipped 62,000,000 pounds of dehydrated vegetables to the AEF. After drying, the vegetables were placed in hermetically sealed cans and were easy to use in field kitchens located near front lines.[39]

To save space and tonnage in shipping beef, bones, excess fat, and unusable portions were removed from the beef which was then packed into one hundred pound molds and frozen. Three types of packages of the de-boned beef were sent. "One set included tenderloins, sirloins, butts, loin steaks, top rounds, and shoulder steaks. Another set of packages contained roasts, including prime ribs, rumps, bottom rounds, and bottom chucks. A third set was for stews, including flanks, plates, blades, necks, shanks, and trimmings."[40] The de-boned beef was generally well received. For cooks it meant much time and labor saved in preparation. For the soldiers it meant they were receiving better meat. With the large refrigeration plants in operation in France, the meat reached the troops in excellent condition. To facilitate more efficient handling of meat, the army developed more efficient methods of meat cutting.

The American military made substantial efforts to provide hot meals for soldiers fighting in the trenches. Usually available in the trenches as part of their equipment were the sealed cans of trench rations but whenever conditions permitted, rolling field kitchens were located near enough the lines that hot food could be carried to the trenches. Crowell

World War I field kitchen. This photograph was taken during 1918 maneuvers at Fort Meade. Courtesy Museum of Missouri Military History (Missouri National Gurard), Jefferson City, Missouri.

writes that prior to America's entry into the war, manufacturers were making "six types of commercial kitchens."[41] Some of these were being produced on orders from foreign armies.

These new field kitchens had been tested prior to World War I through use on the Mexican border during the Mexican Punitive Expedition. By 1918 a standardized design known as the Liberty Rolling Field Kitchen had been adopted. These stoves were produced in two versions, horse drawn and motor vehicle towed. Each field kitchen and the equipment with which it was furnished was capable of cooking food sufficient for 200 men. The complete kitchen contained a bake oven, bread boxes, kettles, and a cook's chest.[42] Much of the testing and development work on the rolling kitchens was done at the Jeffersonville, Indiana, Quartermaster Depot. An engineer there, W.A. Dorsey, developed an oil-fueled burner adaptable to rolling kitchens, field bakeries, army ranges, and Sibley tent stoves.[43]

Food prepared using the rolling kitchen was first transported to the trenches using regular two and one-half and five gallon milk cans. The cans were filled with soup or thin beef stew and some with coffee and were transported as close as possible to the trenches on ration carts, two-wheeled wagons pulled by two mules. The cans were then carried into the trenches on a pole by two men. Using a Yukon pack or Canadian tumpline the can could be carried by one person on his back.[44] It was soon realized however that some type of insulated container was needed. The French were using such a container called Marmite Norvegienne. The army adopted the use of this container to carry hot food to AEF forces in the trenches.[45] Soldiers appreciated the hot meals although the monotony of soup led them to refer to the fare as slum. An article in the *Stars and Stripes* describes the process: "Every night, somewhere between ten and midnight, a hot meal is served out in quantities sufficiently generous to leave a goodly supply of slum and coffee to make another meal heated by the little alcohol cans with which each soldier is provided."[46]

Transporting rations to the trenches proved to be a difficult and dangerous task: "Many a ration runner is killed at his job, and more than once in these past weeks a mess sergeant has returned to the ration pile to find the man he had left on guard there lying dead beside it."[47] The *Stars and Stripes* explained how in at least one instance, even a wrecked ration cart continued to provide food.

> A corporal and six other Marines who, in one forward rush, became isolated in a ravine and held their position there in the shelter of some rocks for a week before the American line moved forward and they were with friends once more. Out in the field near them a battered ration cart lay on its side, and each night one of the marooned Marines would crawl out on his belly and bring back food for the bunch.[48]

In areas of the Western Front where American soldiers were serving with French troops, they sometimes received canned meat from the French as part of their rations. They so disliked the taste of the product they called it monkey meat. It was actually canned beef from Argentina but few troops would eat it unless they had to. It is humorously described in the *Stars and Stripes* as "either boiled llama or some other South American animal which the natives coax from their lair and drive into the can. The can is then sealed up and stored for 30 years."[49]

Soldiers were always on the lookout for ways to supplement and add variety to their rations. The *Stars and Stripes* reported on one infantry battalion that "is jealously guarding an old French wicker cradle in which 60 four-week old chicks are growing up into a promising mess" while an Engineer company is "tenderly cherishing a cow which issues them milk every day."[50]

Both the French and British armies grew vegetable gardens near their front lines and in training areas. Risch writes, "The French had built up a remarkable system of kitchen gardens. Such local production had the advantage of insuring prompt delivery of fresh vegetables and at the same time saving ocean, rail, and motor transportation."[51] In December 1917 plans were made to grow gardens to furnish fresh vegetables. The Quartermaster Corps established the Gardens Bureau as the administrative office in charge of the agricultural pursuit. The bureau distributed seeds and plants for establishment of gardens. While some combat divisions in forward areas were involved in the effort, according to an April 25, 1919, article in the *Stars and Stripes* most of the work was concentrated in "camps and hospital areas of a permanent nature." During the summer of 1918 the Garden Service produced 6,951,000 pounds of vegetables on nearly 1500 acres in cultivation.

The *Stars and Stripes* reported how the gardens benefited one particular group of soldiers.

> Up beyond Chateau-Thierry where the doughboys had been walloping Hohenzollern household guards on a diet of monkey meat and canned Willy, alias wild cat and buzzard something important happened the other day. About the time they began handing out decorations on the strength of those wallopings, a caravan of canvas-colored motor trucks swung into the back areas with the ammunition wagons, and that day monkey meat, canned Willy, wild cat and buzzard all vanished from the doughboys' messes and they

A 1917 Rolling Field Kitchen, used extensively in France. Models to be pulled by mules and by trucks were made. Courtesy U.S. Marine Corps History Center, Quantico, Virginia.

started serving New England boiled dinners. Great kettles full of boiled cabbage, with cauliflower, string beans, and potatoes took the place of the can-opening counters.[52]

Such supply of vegetables to the troops had been the goal of the gardening program in France.

That was a great day because it marked the fulfillment of the self-feeding hopes of the American Army in France, at last, as far as fresh vegetables go. All those cabbages, beans, potatoes, and cauliflower had been planted by doughboys, tended by doughboys, harvested by doughboys and hauled to the front by doughboys. And it had all been done in France.[53]

Coffee

Supplying coffee, long a vital part of the army ration, for over three million soldiers challenged the efforts of the Quartermaster Corps. Initially, coffee was purchased roasted and ground through the competitive bidding process as were other subsistence items. However the length of time it was in storage and transport resulted in coffee with a deteriorated flavor. The answer to the problem was for the army to purchase coffee beans green and roast them in their own plants. The plants operated by the Quartermaster Corps in France roasted and ground sufficient coffee to supply three million men.[54] The

Planting potatoes in France grown by the Quartermaster Garden Bureau. Courtesy Quartermaster Museum, Fort Lee, Virginia.

plant established at Corbeil-Essenes was the largest roasting plant in Europe having a capacity of 1,500,000 rations daily by the war's end. In 1917, the Quartermaster Corps purchased nearly the all of the green coffee available in Europe. Afterwards, shipments had to be made from the United States.[55]

Soluble or instant coffee, a relatively new product at the beginning of the war, came into its own as a result of its widespread use by the armed forces. A soluble product proved to be what was needed by frontline troops in order to have a stimulating and refreshing hot beverage. Soluble coffee made it much easier to provide coffee for front-line troops because it was easier to carry and easier to brew than regular ground coffee. Troops simply had to heat water in their mess cups and add the soluble coffee. It was a part of the trench ration, twenty-five rations being included in each trench ration can. By the end of the war the military required over 42,000 pounds of soluble coffee daily.[56]

Charitable Organizations

Charitable organizations played key roles in providing extra food, nursing, and other services for the soldiers in the AEF. Several different organizations shared in these efforts but most notable and visible in their overseas work were the Red Cross, Salvation Army, and YMCA. Other groups involved with war work included War Camp Community Service, National Catholic War Council, Jewish Welfare Board, and the American Library

Association. This latter list of organizations joined with the Salvation Army in a United War Work Campaign and raised over $170 million by the war's end.[57]

While it is probably better known for its role in the medical care of the sick and wounded and care for war refugees, the Red Cross also helped supply soldiers, sailors and marines with supplementary food, clothing, and comfort items. This role was carried out in two ways, first through its Camp Service which operated adjacent to military bases both at home and overseas. Secondly, its Canteen Service begun in 1917 "provided food and snacks as well as leisure articles to troops primarily when they were in transit at railroad stations and ports of embarkation and debarkation."[58]

Seven hundred canteens were operated in the United States and 130 in France. Statistics for the canteen at Union Station in Kansas City show the magnitude of service at these canteens. Between February 1, 1917, and November 1, 1919, this canteen served the following: 185,000 meals, 420,000 sandwiches, 23,000 doughnuts, 3,575 gallons of coffee, 3,750 gallons of lemonade, 1,800 cases of iced soda pop, 670 bushels of fruit, 8,000 pounds of candy, 10,000 chocolate bars, and 147,000 packages of gum.[59]

However, Red Cross canteens did at times serve men on active duty in the field. Truck mounted rolling canteens which could be taken close to the front lines were operated by the Red Cross. Joe Mitchell Chapple traveled with the rolling kitchens in Italy and described them this way: "They have six places each for spacious set-in kettles, where coffee and occasionally soup may be kept always hot. Under the kettles is an oven burning wood, and once the metal kettles are heated, they will remain hot for sixteen hours at a time."[60] To prevent too much overlap in services, the Red Cross and the YMCA made an agreement in 1918 that canteen operations other than for troops in transit would be operated by the YMCA while those at hospitals run by the YMCA would be turned over to the Red Cross.[61]

Not well known before the war, and associated mostly with street corner bands and efforts to care for the hungry and homeless in cities, the Salvation Army became the most popular organization serving troops of the AEF. Although far smaller in size and scope than the Red Cross, their efforts to provide aid and comfort to soldiers gained high regards for the organization among the troops and the American people. First Sergeant Anthony D. Cone with Battery E, 15th Field Artillery, notes in his diary:

> For the first time we met the Salvation Army and we must say they put more cheer into a soldier than any other organization we met during our entire stay at the front. They were ... only four kilometers from the front-line trenches, and they were exposed to shell fire. The shell fire did not bother them, for the girls said the pies and doughnuts had to be made for the boys and they kept on with their work.[62]

The Salvation Army first arrived in Europe in August 1917 to establish huts in which they operated canteens. Eventually four hundred huts and rest rooms were established. One thing which impressed the American soldiers was the fact that "the Salvation Army followed them right to the front. The women as well as the men went where the troops happened to be, and often were in danger from shells and gas."[63] The following description of how the Salvation Army brought refreshments to troops in the trenches illustrates their commitment and the reason the soldiers held them in such high regards.

> As the soldiers had to work in the night, so the Salvation Army men and women worked in the night to serve them. The Salvation Army men would visit the sentries and bring them coffee and doughnuts prepared in the dugouts by the girls. It was exceedingly dangerous

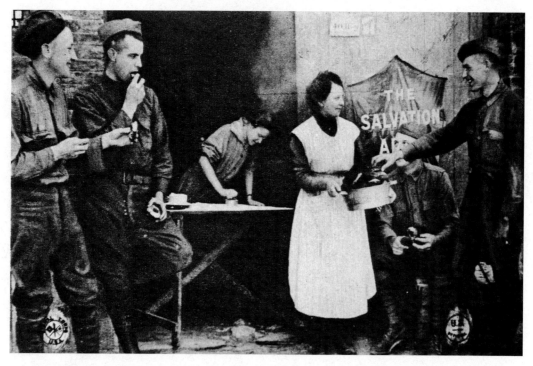

Salvation Army workers passing out doughnuts to soldiers in France. Photograph from Moore and Russell, *U.S. Official Pictures of the War.*

work. They would crawl through the connecting trenches, which were not more than three feet deep, and one must stoop to be safe, and get to the front-line trenches with their cans of coffee. They would touch a fellow on the shoulder, fill his mug with coffee, and slip him some doughnuts.[64]

They served lemonade and coffee along with cakes and pies but "the doughnut became the symbol of the Salvation Army in France."[65] Sergeant Grover Bounds reported to the *Stars and Stripes* that during the St. Mihiel drive the Salvation Army made 8,000 doughnuts which were delivered in trucks to the soldiers "just as they had reached their objectives and were organizing their new lines."[66]

Another charitable organization heavily involved with the military during World War I was the YMCA. In the area of food, their contribution to the AEF was the organization and operation of canteens and post exchanges. The YMCA established post exchanges which sold a variety of articles needed by the soldiers in addition to food. Along with the post exchanges they established "wet canteens for the distribution of hot and cold drinks, sandwiches, and biscuits."[67] The YMCA found that the AEF "had a more intense craving for chocolate, candy and biscuits [cookies], than for anything else except tobacco."[68] Because of their difficulty in establishing a supply of these items the YMCA decided to manufacture them in its own factories in France. Most of the raw materials could be obtained in France, Spain, England, Switzerland, and Brazil, thus not interfering with shipping from the United States. They opened their first factory in October 1917 in Paris and eventually increased the number until they operated forty-four in total. The output from these factories was large; here are a few examples of monthly production: 10,160,000

Red Cross canteen in France. Photograph from Moore and Russell, *U.S. Official Pictures of the War.*

packages of biscuits, 1,000,000 bars of milk chocolate, 3,100,000 cartons of caramels, 2,000,000 tins of jam, 7,400,000 tablets of drinking-chocolate, 3,500,000 bars of sweet chocolate, 3,8000,000 bars of chocolate cream, and 1,500,000 nut-covered chocolate rolls. Even with such production numbers the demand was not fully met. On November 15, 1918, all of the YMCA manufacturing facilities were turned over to the Quartermaster Corps.[69]

Other organizations offering to provide services to troops at the beginning of America's charitable organization involvement in World War I included the Knights of Columbus, Jewish Welfare Board, YWCA, the American Library Association, and the War Camp Community Service. Knights of Columbus clubhouses used the motto, "Everyone Welcome, Everything Free" when they began opening first near training camps in the United States and then in Europe. They provided such comforts as coffee, chocolate, and chewing gum.[70] The Jewish Welfare Board functioned much as the Knights of Columbus but sought to minister to Jewish soldiers.

Soldier Accounts

Letters and diaries written by soldiers in the field provide another perspective on their food. In their letters to family they frequently discuss their food experiences. While troops in rear areas eating the garrison ration generally had good food with sufficient variety, the corned beef hash, or slum as the soldiers referred to it, and canned salmon, nicknamed goldfish, became monotonous for frontline troops. Since they could not have fires in the trenches because the smoke would give their location to enemy artillery these items were often eaten cold. Marine lieutenant Clifton Cates, involved in the battle at Belleau Wood, wrote about food received when in support positions behind the front lines: "We found steak, bread, and potatoes waiting for us—we get one hot meal a day here."[71] Marines in frontline trenches found a way to prepare a special treat for themselves as described by Corporal Fred W. Hill: "This candle fire burns low and clean and we are able to fry bacon and warm beans and coffee even in the very front-line positions. One of the stunts was to fry a piece of bread in the bacon grease and then sugar it. Sounds funny, but I swear I never ate any thing that I enjoyed more than our 'trench dough-nuts.'"[72]

Because of constant shelling by German artillery there were times when frontline troops became desperate for food despite the best efforts to supply them. A soldier in action in the Belleau Wood writes, "Our rations cannot keep up with us very well, so we are hungry all the time."[73] Sometimes soldiers obtained surprising food even at the front lines such as fresh tomatoes. Robert K. Brady wrote August 10, 1918, about this experience in France: "eating ripe tomatoes ... had 3 meals of them right in the front line, can you beat that."[74] Presumably Brady's tomatoes were obtained from either local French growers or through the Garden Bureau since fresh tomatoes would have been too perishable to ship although many canned tomatoes were sent over.

Glen Westover with the AEF in France wrote about a box he received from his family around Thanksgiving 1917.

> You can not really appreciate what it means to me or would mean to any man down here. The meals are very much alike and plain. Now I can answer mess call with a jar of heavenly jam under my arm and a piece of cake or pie for dessert and you don't know how it will add to the meal. The other things—all those nuts and apples and oranges and raisins and pudding and salad and cocoanut and what not—I was simply overwhelmed when I unpacked the box.[75]

Robert K. Brady writes about receiving a package from home this time while in France December 18, 1918.

> Well my Xmas box came yesterday. Was sure glad to get it—everything was in good shape, am now smoking one of the cigars—just got thru eating a piece of cake. Gosh that was good cake and candy. I sure am thankful to you all for the box—it was so good to eat some "home-made" eats.[76]

Perhaps one of the best summaries of doughboy chow comes from a piece written in the *Stars and Stripes* as the "diary of a doughboy's stomach" by "Old Man Stomach himself." The article is signed by "Sgt. C.W. Person." Here are a few excerpts from the piece.

> Monday 7 am—Put on my steel lizzie and waited for coffee. Nothing came down but water, hardtack and goldfish. Wish I had signed with an officer. 12 pm—Hello! What's this, steak and French fries at last? No such luck—got a shower of water and monkey-meat. 6 pm—Called up the speaking tube and asked for steak and onions. Got a lot of goldfish for my trouble. Wednesday 7 am—We got relieved last night at last. Now for some real chow. 7:10 am—Wow! Here it comes—coffee, oatmeal, bacon, bread, jam and more coffee. Seems like old times. 10 am—Steak and French fries. 10:05 am—Rice pudding, doughnuts and cocoa. 6 pm—GAS! Am writing this with my mask on. 6:03 pm—Monday's goldfish is raising the devil with tonight's doughnuts.[77]

The American soldiers had little taste for the dark bread so favored by the French. Edward Van Winkle writes to his wife in July 1918, "You speak of your fine bread. When the next loaf you cut into try to imagine a loaf some 14 × 36 × 5 of black bread. That's what we are getting. Our bakery is not complete yet." But later that year their bakery is operating and he writes about the improvement: "We have white bread now and we make it here. How did you like the pictures, bread loaves that weigh 12 pounds each? They are fine eating."[78] Sometimes Van Winkle found food prepared at a field kitchen surprisingly good as he describes one breakfast: "This is what we had — grapes, fried eggs, steak, coffee, hot biscuits." Later in 1918 after the armistice while with the army of occupation in Germany Van Winkle sometimes found food sparse: "Have lived on hard tack and cold stuff for 3 months."[79]

Glen Westover discovered that even being on K.P. was not always bad, sometimes it enabled a soldier to get extra food: "I was on K.P. yesterday and had quite a time. Ate several nice roast beef sandwiches and steaks between meals."[80]

Soldiers even resorted to foraging at French farmsteads at times although they generally bartered or paid for the food obtained from civilians. Private Roy Sutherland writes about obtaining food in an abandoned town: "New potatoes, green peas, onions, and honey. I had honey that day, but I certainly paid for it. Several of us put on respirators, wrapped up well and invaded the beehives. I finished with eleven bee stings and a great quantity of excellent honey."[81]

By the end of the war, the ranks of the Army had swelled to about 3,700,000, yet rations for World War I era military personnel showed significant improvement from previous periods. The variety of foods was greater and efforts were made to insure the quality. The necessity of supplying such large quantities of food resulted in better cooperation between the government and industry. The understanding of nutrition and improvements in food preservation techniques, particularly canning, contributed to better food.

Post-War Ration Research

In the area of subsistence, a major change occurred in 1920. At the Chicago Quartermaster Depot, the Quartermaster Corps Subsistence School was established in the fall of that year. The purpose of the school was to "instruct selected officers and enlisted men regarding the procurement, processing, inspection, transportation, storage, and issuing of subsistence supplies."[82] The school was also charged with writing subsistence textbooks and assisting the development of food specifications. The school also carried out some subsistence research.[83] In 1922 the school also began training supply officers for the navy followed by the Marine Corps in 1926. Between 1920 and 1936 the school produced fifty-two manuals, their most important publication being *The Army Cook* and *The Army Baker*.

While the trench ration was discontinued with end of World War I, the reserve ration was retained although the Subsistence School proposed some changes in 1920 to its composition. Under their proposal, the ration would consist of the following: corned beef or dried sliced beef — 1 lb; hard bread — 14 oz.; chocolate — 3 oz.; soluble coffee; and tablet sugar. The army purchased 10,000 of these rations, packed in two cans similar to sardine cans. This ration was modified again in 1925 when the amount of corned beef and bread was reduced slightly and the dried beef was replaced with pork and beans.[84] The Depression years of the 1930s halted most subsistence research although the school did experiment with packing the reserve rations in round cans in 1932. In June 1936 the Subsistence School was moved to the Quartermaster School in Philadelphia. By 1936, the unfolding world events made it apparent that the next generation of rations would have to be tailored for an army on the move with the expanding use of airplanes and tanks. Consequently on July 24, 1936, the Quartermaster Subsistence Research Laboratory was established at the Chicago Depot. This facility would be dedicated to ration research and development without teaching responsibilities. Clearly, then, "1936 marked the inauguration of modern ration research."[85]

Changes in the Navy Galley and Chow "Over There"

> *Two thousand sailors ate together.... Mess was served by a white-clad "mess-detail" ... Navy slang is required ... "Java" for tea or coffee, "punk" for bread, and "sand" for salt, and something that sounds like "slumgullion" for any kind of stew.*
> — Joseph Husband, Great Lakes Training prior to going to war

Following the Spanish-American War, as the navy firmly established a solid position as a world sea power, change also came to the table, with improvement in the way enlisted sailors received their meals. J.H. Skillman notes, "One of the results of the War with Spain was the apparent need for a thorough investigation into the methods of subsisting then in vogue."[86] Once again the system of general messing was examined as a better way of messing. J.W. Crumpacker notes that John S. Carpenter, paymaster aboard the battleship USS *Texas*, determined to improve the messing system on that vessel. He "asked for and received the commutated ration money and under his supervision all food was purchased and prepared for the entire crew." According to Crumpacker, "The experiment was a success from the start.... The procedure was soon formalized by General Order 68 of November 26, 1901."[87]

The bill of fare for the sailor also saw welcome changes that led to greater variety. Thanks to Assistant Paymaster Thomas J. Cowie, who served on the training ship *New Hampshire*, items on the ration list established in 1861 were redefined. Crumpacker explains what this redefinition meant to the turn of the century sailor. One change came in the new definition of meat. The new meat included, "although [it was] considered a reckless extravagance ... lamb, veal, mutton, and country sausage." The vegetable category on the bill of fare also took on a new look with lettuce, cabbage, radishes, carrots, and tomatoes being classified as vegetables. Cowie also procured bread from shore bakeries when the ships were in port for a long time.[88]

While changes were being made aboard *New Hampshire,* significant changes to the messing system were also taking place on the battleship *Missouri* under the direction of its paymaster, George P. Dyer. Dyer writes in a 1906 article detailing changes that had been coming to the general mess over the previous two and a half years while he served on *Missouri*. He begins by laying out what he considers to be the "three separate though interdependent parts" of a general mess—"namely, the *procurement* of food, its *preparation*, and its *service*." He provides a concrete illustration to support his list.

Everyone knows that when poor eggs are bought, all possible skill in cooking and art in serving cannot remedy the original fault in purchase; that the best dish may be ruined in the cooking; or that food meant to be warm but which reaches the tables cold, or is otherwise poorly served, is sure to be far from satisfactory.[89]

Of the three interdependent parts of the general mess, Dyer addresses service first. Centralization became a key factor in the new system of messing, whether it was concerned with the organization of eating equipment, delivery of food, storage of condiments, or washing of eating utensils. An interest in sanitation promoted the practice of covering condiments such as butter, molasses, vinegar, and catsup in a designated storage area. Also, an important step forward in improving food service was the introduction of the first dishwasher used in the navy and installed on the *Missouri* in February 1904. Dyer shares the struggles faced with the use of this newfangled machine before it was accepted: "There were days when despair was perilously near victory, and nights when I scarcely expected to find it whole at daylight, such was the force of conservative prejudice against it among the men." However, "After two years and over of continuous operation, its presence is accepted as a matter of course." Dyer also discusses changes that were made in delivery of food to tables from the galley and the management of mess furnishings to keep them off the deck and out of the dirt. This was accomplished by designating a "general mess issuing-room" and by devising mess-boxes for messmen to use in carrying food related items to the tables and back to the storage room.[90]

Dyer addresses food preparation with "attention to details," "modern organization," "changes in arrangement of equipment," and "instruction in cooking" as important elements of the general mess. At the top of his list in the galley is, "*Serve warm dishes HOT, and cold ones Cold*" and "*No STALE food.*" His conclusion about basic food preparation — "Meals timed to the minute, and steaming on the tables are no more an impossibility in the navy than elsewhere."[91]

He enumerates modern galley aids that joined the dishwasher. He mentions a "patent potato-mashing device whose operation requires a plunger to force all potatoes through eighth-inch perforations in a galvanized cylinder." He also lists an automatic meat slicer, a meat-grinding machine, an electrically driven dough-mixer, a forty-quart power ice-cream freezer, an egg-boiler for twenty-one hundred eggs, and an apple peeler and corer for the same number of apples that came to the galley. Not surprising, the ice cream machine was the most popular. The meat grinder added new items to the bill of fare such as "Hamburg steak and pressed beef," and the dough mixer "revolutionized the character of the bread baked on board."[92]

While changes were being made in the messing process, changes in rations were also being made. Crumpacker discusses these changes. The first came July 1, 1902. At this time Congress passed an act "which increased the daily allowance of vegetables and meat and added variety to the menu by providing tomatoes as either a vegetable or a condiment." A second change came with congressional decisions in 1906 and 1907. At this time "eggs, jam, and spices found their way to the general mess and rigidity of issue was modified by permitting the issuance of any article in the Navy ration in excess of the authorized quantity provided there was an underissue of the same value of some other article or articles."[93]

Cookbooks Come to the Galley

At the same time the general mess was being put in place, a significant culinary step forward came to the galley in the form of the development of the first navy cookbook in 1902. As plans were being made to move toward general messing, the need for a standard cookbook became apparent. The development of a cookbook to replace the one in general use, an earlier army cookbook (probably *Manual for Army Cooks, 1896*), became the project of Paymaster Frank Arms at the instruction of Secretary of the Navy Long. At this time the Navy Ration Board added the "enlisted rating of commissary steward, cook, and baker." As well, "In 1902 Arms took over the school for training the Navy's cooks and bakers at Cob Dock."[94] Sharpe believes with the first navy cookbook, "The day of 'salt horse' was doomed, the era of sirloin steak dawned. Nourishing soups, fresh vegetables and fruit, fresh meats and poultry appeared on the menu." He adds, "The Navy cook book, revised from time to time, became the galley bible."[95]

The 1902 cookbook, *Mess Manual and Cookbook*, a rare cookbook, has been made available at the Naval Historical Center website. The cookbook is divided into three parts: Part I, The General Mess; Part II, The Commissary Store; and Part III, Preparation of Food. The cookbook opens with an explanation of the general mess and follows with the duties and the responsibilities of the chief commissary steward or commissary steward, the cooks and bakers and the storekeeper (when a store is established on the ship). The cookbook reads, "It should be thoroughly understood that the general mess is not an organization managed by its members, as was the 'berth-deck mess.'" Also, "Under the general messing system the Government subsists the men entirely, and they have no more voice in the management of the commissary department than in any other department of the ship. The Government, through its authorized officer, provides them with the ration allowed by law. The food is purchased, cooked, and served entirely at the Government expense."[96]

It appears that the intention of the navy in developing a cookbook is to "give the enlisted men three nourishing and palatable meals a day." The aim of the cookbook—"to aid inexperienced cooks in the proper preparation of the stores supplied by the Government. Recipes will serve one hundred men.[97] Sailors reaping the benefits of this cookbook, with a cook determined to follow the recipes, should have been able to sit down to some enjoyable meals.

The navy cookbook continued to be updated. The 1904 version (*General Mess Manual and Cookbook*) continues to include the information about the general mess and adds several recipes calling for tinned products (canned foods). The 1908 *U.S. Navy Cook-Book* drops the general mess information and within the collection of recipes includes two recipes for minced beef. Both are served on toast. It would seem that these recipes are military cousins of the army SOS recipe mentioned earlier. Compared to the 1902 and 1904 editions, the bread, pies, cakes and puddings sections have definitely undergone expansion in this edition. The baking section in this edition read like Mom's cookbook with the exception of much larger yields.

Food for the Navy during World War I

Josephus Daniels, secretary of the navy during World War I, in his book, *Our Navy at War*, offers insight into how many had to be fed during the war: "With more than two

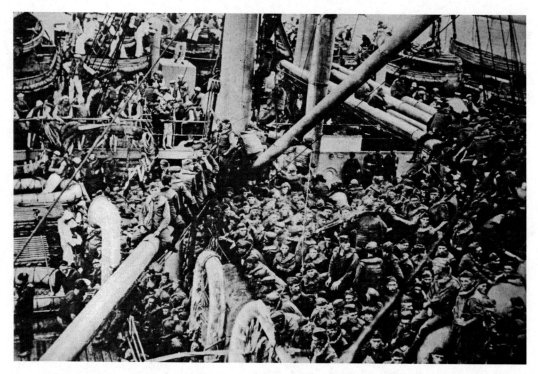

Soldiers crowded aboard the *Leviathan,* a troop transport ship bound for France in September 1918. Many mouths to feed while crossing the Atlantic. Photograph from Moore and Russell, *U.S. Official Pictures of the War.*

thousand vessels in service and 533,000 officers and men, the largest personnel ever possessed by any Navy, our naval operations in the World War literally belted the globe." He points out that of this number, "Eight hundred and thirty-four vessels and two hundred thousand men of the United States Navy were either serving in European waters or engaged in transporting troops and supplies to Europe, before hostilities ended."[98] The distance? Over 3000 miles. "Of the total troop and official passenger movement incident to the war ... the Navy transported more than 2,600,000. He also states, "Not only did the Navy man and operate the United States transports, but provided the food for this vast army of soldiers en route."[99] Daniels praises the commissary branch in its efforts during the war.

> The record of the commissary branch — and this applies to the hundreds of thousands of soldiers transported overseas and back as well as the half-million men within the navy itself — was one of unqualified success from first to last and one of which the service has good reason to be proud. Never were men in uniform so well fed or was so much attention paid to a balanced and abundant ration. "Only the best (with no substitute said to be 'equally as good'), is good enough for our fighting men," was the motto of Rear Admiral Samuel McGowan, Chief of the Bureau of Supplies.[100]

In his discussion of the successful provisioning of sailors during World War I, Allston also focuses on the leadership of the chief of the Bureau of Supplies and Accounts. Commenting on McGowan's initiative to put in place a plan for his bureau to follow in the event of a war that would involve the United States, Allston proposes that his steps

K. P. at Newport Naval Training Center. Photograph from Moore and Russell, *U.S. Official Pictures of the War.*

"led to a degree of preparedness unknown at the start of either the Civil or Spanish-American wars."[101] He credits McGowan with the development of a wartime supply system "based upon readiness to meet the needs of operating forces at a moment's notice" and a department that "organized lists of foods that might be needed on various sizes of vessels" and "purchased supplies in large quantities and stored them until needed."[102]

In his work *A Navy Second to None: The History of U.S. Naval Training in World War I*, Michael C. Besch extensively explores the training and educational efforts that the navy undertook during 1917 and 1918. Several examples of food relating training programs follow. The commissary school in San Francisco trained cooks, bakers and commissary stewards and the Great Lakes facility turned out 1,000 cooks and bakers.[103] Besch writes that St. Helena–Norfolk was the only naval location that trained mess attendants: "St. Helena trained 580 mess attendants and Norfolk trained 232 cooks, 66 bakers, and 2,857 mess attendants.[104] He notes that 249 completed commissary school training at the navy yard at Mare Island in San Francisco,[105] and the Dunwoody Industrial Institute in Minneapolis also trained cooks and bakers.[106]

Additionally, two projects of interest focus on the training of navy cooks and bakers by nonmilitary personnel — one in Philadelphia and Boston and the other in New York. Both programs were operated by women — Mrs. Mary A. Wilson and Mrs. Adrian Iselin, who were associated with cooking schools.

Barbara Kuck, culinary historian and chef, has made Mrs. Wilson's story available on the web at www.wearechefs.com. Wilson's project is detailed in *Philadelphia in the World War*, a book credited to the Philadelphia War History Committee. Mrs. Wilson, who operated her own cooking school, also mentions her work with the navy in her cookbook, *Mrs. Wilson's Cook Book*, published in 1918. Among other credentials, the title page

Recruit camp at Charleston, South Carolina. Typical mess hall and galley. Photograph from Moore and Russell, *U.S. Official Pictures of the War.*

lists that she has been an "Instructor of Cooking for the U.S. Navy." Not only did she serve for five years at Buckingham Palace in the service of Queen Victoria, she also served her own country by training cooks and bakers, at her own expense, for the navy.

The article titled "United States Naval Commissary Schools" in the Philadelphia book explains how she came to be an instructor for navy cooks and bakers: "There had been great difficulty in securing cooks and chefs for the Navy, or at least men who could prepare palatable and nutritious meals, and on June 1, 1916, Frederick R. Payne, Lieutenant-Commander, U.S.N., retired, acting for Captain Hetherington, Commandant, United States Naval Home, conferred with 'her' in reference to the establishment of a school in which cooking could be taught." Convinced that this was something that she would like to do, she started her first class of 50 naval reserves on June 5, 1916. At the completion of their culinary training, they were assigned "to ships and stations and produced palatable meals." A detachment came from the Naval School at Newport next and was followed by additional classes. "The men trained for the first six classes were used as cooks for Naval Base No. 20 in France, on the coast patrol boats in the Fourth Naval District, and on Pier no. 19." She also organized a successful cooking school in Boston where her students received orders from the navy "to supply the boats patrolling the coast as well as the five or six thousand men on the pier." The school in Boston made 2,800 pounds of bread daily.[107]

The article informs that she closed her own cooking school in Philadelphia and "devoted her entire time, day and night, to the training of naval cooks, from June 5, 1916, to December 31, 1918, without compensation ... used the equipment of her school, including ranges, tables and bake ovens, utensils, etc. and from June until October purchased such supplies—flour baking powder, eggs, shortening, etc., for the classes to work with." She was offered a yeoman's wage to cover expenses, but she did not accept this offer.[108] The article seems to be written by Mrs. Wilson.

Besch briefly mentions the work of "'patriotic women' of New York City" who "trained more than 4,000 men."[109] A *New York Times* article dated December 30, 1917, tells their story. The school "an institution of many years' standing in New York" functioned as "a large philanthropic work." During the war, Mrs. Adrian Iselin, the president of the school, and other members of the organization "in conversation with Admiral Usher suggested the classes for the naval men." According to information in the article, students were under the tutelage of three instructors, two women and a "real French chef." While they were at the school, student cooks remained "under control of officers in the navy" with "a regular inspection ... made from naval headquarters once a week." Students were taught how to cut meat, how to prepare menus, and how to purchase. The curriculum also stressed cleanliness and economy in the galley. The article indicates that students left the school as third-class cooks "but many of them are promoted almost immediately to second and first class cooks." Appar-

Mrs. M. A. Wilson, a cooking instructor, closed her Philadelphia cooking school and at her own expense trained navy cooks and bakers, one of at least two civilian efforts to train navy cooks and bakers for shipboard duty during the war. Photograph from *Mrs. Wilson's Cookbook.*

ently Usher reported that "it would have been difficult to fit out small boats and the converted German liners with cooks" without the aid of the New York Cooking School.[110]

Joseph Husband preserves his experiences during the war in *A Year in the Navy*. Early in his memoir, he gives an account of what the food was like at the Great Lakes Naval Training Station. When he arrives, for the first three weeks, he is assigned to one of several camps or barracks. While he is here, food is prepared at the main mess-hall and delivered to each camp. After three weeks he and his comrades move to the main camp. The number of his eating companions increases significantly: "Two thousand sailors ate together in each of the two dining-rooms of the main mess-hall.... At noon a part of the band played, while we ate ... Mess was served by a white-clad 'mess-detail' ... Navy slang is required, and were a bill-of-fare printed, you would see 'Java' for tea or coffee, 'punk' for bread, and 'sand' for salt, and something that sounds like 'slumgullion' for any kind of stew."[111]

The transport ship that Husband served on seems to be a luxury liner that had been converted to transport soldiers and sailors. He describes where the officers ate and also the cafeteria style of messing for the enlisted men and soldiers being transported.

> We lunched in the once richly decorated saloon where men and women had gaily gathered in long voyages to the distant Orient. But today the central table was lined with naval officers, and on either side, at other tables, sat the several hundred army officers who were accompanying us. In the soldier's quarters galley-fires had been long lighted and dinner was being rapidly served to the men. With cup and tin plate in hand, they passed in line before the serving-tables, then scattered about the decks and voraciously devoured their first meal on shipboard.[112]

He adds that on the 3000 plus mile trip, "Meals were served with clock-like regularity to appease appetites sharpened by sea air."[113]

A navy baker carries loaves of freshly baked bread on board the USS *Florida*, 1918. Courtesy Naval Historical Center, Washington, D.C.

Once in France he is assigned to a yacht that patrolled waters for incoming and outgoing freight convoys. Although he doesn't write about his regular meals on this duty, he does, however, mention that when he arrives on the bridge at four in the morning for his night watch he finds that "hot coffee and bread had just been brought up from the galley."[114]

Having great admiration and respect for destroyers in their role of protection, Husband finally gets his wish to serve on one. The destroyer *Benham* has a crew of over a hundred men and eight officers to be fed. Because he eats with the officers, he delivers a first hand description of messing in the ward-room: "Colored and Philippine mess attendants were setting the table, and soon after we sat down to dinner, the 'Captain,' a commander in the regular Navy, at the head, and the Mess Treasurer at the foot." While on duty at night scanning the waters for enemy subs he writes, "A great copper pot of hot, thick coffee was brought up to the bride, and a huge tin cup of it put me on my toes again."[115]

Reginald J. Johnson served from 1917 to 1919 on the battleship USS *Florida* in and out of combat. He regularly corresponds with his mother,

Mess time at Newport Naval Training Center. Photograph from Moore and Russell, *U.S. Official Pictures of the War.*

frequently giving her a report of his bill of fare and of his duties in the galley. During his training at Newport, Rhode Island, he discusses meals and mess assignments. His overall impression in training is that "we get excellent food put out in a clean way." In July 1917 he writes, "Certainly have some big feed Sundays." He is equally impressed with a Fourth of July "feed," indicating that "at mess tables they handed out two plates filled up."[116]

When he was in the "European Waters" (English Channel), one breakfast he especially enjoyed included "two large sugared buns apiece, meat & potatoes, syrup, butter and coffee." Johnson, on more than one occasion, enjoys boxes of fudge and fruitcake sent by his mother. He tells his mother that he had been relieving one of the servants in the chief petty officers' galley: "It was hard work, but plenty to eat. We had 54 to cook for and I had all the pie, cake & beef steak I wanted." He shares a Thanksgiving dining experience while in Rosyth, Scotland. Even though he didn't get turkey, he had a "very good dinner: beef steak smothered in onions, baked potatoes, corn, and peas, canned peaches, cake bread and butter and coffee."[117]

Interviewed in 2005 for the Veteran's History Project, Lloyd Brown, a World War I veteran, briefly explains what the eating situation was like on the ship that he served:

We slept in hammocks that hung from the ceiling of the boat. And get up in the morning, you fold up your hammock, put it away out of the way. And then tables were kept in the ceiling. Bring the table down, set it on the deck and you served your meals. After the meal's over put your table back up in the ceiling so the deck would be clear for other activities.[118]

Loading stores on the USS *New York* at the Brooklyn Navy Yard before 1917. Courtesy Naval Historical Center, Washington, D.C.

Daniels also praises the Naval Overseas Transportation Service, indicating that it was considered to be the world's largest cargo fleet. Called "The Ferry to France," it transported "millions of tons of munitions, guns, food, fuel, supplies, materials to our army and naval forces abroad." Speaking of the efficient service provided by N.O.T.S., Daniels indicates, "Five hundred million pounds of meats, butter, etc., were carried to our forces overseas, only 4,000 pounds being lost on voyage."[119]

Home Front during the War: Food Conservation and Food Production

Conservation and production of food surfaced as hot topics on the home front when America entered the war in 1917. Individuals at home took to heart the concept promoted by Herbert Hoover, administrator of the Food Administration during World War I, that "food will win the war." Education, propaganda, organization, and patriotism became key elements in enlisting those at home in a home front army and in rallying these home front warriors to action. Statistics reveal that "Hoover's program reduced domestic consumption of food by 15% without rationing. For the farmer there was 'fair price' for agricultural products and guaranteed markets for surplus. The result was that U.S. food shipments tripled. He kept the American armies fed and was able to build up surplus stores of food to prevent a post-war famine in Europe."[120]

Two organizations, because of their activities related to food conservation and food production during the war, are explored here—the work of women on the home front and the work of the National War Garden Commission. Both helped to Hooverize, a popular term used during the war, the American home front.

Ida Clyde Clark, in *American Women and the World War*, discusses the involvement of women at this time. According to Clark, "On April 21, 1917, fifteen days after Congress formally declared that a state of war existed ... the Council of National Defense ... appointed a committee of women of national prominence to consider and advise how the assistance of the women of American may be made available in the prosecution of the war." The committee immediately went to work to deliver the messages of the Food Administration to American homes. Each state was encouraged to departmentalize their work with two important departments—Food Production and Home Economics and Food Administration.[121]

The message of conservation was also delivered in numerous government publications distributed to women. The housewife-cook is informed, "These things we must send—wheat, beef, pork, dairy products, sugar." The persuasive appeal continues, "Winning the war rests primarily on one thing: the loyalty and sacrifice of the American people in the matter of food.... Each pound of food saved by each American citizen is a pound given to the support of our army, the allies and the friendly neutrals."[122]

Information on a January 1918 Home Card, an informative war food conservation publication, explains how to voluntarily shape meal plans in support of the war effort.

Two Wheatless Days (Monday and Wednesday) in every week
One Wheatless meal in every day
One Meatless Day (Thursday) in every week
One Meatless Meal in every day
Two Porkless Days (Tuesday and Saturday) in every week
Every day a Fat-saving Day (butter, lard, lard-substitutes, etc.)
Every day a Sugar-saving Day
Use Fruits, Vegetables and Potatoes abundantly
Use Milk wisely
Do not Hoard Food.[123]

A 1918 Food Administration publication, "Victory Breads," explains that "Victory bread is the bread which will be eaten by all the people fighting Germany—100,000,000 people in the United States and 120,000,000 in Europe." Victory bread is defined as being prepared with "80 percent wheat flour and 20 percent substitute." Notice is also given that "Mixed Victory flour will soon be on the market," apparently for the convenience of the cook. Wheat flour will be mixed with barley, corn flour, corn meal, rye or other substitutes.[124]

Amid the plethora of food conservation propaganda, the Food Administration reminds the cook that the key word in food conservation is not just save but more so substitute. An informational chart includes a substitution chart.

The soldiers need	The folks at home can use
Wheat	Corn, oats, barley, rye
Butter, lard	Butter substitutes, cottonseed oil, peanut oil, corn oil, drippings
Sugar	Molasses, honey, sirups
Bacon, beef, mutton, pork	Chicken, eggs, cottage cheese, fish, nuts, peas, beans[125]

The War Garden Victorious by Charles Lathrop Pack shares the story of the National War Garden Commission and the influence it had on food production during the war. In this publication Pack first explains how and why it came to be. By 1917 military conflict in Europe had radically upset the balance of trade between in this area. Men were enlisted in armies. Pack calculates that "altogether, twenty or thirty million men were called away from their usual pursuits. The vocation of the majority of them was farming. Thus, at one stroke, practically all the farms in the embattled nations were swept clear of male workers." As well the "nicely balanced [trade] system" between Germany, Italy, and Russia was destroyed. Add to that the entrance of the submarine which led to the destruction of "thousands of tons" of materials shipped. Pack then indicates, "Thus the burden of feeding the Entente fell very largely upon the United States." He also points out that 1916 "was agriculturally, the most disastrous year the world has known, in recent times" including American production which "fell off by hundreds of millions of bushels."[126]

Pack, believing in the need for Americans to produce some of their own food close to their homes, so that other foodstuffs would be available for American soldiers and America's allies, created the National War Garden Commission. An important element of the commission was "the systematic education of the people" toward the goal of showing them how to produce some of their own foods in their own back yards and in their communities.[127]

Will you have a part in Victory?

WRITE TO THE NATIONAL WAR GARDEN COMMISSION ~ WASHINGTON, D.C. for free books on gardening, canning & drying.

"Every Garden a Munition Plant"

Charles Lathrop Pack, President

THIS POSTER, USED IN 1918, AND WITH DIFFERENT SLOGANS IN 1919, WAS POPULAR WHEREVER IT APPEARED AND DID MUCH TO EXTEND THE WAR GARDEN MOVEMENT

World War I poster promoting Victory Gardens. Photograph from Charles Lathrop Pack's *The War Garden Victorious*. Pack organized the War Garden Commission to motivate Americans to grow food in their back yards and in community vacant lots so that essential food would be available for the military.

The war-garden movement like the food preservation movement organized by the Food Administration also took on a patriotic fervor. Experienced and novice gardeners alike responded to colorful posters designed with thought provoking slogans distributed by the commission: "Sow the Seeds of Victory," and "Can Vegetables, Fruit and The Kaiser too." Considering the gardens grown on "slacker land" (empty or unused ground) in and around cities and communities, the army of gardeners put in 3,500,000 gardens in 1917 and 5,285,000 gardens in 1918. Pack estimates that "more than 500,000,000 quarts of canned vegetables and fruits" were put up in 1917 and 1,450,000,000 in 1918.[128]

Pack explores how "the Soldier of the Soil" serving in a war garden helped the soldier. He mentions the three M's related to war, men, money and munitions: "In the broadest sense, the term 'munitions' includes everything needed by an army, and of all an army's needs the basic and most important is food." With this in mind, Pack offers his conclusions on what war gardens "actually accomplished toward feeding the army." This he believes was shown by "the amount of food which they added to the nation's larder." A tally, based on careful estimates, delivers the following numbers.

Food preservation book published by the National War Garden Commission to promote food conservation.

This [the value of the amount of food added to the nation's larder] was reckoned in 1918 as having a value of $525,000,000. Taking into consideration equivalent food values, it was figured on a conservative basis that our 1918 war gardens grew food equal in body-building power to the meat ration required by an army of 1,000,000 men for 302 days; or the entire ration for 142 days.[129]

Navy Food After the War

Updated navy cookbooks continued to be produced following the war. Following the 1920 edition, the 1927 edition of *The Cook Book of the United States Navy* adds a new section of recipes for the navy cook. This group of recipes for "thickening agents and sauces." A discussion of "food selection" takes a health slant, explaining reasons for

PLANT A VICTORY GARDEN

OUR FOOD IS FIGHTING

A GARDEN WILL MAKE YOUR RATIONS GO FURTHER

World War I poster promoting Victory Gardens. Courtesy Naval Historical Center, Washington, D.C.

certain choices of foods for the bill of fare. A brief discussion of the "destroyer and small craft bill of fare" points out that their menus are "somewhat restricted, particularly in the bakery department." The cookbook includes charts both for stores for 100 men for 30 days and also a chart for a 10 day supply for the destroyer and for other smaller craft. The *Cookbook of the United States Navy* (1932) includes recipes for cooks preparing meals on submarines.

J.H. Skillman was instrumental in developing a new ration put in place by Congress in 1933. He notes changes taking place in the navy: "The Navy was undergoing a decided change, not only in a material way, but as regards personnel." In 1931 Skillman started work on a project to examine the current ration and to tabulate his findings. After tabulating data relating to millions of rations, he identified deficiencies and problems and corrected them in the new ration.[130] The 1933 Ration is as follows.

8 oz. biscuits, 12 oz. soft bread, or 12 oz. flour; 12 oz. preserved meat, 14 oz. salt or smoked meat, or 20 oz. fresh meat, fish or poultry; 12 oz. dried vegetables, 18 oz. canned vegetables, 44 oz. fresh vegetables, or 6 oz. of vegetable juice; 4 oz. dried fruit, 10 oz. canned fruit, 6 oz. preserved fruit, 16 oz. fresh fruit, 6 oz. fresh fruit juice, 6 oz. concentrated fruit juice, or 1 oz. of powdered fruit juice; 2 oz. cocoa, 2 oz. coffee, or one half oz. of tea; 4 oz. evaporated milk, one oz. powdered milk, or one-half pint fresh milk; 1.6 oz. butter; 1.6 oz. of cereals, rice, or starch foods; one-half oz. of cheese; 1.6 oz. lard or lard substitute; 2/5 gill of oils, sauces, or vinegar; 5 oz. sugar; baking powder and soda, flavoring extracts, mustard, pepper, pickles, salt, syrup, spices, and yeast as required.[131]

Efforts to improve the messing system had been tried out prior to the war on board USS *New York*.[132] However, the cafeteria style of messing used during the war faded away after the war. Barboo believes, "It is presumed that the design and the location of the galley were not conducive to cafeteria food service. There were no spaces specifically constructed for crew dining."[133] E.D. Foster reports on a returned interest in the cafeteria style of messing in his article "Cafeteria Afloat" that appeared in *United States Naval Institute Proceedings* in 1937. He discusses the trial use of the cafeteria system, this time in the *Ranger*. The project was so successful that at the time of the article he reports "installations similar to the *Ranger*'s have been authorized for new construction" and "modifications are in the process of being made or have been made to accommodate the

A well cared for World War I Victory Garden. Photograph from *The War Garden Victorious*, Charles Lathrop Pack.

new style of messing in several ships." He believes that as far as he is aware, "The *Ranger's* installation is the first successful application of this system aboard a combatant ship."[134]

The serving of food in the *Ranger* experiment appears to be very much like a modern food bar setup. Steam tables keep hot food hot and cold foods are maintained at correct temperatures. Plates are located on racks close to the food, and eating utensils and other items such as cups and glasses are left at tables. Men, in a mess line, help themselves to food items of their choice, "taking as much or little as they like," and they can return for additional servings. Some foods are served by mess cooks. Foster speculates that one reason for the return to this type of food service came as a result of "new demands, such as for the necessity of instant food service at unexpected hours aboard carriers." In addition to this increased flexibility, he cites self-service, a more varied ration, second servings, choice of foods, sanitary and hygienic control, efficient utilization of messing space, and simplified mess administration as advantageous features. On the other hand, among several possible disadvantages to be considered, he mentions "a long wait in line" and "continued desire for table service."[135]

8

Provisions for World War II

In comparison to other armies we are by far the best paid and best fed.
— 2nd Lt. Robert L. Huber

Types of Operational Rations

By mid–1941 the slow rebuilding of the army that began in the late 1930s had brought its strength to 1.5 million.[1] The only operational ration remaining in the 1930s was the reserve ration consisting of canned meat and bread. Experiments at the Subsistence School resulted in what was named the Logan Bar for Col. Paul Logan, director of the school.[2] In 1937, Logan met with William Murrie, president of Hershey Chocolate Corporation, and Sam Hinkle, chief chemist, about development of a chocolate bar for an emergency ration. Logan told Murrie and Hinkle that there were four requirements: a bar weighing four ounces, ability to withstand high temperatures, high in calories, and tasting just a little better than a boiled potato. Logan was concerned that if the bar tasted too good soldiers would eat it like candy rather than retaining it for emergency use.[3] Hershey packaged the ration as three 4-ounce bars wrapped in aluminum foil and overwrapped in parchment paper; it was never intended for more than an emergency ration. The bars contained 600 calories with three bars making an 1800 calorie day's ration. Following field tests in 1938 and vigorous debate between the quartermaster general and the adjutant general over proper use of the bar, the army standardized it as both reserve and emergency ration.[4]

These discussions resulted in a new system of designation for rations using letters instead of the terms reserve and emergency. Field ration A was the field prepared version of the garrison ration using fresh vegetables and meats while field ration B was basically the same except that no perishable items were used, only canned and dehydrated products. The Logan Bar became field ration D and went into full production in 1941. By the end of 1945 Hershey was producing about 24 million bars per week.[5]

Prior to its entry into World War II, the United States still lacked a nutritionally balanced, palatable, easily transportable ration for combat conditions when field kitchens could not be established. Work began on a combat ration in 1937. The research developed a six-can ration—three meat or M units and three bread or B units packed in twelve ounce cylindrical cans. Following field tests in 1940, the ration was adopted as Field Ration C. The three original M-units included pork and beans, meat and vegetable hash, and meat and vegetable stew. To the bread or B-unit was added a chocolate fudge bar, different from the D bar, and soluble coffee. Eventually hard candy replaced the chocolate bar. The army began large scale purchases of this ration in August 1941, replacing the old World War I reserve ration.[6] The C ration evolved throughout its existence as changes were made to improve its acceptability among the troops. Beverage components added to the B unit cans included soluble coffee, cocoa powder, and lemon powder. The lemon powder proved unpopular and was removed in 1945. Also added were three types of crackers, jam, and a variety of kinds of candy. Beginning in March 1943 cigarettes were included in some of the B unit cans. Later, these along with gum, halazone water purification tablets, toilet paper, and a can opener were placed in accessory packets inserted between the cans in shipping cases.[7]

The P-38 can opener included in the accessory packet is somewhat of a story in itself. The opener, invented by Major Thomas Dennethy at the Subsistence Research Laboratory in the summer of 1942, has been nicknamed the "John Wayne" because of its toughness. Soldiers quickly became attached to their P-38, keeping it on their key rings or dogtag chains. Many retained their P-38 after leaving the

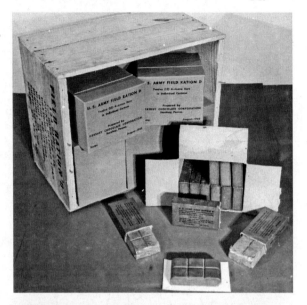

Top: Field Ration D consisted of chocolate bars carried by troops as an emergency ration. *Bottom:* Accessory packets placed between the cans in cases of C rations. Both photographs courtesy Quartermaster Museum, Fort Lee, Virginia.

service and keep it as a valued souvenir. The sturdy device has been found useful for things other than opening C ration cans. It has been used as a knife and screwdriver. According to Colonel Renita Foster, Army Public Affairs, "The P-38 acquired its infamous nomenclature from the thirty-eight punctures around the C ration can required for opening and the boast that it performed with the speed of the World War II P-38 fighter plane."[8]

Two significant problems faced developers of the C ration: finding canned meat products of suitable quality and duplication of B ration meats. A soldier returning from a forward combat position who had been subsisting on C rations might find the same hash or stew being prepared at a field kitchen when he returned to a location behind the front lines. Soldiers grew tired of eating the same foods. The C ration was designed to be used for only a few days at a time, however, "Instances were reported of soldiers being fed the C ration for as long as 90 days."[9] These rations could be eaten cold but were much more palatable when heated, but soldiers often found themselves under conditions where heating wasn't possible and were forced to eat cold rations adding to their dislike for them. The awkwardness of carrying the heavy cylindrical cans was another complaint about the C ration. Soldiers preferred rectangular shaped packages but the C rations retained the cylindrical can throughout their life.[10]

While the C ration provided balanced nutrition and adequate calories, a need still existed for a ration that soldiers could carry with them during active combat or the assault phase of action. In 1940, experiments began with compact rations based on pemmican. The goal was to produce a compact ration that could be carried in the pockets of paratroopers.[11] The K ration met this need. The Subsistence Laboratory received assistance in developing the K ration from Dr. Ancel Keys, a physiologist at the University of Minnesota, who later became well known for his definitive study on the effects of human starvation and for discovering the connection between cholesterol and heart disease. Keys' first collection of items for the K ration looked like what might be placed in a typical lunch bag: summer sausage, canned meat, crackers, cheese, candy, and chocolate. Keys purchased the items at a local supermarket.[12] According to William Hoffman, who interviewed Keys for an article in a University of Minnesota publication, Keys stated, "We bought the stuff down at Witt's, the best market in the Twin Cities in those days."[13] Keys' ration was tested

P-38 can opener being used to open a C ration can. Courtesy the U.S. Marine Corps History Center, Quantico, Virginia.

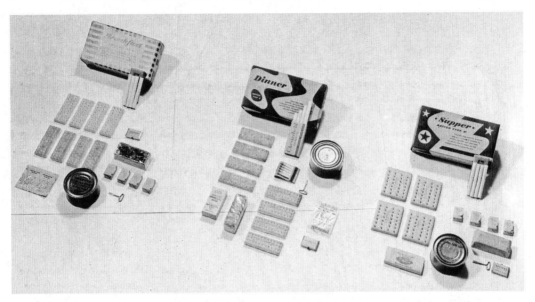

K rations were packed in individual boxes for each meal. Courtesy Quartermaster Museum, Fort Lee, Virginia.

first with a few soldiers at Fort Snelling, Minnesota, followed by more extensive testing at Fort Benning, Georgia.

The first version of the K ration issued to paratroopers contained twelve pemmican biscuits, D bar chocolate, a canned meat product, and lemon or orange drink powder.[14] Later development involved making three distinct units, labeled "breakfast," "dinner," and "supper." The K ration went through several modifications during the war but in general the units were as follows:

> The breakfast packet contained a canned meat product, biscuits, a compressed cereal bar, soluble coffee, a fruit bar, gum, sugar tablets, four cigarettes, water-purification tablets, a can opener, toilet paper, and a wooden spoon. The dinner carton had a canned cheese product, biscuits, a candy bar, gum, a variety of beverage powders, granulated sugar, salt tablets, cigarettes, and matches, a can opener, and spoon. The supper packet included a canned meat product, biscuits, bouillon powder, confections and gum, soluble coffee, granulated sugar, cigarettes, can opener, and spoon.[15]

In 1944 the army purchased more than 105 million K rations.[16] Like other operational rations, K rations were intended to be used for only a few days but in practice, conditions sometimes forced soldiers to use them for a much longer time. The long term use led to complaints about K rations and their discontinuance in 1946. Although originally designed with paratroopers in mind, the ration came into full use by all troops, not just paratroopers.

Some confusion persists about the designation "K" ration and whether they were named for Dr. Ancel Keys. Officially the Subsistence Laboratory explained that there was no significance to the designation; it simply used an alphabetical designation to differentiate this new ration from the C and D rations.[17] Keys stated that "I was surprised when I saw the packages start to roll in with 'K' on them. I got a letter from Colonel Logan ... saying he hoped I wouldn't mind."[18]

Early in the war, planners perceived the need for specialized rations to feed small groups of troops in unusual service conditions. Three such rations were developed by the Subsistence Laboratory: the Mountain Ration, the Jungle Ration, and the 5-in-1 Ration. The Mountain Ration and the Jungle Ration both included canned meats, dry milk, biscuits, cereal, hard candy, and dry drink mixes. Packaged as meals for four men for one day, both rations were used only in 1942 and 1943.[19]

The Subsistence Research and Development Laboratory produced a third group feeding ration, the 5-in-1, in early 1942. Its intended use was for motorized units in desert conditions. It consisted basically of B-ration items such as canned vegetables, meat, evaporated milk, fruit juice, fruits, dehydrated soups, cereal, biscuits, hard candy, salt, sugar, and toilet paper. They were packed to provide meals for five men for one day. Production of this ration stopped in 1943 but remaining stocks continued in use throughout the war.[20] Historians William F. Ross and Charles F. Romanus write, "By far the most popular combat ration in North Africa was the 5-in-1."[21]

In 1943 work began on another group feeding ration called the 10-in-1. It consisted of basically five menus of food for ten men. The menus typically contained butter spread, soluble coffee, pudding, meat units, jam, evaporated milk, vegetables, biscuits, cereal, beverages, candy, salt, and sugar. Additional items included cigarettes, matches, can opener, toilet paper, soap, towels, and water purification tablets. The dinner or noon meal portion of the 10-in-1 ration consisted of the dinner portion of the K ration and was issued on an individual rather than on a group basis. This was the largest complaint against the 10-in-1. The ration was in use from 1943 until end of the war.[22] Later in the war the Subsistence Laboratory added new meat items, expanding the menu options. These items included hamburger, pork tenderloin, pork and corn, pork and apple, and sausage and apple.[23]

Special Rations

As a result of the numerous amphibious assault landings in the Pacific, the army perceived a need for a light, concentrated ration to be given to soldiers just prior to entering combat to sustain them until the normal supply operations could be established. The result of experimentation was the development of the Assault Lunch, basically a candy ration. It contained chocolate bars, caramels, dried fruit, chewing gum, peanuts, salt tablets, cigarettes, matches, and water-purification tablets. The Assault Lunch ration was discontinued after 1947.[24]

World War II brought a greatly expanded role for aircraft and consequently the need for special rations to be used by aircraft crews. In 1943, the first such ration was established, known as the Aircrew Lunch. The ration consisted of a variety of hard candy, candy bars, and gum and continued to be used throughout the war. For missions involving longer time in flight the Army Air Force Combat Lunch was used. Items included consisted of dry milk, chili powder or tomato paste, bouillon cubes, hard candy, gum, precooked rice, salt, tea tablets, and a can opener. The meal was to be prepared on board the airplane. Small amounts of this ration were purchased in 1943 and 1944 but by mid–1945 it was discontinued and criticized by the Subsistence Laboratory. Food was also needed for situations when an air crew was forced to bail out of their aircraft. The first so-called bailout ration was procured in 1942 and contained D bars, fruit bars, hard candy, lemon juice powder, and K biscuits. In 1943, the ration was modified to the Parachute Emergency Ration consisting of sweet chocolate, hard candy, dehydrated cheese and crackers, bouillon cubes, sugar, cigarettes, water-purification tablets, soluble coffee, gum, and a bag in which to store uneaten food after opening the can. This ration remained in use until 1952.[25]

The Air Force also sought rations to stow on lifeboats which rescuers dropped to crews of aircraft crashes in water. This ration, the Airborne Lifeboat Ration, contained B units from the C ration along with canned meat and condensed soup. These rations were not procured after 1944. The Quartermaster Corps developed a much smaller Liferaft Ration consisting of hard candy and vitamin pills. The Coast Guard and merchant marines used a liferaft ration beginning in 1942 which contained C biscuits, pemmican, chocolate tablets, and milk tablets. The components of the ration were obtained through the Chicago Quartermaster Depot.[26]

Three other special ration packages were assembled by the Quartermaster Corps during the war. One was a Kitchen Spice Pack consisting of spices, flavorings, and condiments to augment the palatability of B rations. In 1943, the Subsistence Laboratory developed a hospital supplement ration with canned fruit, canned orange juice, evaporated milk, coffee, dehydrated soup, and sugar. This supplement was designed to be used at evacuation and base hospitals. It was revised in 1944 with the substitution of soluble coffee for ground roasted, powdered milk for evaporated, and condensed soup for dehydrated. Also added were cereal, cocoa beverage powder, malted milk tablets, tea, and tomato juice. The third special ration was the Aid-station Beverage Ration which contained components recommended by the Surgeon General. These included coffee, tea cocoa beverage powder, evaporated milk, and sugar.[27]

Cooked Rations and Fresh Foods

Army regulations specified three types of hot, cooked rations for troop feeding depending on the location of the troops and conditions. During peacetime at established bases, organized messes used the garrison ration. Cooked fresh, canned, and frozen foods made up this ration. The basic components included bacon, fresh beef, pork, and chicken; fresh eggs; beans, rice, oats; fresh and canned vegetables such as string beans, corn, onions, peas, tomatoes, potatoes; fruit, jam, and preserves; coffee, cocoa, tea, milk; butter, macaroni, cheese, sugar, spices, syrup, vinegar, and pickles. The garrison ration was issued as money credit to each mess which could be used to purchase any food either from the commissary store or local markets. The amount of money credit was based on the quartermaster's calculated price per ration. If a mess did not use the full amount in any one month it would be added to the company fund and could used at any time on additional food. This was referred to as ration savings.[28]

All field rations were issued in kind, that is the actual food. The Field Ration A consisted of fresh foods and was essentially the same as the garrison ration. It required the use of refrigeration. There were no ration savings under the A ration. Field Ration B was very similar to A except for the use of nonperishable items. It provided a hot cooked meal but did not require refrigeration. In place of fresh meats, fruits, and vegetables, canned and dehydrated items were substituted. One of the canned meat products included in the B ration has merged into World War II folklore. In 1937, Hormel introduced a canned meat product called Spiced Ham. Later the company renamed the product SPAM Luncheon Meat. It consisted of pork and ham and was well suited for use by the military since it did not require refrigeration. The product was used extensively by the military and was also used to supply civilians in both Europe and the Pacific who were short of food because of the war. Hormel packaged SPAM in six pound cans for the military and smaller twelve ounce cans for civilian use.[29] World War II troops who sometimes ate canned meats for three meals a day for weeks grew tired of such products. The army purchased canned meat from several suppliers, however all such products came to be called SPAM although Hormel insisted their version was of better quality. One unknown writer even penned a short poem about SPAM.[30]

To meet the demand for fresh foods, the Market Center Program (MCP) was established in 1941 under the Office of the Quartermaster General. Historian Herbert Rifkind describes the program as being "the rational and coordinated procurement, storage, and distribution of perishable subsistence to the armed forces of the United States during World War II.[31] He explains further that the agency "can be considered a cooperative undertaking participated in by the Army, other Government agencies, and representatives of the commercial perishable food trades."[32] The Market Center Program began operation in April 1941 with six centers. Eventually the program operated more than forty centers with the headquarters in Chicago being designated as the administrative headquarters.[33] The centers were established in areas where particular kinds of fresh produce were grown. For example, centers in California and Florida would have access to citrus fruits and vegetables.

The MCP expanded to also become the primary supplier of perishables to the navy, marine corps, and coast guard. The joint procurement of ration items among the military service branches increased efficiency and prevented competition for products between the various services.[34] Purchases of canned meat, boneless beef, poultry, and fish also became part of the Market Center's activity. Other items procured by the Market Center which were not originally planned were frozen fruits and vegetables and milk. To insure the quality of its purchases, all items were inspected by either the Veterinary Corps or Agricultural Marketing Service, part of the United States Department of Agriculture. By 1944, the Veterinary Corps made all inspections of animal products.[35] As shortages began to appear for some food items, the government took steps to exercise control over the economy to prevent excessive prices; thus the MCP had to coordinate its purchases with the War Production Board, Office of Price Administration, Food Distribution Administration, and War Meat Board.[36] One of the most important items purchased by the MCP was beef. Frozen boneless beef first appeared as a ration item toward the end of World War I. It saved a great amount of shipping space and weight when supplying American forces in France. However, no further development work was done on the product until the late 1930s. The Subsistence Laboratory received assistance from both Armour and Swift to develop de-boning and packaging techniques. As in World War I, the goal was to save shipping space and weight. Packed in easily stacked boxes, the boneless beef proved popular with cooks in the theaters of operation since it was packaged according to use: roasting and frying, stewing, or ground meat. In addition, it eliminated the need for butchers to cut up carcass beef.[37]

Dehydrated products once again came to the forefront of subsistence supply. Largely ignored by the military following World War I, their shipping weight and space savings advantages were quickly realized and extensive research was carried out on their use and production. Work with dehydrated products extended not only to fruits and vegetables but also to milk and eggs. While an effort was made to instruct cooks on the proper preparation of dehydrated foods, among the most universally disliked foods in the military have been dehydrated milk and eggs.

Butter was an item desired by soldiers but one difficult to store and ship. It quickly becomes rancid without refrigeration and will also melt at high temperatures. The Subsistence Laboratory worked with Kraft Cheese Co. in 1941 to find a more stable product. The result was a combination of butter and hydrogenated vegetable shortening known as Carter's Spread. The taste and consistency did not receive high marks from troops in North Africa, the first to use it. Further collaboration with Kraft produced a new one which was a combination of butter and cheese known as Army Spread. This new product was much better accepted and was widely used throughout the war.[38]

Because of issues of increasing food shortages, the Office of the Quartermaster General established the Food Service Program to address food conservation in troop messes, supervise the preparation and serving of food, and to provide properly trained mess personnel.[39] This program began at the end of July 1943 with the establishment of the Food Service Branch, Subsistence Division. There were five sections in this branch: Bakery, Schools for Bakers and Cooks, Mess Supervision, Refrigeration, and Mess Equipment. Food Service Program personnel helped solve problems at various types of mess facilities by observing conditions at the site and making recommendations to improve feeding efficiency and food quality. The War Shipping Administration asked for help from the Army Food Service Program to improve troop messing on transport vessels. Other activities included the publication of a manual on handling, storage, and brewing of coffee and the organizing of weekly drives that featured some aspect of messing. Some examples of the kinds of drives organized were use of leftovers, coffee brewing, attractive food service, preparation of fresh and frozen vegetables, the cooking of meats, and making gravy. The Food Service Program also promoted victory gardens at army posts. One particularly interesting study conducted revealed the differences in food preferences between women and men in the army. The result was modification of menus providing a 15 percent decrease in bacon, 20 percent in veal, 30 percent to 50 percent in eggs, 20 percent in bread, and 25 percent in coffee but also allowing a 50 percent increase in fruit cocktail, 100 percent in pears, and 50 percent in apples.[40]

Supply and Troop Transportation

With the massive number of troops deployed in World War II, the U.S. military faced an onerous task of transporting both personnel and supplies, including food, to diverse destinations. To better manage issues of shipping President Roosevelt established the War Shipping Administration in February 1942. Troops and supplies were ferried to overseas points by a variety of ship types. Some were navy vessels while others were those owned or chartered by the Army Transport Service or were privately owned ships. The ships were operated by navy, coast guard, or merchant marine crews. Under the direction of the War Shipping Administration, the nation took on the task of building additional ships to meet the crisis. The so-called Liberty ships were built in large numbers and proved invaluable in supplying as well as transporting troops.[41] World War II marked the first war in which the movement of supplies in the field was carried out primarily by motorized vehicles. Although, the army found that mules greatly facilitated the transport of ammunition, water, and food in rugged, mountainous areas where few roads existed. Troops in Tunisia, Sicily, Italy, and the China-Burma-India Theater used mules extensively.[42] As well, railroads provided an invaluable service in transporting both supplies and personnel across the country to ports of embarkation. To meet the demand for cars, the Office of Defense Transportation contracted with the Pullman Company and American Car and Foundry to build troop sleeper cars and troop kitchen cars.

One of the most remarkable efforts at providing food and refreshments for troops took place at canteens established by community volunteers in railroad stations across the country. According to Scott Trostel writing in *Angels at the Station*, "At approximately one hundred twenty-five cites, canteens served the troops."[43] These canteens met troop trains and provided free of charge sandwiches, cookies, candy, fruit, hot coffee, and cold milk along with newspapers and magazines. In some cases it was a sacrifice for the volunteers providing food because of the food rationing during the war.

The first community canteen to be established was at Neodesha, Kansas. The largest and perhaps best known was at North Platte, Nebraska. Troop trains passed through North Platte from 5 A.M. until after midnight each day during the war. Members of the community decided to greet the soldiers, sailors, and marines passing through with a warm welcome and food and beverages. Citizens of North Platte and surrounding communities provided all of the food themselves and received no government aid. By end of the war, 6,000,000 men on troop trains had passed through North Platte and were provided refreshments by the canteen during the ten minute stops. The program began on Christmas Day 1941 following which every troop train passing through North Platte was greeted.[44]

Cooks and Bakers Schools

At the beginning of the war the army operated nine schools for cooks and bakers, each offering a four month course. Eventually this number expanded to ninety-five. Specific courses were modified throughout the war period. In 1941, two courses for officers were offered, one for the training of mess officers and the second for the training of officers as instructors in mess management. Enlisted men were trained in the following schools: army cooks, graduate cooks to become mess sergeants, army bakers, and graduate cooks to become pastry bakers.[45] The increased use of new foods, especially dried products, necessitated the courses to train mess personnel in the preparation and use of these foods. The quartermaster general also made use of civilian resources to assist in training cooks. The National Livestock and Meat Board sent experts to all of the schools to provide instructions on the most practical methods of cutting and cooking meat. Periodically throughout the war, the Subsistence Research Laboratory in Chicago offered special courses for both officers and enlisted personnel.[46]

Coffee

Long a part of military rations, coffee was used widely during World War II. It was a component of all operational rations except D rations and lifeboat and life raft rations. Field operational rations such as C and K included soluble or instant coffee packed in individual foil-acetate packets. Each packet was enough to make eight ounces of coffee. This widespread use of instant coffee during World War II led to the growth of its popularity following the war among consumers. In rations designed for group feeding, instant coffee was packaged in cans.[47]

During World War II the army, navy, and marine corps all roasted their own coffee. In addition to its own roasting plants, twenty-two commercial plants signed contracts with the government to process coffee. One hundred twenty-five roasting plants were also set up overseas. Many of these were mobile units which could be moved. Five plants were operated by the army: Atlanta, Seattle, Brooklyn, Chicago, and Memphis. Two were operated by the navy: Oakland and Brooklyn. The marine corps operated a roasting plant in Philadelphia. The ground roasted coffee was placed in either bags or vacuum sealed cans ranging in size from one pound to twenty pounds.[48] The vast majority of the coffee used by the military came from Brazil and Colombia and was a blend of Santos Brazilian and Colombian coffees. The blend ranged from 50–50 to 70–30 Santos to Colombian. After 1950 the blend was standardized at 70–30.[49]

Cooking and Subsistence Manuals

With the immense size of the army during World War II it is not surprising that the War Department published a large number of cooking and subsistence manuals. *The Army Cook*, first published in 1928, was revised in 1938, 1941, and 1942. The 1942 version, published as TM 10-405, was used throughout the war. The book is divided into two sections. The first half discusses food and nutrition principles, various cooking methods, kitchen management, and field cooking equipment. *The Army Baker* in its 1942 edition was the primary baking manual throughout the war period. In March 1943 the National Live Stock and Meat Board published for the army the *Baking Manual for the Army Cook*. This manual contains recipes for all types of bread, rolls, sweet rolls, pies, crusts, and fillings as well as cakes, cookies, and icings. One obvious emphasis of the publication is to encourage the use of lard. Another manual published for the army by industry was the *Canned Food Manual*, published by the American Can Company in 1942.

Cooking Dehydrated Foods was published in 1943 "to furnish a clear and complete source of information ... on the best method of cooking dehydrated foods."[50] Recipes in the manual show ways of combining dehydrated products with canned foods. For example, the cook is shown how to prepare dehydrated eggs and luncheon meat (SPAM) and how to used canned corned beef and dehydrated potatoes and onions to make a hash.

Increased purchases of food by the army meant a need for more individuals trained to inspect subsistence supplies. To that end, the War Department released in 1940 TM 10-210, *Inspection of Subsistence Supplies. Mess Management and Training*, TM 10-205, first appeared in 1940 and was reissued in 1941 and 1944. This manual also covers inspection of supplies along with procurement procedures, food conservation, sanitation, accounts and records, mess personnel, rations, nutrition and menu planning, and procedures for messing on troop trains, in garrison, and in the field.

One particularly interesting publication made by the Women's Interests Section, War Department, Bureau of Public Relations, was titled *The Soldier and His Food*. The booklet is directed toward mothers, wives, and sisters of soldiers, seeking to reassure them that their soldier is being well fed in the army. Information is provided about how menus are prepared, how cooks are trained, and details about both garrison and field rations. The booklet also discusses how food for the army is procured and concludes with a brief history of army rations through time.

Field Cooking Equipment

A major improvement in field cooking equipment occurred with the introduction of the M-1937 field range. Developed at the Jeffersonville Quartermaster Depot, the stove could be mounted in the bed of a 2½ ton truck. This unit used gasoline for fuel rather than the wood or coal utilized by World War I era field ranges. Mounting the M-1937 stove in a 2½ ton truck made a highly mobile field kitchen which enabled cooks to prepare cooked meals for troops near the front lines. These trucks usually had two or three stoves along with all necessary cooking pots and pans and other kitchen equipment. The kitchen truck also carried an icebox usually constructed of wood. The trucks could also pull a trailer to carry additional subsistence supplies.[51]

In many instances soldiers found themselves away from organized messes for extended periods of time. Particularly in cold climates these men needed a method of heating food. In mid–1941 the Quartermaster Corps asked the Coleman Lamp and Stove Company to produce a lightweight gasoline stove. It was primarily intended for ski troops, paratroopers, and small groups of soldiers behind enemy lines. This stove was designated the M-1941.[52] The small one-burner stoves became almost legendary and brought great success to the Coleman Company.

Members of Veterinarian Corps inspecting cheese before purchase for U.S. forces. Photograph made in Iceland in 1942. Courtesy Quartermaster Museum, Fort Lee, Virginia.

Eventually these small stoves "were used in every battlefield in both the European and Pacific Theaters."[53]

One of the biggest morale boosters for troops was having fresh bread: "Fresh bread, many field commanders maintained, was the most important component of the ration."[54] At the beginning of World War II, however, army field bakery companies still used the World War I era No. 1 field baking oven. The 3,714 pound oven had to be assembled in the field and was heated with wood, making it difficult to move and set up quickly. All mixing and preparation of the dough was accomplished by hand.[55] A new gasoline fueled oven, the M-1942, appeared in 1942. This oven featured a dough mixer powered by a gasoline engine.

While the M-1942 oven represented an improvement, moving a bakery company was no simple task. About forty-five 2½ ton trucks were required for the move. A bakery company consisted of thirty-two ovens, sixteen dough mixers, sixty-four insulated fermentation cans, and other equipment. A bakery company could average about 24,000 pounds of bread daily.[56] The American field baking equipment stood in contrast to the British equipment which was all mounted on trailers and required only nine trucks to move, making a bakery company highly mobile. In 1943, the decision was made that all future baking equipment for the European Theater of Operations would be of the British type.

Bakery companies dealt with particularly difficult conditions in the South and Southwest Pacific. They sometimes faced shortages of flour, milk, yeast, and baking powder. Hot, humid weather damaged yeast and flour so that much was lost to spoilage. Bakers were resourceful and unrelenting in their efforts to supply bread as evidenced by one occasion in the New Hebrides when they were without ovens so they built ovens out of fifty-five gallon barrels. In New Guinea some bakers used fermented coconut milk when yeast was not available and on Guadalcanal they extended the short supply of flour by mixing half and half with wheat cereal.[57]

Feeding Troops in the Field

The goal of troop feeding for frontline soldiers was to provide hot, cooked meals as often as possible. The kitchen truck helped in meeting this goal. Detailed instructions were provided in mess management guides such as TM10-205 about using the kitchen truck. Cooks prepared a hot meal in a rear bivouac area and then carried it forward in the kitchen truck at dark to each company mess location. If some troops could not come to the company mess location then carrying parties took food containers to them. The containers were recovered and the trucks returned before daylight. Breakfast might be prepared in the company mess location and served in time for the trucks to return under darkness. Lunch usually consisted of a meal prepared from rations served cold.[58] Food and hot drinks were carried forward in Marmite cans. One-quarter-ton trucks with trailers were used to carry the containers and mess gear as far forward as possible.[59] Even when troops were forced to subsist on operational rations, quartermasters made an effort to see that these were supplemented with fresh bread thus making them more acceptable. Ross and Romanus note, "Fresh bread issues were habitual in the combat zone in the ETO."[60]

Trucks like this 2½ ton GMC served as mobile kitchens when properly equipped and could also carry mobile refrigeration equipment. Photograph from U.S. Army Manual, TM 10-1269.

In spite of the efficiency of the kitchen truck, conditions of weather, terrain, or battle sometimes prevented bringing food to front line troops. Under these conditions troops were forced to subsist on C, K, D, or 10-in-1 rations. While these rations were intended to be used for only short periods of time, the necessities of combat conditions sometimes meant they might be forced to rely on them for weeks.

> Hot food was highly important, for it gave soldiers' morale a lift seldom imparted by cold food. Yet to provide it was not an easy task. During an amphibious operation the low landing priorities for rations and for cooking equipment, the unsorted state of supplies on beachheads, and the narrowness of the initial combat zones sometimes precluded the establishment of kitchens for ten days or more. If operations became mobile, kitchens could seldom keep pace with the constantly moving troops, and this circumstance alone might prevent the supply of hot food. The absence of roads rendered impossible using trucks to take to the front marmite cans filled with hot provisions.[61]

A new method of supplying troops in difficult to reach localities emerged during World War II. That method was dropping supplies from airplanes. The technique met with mixed results in the European Theater. According to quartermaster historian Dr. Steven Anders, "Air supply was widely used in the ETO, but it was mostly air-landed rather than airdropped."[62]

Local Procurement of Subsistence

The numbers of troops to be supplied, the distances involved, and the relative shortage of shipping capacity made the ability to obtain subsistence supplies near combat area important in all theaters in World War II. Often the ability to procure supplies locally meant the difference between having fresh foods and relying almost entirely on operational rations.

In the Mediterranean region important fresh vegetables were obtained from Morocco and Algeria. Ross and Romanus cite information indicating that "between February and June 1943, thirty percent of the vegetables consumed by American troops were purchased locally."[63] Sicily fell in the late summer of 1943 making citrus and other fruits available. Sometimes quartermasters could become overzealous in their procurement efforts. In one month the Fifth Army's quartermaster office requested 6,000,000 pounds of lemons. By the time only half of the contract was received this amounted to one bushel for every soldier in Italy. Without local procurement, the Fifth Army would have not have been supplied with the quantities of fresh vegetables they received.[64]

In less than one month after the Normandy invasion purchases of fruits and vegetables were being made in France. In April 1945, 30,600 tons of fruits and vegetables were purchased. The French government also made available food processing plants including plants for roasting and grinding coffee and making macaroni. In addition to France, subsistence supplies were also purchased from Spain, Portugal, Belgium, and Luxembourg.[65]

Local procurement played perhaps an even larger role in the Pacific Theater. The bulk of local procurement in this area came from Australia. While Australia had the potential to produce and process a wide variety of food items, it lacked technical expertise in agricultural production and canning and dehydrating industries. With the establishment of a subsistence depot in Australia in 1943, specialists were brought in to collaborate with Australian officials in providing technical advice to farmers, canners, and dehydrators and to provide inspection of locally purchased food.[66] Australia thus became an important subsistence provider in the Southwest Pacific Area, furnishing up to 90 percent of some items, especially fresh foods since it was difficult to ship these from the United States. Stauffer concludes, "Had not Australia filled this gap in military supplies, American soldiers would have been forced to live out of cans much more that they did."[67] New Zealand also was an important Pacific supplier of fresh supplies. In addition to meats and vegetables, New Zealand also supplied dairy products, especially butter and cheese. Other sources of subsistence supply for Pacific troops included Hawaii for fruit and coffee, New Caledonia supplied coffee, the Fiji Islands supplied primarily fruit.[68]

Perhaps somewhat surprisingly, the army pursued some agricultural activities during World War II to supplement its supply of fresh vegetables. Troops in the United Kingdom cultivated more than 15,000 acres in 1943.[69] The produce could be used locally or sold with a profit credited to post funds. An Agricultural Branch in the Service Installations Division of OCQM provided seed, tools, and informational literature.

Several Quartermaster farming efforts were made in the Pacific. Efforts were often handicapped by lack of fertilizers, insecticides, proper tools and equipment, and a lack of adequate irrigation. The largest effort was on Guadalcanal. First plantings were made in 1943 and eventually 1,800 acres were in cultivation. Hospitals were given first priority on the use of vegetables produced. Other farming efforts were made on Espiritu Santo, Efate, Bougainville, New Georgia, and New Caledonia. Farms produced a variety of vegetables including cucumbers, corn, eggplants, watermelons, cantaloupes, peppers, radishes, tomatoes, okra, and onions. Ross and Romanus attribute the limited success of these operations to "expert supervision, use of a sizable tract of land, and the employment of a large body of civilian laborers." However, these efforts "never attained more than local importance," and they conclude that "agricultural projects thus became largely hit-and-miss affairs of individual bases and units and seldom produced worthwhile results."[70]

Refrigeration

Adequate refrigeration equipment was essential for feeding the troops during World War II. One solution for mobile refrigeration was the 10-ton refrigerated semi trailer pulled by a 4 or 5 ton 4 × 4 tractor. These units could provide refrigeration or keep frozen up to 10,000 pounds of food. Their drawback was their weight, slowness, and lack of maneuverability. To provide more mobility, the Quartermaster Corps worked with several manufacturers to develop a one-hundred-fifty cubic foot refrigeration unit that could be hauled in a 2½ ton truck. This unit could be used as either a refrigerator or freezer depending on which foods needed to be handled. Two models were manufactured, one using a gasoline engine for power and another using an electric motor.[71]

Home Front Activities Related to Food

Feeding the large number of American troops combined with supplying food to our allies facing shortages because of the war strained the nation's food supply. The concern over actual shortages plus the ever present threat of uncontrolled inflation led to the establishment in 1941 of the Office of Price Administration (OPA). Food shortages came about in two ways, first, through an actual reduction in supply and second, from a lack of cargo space for shipping. These conditions can be illustrated by a couple of examples. When the Japanese captured the Philippines, sugar supply from there was lost and coffee supplies were reduced because of a lack of a means of shipping adequate supplies from Brazil. Reduced supplies called for sacrifice on the part of Americans on the home front. The OPA began rationing in 1942. It established some 8,000 local boards to carry out the rationing program. Food items included in the rationing program were sugar, coffee, meat, butter, and even some canned goods.

Rationing was administered in several ways—by the use of coupons, stamps, coins, and a point system with numerous changes being made throughout the war. The rationing program caused inconvenience for consumers and created extra work for grocers and other businesses. Although a black market developed through which individuals could buy rationed items at a higher cost, in general the system was successful in controlling both supplies and inflation. Food prices increased only 4 percent from 1942 until the end of the war.[72]

The government went to great lengths to publicize and promote rationing, conservation, and recycling for the war effort. One of the primary avenues used for promotion was posters produced by the Office of War Information. Millions of posters were printed and distributed urging these actions. Also strongly promoted to extend food supplies was the planting of victory gardens as had been done during World War I. It has been estimated that 20 million victory gardens were planted, producing nine to ten million tons of fresh vegetables during the war, thus making an important contribution toward the wartime supply of fresh fruits and vegetables.[73]

Major American manufacturing corporations and industry organizations supported the government's conservation and rationing efforts by publishing cookbooks that enabled housewives to prepare meals using the foods and cuts of meat most readily available and offering menu planning tips built around the rationing program. Also included were ideas for extending ingredients that were in short supply such as meat, shortening, and sugar. Most also encouraged the planting of victory gardens. These publications equated food conservation efforts at home with being as much a part of the war effort as the soldiers in combat.

Charitable Organizations Overseas

In World War II as in World War I charitable organizations played important roles in soldier morale through the food and drink they provided. In addition to its work in providing nurses in military hospitals and efforts to aid prisoners of war, the Red Cross was relied upon by the military to provide recreational services. Overseas, this organization established permanent service clubs in major cities and small towns in both the European and Pacific theaters. The larger facilities even offered overnight lodging as well as meals and other services while smaller clubs had only food. As in World War I the ever popular doughnut and cup of hot coffee became the trademark item that awaited weary soldiers, sailors, marines, and airmen at canteens, not only those operated by the Red Cross, but also by other organizations such as the Salvation Army. Such facilities were often referred to as Donut Dugouts.

In addition to permanent facilities, the Red Cross began operating what were called clubmobiles. First started in Great Britain using converted buses, these vehicles were equipped with a coffeemaker and doughnut machine. Clubmobiles were also built on 2½ ton trucks. The clubmobiles and the American women who were in charge of them became extremely popular with the soldiers and not to disappoint the troops, they kept up, sometimes dangerously close to the front lines. George Korson in his book *At His Side: The Story of the American Red Cross Overseas in World War II* describes the first clubmobiles in France after D-Day: "Rolling on to the Normandy beachhead at 5 A.M. July 19, these ... clubmobilers were serving doughnuts and coffee twenty-four hours later only three miles behind the front lines." According to Korson the question persistently asked throughout northern France the first few weeks of the invasion was, "When are the clubmobiles coming?"[74]

Canteens and clubs were established in the Pacific Theater as well. The clubmobile also made its appearance there. The jungle environment presented added difficulties of tropical diseases and insects for soldiers and Red Cross workers alike. Korson notes that in July 1944 on New Guinea and neighboring islands thirty-two on-post clubs, seven canteens, and eleven clubmobiles were in operation.[75] Some canteens were established in truly difficult to reach localities. For example, a roadside canteen was established on the Ledo Road leading from India into China and connecting with the Burma Road. Six miles below Ledo a Red Cross club was opened in 1943. This club served twelve hundred soldiers a day.[76]

As had been the case during World War I, other charitable organizations made efforts to provide morale boosting meals and refreshments for troops serving overseas. The Salvation Army, well known for its doughnuts during World War I, took up that mantle again but this time in concert with five other agencies. As a result of President Franklin Roosevelt's request that private organizations provide on-leave recreation activities for the military, six organizations, the Salvation Army, YMCA, YWCA, National Catholic Community Services, National Travelers Aid Association, and the National Jewish Welfare Board, pooled resources and coordinated efforts thus forming a new organization, the United Service Organization or USO.

The USO operated clubs in 3,000 communities near bases in the United States. Overseas the USO established clubs providing various types of entertainment, a place for letter writing, religious counsel, or free coffee and doughnuts. Mobile canteens operated by the Salvation Army continued the tradition of bringing coffee and doughnuts near to troops in forward areas.[77]

Post Exchanges

Post exchanges which sold such things as chewing gum, soft drinks, candy, and razors and other toiletry items had been a part of army bases within the United States since 1895. However, through World War I they had not been established in overseas areas. Thus doughboys of World War I had to rely on packages from home or items that were supplied at canteens established by charitable organizations. That changed with World War II. The Army Exchange Service which operated the Post Exchanges accompanied the troops to all theaters of war. They also usually had a soda fountain where a GI could get a hamburger and Coca-Cola.

Closely allied with the PX system was Army Special Services, which established service clubs for soldiers. These usually featured female hostesses and offered organized dances and other activities as well as a place for soldiers to relax and eat a sandwich and enjoy a beer or soft drink when off duty.

First Person Food Accounts

Soldiers' personal experiences with military food, particularly during wartime, give insights into the effectiveness of the operational rations and methods of providing meals to soldiers in combat as well as illustrating the resourcefulness of soldiers in supplementing their regular rations. It also highlights the importance of receiving packages from home and their ventures into trying foods in other cultures.

Jim Boan with the Sixth Marine Division Reconnaissance Company remembered short rations on the USS *Nobel* headed for the South Pacific: "The troops were on short rations, maybe a sandwich and an apple for a meal."[78] In contrast, some soldiers had positive experiences with shipboard voyages. Everett Farmer, a technical sergeant with the army's 6th Infantry division in New Guinea recalled that his trip to New Guinea was not unpleasant: "We had three meals a day and the food was good."

There were occasions when troops faced the situation of actually being without food.

Packages from home. GIs of an infantry division fighting in Hurtgen Forest, near Zweifall, Germany, open first batch of Christmas packages, November 14, 1944. Courtesy Quartermaster Museum, Fort Lee, Virginia.

Troops on New Guinea particularly suffered ration shortages, unbalanced rations, and inequitable distribution among the bases there. Farmer commented, "In New Guinea there were several occasions when we went as much as three days without food."[80] Jim Boan wrote about an occasion when "we had no food, no blankets, no potable water, not even a shovel. Seeing our plight, regimental marines shared what little they had — about three spoonfuls each of C-ration hash, and water."[81]

In mess halls and even in the field when troops were located close enough to be served by the truck mounted field kitchens most soldiers were reasonably satisfied with the food available. Farmer noted that "the food was always good and plentiful in the mess halls."[82]

Frederick Lafferty with the army in New Caledonia recorded in his journal some of the meals served there: "We had a large patty for dinner made up of chopped beef I guess. Lima beans, peas, pickles and the cream puff for desert. Cocoa was the drink. For supper we had frankforts [sic], beans and a swell biscuit and mixed fruit for dessert. In the tent we ate cheese and bananas." On another day he wrote about supper: "For supper we had spam camouflaged into an omelet which was pretty good, corn, string beans, and

Using steel helmets to heat rations on Guadalcanal, January 15, 1943. Left to right, Pfc. Joseph Lebert, Pfc. Peter Rendels, and Sgt. Fred Dispensa. Courtesy Quartermaster Museum, Fort Lee, Virginia.

two delicious pieces of chocolate cake." Yet another day supper consisted of "salmon served in a cream with Idaho (shreds) potatoes and lovely lemon pie — I had two pieces of it."[83] Paul Alexa, who was with an antiaircraft artillery battalion, remembered his first hot meal in France after his unit had been on C and K rations for several weeks: "A truck pulled up and [someone] said, 'Hot chow.' Somewhere they got some oatmeal and some powdered milk and sugar and they were dishing this out. These guys were just hitting seconds and thirds. I have loved oatmeal ever since."[84]

Soldiers sometimes obtained sustenance by foraging or purchasing food from local residents. Farmer noted that he never ate any locally prepared food in New Guinea but that "we would kill wild hogs and the cooks would grind everything into sausage. It was pretty good. At least something different."[85] He also shared that they would use explosives to kill fish: "Native boys would swim out and gather up the fish. The cooks would fry them for us." Wilbert Amos, with the army in Europe, noted that he sometimes would find "some chicken coops and get an egg or two." He would also go up in the attic of farmhouses and sometimes find "some of that good old German summer sausage."[86] Jim Boan reported some of the 6th Marine Division's efforts at foraging on Okinawa: "An old red rooster and a half-grown chicken were killed and boiled in helmets. A pig was dressed and roasted over an open-pit fire. The cooks' culinary efforts didn't add to their reputations, because salt and seasonings were scarce. And the two men who owned the borrowed helmets were furious because the straps had been burned off."[87]

Opinions varied on their like or dislike of C and K operational rations. Soldiers also found ways to modify, heat, and cool rations. Farmer commented that "I liked the canned beans and wieners and especially liked fruit cocktail." He also noted, "We heated cans on the manifold of vehicles or by using alcohol heaters (sterno)." Farmer added, "We would bury cans of fruit cocktail in the sand on the beach to cool them. We did the same with beer or soda when we had them. We would place a flag where the can was buried."[88] Benjamin Armour with the 661st Tank Destroyer Battalion in the ETO recalled heating C rations using C-2 explosives: "C-2, you can take and break that out and set it on fire and heat your stuff, and it won't

An improvised ration heater made from C ration cans and Sterno. Courtesy Quartermaster Museum, Fort Lee, Virginia.

blow up." Armour's unit also had a unique method for chilling Cokes using the fire extinguisher from the tank destroyers. "We put them together [Cokes] in ... a tub or whatever. We put them in there, and shoot that dude [CO2 fire extinguisher] ... and it would instantly [cool them], you couldn't shoot it too much. It would freeze them.[89]

Keith Burlingan Hook, a lieutenant with the army serving in the South Pacific, had his own method of making a chocolate drink by using the can from the C rations that contained hard candy and crackers and cocoa powder. Hook explains, "I take the candy and crackers out, pour about one half inch of water from my canteen. Then empty cocoa powder in, and mix — then fill two thirds of can with more water and use chocolate beverage to wash down the crackers." Hook describes heating his C ration hash: "I usually eat the hash in the morning, if time, and then try to chisel a little alcohol from the Battalion Aid Station and a little gauze — then, I light that and heat the Hash. However, at least half the time I eat the hash cold."[90] Both Farmer and Hook mentioned the occasional use of D rations. The most serious problem with the rations was their long term use. Paul Alexa's comments summarize the feeling of most soldiers: "After you're on that [C or K rations] for four or five weeks day in and day out ... we got tired of it."[91]

While all theaters of operation during World War II experienced supply difficulties, problems were especially troublesome in the China-Burma-India Theater as a February 1944 letter written by Lieutenant Lyndell Highley, a navigator with the Army Air Corps, indicates: "In other theaters of war the idea of eating Spam or corned beef is revolting but we are glad to get our hands on the stuff." Highley reported that his 1943 Thanksgiving dinner "consisted of cheese and corn beef eaten about twenty thousand feet in the air." Troops in this region obtained at least a portion of their food locally and Highley was excited to report that "a little more American food" was coming their way. Highley wrote, "Usually we eat Chinese vegetables and some kind of tough meat and most always canned butter."[92]

One of the most important things for keeping up morale among troops was receiving packages from family and friends at home. Here are a few examples. Farmer noted that "I received a package with cookies about twice a month. About once a month my mother would send a package with olives. She would get bulk ice cream cartons from the drugstore and put a jar of olives in it and pack paper around it."[93] Paul Alexa came up with the idea of his family numbering packages, "I told by mother and mother-in-law and my wife, and I gave them numbers from 1 to 10, 11–20, and so on. I said you number your packages, and I'll always know when I'm going to get a package from home."[94] Often fruit sent in packages did not weather the trip well while other items were quickly consumed as Gordon Hansen reported: "Apples in sad state [but] brownies gone almost immediately. We ate them in our long johns with pots of coffee."[95] Sometimes food items from home were used to conceal other things not legal to send. Jake Alabaster told about one package he received: "During the Battle of the Bulge I got a package from my mother. It was a big baked [loaf of] bread and inside the bread there was a canteen of wine that she made."[96]

While the American military certainly never achieved perfection in feeding its large number of troops during World War II, they arguably received the best food of any nation's military in spite of the great distances to overcome and the sometimes almost insurmountable conditions of combat, roads, and weather. Perhaps Second Lieutenant Robert L. Huber with the Army Air Corps summarized it best. "In comparison to other armies we are by far the best paid and best fed. I really feel sorry for all the other soldiers. We are really fortunate in being Americans."[97] Those who study the complexities of World War II will see the challenges that had to be addressed in supplying and provisioning those in the military during that time.

World War II Navy Chow Delivered

Frozen strawberries shipped in 5–25 pound cans ... according to those making the deliveries, from the view point of the blue jackets, far away in the Mediterranean ... appeared to bring home just a little closer.
— Captain Chambers, provisions stores ship *Tarazad*

The navy had to feed its sailors in far reaching areas in the Pacific and once again as they had during World War I in the Atlantic. Fleet Admiral Ernest J. King, commander in chief, United States Fleet and chief of naval operations during World War II, comments on the navy following World War I and leading up to World War II. Because of the perception that war seemed to be remote, the size of the navy at that time was "comparatively small." A "modest" and "adequate" navy at that time meant "an average of about 7,900 commissioned officers ... and 100,000 enlisted men more or less." By December 1944 the number had increased to 3,227,525. By the same date the marine corps had grown from 19,701 to 472,682 and the coast guard numbers to 169,832 in 1944.[98]

King overviews the supply operations in his reports, first mentioning "the so-called 'Fleet Train' composed of tankers and other auxiliary vessels specially designed" for "replenishing fuel, food and ammunition at sea" which had been operating "as far back as 1916." He indicates that supply of operations in the Pacific were the most difficult "due mainly to the absence of port facilities in the island bases ... captured ... and to the distances involved." The Atlantic he sees as less difficult "because of the more highly developed nature of the ports we have occupied."[99]

Provisioning the Navy in the Pacific

In his book *Beans, Bullets, and Black Oil: The Story of Fleet Logistic Afloat in the Pacific During World War II*, Rear Admiral Worrall Reed Carter discusses the origins, growth, and duties of the Service Fleet. At the end of World War I, the "principal part of the U.S. Fleet" was transferred to the West Coast and "a Base Force was formed as part of the fleet." There, "The fuel-oil tankers, fresh and frozen-food ships, repair ships, fleet tugs, and target repair ships were administered and operated by the Commander Base Force." Moving forward, he indicates that "by 1925 the Navy had expanded to 234 vessels" and "by 1940 ... 344 fighting ships and 120 auxiliaries of various types. His concern was that the navy at that time was expanding its ship numbers but not developing service to them "in a balanced manner." He adds, "Still no one seemed to give much consideration to the delivery and distribution of supplies to ships not at those bases to receive them."[100]

As the war became a reality and more and more vessels were constructed and converted to wartime use, steps were taken to step up service to them: "The early Service Force was organized around four squadrons: Two, Four, Six, and Eight" with Squadron Eight being responsible "for the supply and distribution to the fleet of all its fuels, food, and ammunitions." The name Service Force was changed to Service Forces Pacific Fleet and the number of vessels continued to grow as additional vessels were added to the fleet which would have to be provisioned and serviced.[101]

Both dry provisions and fresh and frozen provisions had to be delivered to ships in the battle areas. Because of a shortage of fresh and frozen food ships, this type of provision wasn't always able to be delivered in requested quantities. Carter notes that these shortages became apparent in March 1943 in the South Pacific area: "Additional refrigerator ships had already been requested, and efforts were being made to procure more fresh provisions from New Zealand. In the meantime, tinned and dry provisions had to make up the difference." He indicates that the forces afloat "could not expect to be provisioned oftener than every 30 days until more refrigerator ships became available."[102]

The establishment of advanced bases, when the military gained control of land areas, allowed the delivery of provisions and supplies at great distances from the U.S. Carter mentions Lion One, which he defines as "a large advanced base unit consisting of all the personnel and material necessary for the establishment of a major all-purpose naval base." As an example, Espiritu Santo, an advanced base for the South Pacific, stored provisions for the navy in that area: "At this time, late in 1943, the supply storage space approximating 400,000 square feet was filled with supplies of all kinds. The fleet provision unit, with 24 large 'reefers' (refrigerator boxes or rooms), and 5 warehouses had been

Realizing it was going to be a busy day, a crewman aboard a U.S. Navy aircraft carrier garnered himself this pile of sandwiches on June 14, 1944, during action off Saipan. Courtesy Naval Historical Center, Washington, D.C.

receiving and issuing quantities of both fresh and dry provisions. Storage capacity was 2,500 tons of dry and 1,500 tons of fresh and frozen provisions."[103]

Carter discusses the challenging extent of the provisioning process in the South Pacific: "The important supply of fresh and frozen foods was furnished by the fleet provision unit with 24 reefers and 5 warehouses and Espiritu Santo ... and 10 ships working out of Auckland to carry their vital freight wherever it was needed. Even this was not enough as our effort grew. In September 1943 the Commanding Officer of Service Squadron South Pacific estimated that he had exactly half enough ships to carry the provisions contracted for in New Zealand for 1944." As the ships moved too far from friendly land sources of supply the navy had to rely on provision ships and on provisions from supply depots on advanced bases such as Espiritu Santo.[104]

Oilers also delivered provisions in addition to their primary loads of "fuel, bottled gasses, aviation gasoline, and sometimes airplanes and boats on their decks." Carter notes that the oilers brought canteen stores and even ice cream to the smaller ships. On one day's deliveries, the tanker *Neosho* supplied several heavy cruisers with a total of 63,485 pounds of provisions and 9,360 candy bars in addition to quantities of military supplies listed above.[105]

Giving insight into the provisioning process during the war, Carter explains how the Alaskan-Aleutian sector received provisions. Three provisions ships delivered to that area, *Bridge*, *Antigua*, and the merchant ship *Plantano* formerly operated by the United Fruit Company. "Some food stuffs were supplied to the ships of the task forces by direct contact while in port, others by storage barges which had been stocked from the provisions ships." He adds, "So far as having enough to eat was concerned, provisions were never any considerable problem; but to obtain the amount of fresh and frozen foods the ships wanted was entirely out of the question. Throughout the war there were never enough to keep them stocked to their liking. The days of dry stores, bully beef, and canned foods were not relished by our crews."[106]

The Service Squadron system had as a goal to be able through the Service Force to develop the capability of supplying and provisioning vessels for indeterminable time periods when they were away from permanent bases. Extensive coordination and organization were required to accomplish this feat. Carter explains that during the first 2 years of the war, provisions ships of Squadron Eight carried balanced loads, meaning fresh,

Galley of USS *Texas*. The ship served from 1911 until 1948.

frozen and dry provisions. In 1944 Squadron Eight was not able to keep up with the fresh provision needs. Consequently, War Shipping Administration vessels, under the administration of Squadron Eight, began carrying provisions. Additionally, because of the shortage of refrigerated ships, the practice of balancing provisions was changed to having refrigerated ships carry "the absolute maximum of frozen and chilled items." When they did this, they didn't have enough space for dry provisions. The navy addressed this problem by coordinating the arrival of other vessels making deliveries so that both dry and fresh provisions would arrive "at the same anchorage or bases." He notes that a dry-provision vessel such as a Merchant Marine Liberty ship "carried approximately 5,300 tons ... of bulk provisions" in addition to other types of supplies.[107]

Of interest are the "special type ships" controlled by the Service Squadrons. Carter indicates that there were "13 concrete barges that were 366 feet long and had crews of about 55 men and 3 officers" that were involved in the provisioning process. Because they had "substantial Diesel-electric power aboard," they had refrigeration and cooking capabilities. The concrete barges were used for "the stowage and issue of large quantities of dry provisions" in addition to various supplies needed by vessels. Carter adds, "On several of the barges there were large bakeries and butcher shops as well as refrigerated storage designed especially to permit small craft and patrol vessels to receive as good a diet and as many so-called luxuries as were furnished on the larger self-contained combat ships."[108]

Galley of USS *Brooklyn* in 1938. Courtesy Naval Historical Center, Washington, D.C.

A second type of special ship, the distilling ship, addressed "a major problem in the middle of the largest of all oceans," the need for fresh water. To deal with the immediate problem of supply of this very important item "several new tankers ... were employed for more than a year solely in transporting pure water from supply points at Oahu, Guam, and Manus to anchorages where the fleet was temporarily based." At Iwo Jima "22,000,000 gallons of water were supplied to the participating vessels." The navy next developed distilling ships. The first two distilling ships were merchant marine Liberty ships. These ships had a "distilling capacity of 120,000 gallons a day and storage for 5,040,000 gallons."[109]

Julius August Furer, in his book on the administration of the Navy Department in World War II defines the two basic categories of foods already mentioned: "Subsistence items were divided into two basic categories: perishable and non-perishable. The latter term covers those items that are canned, dehydrated, dried, or otherwise processed for ordinary storage. Sixty-eight items were canned in this category prior to the war, and procured by the Bureau [Bureau of Supplies and Accounts] periodically through competitive bidding." As the war continued, "The list of non-perishable subsistence supplies soon grew to 122 items with the addition of new items required." He notes that "eighty-six of these were purchased under the Joint Army-Navy procurement program, 33 by the Navy, and 2 by the War Food Administration."[110]

Furer discusses steps taken by the navy to assure that adequate supplies of dry provision would be available for disbursement. He mentions the enlargement of existing facilities, the establishment of naval supply depots at Bayonne, New Jersey, and at San Pedro, California, in 1942, the development of feeder depots at Mechanicsburg, Pennsylvania, and Clearfield, Utah, in 1942 and 1943. "Stocks of dry provisions for issue to ships and stations were maintained in the United States at 9 supply depots, 2 navy yards, and 2 inland feeder depots. Also, 12 large training and air stations received direct shipments from contractors in carload lots."[111]

Furer notes the contribution of research and development in meeting the needs of "new problems in subsistence" which developed during "actual war conditions." Examples developed for use of the navy during the war included "revised and greatly improved" abandon-ship and aircraft rations. Additionally, he mentions that "a battle-ration was developed for use when it was necessary for men to remain at battle stations." Likewise, "Ration lists were prepared for special expeditions sent to remote sections of the world" and "dry and powdered provisions were highly developed and utilized."[112]

Provisions for the Atlantic Side of the War

Carter with Rear Admiral Elmer Ellsworth Duvall include in their book, *Ships, Salvage, and Sinews of War*, details of the process of provisioning ships in the Atlantic including the "Battle for the Atlantic (German submarine and raider activities for the first 2 years of the war) and then operations in North Africa, Sicily, Italy, and France."[113] As it was in military operations in the Pacific, food was delivered by provisions stores ships and food was prepared by sailor cooks and bakers trained at specialty schools.

One of the responsibilities of Task Force 9, the Service Force of the Atlantic Fleet, was to deliver provisions to the Atlantic Fleet. As in the Pacific, provisions other than dry and field rations ships had to have refrigeration capabilities. In 1941, provisions stores ships in Service Squadron 7 for the Atlantic Fleet included *Yukon, Polaris, Uranus, Pastores, Mizar,* and *Tarazed,* the last three being former United Fruits ships that were "well designed and equipped to carry refrigerated food in large quantities."[114]

Carter and Duvall explain that "by the fall of 1942 most of the refrigerated storage facilities at the bases, except at Iceland, had been completed, and the Service Force ships usually unloaded into these: the fleet units then got what they needed from the shore bases." Until refrigeration storage units could be arranged in Iceland, the refrigeration ship *Yukon* was sent there to for a time to serve as a "storage and distribution unit."[115]

Certainly acquisition and delivery of provisions to so many areas sometimes met with problems to be solved: "There were complaints here and there over shortages of certain items and grumbles about one detachment of command getting something better or more of something than other, but no one went hungry." As well, "There were experiments in battle rations, experiments in loading and in packaging, and substitutions of one thing for shortages in something else." Another problem to be dealt with was the problem of not enough escorts for the provisions ships. At times the authors indicate that ships were sent without escorts in order to meet the demand for fresh provisions. They explain, "Our modern sailors could survive, but would not be content with the kind of dry and canned provisions that formerly were good and sufficient for 'round the Horn' sailors, even though the wartime quality of such canned chow was far better than in those long voyages of earlier days."[116]

On a run from the United States, a provisions ship, carrying approximately 1,700 tons of "fresh and frozen" foods would have scheduled stops at bases. Deliveries and transfers were also made directly to other ships. What types of fresh and frozen food might be carried on a provision ship? Carter and Duvall explain the load carried on the *Tarazed* on one of her runs.

> Among the frozen meat carried by the *Tarazed* were turkeys, chicken, mutton, frankfurters, and boneless beef. The latter was packed in 33-pound containers. Beef, in boneless form, saved shipping space and, a Captain Chambers said, was therefore more economical and more readily useful to a consignee, particularly to a vessel of smaller type. In illustrating this point Captain Chambers cited the difficulty that a destroyer had in "juggling" a quarter of beef, and in disposing properly of its large bone. Among the frozen vegetables carried by the *Tarazed* were Brussels sprouts, peas, beans, and squash; these were in 2-pound containers. Apples, oranges, lettuce, peas, celery, and cabbage were some fresh fruits and vegetable transported.[117]

The same captain expressed satisfaction when his ship was able to bring fresh fruits and vegetables, particularly when men of those ships had just experienced a long spell of C rations. They also mention the delivery of "frozen strawberries, (shipped in 5–25 pound cans)." According to those making the delivery, "From the view point of the blue jackets, far away in the Mediterranean, strawberries appeared to bring home just a little closer."[118]

Carter and Duvall explain the quantities of provisions carried on a stores ship. After loading at the Naval Operating Base, Norfolk, Virginia, *Merak* took provisions to bases and ships in the Mediterranean. She carried slightly over 1500 tons. Described here in short tons, she carried the following provisions: "Fresh fruit (175), potatoes (500), other fresh vegetables (175), smoked meats (140), boneless beef (225), other fresh meat (228), butter (45), cheese (18), and 100,000 dozen eggs."[119]

U.S. naval training facilities during World War II relating to food include several cook and bakers schools (Gulfport, Mississippi; Pensacola, Florida; Jacksonville, Florida; Treasure Island, California; San Diego, California; Great Lakes, Illinois), a chief commissary steward school (Jacksonville) an officers cooks and steward school (Annapolis, Maryland), and a meat specialist school (Great Lakes, Illinois). Cooks and bakers were also trained in the college or university setting.[120]

As an example of a university program, Iowa State College (now Iowa State University), located in Ames, Iowa, included a cooks and bakers school at its naval training school. A written history of the training program during World War II is currently held at Iowa State University. Information in the section of the history of the cooks and bakers school was taken from a report written by Miss Fern Gleiser, director of the Navy Cook and Bakers School and formerly head of the department of institution management.

According to the report, the establishment of such a school was proposed to the Advisory Committee at the college on October 6, 1942, and put into operation on October 12 with twelve men in the first company: "A new company arrived every four weeks thereafter and after February 13, 1943, a company graduated every four weeks. Twenty-three companies completed the course and a total of 280 men graduated."[121] The administration of the cook and bakers school was a cooperative effort of the institution management department and the Memorial Union. Gleiser reports that "the assignment of cooks and bakers schools directed by civilians in civilian organizations has been a new departure for the Navy. No curriculum was available for a guide in teaching the principles of quantity cookery applied to Navy cooking procedures." She continues to explain the plan adopted: "Therefore a course was planned and developed by the Institution Management and Memorial Union foods staffs. The laboratory work was carried on through the facilities of the Memorial Union, Friley Hall and the College Meat Laboratory which was used for the cutting and storing of meat served at Friley Hall and the Memorial Union."[122]

Navy bakers in training at Iowa State University. Courtesy Iowa State University Library/University Archives.

The instruction involved the following assignments. Students spent 4 weeks in classroom instruction. By the time they graduated, their laboratory assignment would have included "four weeks in the galley, four weeks in the bakery and the third four weeks divided to include one week in the salad department, one week in the issue room, and two weeks in the meat laboratory."[123] In the curriculum included in the history, references are made to the use of a *Quantity Cookery* publication; *Qualifications and General Instructions for Ship's Cook, 3c*; *Canned Food Manual*; and *The Cook Book of the U.S. Navy*. The classes also viewed educational films on meat cutting tools and equipment, cutting forequarters of beef, and cutting hindquarters of beef — all army productions.

It would seem that by the time the class was completed that student cooks and bakers had pretty well cooked and baked their way through the navy cookbook and should be able to find their way around whatever galley to which they might be assigned. The report states that graduates, supposing that they met physical qualifications, "have been assigned to submarines, P.T. boats, amphibious boats, aircraft carriers, troop transport ships and shore stations."[124] The course trained them to pass tests to qualify for the ratings of ships cook 3c or baker 3c.

World War II Era Navy Cookbooks

Navy cookbook editions published in 1944 and 1945 include recipes using a variety of dried, dehydrated, and evaporated ingredients. In the 1945 edition, W.J. Carter, chief

Lemon pies in the bakery on the USS *Missouri* during her shakedown period, summer of 1944.
Courtesy Naval Historical Center, Washington, D.C.

of the Bureau of Supplies and Accounts, delivers information on wartime food preparation. He explains, "In an attempt to assist with some of the feeding problems of the forces afloat and at advance bases, more recipes for dry provisions have been added in this edition."[125] This edition brings the information on dehydrated foods up to an early part of the cookbook.

In this section, navy cooks receive information about dehydrated (dried) and specially processed foods. The section delivers a brief explanation about the dehydration process and then moves on to the advantages of its use in the navy. Because of their reduced volume dehydrated foods save storage space, and if properly cared for, they will keep indefinitely. The information then moves the cook to "the process of restoration" or reconstitution of items. Cooks are urged to read directions on containers carefully because "as the process of dehydration is further developed, changes in the methods of reconstituting and cooking may be somewhat changed."[126] The section details information about powdered eggs and a table of equivalents for fresh, frozen, and powdered eggs. A handy chart explains how to use evaporated, dry whole milk or dry skim milk in food preparation.

The dessert section of the 1944 navy cookbook explains that "ice cream should be a 'regular' on the Navy menu. In addition to being one of America's favorite desserts, ice

Some World War II era Navy ships featured soda fountains with ice cream. Photograph taken in 1945. Courtesy Naval Historical Center, Washington, D.C.

cream is nourishing and economical."[127] The cookbook includes fifteen different variations of ice cream (and seven recipes for different versions of sherbet), some made with powdered whole milk and powdered whole eggs. Each recipe yields five gallons.

One veteran at the Veterans History Project mentions ice cream when thinking back on his food experiences in the navy during World War II. Norbert Wooley served on USS *Wasp* (CV-18), an aircraft carrier. He explained that when their planes were shot down, they would try to find downed pilots. When they did, "A destroyer would come up, and they'd pick them up ... you'd hook up to a rig, and they'd transfer them from the destroyer to the aircraft carrier." He continues, "Now aircraft carriers had the facility to make ice cream so every time they brought us back pilots, we'd send them over five gallons of ice cream."[128]

Additional information in the 1945 cookbook provides insight into foods prepared in the galleys. Quick-frozen foods were mentioned. Notes on the use of frozen eggs explain that the whites and yolks are frozen separately and that whole eggs are made from combining the two in proportion of 2 parts whites to 1 part yolk. Recipes deliver directions for preparing dishes using dehydrated, canned, and fresh fruits and vegetables.

The meat section features recipes for a variety of meat types using the substitution process. Recipes explain how to use boneless, frozen beef packaged in 50 pound packages. Instructions detail how to use canned meats when the supply of fresh meats is "limited, unavailable, or impractical." According to information in the cookbook, a positive feature of canned meats for the navy is that they require less storage space and most of them require no refrigeration. About cooking techniques, canned meats can be eaten straight from the can or heated. Heating suggestions include either heating the unopened can in boiling water or a safer suggestion to heat it in a oven.

Luncheon meat (packaged in 6-pound cans) made an appearance in numerous recipes. Just to mention a few, it could be baked with sugar and orange juice or with barbecue sauce or with tomato sauce poured over it. Cut into ¼ inch thick slices, it could be pan-fried in fat or in a fat and prepared mustard mixture. One recipe calls for it to be baked and basted with a mustard, sugar, cinnamon, corn syrup, and vinegar glaze. Still additional variation has canned luncheon meat made into meatballs by breaking it into small pieces, adding rice, eggs, and pepper. The meatballs are then baked in tomato juice. Another recipe guides the cook to prepare escalloped luncheon meat and corn prepared with either whole kernel corn or cream style corn. And luncheon meat can also be substituted for a frankfurter in a blanket if it is "cut ... in finger length pieces ¾ × ¾ × 3½ inches."

Apparently a scarcity of fresh fruit didn't stop navy cooks from baking pies. Three versions of the all American apple pie were available for the pie baker. The first recipe requires 3½ gallons of canned apples, a second recipe requires 4⅜ gallons dried apples reconstituted with 4⅜ gallons of water, and a third is made with 1¾ gallons of dehydrated apple nuggets reconstituted with 3¼ gallons water. All three recipes result in 17 (10-inch) pies with ⅛ of a pie being a serving. If fresh or canned cherries are not available, the pie section includes a recipe for mock cherry pie made with dehydrated apple nuggets and dehydrated cranberries.

In *Swabby: World War II Enlisted Sailors Tell It Like It Was!* Jack Haberstroh records the experiences of numerous sailors during World War II. When thinking back about their experiences in the navy during the war, food often becomes the subject of their reflections. They remember their food experiences—favorably and negatively. Sailors were surprised when they learned that beans would be served for breakfast. Some indicate that beans were served on Saturday or Sunday for breakfast. Others remember Wednesday as bean day. This meal became a favorite meal for some of the men. Sailors also enjoyed fresh bread on mornings after the baker had been busy in the galley the night before and also pies with their meals. Learning how the meal system worked while involved in battles, Walt Keiper aboard the USS *Petrof Bay* (CVE-80) is surprised when a cook shows up "with a big basket of sandwiches and coffee" when there was a lull in the attacks by the Japanese kamikazes.[129]

Swabby's accounts range from unexpected ingredients that turned up in bread to dehydrated foods to bad weather foods. Bakers and sailors dealt with critters in their bread in a variety of ways. Mention is made of "holding bread up to the light" to determine if the bread of the day had been inhabited and also bakers adding raisins to camouflage the weevils or bug parts. Unpopular food items and repetitive meals caused grumbling among some of these World War II sailors. Powdered milk and powdered eggs definitely did not make the favorite food list in this group of sailors. One swabby indicates that "when the seas became so rough that cooks had to suspend their activities, they served sandwiches, candy bars and coffee."[130]

In Haberstroh's collection of narratives, sailors sometimes offer overall ratings of food on their ships that range from "very good" to "wasn't too bad," to "more than adequate," to "excellent." It seems that food desirability varied from ship to ship. Food aboard the USS *Missouri* (BB 63) received high praise attributed to "large frozen food lockers" and an "ice cream machine that was always on" and "plenty of fresh apples and oranges."[131] One sailor felt the food on his ship was too greasy and that the canned vegetables were overcooked and was disappointed they had very little fresh fruit.[132] Ronald Graetz, who served on the USS *Enterprise* (CV 6) said that his ship was "the best feeding ship in the Navy."[133] Marlo Sivilli aboard the USS *North Carolina* (BB55) recalls going through the food line one day, tossing a comment over his shoulder to the effect that he hoped the "chow is better today." He heard the man behind him say, "It will be." When he turned around, he saw his captain "in dungarees, tray in hand, checking on the crew's chow." Sivilli notes that it was better that day and that the captain "sat and ate with us."[134]

Meals for the Seabees

This project would be remiss without a discussion of the role played by Seabee cooks who performed their culinary duties under trying conditions during the war. "The Seabee ratings in the Navy are an outgrowth of World War II, but they did have an earlier counterpart." Details at the Naval Historical Center website refer to "construction and maintenance of 10 separate camps at Great Lakes Naval Training Center" and "construction duties in France" during World War I. At this time skilled civilians and enlisted men were used in military construction efforts.[135]

Seabee museum information at their website explains the rationale for the change to using specifically enlisted men for war related construction projects. Once war was officially declared following the Pearl Harbor attack, "Civilians were not permitted to resist enemy military attack. If they did they could be executed as guerillas." Consequently, authority was given by the navy "to activate, organize, and man a unique, very special organization that would support the Navy and Marines in remote locations and defend themselves if attacked — the Naval Construction Battalions."[136] William Bradford Huie's *Can Do! The Story of the Seabees*, published in 1944, was written when the Navy Construction Battalion was in its infancy. Huie, a writer by profession and a Seabee at the time the book was written, was given the task as a public relations officer to write the story of the birth and development of this new part of the navy as it replaced the practice of using civilian workers on advanced military bases not in the United States.

Seabees do their work on land. As they move from ships to beaches and to work areas where they are involved in construction of projects vital to war efforts such as building roads, docks, bridges, airports, and hospitals, often under dangerous conditions in times of war, their cooks move with them. Seabee cooks are known for aggressively getting their chow lines up and running, even in adverse conditions. By the same token, if they are needed outside the galley, they are quick to respond.

Consequently, the Seabee cook's day in times of war doesn't always go as planned. Huie details a situation when Japanese bombers arrived during World War II where Seabees had arrived to do their job: "Our galley equipment, most of our supplies, and all the men's seabags and personal belongings were destroyed." However, when the situation improved, cooks were able to borrow three stoves from the army and marines and began providing hot meals. On another work site, an airstrip that the Seabees were working on was being bombed by the Japanese. Food was put on hold because the cooks were helping repair bomb craters in the airstrip.[137]

Huie gives additional insight into the details of World War II Seabee cooking. Of importance to the cook was one particular piece of equipment, "a portable electric refrigerator" described as "150-cubic-foot boxes—called 'reefers'" that "contain a gas refrigerating unit which enables them to operate in transit." After transferring them to the mess area on the beach, they are hooked up to the power supply there. Riding in the reefers to Kiska Harbor, the location of this particular assignment, were "ten tons of fresh boneless steaks, chops and roast." He indicates that on the first day on the beach, "Chow was sent to us in twenty-gallon aluminum containers from the ship's kitchens." The next day in the mess tent they enjoyed "bean soup, Yankee pot roast, browned potatoes, brown gravy, green snap beans, Bartlett pears, bread, butter, and coffee."[138] Huie points out that "because Seabees stick to the beaches ... they almost always have hot food" while the army moving inland uses canned rations. Commenting on Seabee hospitality, he explains that they feed "everybody in line as long as the food lasts." This food line at that location served food to "men from half a dozen Army units, the Amphibious Force and Canadians, as well as its own men."[139] When the marines and Seabees came in behind the first marines at Torokina Point, Bougainville, the cooks had hot food ready to be served within hours after their arrival on the beach. This included food for "the Marines in the most advanced positions."[140]

Never knowing exactly what they will be facing in stressful and ever-changing situations, Seabees necessarily are innovative. Working frequently with pontoons, Seabees pride themselves in is their ability to "build anything with them." Case in point was Joe's Hamburger Stand "located just off an airstrip in the Russell Islands." According to Huie, here, Joe, the chief commissary steward of the 33rd Seabee Battalion, served "the most delicious hamburgers and hot cakes." He managed to do this with "improvised cooking equipment" made out of "battered pontoons." One served as an oven and the other as a grill. Locating a herd of cattle on the island, he convinced the navy to purchase them and set up a slaughterhouse. "He grinds 400 pound of beef each day on a hand grinder" in order to turn out grilled hamburgers each day.[141]

9

The Modern Military Menu

*Today the dining facilities on large bases in Iraq and Afghanistan resemble the food
courts on a college campus ... with a variety of choices.*
—Mark Cancian, USMCR, Ret.

Post-War Ration Review

Although rapid downsizing of the military following World War II left a dearth of
experienced personnel in many areas of the army, subsistence research did not come to
a halt as might have been expected. The quartermaster general convened an Army Food
Conference in Washington, D.C., in April 1946 to review the World War II experience in
subsistence and to identify deficiencies and also to outline objectives of ration research
and development during peacetime. This conference reviewed the merits of the C and K
rations and sought to keep those parts of each that worked well and discard those that
were not liked. It concluded that the K ration should be abandoned and that while the C
ration had ultimately been more popular and provided adequate nutrition, there were
numerous problems with it. Among the problems noted were unappetizing meat units
when eaten cold, meat items duplicated in the B ration, and the need for a fruit component and a need for a self-heating unit. Accordingly, the conference recommended the C
ration be discontinued and be replaced with a combat ration with the E designation to
give it new identity.[1] The letter E came at the suggestion of the Subsistence Laboratory,
which was renamed the Quartermaster Food and Container Institute in 1946. The E ration
was in reality a modification of the C ration. It had one meat unit and one B unit eliminated and, in their places, canned bread and fruit were substituted. The ration included
an accessory pack containing gum, salt, salt tablets, toilet paper, a wooden spoon, hexa-
methylene-tetramine heat tablets, matches, and a can opener in four packets in each case
of eight rations. In the summer of 1946, 300,000 rations were obtained for field testing.
While test reports were generally positive, the potential for *Clostridium botulinum* food
poisoning was discovered in the canned white bread. This brought to a halt the procurement of the E rations. The Office of the Quartermaster General preferred to drop the E
ration and return to modifications of the C ration.[2]

C rations delivered by air to troops in Korea in 1951. Note the number after the "C" on the boxes. This indicates the procurement number. Each procurement brought changes to the C ration menu. Courtesy Quartermaster Museum, Fort Lee, Virginia.

Another significant post-war development in quartermaster research for the military was the establishment of the Quartermaster Research Facility at Natick, Massachusetts. Congress authorized the construction of research laboratories there in the fall of 1949. The Food and Container Institute moved to the Natick laboratories in 1963. The facility underwent several organizational and name changes through the years, but now all military subsistence research along with other research related to sheltering, clothing, and equipping the warfighter[3] is carried out there and the laboratory is known as the U.S. Army Natick Soldier Research, Development, and Engineering Center (NSREDC).

C Ration Modifications and
Subsequent Individual Combat Rations

Following the return to the C designation for the combat ration the official name became, Ration, Individual, Combat, C. A number following the C indicated of which procurement the ration was a part. Up to ten procurements of the C ration were made until 1958. Improvements continued to be made, in part based on field reports from Korea. Efforts were also made to add variety to the menus and eliminate those items having the least acceptability.[4]

One small controversy arose over the rations during the onset of the Korean War. The Quartermaster General questioned the need to include spoons in the rations. Wooden spoons were included in C rations in 1945 while plastic spoons were substituted at the beginning of the Korean War. The Army Field Forces, the marine corps, and the Army Medical Service all maintained that three spoons should be a part of the ration and ultimately that pattern was maintained.[5]

The 1960s brought a change in the packaging and nomenclature for individual combat feeding. The term meal was substituted for ration when referring to this item and it was no longer officially referred to as the C ration but instead as Meal, Combat Individual (MCI). It was packed as individual meals which could be issued in multiples to make a complete ration. Other than the method of packaging, the components were the same as the improved C rations which continued to be issued until stocks were exhausted. Each meal contained a meat item; canned fruit; a bread or dessert item; a B unit containing such components as crackers, candy, cookies, peanut butter, cheese spread, jam, and cocoa beverage powder; and an accessory pack with cigarettes, matches, chewing gum, toilet paper, coffee, cream, sugar, salt, and a spoon. As with all canned meats, the MCI was much better heated than when eaten cold as was sometimes necessary.[6]

The MCI became the principal combat ration of the Vietnam War where it continued to be referred to by soldiers as C rations or Charlie Rations. Troops of this era also learned a new way to spice up otherwise dull rations. In 1966, the chief executive officer of the McIlhenny Company, manufacturer of Tabasco pepper sauce, was Walter S. McIlhenny, a Marine Reserve brigadier general and World War II veteran. Based on his experience with C rations, McIlhenny decided to publish a cookbook known as *The Charlie Ration Cookbook or No Food Is Too Good for the Man Up Front*. The cookbook was shipped in a canister wrapped around a two ounce bottle of Tabasco Sauce with several P-38 can openers included.

A major change took place in field rations in 1983 with the introduction of a new ration to replace the MCI. This was the Meal, Ready-to-Eat, Individual or MRE. The first MREs were basically MCI meals in flexible packaging which greatly reduced the weight and bulk of the meals. The MRE has been under continuous improvement since its introduction and is used by all military branches. An MRE contains about 1300 calories and its nutritional content is suitable to sustain soldiers for twenty-one days or more. Three MREs make a complete ration. Each meal consists of an entrée, starch, spread (cheese, peanut butter, jam or jelly), dessert, snacks, beverages, hot beverage bag, accessory packet, plastic spoon, and since 1993 a flameless ration heater. To use the heater, the entrée or hot beverage bag is placed in the heater pouch and about 1 ounce of water is added which reacts with a magnesium-iron compound producing enough heat to warm the food or beverage.[7] Here are four examples of the current menu offerings: Southwest beef & black beans, Mexican rice, cookie, cheese spread, cracker (veggie flavor), and picante sauce; pot roast with vegetables, dried fruit, pound cake, chocolate peanut butter spread, cracker, steak sauce, cocoa; spaghetti with meat sauce, cherry-blueberry cobbler, baked snack cracker, cheese spread, chipotle snack bread, candy; chicken pesto & pasta, fruit (wet pack), pudding, bacon cheese spread, wheat snack bread.

Researchers at Natick take note of warfighters' likes and dislikes in MRE menu development and continually make changes to produce a more acceptable ration. Nutritionists express concerns that unless the entire ration is consumed soldiers fail to receive a balanced diet. There are twenty-four menus and even ethnic and vegetarian choices. Like the C rations, the MRE has also received help from Tabasco. In 1984 the company issued a booklet called *The Unofficial MRE Recipe Booklet* to provide recipes made by combing various components of the MRE.

Group and Small Detachment Rations

The popularity of the 10-in-1 World War II ration led to the 1946 Army Food Conference recommendation for the continuation of a small detachment ration although it came to be packaged in one-half the size or a 5-in-1 ration.[8] Several changes to the components were made prior to the Korean War. One significant departure from the World War II 10-in-1 ration was the removal of the K ration type of noon meal and replacement with a full meal. Initially canned bread again made an appearance as part of the 5-in-1 ration. However, with continuing concern over *Clostridium botulinum* poisoning this item was removed and crackers substituted beginning with the 1947 procurement.[9]

In 1949, the Office of the Quartermaster General proposed dropping the 5-in-1 ration but the Quartermaster Food and Container Institute argued for its continuation as did both the navy and air force. Thus the nation's military entered the Korean War with a much improved small group ration.[10] During the conflict, over twenty-two million 5-in-1 rations were procured.

The ration proved popular in Korea, particularly in the early phases of the war. Field reports caused minor changes to continue to be made through 1952 including the restoration of canned bread as a component. The changes removed less popular items and were generally aimed at adding variety to the ration. As with most rations, complaints emphasized the lack of palatability when eaten cold and that the larger sized cans in the 5-in-1 ration made heating more difficult when cooking facilities were not available.[11] The 5-in-1 ration remained a part of the operational ration list until 1963.[12]

A new group field feeding ration known as the T-Ration emerged in the early 1980s through research at Natick. The T-Ration consisted of pre-prepared items sealed in tray packs packed in units for eighteen men. The trays could be heated unopened in boiling water or opened in an oven. Menus consisted of meat, vegetables, dessert, and beverage powder. The army began phasing out the T-Ration in 1998 and the marine corps continued its use into the early 2000s when it was eliminated.

Group feeding in the field is now accomplished with what Natick refers to as Unitized Group Rations (UGR). First introduced in the mid–1990s, these rations are produced in several types: UGR-Heat & Serve, UGR-A, UGR-B, and UGR-Express. One major advantage to the unitized rations is that all items needed for one meal can be ordered under one stock number, thus, food service personnel do not have to order individual items and not be sure of them all arriving at the same time.[13]

The UGR-H & S is packaged in sealed trays that are heated by submerging them unopened in boiling water. They are prepared by trained food service personnel. Three breakfast and fourteen lunch and dinner menus are available. These usually comprise the first group rations soldiers receive in a theater of operations.[14] A meal similar to freshly prepared is provided by the UGR-A ration which is shipped in complete modules to serve fifty. However, it uses perishable and semi-perishable foods requiring refrigerator and freezer availability. Trained food service personnel prepare the seven breakfast and fourteen lunch and dinner menus. The modules also contain condiments, serving utensils, and trash bags.[15] The UGR-B is a marine corps ration that like the UGR-A is prepared by food service personnel but consists of all canned and dehydrated items that require no refrigeration. The UGR-B features five breakfast and fourteen lunch and dinner menus. In both the A and B versions, many familiar brand name items are included. The final type of UGR ration is the UGR-Express (UGR-E). This ration fills the niche formerly filled with the 5-in-1 and 10-in-1 rations. It provides a hot meal through a self heater using technology similar to the flameless ration heater for the MRE. It contains a complete meal for eighteen soldiers and includes an entrée, starch, vegetable, and dessert along with condiments, utensils, napkins, and trash bags. The food is contained in sealed polymeric trays. This ration enables troops in remote locations to have a hot group meal when they do not have access to kitchen facilities or are in situations that prevent bringing hot food in insulated containers. The UGR-E has four breakfast menus, eight lunch and dinner menus, and a holiday meal. Some of the entrée items included are chicken breast with gravy, pork carnitas, and chicken pot pie. The UGR rations provide several advantages for mess service personnel. Not only do these rations simplify ordering, preparation time is reduced as well through the use of pre-prepared frozen entrees that only require heating.

The Frigid Trail Ration

The Frigid Trail Ration was a post World War II development and emerged following arctic tests of the 5-in-1 ration and the C ration. Tests revealed these rations might not be readily adaptable to arctic conditions. In December 1947, the quartermaster general directed the Food and Container Institute to begin work toward developing such a ration.[16] Efforts were directed toward developing a ration that would be compact and lightweight, could be used with minimum preparation, and could be eaten either hot or cold. The Food and Container Institute proposed the following components: meat bar, luncheon meat, cereal bar, biscuits, bouillon powder, chicken soup mix, bean soup mix, fruit bar, margarine, soluble tea, soluble coffee, dry cream and sugar, cocoa beverage, and confections.[17] The ration was first tested during the winter of 1949 and 1950. Tests resulted in general acceptance of the ration although several changes were suggested, especially in the taste of the meat bar.

Two procurements of the Frigid Trail Ration were made during the Korean War, although the ration's actual use in Korea was rather limited. Post-war tests brought minor adjustments to the components and changes in packaging to make the ration more compact and easier for soldiers to carry. By the mid–1950s the military had a well tested, practical trail ration for use under conditions of extreme cold. However, the ration was little used except in tests and was discontinued in the early 1980s.

A specific cold weather ration did not reappear until 1989. Known simply as Ration, Cold Weather (RCW), it was developed at Natick in the late 1980s at the request of the marine corps but was also used by some army units such as the 6th Infantry Division and the 10th Mountain Division. It consists of dehydrated entrees, drink mixes, and soup packed in a flexible bag.[18] In the 1990s, a redesign of the cold weather ration took place

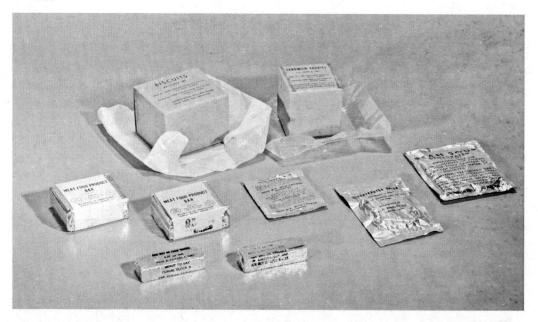

The Frigid Trail Ration, designed for use in cold climates, was developed after World War II and consisted of biscuits, meat bars, cereal blocks, dehydrated chicken soup, dehydrated bean soup, and dehydrated onions. Courtesy Quartermaster Museum, Fort Lee, Virginia.

which resulted in twelve menus issued as individual meals rather than in ration packets. The new design was named Meal, Cold Weather (MCW). Like its predecessor, the MCW consists of dehydrated items along with crackers, cookies, sports bars, nuts, candy, and powdered beverages.[19]

Assault Food Packet and Special Operations Rations

The Assault Food Packet evolved as a successor to the World War II Assault Lunch, basically consisting of various candies. The 1946 Army Food Conference emphasized the need for a food packet that could be carried by the individual soldier during the initial phases of combat action when supplying regular rations would not be possible. However, an assault food packet was not to be considered a ration, which is defined as food for one soldier for one day. Some confusion over terminology occurred in the development phase when the designation ration was used in naming this food packet.

The Individual Assault Food Packet developed in 1948 consisted of one can of meat, one B unit, and one accessory packet. The B unit contained chocolate-chip oatmeal cookies and crackers. Food items included in the accessory packet were chocolate bars or one starch-jelly bar, gum, soluble coffee, and sugar. Canned meats used were beef and corn, pork and applesauce, beef and pork, ham and eggs, hamburgers, chicken, pork sausage patties, and cheese with bacon.[20]

The assault packet was generally well received by soldiers and over 22 million of the packets were purchased for use in Korea with improvements being made for each procurement. Improvements took the form of the elimination of items not liked by the soldiers and better packing and packaging.[21] Efforts to retain the assault packet found support from the marine corps in 1951 which recommended it be adopted as standard for marine corps use during assault portions of operations.[22] This ration however disappeared from the list of operational rations in the early 1960s.

Work began in the 1960s to again provide an assault food packet requested by the marine corps. The result was the Long Range Patrol (LRP) food packet which functioned to provide food during assault phase of action and for troops on patrol and reconnaissance missions where resupply would not be possible. First used by the army in 1968, the LRP was the first flexibly packaged ration used in the military ration lineup and was made possible by advances in freeze-dried food technology. The LRP was used extensively during the Vietnam War. The entrée could be reconstituted with hot water. Other items included a confection, a cereal or fruitcake bar, coffee, cream, sugar, toilet paper, matches, and a plastic spoon. Some of the eight entrees were beef hash, chicken stew, and pork with escalloped potatoes.[23] The packets were issued one per man each day. Early versions contained 1100 calories but by 1990 the caloric content had been increased to 1560.

In 2001 the LRP was combined with the MCW as one ration, the LRP being packed in tan packaging and being issued as one packet per day, while the MCW portion is packed in white plastic and three packets are issued per day. The combined ration has been expanded to twelve menus.[24]

Two other assault-type rations are used by warfighters. The First Strike Ration (FSR) was first available in 2008 and is designed to provide a lightweight ration to use in the first three days of combat in highly mobile situations. The FSR contains pocket sandwiches, energy bars, high energy drinks, beef jerky, dessert bars, and Zapplesauce, a high carbohydrate version of applesauce. The Go-To-War (GTR) Ration developed after Operation Desert Storm is designed to supplement other rations and to be used in early stages of combat mobilization. It consists of commercially produced items including an entrée, fruit snacks, spread, condiments, and beverages.[25]

Special Rations for the Air Force

Little interest was shown in further development of an aircrew ration until 1948 when the Food and Container Institute assembled two sample types, one with candy bars and loose candies and the other with cookies and loose candies. In 1950, the air force made a limited procurement of one type, named Food Packet, Individual, Fighter Pilot, consisting of a candy bar, a two-ounce bridge-mix of loose candies, and two candy-coated chewing gum tablets. The candy bars included four varieties: sweet chocolate, coconut, caramel nougat, and starch-jelly. The final procurement for this item was in 1951.[26] With surpluses on hand, the transition to jet aircraft, and the relatively short flights in Korea officials saw little need for further development of the food packet as it existed. Yet, the air force believed there was still a need for a ration for in-flight crew feeding during long flights.

By 1948 the Food and Container Institute had developed an in-flight food packet based on selecting items from the C rations. Included were one can of meat item, a B unit, a can of fruit, and an accessory pack. This food packet was procured in several versions until 1954. Each procurement brought refinements in the components and packaging based on user comments. This ration was in place until the 1980s when it was replaced with the MRE.

Survival Rations

Following the Army food conference of 1946, Quartermaster researchers began to develop a new survival ration in connection with the air force's request for such a ration. The Food and Container Institute eventually produced two versions, one for cold weather conditions known as the SA (arctic survival) and another for warm conditions, ST (tropical survival). The SA in particular went through several revisions before it was accepted. The ration was stowed on aircraft flying over arctic regions, placed in the parachute pack, formed into a seat in fighter planes, and stored in rubber life rafts or emergency kits on larger aircraft. The ST ration was employed in the same way except in planes operating in tropical regions.[27] The basic composition of the ration was compressed cereal and cheese bars, fruitcake bars, chocolate bars, starch jelly bars, soluble coffee, soluble tea, gum, sugar, dry milk, and water purification tablets.[28] The components included starch jelly bars, soluble coffee, soluble tea, candy-coated chewing gum, sugar, cigarettes, matches, and water purification tablets.[29] In 1961, these two rations were replaced with a single general purpose survival food packet consisting of food bars, instant coffee, sugar, and instant soup. In 1993, this ration was updated and improved.

During the Korean War, the navy continued a life raft ration originating in World War II, designating it the Liferaft Tablet Ration (Abandon Ship). This ration consisted of sucrose-citric acid fruit flavored tablets, sucrose-lipid-citric acid tablets (butterscotch flavored hard candies), sucrose malted milk tablets, multivitamin tablets, and chewing gum tablets.[30] In 1952 a new Abandon Ship Food Packet was introduced containing both hard candies and food bars. The ration was stored on life boats.[31] The currently available Abandon Ship food packet was updated in 1997 with non-thirst-provoking commercial food bars. A final type of survival food packet is used in small quantities by the navy. This is the Food Packet, Survival, Aircraft, Life Raft, used "to sustain personnel that survive aircraft disasters. The packet, along with other essential equipment, is supplied in the emergency kits carried aboard naval aircraft."[32] It is supplied in two types: type I consists of hard candy and candy coated chewing gum; type II contains survival food bars.

The First Strike Ration is a lighter weight version of the MRE and contains pocket sandwiches, energy bars and drinks, beef jerky, dessert bars and Zapplesauce. Courtesy U.S. Army, Juan R. Melandez, Jr., photographer

Ration Supplements

Four supplement packs which originated in World War II continued to be supplied afterwards: the hospital supplement, aid station pack, sundries pack, and kitchen spice pack. As was done with the operational rations they supplemented, these packs continued to be improved both in content and packaging. The supplements persisted in various forms until the early 1980s when they were made obsolete by changing supply systems.

Throughout military history, fresh bread has been an important morale booster for troops. The same is true today. The army no longer operates the large garrison and field bakeries it did in the past since bread is usually obtained from commercial sources. However, operational rations are still supplemented with fresh bread. Technological advances allow warfighters to be supplied with fresh, split top loaf bread packed in a pouch, which is shelf stable for two years. To provide an energy boost, Natick developed a carbohydrate supplement (Carbopack) consisting of beverages and a carbohydrate rich bar (Hooah Bar). The Hooah Bar was developed in 1996 by the Natick labs in cooperation with M & M Mars. It has become extremely popular not only within the military but is now marketed to civilians.

Supply System Changes

The Market Center system for the centralized purchasing of perishable food for all branches of the armed forces which proved so effective during World War II expanded in the 1950s to the make centralized procurement of semi-perishable items as well. The increasing number of troops in Korea combined with the effort to provide two hot meals a day for them greatly increased the demand for perishable and nonperishable subsistence supplies. This led to the establishment of the Defense Subsistence Supply Center in Chicago through which all branches of the armed forces placed orders for subsistence supplies. More centralized procurement of supplies used by all military services occurred in the 1960s with the establishment of the Defense Supply Agency. This allowed better inventory control, simplified ordering, and prevented duplication of purchases. In 1965, centers for purchasing subsistence, clothing, and medical supplies were consolidated with the establishment of the Defense Personnel Support Center in Philadelphia, renamed Defense Supply Center Philadelphia in 1998. Continued consolidation and refinements in organization occurred through the 1970s and 1980s. In 1977, the Defense Supply Agency's name was the changed to the Defense Logistics Agency. The DLA now handles most contracts with vendors for military supplies through its various supply centers, with subsistence procurement for all armed services being made through the Defense Supply Center Philadelphia.[33]

Cooking Manuals and Cook Training

Following World War II, all branches of service continued to publish manuals with recipes, information, and instructions dealing with various aspects of subsistence. Many of these were simply revisions and updated versions of manuals previously published during World War II. The air force, after it became a separate branch of service, published subsistence manuals although many have been joint publications with the army. Increasingly, beginning in the late 1960s, cooking and subsistence manuals became joint publications used by all branches of the military. One particularly significant change occurred in 1969. Beginning in February of that year all services began using the same set of recipes for preparing garrison and A rations. The recipes were written for one hundred portions but instead of being printed in a book format they were printed on 5-by-8 inch cards. This became known as the Armed Forces Recipe Service. The set of recipes is updated frequently with the addition of new recipes and removal of others based on research done at Natick, where all recipes are now developed. These recipes are even available to the public online for use by food facilities serving large numbers. The number of cook and baker training centers for all branches of the military dwindled after World War II. Both army and marine food service training was eventually concentrated at Fort Lee, Virginia, where other Quartermaster schools are also located while the air force cooking school was based at Lackland Air Force Base. In 1996, the navy moved its culinary specialist school from Athens, Georgia, to Lackland. However in 2006, the navy moved its training facility to Great Lakes Naval Training Center. The 2005 Base Realignment and Closure plans enacted by Congress made significant changes in the location of several military schools. Under these plans, what had been known as the Army Center of Excellence-Subsistence (ACES) at Fort Lee became the Joint Culinary Center of Excellence where training for food service personnel from the army, marine corps, navy, and air force will be carried out.[34] The coast guard retains its Food Service Specialist School at Petaluma, California. Two courses are offered at Fort Lee, a basic and an advanced. The basic is an eight week course covering cooking, baking, dining facilities operation, and field feeding. The advanced course is approximately three weeks in length and is designed to enhance the skills of an experienced cook. In addition to the two cooking courses, the JCCoE also offers courses in dining facility management and supervision.

Cooks completing the advanced course achieve a high level of proficiency in the culinary arts and after leaving the military are well equipped to pursue careers as chefs in civilian life. Today's military places much emphasis on advanced training for cooks and allows them to achieve exceptional levels of culinary skills. Military chefs wanting to further their competency have the opportunity to pursue certification as a professional chef through courses offered by the Culinary Institute of America and the American Culinary Federation. Certification through these programs can be gained at five different levels of professional skill. Personnel who have completed culinary training may also apply to take the Enlisted Aide course after which they may become an aide to a general officer.

To foster excellence in military cooking and to recognize outstanding chefs the JCCoE sponsors annual chef competitions at Fort Lee. The competition features military chefs from all branches of the armed forces with approximately 180 entrants. The highest individual award is Armed Forces Chef of the Year. Held since 1973, the event is the largest chef competition in the United States and is sanctioned by the American Culinary Federation. The event provides a way for each branch to build a reputation for its cooking skills and the quality of its food. Even before becoming an independent branch of service, the air force has enjoyed the reputation among many members of the armed forces as having the best mess hall food. Each branch of the armed forces has its own culinary competition open to all units within that branch having an organized food service.

The awards are as follows: army — Phillip A. Connelly Awards; air force — John L. Hennessy Award; marine corps — William P.T. Hill Award; navy — Edward F. Ney Award; coast guard — Coast Guard Excellence in Food Service Award. These awards are sponsored jointly by the service branches and the International Food Service Executives Association.

Field Cooking Equipment

Field cooking equipment changed rather slowly following World War II. In 1959, a new field range, the M59, was introduced. A new burner, the M2, accompanied this range. The M2 burner had to be removed from the range and taken several feet away from the cooking area to be lit. The lit burner then had to be carried to the range and carefully placed in it. The use of this burner resulted in numerous injuries through the years. However, it remained in use until 1999 when the Modern Burner Unit (MBU) was introduced. This burner could replace the M2 in existing

Armed Forces Chef Competition at Fort Lee. Pfc. Jacob Paul completes a dish as judge Ronald Schaeffer watches during the competition. Courtesy U.S. Army.

ranges and is an important improvement. The MBU uses JP8, a kerosene based fuel which both the army and marines plan to use as the sole fuel for all battlefield equipment, including tanks and trucks, thus eliminating the need to supply several different fuels. One MBU will replace two M2 units and burns more efficiently and is safer to use and easier to light with its electronic ignition.

The only mobile cooking facility for the military was the truck mounted kitchen first used in World War II until the 1975 introduction of the mobile kitchen trailer (MKT). The MKT can be towed with the 2½ ton truck and set up in thirty minutes. Many MKT units are still in use but have been improved by adding the MBU to ranges, increasing the size of the ice chest, using a generator to allow fluorescent lighting to replace gasoline lanterns, and provide a ventilation system. Late in the 1999 fiscal year some units began receiving the Containerized Kitchen (CK), a new mobile field kitchen. One CK can replace two MKT units and provide three hot meals a day for 550 soldiers. The CK contains both standard military equipment and newer commercial equipment including

Fort Lee's Staff Sgt. Marcus Hughes and Staff Sgt. DeAndre Brown cooking in a mobile kitchen trailer. Courtesy U.S. Army, Mike Strassner, photographer

a thirty-three cubic foot refrigerator and storage for fifty gallons of water for food preparation. The entire unit fits into a twenty-foot container which can be hauled on a trailer.[35] Another change in the method of getting cooked meals to soldiers is the Kitchen, Company-Level Field Feeding-Enhanced (KCLFF-E). This system is designed to provide one heat and serve ration each day for as many as 200 warfighters. The equipment is loaded on an easily mobile trailer pulled with the military's multipurpose vehicle, the HMMWV.[36]

Supplying Rations During the Korean War

The United States entered the Korean War with quartermaster unit troop strength below the level needed. A lack of transportation facilities was a critical problem in Korea. An inadequate railroad network and poor roads made movement of supplies difficult, especially when combined with the mountainous nature of much of the terrain.[37] The rapidly changing combat conditions forward and retrograde, particularly early in the war added to supply management difficulties. One advantage, however, was having a quartermaster depot located in Tokyo, Japan. The goal of feeding troops in the field in Korea was to give them at least two hot meals a day. A wide variety of fresh products added to the normal B ration fare of canned and dehydrated foods gave soldiers better meals.[38]

While most of the food sent to the Eighth Army in Korea came from the United States, local procurement was important in supplying eggs, fish, and fruits. An important source of fresh vegetables for troops in Korea came from what a somewhat surprising source. The Quartermaster Corps operated hydroponic vegetable farms in Japan. The vegetables were grown in concrete troughs filled with gravel and watered several times a day with a nutrient solution. Army medical personnel preferred such a source instead of buying produce grown locally in soil because of the common practice in Asian countries of fertilizing crops with human waste, commonly referred to as nightsoil. The vegetables grown by this method included lettuce, green onions, radishes, cucumbers, tomatoes, eggplant, Chinese cabbage, and green peppers. Millions of pounds of such produce were sent to Korea aboard daily flights by air force cargo planes.[39]

A soldier is having a hot meal in the field during the Korean War. Courtesy Quartermaster Museum, Fort Lee, Virginia.

Another item furnished in greater frequency than ever before was ice cream. A powdered ice cream mix prepared in freezers at division areas and at Quartermaster rations supply points made this possible. The ice cream was then packed in insulated containers for transport to frontline troops.[40]

Major Lawrence Dobson, an observer for the quartermaster general in Korea, visited numerous units and conducted interviews about soldier likes and dislikes in the rations. He found that the 5-in-1 ration was not desired because of the difficulty in heating the individual items. He recommended that it be used only as an emergency B ration where it could be prepared by organized company kitchens. He found the C ration to be the most acceptable operational rational when troops were not receiving the kitchen prepared B ration. Dobson learned that beans and frankfurters along with fruit had the highest acceptance rating while corned beef hash and beef stew had the lowest.[41] He also discovered that cooks were not receiving enough spices and seasonings. Soldiers going on rest and recreation to Japan were sometimes given money from the company fund to purchases items such as nutmeg, cinnamon, cloves, vanilla, and maple. Dobson praised the cooks for their skill in preparing dehydrated eggs, milk, and potatoes and for baking pastry and rolls far more often than required.[42] Dobson observed that "the farther forward you go in Korea, the better you eat." This meant that the best food is sent to the most forward troops. He gave good marks to the bakeries but found they had maintenance problems with ovens and the bread had to be transported distances up to one hundred and thirty miles over dusty roads. The bread was packed in kraft-paper bags which sometimes became torn in transport. Dobson reported that the bread was five and sometimes seven days old before it reached the troops.[43]

Dobson described the general manner in which forward troops received their meals.

> The meals are cooked in the battalion areas, then carried forward in jeeps as far as possible, and finally packed by the Korean bearers using carrier straps or A-frames. Bearers cannot carry water up to the top of the hill except for drinking, and they cannot carry a stove to heat mess-kit water, so no one on the hill keeps his mess kit. The kits are all kept back in the kitchen are carried forward with the food.[44]

The ability to drop supplies to isolated troops by parachute greatly aided Quartermaster resupply efforts in Korea. While the technique had been used successfully in World War II it became a much more refined and routine effort in Korea. The lack of adequate roads and sometimes rapidly changing combat situations made this method particularly useful there.

Personal Food Accounts in Korea

While the goal of troop feeding in Korea was to provide two hot, kitchen prepared meals a day, some men don't remember that being their experience as James Hayes with the 1st Marine Division recalled, "From the time I got to Korea, I think we had in a year, three hot meals. That was like Christmas and Thanksgiving, the rest of the time we were on C rations all the time."[45] Extra effort was made to provide special meals for Thanksgiving and Christmas but the weather could cause problems. Sergeant First Class Bobby J. Martin with the Army First Cavalry Division recalls his experience.

> Thanksgiving Day saw the army go all out to provide the troops with a really good meal, a complete turkey dinner. The problem was eating it before it froze. I remember the meal sat on burners in the serving line, but by the time we got it on our trays and sat down to eat, much of the food would be ice cold. By the time I got to my fruit cocktail it had actually frozen."[46]

During a retreat just after Thanksgiving 1950, Martin's outfit became separated from the cooks. He explains how they were forced to forage for food.

> We did find some rabbits and a four hundred-pound calf in a village. We confiscated both the rabbits and the calf. After butchering the calf, we gave half of it back to its owner. We kept the two hind quarters and cut them into steaks, so we ate pretty good for a little while.[47]

Corporal Harold L. Mulhausen, Seventh Regiment, First Marine Division, tells about receiving hot food in the Chosin Reservoir area under extremely difficult conditions:

> Miraculously, during all of this we managed to get some hot food. The cooks set up a field kitchen, and we were allowed to go down the hill two or three at a time. We got sausage, bacon, scrambled eggs, hot cakes, and big old cup of coffee. Boy, did it taste good.[48]

Rations and Subsistence Supply in Vietnam

As the number of American forces in Vietnam escalated rapidly in the early 1960s, reaching 490,000 by the end of 1967, logistic planners had a significant task facing them because of the long distance between Vietnam and the United States. Perishables were shipped by air while nonperishable items arrived monthly via LSTs. Orders were placed directly with the Defense Personnel Support Center and were sent to ports such as Vung Tau, Cam Ranh Bay, Nha Trang, and Qui Nhon. In 1969, the Defense Automated Addressing System was established to handle all requests for logistical supplies and direct them to the appropriate supply center rather than requests being made to individual supply centers. That basic system is still in place today and is part of the Defense Logistic Agency.

During the early part of the war, field units had only B rations or the MCI while units in large base areas such as Saigon, Cam Ranh Bay, and Vung Tau received A rations. A special twenty-eight day menu cycle was developed for use by troops in Vietnam to coordinate with the cycle of shipment of supplies. Fresh fruits

Preparing 5-in-1 rations using a one burner stove in Korea, 1950. Courtesy Quartermaster Museum, Fort Lee, Virginia.

and vegetables were procured from Western Pacific countries and from sources within Vietnam to supplement those shipped from the United States. In order to provide more fresh rations to troops in the field the Sea Land Corporation started a refrigerator cargo service to South Vietnam every fifteen days. This enabled troops in forward areas to receive A rations at least part of the time.[49] Pre-fabricated refrigerated storage units holding 1,600 cubic feet augmented permanent cold storage facilities to make it easier to supply fresh products to forward troops.[50]

Contracts with Foremost Dairy and Meadowgold Dairies brought the construction of milk plants in South Vietnam in order to supply troops with fresh milk and ice cream. Additional small ice cream plants were built to provide ice cream to troops as far forward as possible. At one point during the conflict, there were as many as forty such plants in operation.[51]

Vietnam Food Accounts

Troops in Vietnam had a variety of food experiences. How and what they ate largely depended upon their location. Soldiers at large bases near such cities as Saigon and Cam Ranh Bay had access to local restaurants as well as A rations in dining facilities that

Airlifting C rations to troops in Vietnam, 1966. Courtesy Quartermaster Museum, Fort Lee, Virginia.

included steak and seafood along with fresh fruit and vegetables. At bases in more remote locations, hot meals might be confined to B rations consisting of canned and dehydrated items. While on patrol meals would be limited to the MCI or LRP.

Even with local Vietnamese food available, it was wise for soldiers to be careful about indulging as Robert Kattness, an army medic, explained his reason for avoiding local food: "It did not do well to drink their water or to eat their foods unless you wanted to take on the very high probability of a good case of dysentery, worms and other such ailments."[52]

An effort was made to get at least one hot meal a day to troops even in remote areas. The use of helicopters was the only reason this was possible in some areas because of distances and poor roads. Douglas Kathary who was with the army's 25th Infantry Division recounts, "They had a helicopter run and we did have one hot meal a day. It was not always the best hot meal, but it was a good hot meal." Kathary explained that his unit was never sure which meal they would get, breakfast, lunch, or dinner, but they were assured of one hot meal a day. He added, "You may not always like what you ate, but you didn't go hungry."[53]

While on patrols troops utilized either C rations or the LRP, also referred to as the LRRP for long range, reconnaissance patrol or by the soldiers themselves as Lurps. Dave Augustyn with the 1st Air Cavalry noted that he was in the field most of his four and a half months in Vietnam and usually consumed C rations.[54] Many soldiers seemed to prefer the LRP rations over MCI rations as Phillip Kaiser with the 17th Air Cavalry remembered: "When we started getting them [LRP rations] that was really good food." Kaiser also recalled a common problem for troops trying to eat in the field in Vietnam during the monsoon season — the persistent rain soaking your food: "While you are eating, your food's floating in your plate."[55] Edward Allen with the army's 15th Artillery also mentioned the rain: "I remember going up and getting me some food and carrying it back.... It was sopping wet the entire time."[56]

Innovation on the part of the cooks and soldiers helped to improve meals. Edward Allen talks about the good cook his unit had: "We had the best chief cook. He would take things he knew we didn't eat and take them down to the village and trade them. I have to give him a lot of credit." Allen then shares how he and his friends would get supplies from the mess hall to cook: "You might go over [to the mess hall at night] and get a couple pounds of potatoes and four or five eggs and some bacon. We had an electric skillet."[57]

Meal Ready to Eat. Introduced in 1983, MREs were a significant improvement in operational rations.

Post Vietnam Conflicts

In the time between the Vietnam War and Desert Storm, the military in general and the army in particular underwent dramatic changes. Of major significance was the end of the draft and the army's transition to an all-volunteer force beginning in 1973. Another important change during this period was the inclusion of more women in all branches of the military and an expansion of the positions to which they could be assigned. Concomitant with the volunteer army was a shift toward the hiring of civilian employees to handle many of the more menial tasks formerly carried out by soldiers such as cutting grass, painting, and kitchen police in mess halls. A better paid but smaller force meant that the army did not have manpower to spare and needed the now higher paid soldiers to devote more time to honing their military skills.[58]

Desert Shield and Desert Storm

The first troops left for Saudi Arabia August 8, 1990, to begin preparations for the invasion of Kuwait. Initially, the deployment of combat forces received priority over the movement of support units. Since combat units had their own logistic capabilities and were to bring their own supplies, planners believed that for short periods of time they would not need additional support.[59] However, in early August it was realized by commanders that a much better developed logistics system would be needed. Lt. General William Pagonis was placed in charge of logistics. General Pagonis found that the rapid influx of combat troops had exceeded the capacity to house them and it was even difficult to provide adequate meals.[60] Fortunately, in mid–August the army had pre-positioned four ships loaded with rations, tents, blankets, medical supplies, refrigerated trailers, water purification equipment, and other equipment off the coast of Diego Garcia in anticipation of a crisis in southwest Asia. The arrival of these ships eased the immediate problems and a better logistics organization was put into place with the army coordinating food, water, bulk fuel, ground munitions, port operations, inland cargo transportation, construction support, veterinary services, and graves registration for all American forces.[61]

Many of the first troops arriving in Saudi Arabia did not have their normal supply of rations, usually the MRE, to subsist them for several days until more organized messes could be arranged. CWO4 Wesley C. Wolf, selected as food service advisor for Desert Shield and Desert Storm, effectively improvised the feeding of incoming troops with the assistance of an innovative mess sergeant. Bags of hamburgers from a Hardee's near the Dahahran airport helped meet the shortfall.[62] Because of the popularity of hamburgers, roving hamburger stands were set up and made their rounds among the troops. These were sometimes referred to as the Wolfmobile after CWO4 Wolf. The original plan for troop feeding was to use either two MREs per day and one T ration or one MRE and two T rations. In the early part of the war, many troops subsisted entirely on MREs.

Wolf wanted to add more A ration meals as a morale booster. He made arrangements with Saudi contractors to operate dining halls. Initially these contractors prepared Saudi cuisine not much liked by the troops; however the contractors eventually learned to prepare American food according to the army's ten-day A ration menu. Army veterinarians inspected all food obtained locally from Saudi sources.[63] As the operation progressed to the combat phase, MREs were the main food source for troops in the field.

Troops had mixed reactions to MREs. Michael Harris with the 82nd Airborne Division remembered that the "chicken a-la-king was pretty good." However he found that "the pork patty was just the most awful thing ... you actually had to pour water in it to get it to re-hydrate, and it tasted just awful." At the time of Desert Storm, MREs did not yet come with the flameless heater so the troops found ways to heat them. Harris learned that the food packets could be placed, "on top of the engines and close to the hoods to heat them up." He also noted that when his unit was served hot meals, "The food was actually pretty good."[64] The dusty desert environment also affected food quality. Some marines and soldiers have remarked that the hot food brought to forward areas was good but often items such as scrambled eggs would be gritty from the sand.

Enduring Freedom and Iraqi Freedom

One of the biggest handicaps to efficient supply in Afghanistan was the poor road system combined with rugged, mountainous terrain. With less than 2,000 miles of paved roads, movement of supplies by truck was difficult. In addition, Afghanistan has no seaports.[65] Food supplies arriving by ship from the prime vendor must go to Karachi, Pakistan, and then be trucked to bases in Afghanistan while fresh fruits and vegetables were shipped twice weekly using commercial air carriers.[66]

In the early phases of the operation, troops typically used primarily MREs but as bases became established the use of the Mobile Kitchen Trailer and the Company Level Field Kitchen allowed hot meals to be prepared using UGR rations for troops even in remote areas. Eventually, through the use of private contractors, dining facilities were established at larger bases. These provide a variety of food choices in a comfortable setting.

The attack phase of Operation Iraqi Freedom began March 21, 2003. As troops began their movement into Iraq, they carried at least five days' supply of food (MREs) and water with them. Plans called for resupply after two days, but because of sandstorms, congested roads, and a shortage of trucks, supplies were sometimes delayed in reaching the fast moving combat units.[67] Like action in Afghanistan, as the operation in Iraq changed, troops in forward positions were fed through the use of containerized kitchens or company level kitchens serving UGR rations sometimes supplemented with fresh vegetables, while at large bases, contractor-run dining facilities were established.[68]

Food Accounts—Afghanistan and Iraq

One comment made by most soldiers is the problem of long periods of time that they had to use MRE rations. Eric Lathrop with the 101st Airborne Division in Iraq noted that his unit ate MREs "about three months or so."[69] Todd Walton with the 1618th Transportation Company in Iraq observed the improvement in meals as time went on beginning with all MREs, then, "For a while we would eat out of a Mobile Kitchen Trailer and have one or two hot meals a day. Then it just kept getting better. They'd have the chow hall you'd go through [the line and] they'd [the contractor cooks hired by the military] try to make American meals."[70]

Marissa Pelke with a forward support battalion of the 10th Mountain Division in Afghanistan experienced both MREs and UGR-A rations: "[We] started out [with] MREs [then] we used what were called UGR-A rations ... which were not bad, really beat the heck out of MREs." She also noted that "every now and then you did get some fresh vegetables."[71]

Some troops also tried local food but most knew to do so cautiously like Marissa Pelke. "I went out and bought from local vendors ... but you have to be careful. If you ever find yourself in a situation where you need to eat meat, it needs to be charred beyond recognition. You go around open markets in the sun and you see flies buzzing around big cuts of meat."[72] Shannon Wilde with the 735th Main Support Battalion, Missouri Army National Guard, in Iraq found that his dining facility provided excellent food: "We actually had an awesome dining facility ... a main line ... served fried chicken and roast beef ... they had a short order line where they had cheeseburgers and hot wings and ... a deli section ... huge salad bar ... ice cream bar. On Fridays they had prime rib and lobster and crab legs so no complaints about the food at all."[73] James Monk remembers eating local lamb, chicken, and vegetables in Iraq and notes, "I didn't really get sick a whole

Large contractor operated dining facility in Iraq featuring multiple food bars. Courtesy Museum of Missouri Military History (Missouri National Guard), Jefferson City, Missouri.

lot." But he drank local water against his better judgment much to his regret later: "This nice, elderly lady showed up with a cool pitcher of water, and I kept saying no and my throat was saying please. And I drank it, and I lost about forty pounds in a week."[74]

Private Contractors

The transition to an all-volunteer army beginning in 1973 along with a national emphasis on reducing the size of the military required the expanded hiring of civilian employees and contractors. The nation's large commitment in the Middle East has since greatly expanded the use of contractors for a variety of functions including security, transportation, and food service. Part of the reason private contractors, or mercenaries as they are sometimes despairingly referred to by the media, have become necessary is the restructuring of all armed forces, especially the army, since the Cold War era to emphasize combat units over support units. The nation's military simply does not have a large enough force to provide all support services within its own ranks. Private contractors now fill that gap. As of 2008, there are about 265,000 personnel doing contract work for the military in Iraq and Afghanistan.[75]

In the area of food for the military, contractors fill two roles. One is in the transportation of food supplies and the second is the preparation of food. Today, in Iraq and Afghanistan there are dozens of dining facilities, all of which are operated by private contractors employing thousands of third country nationals. Cooking by military personnel is generally confined to troops in more remote locations where mobile kitchen facilities are used. These contractor-run dining facilities bear little resemblance to chow halls of the past. As Mark Cancian (USMCR Ret.) writes in *Parameters*, "Today the dining facilities on large bases in Iraq and Afghanistan resemble the food courts on a college campus, with main-lines, short order-lines, salad bars, and a variety of choices."[76] The Houston based firm of Kellogg, Brown, and Root (KBR) is one of largest contractors operating dining facilities in Iraq and Afghanistan. Even the dining facilities on many military installations within the United States are now run by contractors.

The army's program to establish on-going contracts with service providers is known as the Logistics Civil Augmentation Program (LOGCAP). Basically this works by having the contractor keep a list of qualified personnel it can recruit quickly. In the absence of a conflict, there is little cost to the government but since a contract is already in place, in the event of conflict, assistance to the military can take place quickly.[77] The use of contractors has not been without its problems, including fraud, and overcharges, largely due to a lack of oversight of the contracting process. Cancian writes, "Contracts were poorly structured, improperly priced, and inadequately supervised."[78] The Department of Defense and the Department of State now have in place an agreement which establishes stronger control of contractors.[79] It is unlikely that it would be possible to replace contractors with military personnel. Cancian cites Congressional Budget Office reports showing that the use of military units instead of contractors would cost 90 percent more.[80]

Subsistence Supply Chain

The Defense Supply Center Philadelphia (DSCP), a part of the Defense Logistics Agency, has the responsibility of acquiring and distributing food worldwide in support of military dining facilities and ships' galleys. This includes fresh, refrigerated and frozen items, semiperishable and market-ready items, and operational rations. The DSCP also procures, distributes, services, and installs food service equipment for dining facilities.[81]

The Subsistence Prime Vendor is a program instituted in 1993 by the Department of Defense to facilitate transportation of subsistence supplies to dining facilities. The program uses commercial distributors such as Sysco that supply restaurants and other commercial outlets with a wide variety of foods and beverages. The Defense Logistics Agency handles all contracting but under the Prime Vendor program, a dining facility manager places an order directly with the contracted vendor and the vendor then transports the items directly to the dining facility rather than to a depot point and the military then having to arrange for transportation to the dining facility.[82]

Prime vendors must also interface their computer software with a government program, Subsistence Prime Vendor Interpreter, which allows a military installation to order directly from a contracted supplier while also giving the DSCP a record of all orders. Information technology has aided transporting military supplies in another way. One significant problem has always been to know exactly where a shipment was during transit and when it could be expected at its destination. Since Desert Storm, the Defense Logistic Agency attaches radio frequency identification tags to containers so they can be tracked in transit. This allows the destination to even be changed if needed to meet the needs of fluid battlefield conditions.[83]

One other aspect of subsistence supply that needs to be mentioned is the commissary. Today's commissary store evolved from the necessity of providing a means for soldiers to purchase items not provided in their regular ration. The need was first met by the sutler and post trader. To replace the private traders, the army allowed officers in 1841 and by 1867 enlisted men as well to purchase items from the commissary warehouse at cost. The commissaries stocked food items not part of the ration. Commissary stores were opened around the world by the early 1900s as the military began to have a presence in more locations. Navy and marine commissary stores opened in 1909. Following World War II when the air force became an independent branch of service it simply took over army air force stores. Until 1990 each service operated its own system. At that time the Defense Commissary Agency was established so that all commissary stores are under one agency. Commissaries sell items at cost plus a 5 percent surcharge to pay for new stores and upgrades to existing facilities. The stores are open to active-duty personnel, retirees, national guard, and their immediate family members. Shoppers usually realize a savings of 30 percent on their grocery bills over buying at commercial stores.[84]

The Modern Navy Menu

During the morning as we were on patrol, the can blew up and the boat captain thought that we were taking fire. The engineman found burnt spaghetti all over the engine.

— Bill Monroe on a river patrol boat in Vietnam

At mid-century changes were in store for the navy cookbook following World War II. The Navy Cook Book Task Committee, a "subgroup of the National Security Industrial Association," was organized in 1948 with the goal of helping the navy revise its cookbook. "Expert women and men technologists, home economists, and dietitians from most of the nation's leading food processing corporations" were a part of the group that assisted in "developing and testing food formulaes" that were to be incorporated in what was to become the Navy Recipe Service.[85]

An important decision that came out of the study was a change in the format of the cookbooks. The traditionally bound cookbook became a file of recipes, printed on 5 × 8 inch cards for convenient use in the galley. According to Sharpe, at the time of his article in 1954, it seems that the successful switch in cookbook format has been made. He writes, "Today's Navy recipes appear on handy 5-by-8-inch cards. They meet the Navy needs as the most modern type of recipe information and are endorsed by leading institutions and group feeding authorities."[86] A collection of 5 × 8 inch cards, in the author's possession, stamped "U.S. Naval Training Center, Commissary Department, Great Lakes, Illinois," has specific dates during 1945 and 1946 on several of the cards. This seems to indicate that cards of this nature were already being used in at least one naval training facility before the 1948 study.

The navy continued to be involved in food studies and food improvement programs during post World War II years. In 1953 navy and marine corps experts developed "a new 15-day field menu series composed entirely of non-perishable foods." Additionally the creation of the "field food service team" in three areas—navy cooks, bakers, and meat cutters—provided "on the job training" for "commissary men who operate general messes." The goal of the program was "to standardize and improve methods of food preparation and service, thus insuring continuing high quality of Navy messing." Efforts were also made to address sailor complaints of long mess lines. Of interest is a study conducted on the large battleship USS *New Jersey*. The results of the study showed that by using four serving lines in the area of the galley, "Crews are served at a rate of approximately 20 men per minute in each line." The study looked at "where and how foods were placed and/or passed out." As an example, to conserve time in the dessert area of the line, instead of having bakers replenish dessert choices more frequently, "Faster pastry and bread service was obtained ... by building a rack capable of holding 1200 rations of pastry and three pans of bread [1314 slices]."[87]

Feeding the Navy during the Korean War

Historians at the Naval Historical Center discuss the food delivery plan during the Korean War: "When the Korean War began in June 1950, underway replenishment of the combat ships was, though not a lost art, very hard to come by in the western Pacific." They explain that a "severe shortage of auxiliaries" to supply "needed fresh supplies of ammunition and provisions" meant that warships in combat situations had to "retire to ports in Japan" every few days to restock. The situation was soon under control as necessary auxiliary ships began arriving in the war area: "By Autumn, replenishment at sea was again the routine undertaking that it had been during the great Pacific war just a half-decade earlier."[88] The same information explains that the distance that food had to be delivered is about 5000 miles, from San Francisco to Korea. It took a ship traveling at fifteen knots approximately two weeks to carry supplies to Korea and two additional weeks for the return trip.[89]

Korean War veterans interviewed share their thoughts about navy food. Frank Mireles served on USS *Orion* (AS-1), a submarine tender: "We were a mother ship of 16 submarines and 1 submarine rescue vessel." He describes the food set up on his ship: "We had the best cooks in the world." He tells about the lunch and dinner food lines.

> For lunchtime, we had a hot and cold line. A cold line was sandwiches and all kinds of lunch meat, cold drinks. And in the hot line you had your regular hot meal. You could be having chicken or pork chops or roast beef or all these hot meals. Same with dinner ... so if you was in a hurry and didn't want to stand in the hot line, you went to the cold line and then got your sandwiches and ate, and then you would take off.[90]

Dale McKinley served on USS *Cronin*, a destroyer escort. After saying, "Never was hungry in my life in the Navy," he tells how he and some of his friends on the ship supplemented their food.

> Whenever they'd stop to [receive]—what we always call stores—to load groceries on ... we'd have to send someone to help ... two or three to carry them on. And they'd pass over this hole ... the ladder where we had to go down to where we'd work. And they'd say "Heads up." Well, here'd come a canned ham or something like that. We'd catch it ... put in down in the bilges ... what's [the part of the ship that is] underneath the water.[91]

Eldon Morrison spent his time during the Korean War on LST 1101, a ship that hauled supplies, ammunition, equipment, and troops. He recalls his LST and several others picking up army men who had been fighting for some time in one area of Korea. He had

Crewmen say grace as the chow line is opened for a meal on board USS *Wisconsin* off Korea, March 1952. Courtesy Naval Historical Center, Washington, D.C.

noticed earlier that his LST had taken on extra rations and also as much fresh water as the tanks would hold. Once the men were on board, the captain announced on the PA system that the showers and galley were open. "There's hot coffee in the galley. You go through the galley. You're not getting to eat just regular chow. You go through, you tell the cooks what you want to eat."[92]

Wayne Rudisill on the USS *Niobrara*, an oil tanker, makes this observation: "At the time it was still segregated. We had three or four blacks, but they had to be in their own area, you know, the sleeping quarters. They were our cooks, and so ... they did eat with us and everything."[93]

Navy Food during the '50s and '60s

In his study of navy food, Samuel Barboo discusses changes in navy food in the '50s and '60s. An amendment to the 1933 ration by Congress in 1951 "authorized monetary limits of rations issues in lieu of the unwieldy issue-in-kind allowances." In 1958 because of the unpredictable schedules of pilots, adjustments were made in meal time offerings. "The first extended messing hours for the continuous feeding of personnel for a daily period for 18–24 hours" was first tried out on USS *Bonhomme Richard* and USS *Forrestal*.

He adds that "this messing arrangement proved successful, and by 1965, 80 per cent of aircraft carriers provided extended messing hours." He also notes that a previous amendment in 1942 had been made to the 1933 ration providing for "authorized aircraft flight rations."[94]

"Shipboard habitability" seems to be an important feature of mess halls at this time with efforts made to "improve the visual surroundings" in eating areas. Barboo mentions decorated salad bars, music, flower arrangements, and upholstered chairs. Even though the areas seem to be more appealing, sailors didn't have time to sit and visit after eating because "seating capacities necessitate the successive use of each seat by at least two men during each meal."[95]

While on cruises, ships were re-supplied in various ports. Bob Carter was in the navy from 1958–62. One assignment put him on USS *Point Defiance* on a cruise to WESTPAC for six months where they "practiced war games." Food on the cafeteria line was "pretty good" and he enjoyed the homemade pies. He does remember a stop in Hawaii when they loaded up with pineapples and pineapple juice. The cooks "burned us out on pineapple pies." He remembers having "steak a lot, SOS — sausage gravy and biscuits and also one [SOS] made with a tomato base — also served on toast." When he was on night watch, he would visit the night baker and "get a loaf of fresh bread and some butter for a snack."[96]

During the Cuban Missile Crisis in 1962, Bill Orr performed his duties as an electrician aboard a "tin can" Class 2100 destroyer with 200 to 250 other sailors. Thinking back through his food memories, he remembers powdered eggs and powdered milk, peanut butter and crackers, and cheese. Some of the meat choices he hasn't forgotten include "hash made with canned meat, Spam fried, or sandwiches made with raw Spam with a piece of cheese for a sandwich (which was not bad), and S— on a Shingle [SOS that he describes as] canned meat in white gravy served on toast." As well, "We had a lot of bread pudding — better to use left over bread than throw it over the side." The carrier that his destroyer traveled with "had more refrigerator space and they would cable provisions over to us ... on a line. They could carry more fresh provisions." He also remembers time spent off the coast of Hong Kong where "some provisions were brought from there" and while they were there he "tasted squid for the first time in his life."[97]

Bread just coming out of the oven on the USS *Alabama* in 1960. Courtesy Naval Historical Center, Washington, D.C.

Navy Food during the Vietnam War

Information at the Naval Historical Center also addresses the naval involvement in the Vietnam War. Explanations indicate that Navy involvement in support of South Vietnam included a Coastal Surveillance Force (MARKET TIME), SEAL (Sea, Air, Land) Teams, GAME WARDEN (The River Patrol Force) , and Mobile Riverine Force (a joint Navy-Army operation). At one point, all of the above were joined in operation SEA LORDS.[98]

Distance again became an important issue in feeding the navy in Vietnam. This time the sailors to be fed were 7000 plus miles away from the West Coast. Edward J. Marolda defines the responsibility of the navy at this time in the war: "The Service Force, U.S. Pacific Fleet (SERVPAC), which controlled or coordinated the actions of the logistic ships and shore support facilities throughout the Pacific area, supplied the Navy in Southeast Asia." He points out that "95 percent of the supplies" came to Vietnam by sea." The process of underway replenishment — getting food to sailors — involved "improved and new equipment and techniques." One technique developed was "vertical replenishment by shipboard helicopters." He points out that "in a typical year, from 70 to 97 percent of the deployed fleet's requirements for fuel, ammunition, and provisions were satisfied by sea transfer." Marolda notes that this feat was accomplished using "modern, multifunction logistic ships." He adds that the successful execution of underway replinishment "by shipboard helicopters, enabled the ships to operate for long periods at Yankee and Dixie Stations, on the Market Time patrol, and on the naval gunfire support line."[99]

Ray Nabors, navy hospital corps, served in the navy from 1970 to 1975. The location of one of his assignments was in the Pacific on the aircraft carrier USS *Ranger* during the Vietnam War. He remembers, "With 4,500 mouths to feed, the lines for lunch and supper were long." He found that he often could not take time away from his job to stand in line for some of his meals. He recalls the mess halls and everything in them were "spotlessly cleaned with Clorox solutions between meals ... even the deck." About the kitchen equipment necessary to prepare food for this many, he compares the four bread machines and the mixers on the *Ranger* to large kettle drums. He notes that "we always had all the dairy products we wanted and could eat a pound of butter if we wanted to, and I often wanted that much ... and we had free access to milk and cheese."[100]

One of his jobs was to inspect food on the ship. He recalls, "When I inspected food on the ship, the wheat flour had flour beetles." Nabors, now a trained entomologist, explains that today they are "in all grain products i.e. cereal, bread, cakes, pies etc." He remembers that the sailors asked why the cooks put pepper in the bread. "These pests have nutrients and protein and pose no health risk ... however ... not a good thing to think about." He also recalls that fresh fruit deteriorated quickly aboard ship.[101]

Even though they never were involved in a battle in the Vietnam conflict, they did send planes off the ship. He said they were called to battle stations more than once. "You left the mess hall between bites. If you stayed more than 3 hours, they delivered packaged rations." Evidently more impressed with the chow line than with this type of military food, he recalls that the package included "a can of mystery meat, a cube of dehydrated fruit, and a vegetable medley pack — 2000 calories of mystery food, including a dessert."[102]

Regarding packages from home during this time he said, "Food from home is appreciated beyond belief. Men that get such a package share with their friends who are jealously wanting one of their own. I've seen a wounded man in a Naval hospital cry over Mom's cookies."[103]

Nabors recalls his Thanksgiving dinner in 1973 when was stationed at the Jacksonville Naval Air Station.

> Our clinic had sailors, families, and retired military in line since 7 A.M. with not a minute to eat for any of us medical technicians. No food since supper the evening before. The chow hall is off limits after 1 P.M. The cook, our friend, had fixed us a turkey sandwich at 3 P.M. because we were hungry and it was a holiday. In walks the Captain. "What are you doing in my chow hall!" The cook, under stress replied, "These men could not get to dinner because they worked through." Then the Captain ordered, "Cookie, I want turkey, dressing, cranberries, pies ... everything on this table for my crew on the double." The cook smiled, snapped to salute and said "Yes sir!"[104]

Bill Monroe served in the navy from 1970 to 1973, getting his "first taste of service food" at Great Lakes where did his basic training. About that food he said, "It was an assortment and was done in large quantities. It was not like home cooking." After additional training, he first served in Vietnam in the Brown

Sometimes sailors must eat their meals while manning gun stations. Roberto V. Salinas pictured at a forward starboard gunnery and lookout station eating breakfast March 13, 1966. Courtesy Naval Historical Center, Washington, D.C. JOC R. D. Moeser, photographer.

Water Navy, patrolling the inland rivers on a PBR (Patrol Boat River), assigned to River Division 594 in Tay Ninh province. The navy base there consisted of 4 or 5 barges along the side of the river. Monroe recalls the eating arrangements while on this duty. The chow hall and barracks were constructed on the barges. Commissary men prepared meals in much the same style using the same supplies as would be found on a ship. The men were served meats, vegetables, fruits, bread baked in house and desserts—all cafeteria style. "You could take as much as you wanted, but you could not waste it."[105]

He discussed his meals when he was out on patrol. "When on patrol in Vietnam, we ate sea-rations [C ration] at times that were sealed in the 50s." He adds, "The only problem that I had concerning the food was when I had rations. One of the meals was beef stew with little round potatoes. I do not care what you did to them, they would not soften up. I think they were golf balls in disguise." If they got hungry when on night patrol, they would come back to the chow hall for sandwiches and soup. As on other navy vessels, the baker baked at night for the next day.[106]

Men of the USS *Okinawa* having a picnic on the deck. March 16, 1975. Courtesy Naval Historical Center, Washington, D.C. Peter A. Hoffmann, photographer.

He explains how they handled the matter of heating food when they were going out on a day patrol.

> We would pick out the sea [C rations] that we wanted for lunch and would put them on the manifold so that the main meal would be hot when we had a break. I picked out a can of spaghetti and meat balls one day. During the morning as we were on patrol, the can blew up and the boat captain thought that we were taking fire. The engineman found burnt spaghetti all over the engine. I was not allowed to do that anymore. It makes a hell of a noise when it blows up.[107]

Post Vietnam Navy Food

Michael Marmon served on the aircraft carrier USS *Ranger* from 1977 to 1979. By that time he had been promoted to CWO2. As the food service officer, he managed a large budget, bought the food supplies, and directed the food service operation. While he was on duty there, the fast food line was added.

> I had some 60 cooks from ship's company and 60 cooks from the air wing, plus 120 men assigned as mess cooks (cooks helpers). We fed approximately 5000 men. In a large opera-

Opposite page, top: Wardroom mess on USS *Dixon*, November 20, 1978. These are members of the first group of female officers to be assigned shipboard duty. *Bottom:* Enlisted mess on USS *Dwight D. Eisenhower*, May 29, 1988. PH2 Kevin E. Farmer, photographer. Both photographs Courtesy Naval Historical Center, Washington, D.C.

tion, we served regular meals in the after galley and mess decks—from the forward galley we ran a fast food operation. Hamburgers, French fries, milk shakes—we even had conveyor broilers to help keep up with the demand. That operation was called the Minute Man Inn, and operated 23 hours a day. It was certainly the most popular place to eat. We would change the menu from time to time, to chicken, shrimp, or steak sandwiches. The storeroom we had to store just the paper items was bigger than a house.[108]

He explains the manpower necessary to feed 5000: "On the *Ranger* it took a small army of folks to get the job done. The after galley had 20 cooks, 10 in the bake shop, 4 in vegetable prep, and 10 working in the storerooms, just bringing the food items to production. The forward had another crew of 20." Marmon indicates that "we had regular chow lines at scheduled times, plus we had separate eating places—the Chiefs' Mess for E7 plus, and Wardroom for officers. The Captain had his own mess, and then there was the forward galley with its fast food operation." The fast food operation was added while he was assigned to the *Ranger*.[109]

The *Ranger* could carry enough food for about 40 days or so: "We would meet a resupply ship every 30 days or so." He recalls the planning necessary for UNREP—underway replenishment: "We would bring 30 days of everything on deck and have to clear it

Mess management specialist cooking hamburgers in the galley of one of the two enlisted mess decks on the USS *Dwight D. Eisenhower*, January 1990. Courtesy Naval Historical Center, Washington, D.C. JO3 Oscar Sosa, photographer.

off so they could launch planes, and there was never enough people to help get it put away."[110]

Feeding during the Gulf Wars

With the Vietnam War less than two decades in the past, the navy, as it had in past military engagements, continued to fulfill its responsibility of feeding men and women on vessels during the Persian Gulf War. A navy report details supply actions taken at the beginning of the war. As the navy was preparing for deployment of ships at the start of the war, "Naval Supply Center (NSC), Norfolk ... was flooded with requests from ships gearing up for deployment. Dozens of Norfolk-based ships were scheduled for short notice deployment. The USS *John F. Kennedy* (CV 67) battle group had to accomplish the normally 30-day process of locating and storing the supplies necessary for a six month deployment in just four days." As an example of what it took to supply just one ship and her escorts headed to the Persian Gulf, "*John F. Kennedy* [an aircraft carrier] alone requested some 700 pallets of food. By the time she departed, in company with her escorts, NSC Norfolk had provided the group with 2 million fresh eggs, 185,000 pounds of hot dogs, 250,000 pounds of chicken and 400,000 pounds of hamburger."[111]

Furthermore, the report explains the extent of the supply operation to be handled During Desert Shield and Desert Storm.

> Keeping up with 115 combatant ships battle ready was a full-time job. Most resupply operations were carried out at sea by combat logistics force (CLF) ships, which were in turn supplied through expeditionary forward logistics sites. The CLF ships deployed during DESERT SHIELD/STORM, along with various Military Sealift Command and Ready Reserve Force ships, had the monumental task of supplying six carriers, two battleships, two command ships, two hospital ships, 31 amphibious ships and 40 other combatants including cruisers, destroyers, frigates, submarines and mine sweepers.[112]

Currently, navy ships at sea continue to be replenished by the Naval Fleet Auxiliary Force, one of the four mission areas of the Military Sealift Command. Information at the Military Sealift Command web site provides details about the history of the MSC. The Military Sea Transportation Service, so named in 1949 after World War II, during the Vietnam War was renamed Military Sealift Command.[113]

"These ships provide virtually everything that Navy ships need, including fuel, food, ordnance, spare parts, mail and other supplies." In the ongoing tradition of navy supply at sea, these support ships "enable the Navy fleet to remain at sea on station and combat ready for extended periods of time."[114] The Naval Fleet Auxiliary Force (NFAF) continues to use two types of ships, previously discussed, to insure the delivery of food to Navy to ship at sea — the combat stores ship and the fast combat support ship. The first is being replaced by dry cargo-ammunition ships. This new type of ship is able "to deliver ammunition, provisions, stores, spare parts, potable water and petroleum products to the navy's carrier strike groups and other naval forces worldwide." The second has speed, also mentioned previously, as a valuable ability, contributing to "one-stop shopping for the fleet." These ships deliver supplies though either vertical replenishment (using helicopters), connected replenishment (passing supplies using cables from one ship to the other), or underway replenishment (delivery from ship to ship while both are moving). In addition

Connected underway replenishment of USS *Abraham Lincoln*, February 5, 2010. This system allows ships to be refueled while underway without returning to port. Replenishment is carried out by the Military Sealift Command. Courtesy U.S. Navy. Mass Communication Specialist 3rd Class Kat Corona, photographer.

to other war related materials, a fast combat support ship can carry 500 tons of dry stores and 250 tons of refrigerated stores.[115] "All NFAF ships are government owned and crewed by civil service mariners. Some of the ships also have a small contingent of Navy personnel aboard for operations support, supply coordination and helicopter operations."[116]

Submarine Food Then and Now

The diesel submarines in the fleet during World War II and in years following the war were joined by and eventually replaced by two types of nuclear powered submarines—Fast Attack Submarines (SSN) and Ballistic Missile Submarines (SSBN). These two types, with advanced technology, are now able to remain submerged in their assigned positions and are able to move from location to location for extended periods of time, limited only by their supply of food.

During World War II Robert Burrell served on two submarines—the *Nautilus* and the *Boarfish*. Food seemed to be a very positive experience for him: "That's one thing about submarines we always had good chow. I mean even if we stayed out long and ran out of some food, the cooks and the bakers we had could scramble up something, fix something up." And he adds, "We could make our own ice cream."[117]

Vertical replenishment of aircraft carrier *George Washington* by the Military Sealift Command, August 28, 2008. Dry cargo is handled in this manner. This allows ships to remain at sea while being resupplied. Courtesy U.S. Navy. Mass Communication specialist 3rd Class Najah M. Zenthoefer, photographer.

According to information in a promotional brochure located at the Arkansas Inland Maritime Museum (AIMM), USS *Razorback*, launched in 1944, is the longest-serving submarine in the world. It served in World War II and in the Vietnam War and was sold to the Turkish Navy where it served actively until 2001. It was then sold to the City of North Little Rock in 2004 where it is now the feature of the AIMM in that city where it lies in the Arkansas River.[118]

Maurice Barksdale, who at 23 was the youngest second class commissaryman in the navy, served as a cook on the USS *Razorback* from 1961 to 1963. In an interview on line at the AIMM website, he explains what his average day was like in the galley: "There were three Cooks. One Cook cooked all day, a 24-hour period. One guy baked all night and one guy relieved the second cook on the third day." His day started when he would get up at 4:00 A.M. to start the breakfast meal. As the day progressed, he prepared the noon meal, then snacks for mid-afternoon (mid-afternoon rations), followed by the evening meal and the "Mid-Rats"—"Midnight Rations ... cold cuts, sliced cheeses, and condiments to allow crew members to make their own sandwiches." His day ended at this point and the night baker would take over the galley area and "cook all the breads, cakes, pies, rolls and everything that would be needed for the basic three meals for the next day." His work day in the galley added up to "12–14 straight hours of working" as he moved from one meal or snack to the next.[119]

He talks about fresh foods. They took on as much fresh food as possible when they went to sea. However, "The fresh food would run out after about thee weeks. So you could forget about tomatoes, vegetables, all that." That was when he started using dehydrated foods such as dehydrated eggs and dehydrated milk. A long time submarine cook taught him how to make scrambled eggs in a way that "the guys would never know when we ran out of fresh eggs ... and ... started using dehydrated eggs."[120]

He recalls an unfortunate situation that happened while he was cooking on the *Razorback*. Their fresh meat locker refrigerator system failed so they had to throw overboard to the sharks meat — and fresh vegetables that had been stored close to the meat. Because they had to stay at sea for an additional month, their meat supply was limited. "The only meat we had on board was Spam — old, green cans of Spam. On these cans were stamped ... 'Guam —1943' and 'Saipan —1944' ... from World War II." So he served various versions of Spam for breakfast, lunch and supper to a not so happy crew.[121]

When asked about methods of cooking, i.e., prepared vs. scratch methods, Barksdale comments, "We were submarine cooks!!!" This meant that, Barksdale informs, "All breads, rolls, etc. were made from scratch." He discussed problems the bakers had with yeast on a submarine. "When we were snorkeling ... the pressure changes would affect the yeast." He explains. "The bread would have to 'rise' twice and many times a pressure suction would occur just as the bread completed the second rise. Consequently, we did have funny looking bread on some occasions." He also notes that "officers did not taste the meals before serving. Officers consumed the SAME food as the enlisted men."[122]

Barksdale explains the organization behind feeding the crew on a submarine: "We would take ninety days rations to seas. We prepared our menus on the boat and they were submitted to Division for approval. They had nutritionists on staff who checked the menu for the entire ninety days to make certain they were healthy and in compliance with regulations."[123]

He explains the loading procedure: "We had to 'load' the boat according to the menu.

Galley of the USS *Razorback* (diesel submarine) located at the Arkansas Inland Maritime Museum, North Little Rock. Galleys were very small and according to Maurice Barksdale, cook on the *Razorback* from 1960 to 1963, "All cakes, pies, pie crust, cookies, puddings etc. were made from scratch."

The meat was frozen and loaded in the freezer with the meal for the 90th day loaded first." With their menus in hand, they "would then continue backwards with the first day's meal being the last item loaded. Fruits and vegetables were loaded in the cooler in front of the freezer."[124] The cooler was located below the floor of the galley.

He continues to reflect on his cooking experiences. About serving soups, "We had to be careful with soups because a submarine is pitching and rolling on the surface. Soup was fine when we were submerged and that was most of the time. The 'main meat menu items' were the same as any Navy ship. We had beef, chicken, pork, and everything that would be on a regular Navy menu."[125]

Prior to his service on the *Ranger* from 1977 to 1979, Mike Marmon, mentioned earlier, worked as a cook in the '60s and '70s on diesel submarines as well on ballistic missile submarines, referred to as boomers. He recalls his submarine cooking experiences. Comparing the size of the cooking area on the two types of submarines, the cooking space of a boomer galley was about two to three times bigger than a diesel galley. "Boomers are bigger boats, more room, bigger freezer/chill box and a lot more cooking space." This space he welcomed and indicates that both types generally had about 125 in the crews. "On a submarine we loaded everything we needed for the trip. Once we were at sea, if you didn't have it you got along without it."[126]

Meals were primarily served family style: "The cooks dished up platters and bowls and placed them on the table and the crew would come in, sit down and eat. We would refill any empty bowls. We could feed sixteen at a time and then clean up, reset, and continue till all were fed." In contrast, "The boomers could seat 30 or so per setting ... the same family style except where I did restaurant style." He explains how that style of messing worked: "We offered 4 entrees, 3 starches, 2 vegetables, 2 or 3 desserts, plus, coffee and tea and we served 24 hours a day. The crew member would select from the menus and we would fix his plate any time." He adds, "The crew loved it ... the cooks not so much. It was hard to pull off, but the rewards were worth it."[127]

Speaking of his submarine cooking experiences, he explains, "I took the lessons I learned in my Mom's kitchen and expanded them to feed the crew. There is not much to keep you up in spirits when you are under water a lot. Real good food was a plus. We were small crew and we were close, and extra effort to make other people's day better was appreciated—from good fresh coffee to omelets made to order. We made personal birthday cakes, and any special meal a crew member wanted." He believes that food impacted the crew morale.[128]

Marmon recalls problems that he faced while cooking on submarines. He mentions not enough fresh vegetables, milk and fruit and also not enough storage space. "On the old boats, we put stuff wherever it would fit — 35 lbs flour/sugar outboard of the engines. I stored potatoes/onions in a bilge of the missile compartment." And then there were problems with identifying canned items when "labels ... in the storerooms would come off, so the vegetable of the day could be a lucky guess." Eggs sometimes presented a problem. "On Boomers I would go to sea with 30 cases of eggs in the back of the mess decks." He would move them to the chill box whenever room became available, which sometimes was not soon enough judging from this experience: "These eggs made for some very exciting eggs to order. You know what a rotten black egg broken on a hot grill smells like? The smell would get caught up in the ventilation system, and nobody wanted eggs after that."[129]

Food for holidays sometimes presented challenges: "When you are under water for Christmas, it's hard to get in the spirit. I found that some hand carved prime rib with all the trimmings helped out a lot." He recalls a Christmas when he was in the shipyards: "We got all the turkeys cooked off ahead of time." However, "During the watch change some of the turkeys walked off with some turkey." He solved the problem: "That's the first time I ever deep fried a turkey — a long time before it became so popular."[130]

Joseph Mathis details his food experiences during his career in the navy from 1983 to 2005. Mathis served on fast attack submarines. He notes that a submariner had two eating location options—either the galley–chow hall, which is the dining facility on the base, or the mess deck on the submarine. When he was in training or on shore duty he ate at the former. Here meals were served cafeteria style. "I remember early in my Navy career that food was served on trays, the ones with individual compartments for the food, like TV dinners. Later ... meals were served on standard round or oval plates. You usually had a choice of entrees and sides where you got a full square meal. Or, you could choose the speed line, where you got either hamburgers or hot dogs and fries."[131]

He preferred eating on the submarine: "The food is prepared in bulk, but not on such a grand scale as the shore galley. The cooks were more personal with the preparation and we got better food. The meals were served on plates as you came into the mess decks." In both locations, "Desserts, salads, drinks and condiments were self service," and mess attendants "assisted the cook in preparation of the meals, cleaning the dishes and mess deck, serving drinks or seeing to the patrons' needs."[132]

Mathis also believes that food "definitely has an effect on the morale of the sailor and crew as a whole." He adds, "The cooks that I worked with took pride in preparing the meals. Our supply department tailored the menu to the crews' likes and dislikes. If a meal didn't go over very well ... that meal wasn't served again." Sometimes their food choices were affected by where they re-supplied. One example of an interesting food loaded — "We had kangaroo burgers one time after a food load in Australia. I knew they tasted different, not quite like beef, but not bad either."[133]

He also recalls one of his not so favorite responsibilities as a submariner ... the loading process in preparation for a 90 day deployment for 120 for 4 meals a day.

> On a submarine, everyone loads the food. It's an all hands evolution. By all hands, I mean all hands: from the lowest ranking person up through the Chief's quarters and even junior commissioned officers. You eat it, you load it. We would load in all kinds of weather; heat, rain, cold, it didn't matter. You were up on deck or on the pier or in a passageway all day passing cans and boxes and bags from hand to hand until it got to the proper place. We would take a break for meals. Everyone got to go home only after all the food was loaded.[134]

He explained specifically how the food was stored: "On the first 2 boats I served on, when we did a 90 day loadout, we had #10 cans stacked everywhere. In practically every berthing area, the deck was covered with a rubber mat, cans were stacked on the mat and a piece of ½ inch plywood was placed over the cans to create a walking surface. Our larger #5 cans of coffee, shortening, sugar and flour were stacked against the hull in frame bays. A frame bay is space between the ribs of the submarine hull. They are about 6 feet apart and about 8' or so tall and curved like the hull. You can put a lot of those big cans in a frame bay."[135]

Recalling favorite submariner foods, "Everyone's favorite food was sliders ... hamburgers and cheeseburgers with fries and sometimes baked beans on the side ... usually a Friday or Saturday lunch after our weekly field day (field day is massive ship-wide housecleaning period, usually 4 hours)." He also mentions surf and turf, crab legs or lobster tails as crew favorites, and hard pack ice cream (especially on deployment). "We always have ice cream, but when the hard pack ran out, we had soft serve from the machine." He also mentions SOS as a "military standard, not just Navy ... I didn't care for it too much, but others did." He mentions that "SOS stands for Same Old —" with a little variation on the usual expletive here.[136]

Researchers at the Submarine Research Canter, U.S. Naval Submarine Base in Bangor, Washington, in their book *Submarine Cuisine*, comment on food service in today's submarines. They point out that food is now purchased from "wholesale vendors called prime vendors," mentioning two such operations— Sysco Corporation and King's Bay System. A change they mention that Morman indicates would have made his job easier in ordering food is the advent of the computer. The researchers indicate that "normally, food is delivered seventy two hours after an electronic order has been placed" and the culinary specialist's (what the cook is now called) PC is "his primary tool in record-keeping."[137]

Continuing their discussion of modern food service in submarines, the researchers believe that health trends and health awareness in the navy have come to the submarine galley. They mention the navy's interest in food choices relating to physical fitness, limitation of areas of smoking, and in some cases limitation of fried foods to keep "hydrocarbons out of the boat's atmosphere." The researches conclude that "modern submarine cooking tends to emulate civilian cooking standards," and there appears to be "a better variety of food." With this said, they believe that one thing about submarine cooks "has remained a constant: submarine cooks are proud of their work and the quality of the meals served by them."[138]

21st Century Cooking in the Navy

Who is cooking in the galley in the twenty-first century and where are they being trained? CDR Jeff Baquer, SC, tracks the rating of those responsible for preparing navy chow. The historical rating of individuals preparing food in the galleys has changed over the years from cook (1797) to ship's cook (1838) to commissaryman (1948) to mess management specialist (1975) and as of January 2006—culinary specialist. He believes that the current name change "more appropriately describes the duties and mission for the rating, aligns the rating with today's commercial culinary profession and enhances the rating's professional image." He adds that the navy's culinary specialists (CSs) are "responsible for the culinary operation and management of Navy messes, galleys, and living quarters established to subsist and accommodate Navy personnel." Additionally, they "provide food service catering for admirals and senior government executives." Navy culinary specialists also "operate the White House and Camp David messes for the president of the United States."[139] Currently culinary specialist training is conducted at Training Support Center at Great Lakes, Illinois. "Under BRAC 2005, the Quartermaster School [located at Fort Lee] was selected to become the Joint Culinary Center of Excellence for all of the armed services."[140] Therefore, the navy food service basic and advanced training is scheduled for a move to Fort Lee.

Navy culinary specialists in the 2009 Commander, Navy Region Southeast Iron Chef Competition. Photograph by Mass Communications Specialist 1st Class Rebecca Kruck. Courtesy U.S. Navy.

Aside from basic and advanced culinary classes, CSs have a variety of programs and competitions that they can participate in to hone their

Top: Chef at sea. Chef Ray Duey instructs Culinary Specialist Seaman Keyon Burrell aboard the USS *Kitty Hawk.* Photograph by Mass Communication Specialist 3rd Class Juan Antoine King. Courtesy U.S. Navy. *Bottom:* Marines and sailors aboard the USS *Iwo Jima* having Movie Night on the ship's mess deck.

culinary skills. Annually 18 messes out of over 300 messes in the navy make it to final competition for the coveted Ney Award (named after Capt. Edward F. Ney, who was responsible for supervising the procurement of food for the United States Navy during World War II). This award was established by the navy and IFSEA (International Food Service Executives Association) to improve and recognize the quality of food service in the navy.[141] CSs also benefit from the Adopt-A-Ship program where professional chefs spend

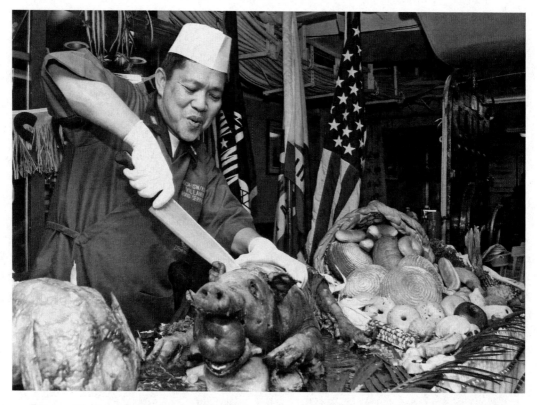

Master Chef Mess Specialist Arsenio Villanueva prepares to serve Thanksgiving dinner aboard the USS *Constellation*. Courtesy U.S. Navy. Photographer's Mate 2nd Class Charles E. Alvarado, photographer.

time on navy ships and submarines sharing their culinary skills. They have additional opportunities to improve their cooking skills through the Chef-at-Sea Program. In this program the navy brings the instructor or chef to the ship. Such courses, in addition to improving the quality of the food service, allow CSs to earn college credits toward their certification as a chef.[142]

Today, twenty-first century sailors, as they pass through their chow lines, are benefiting from a variety of changes directed by the navy. These changes affect not only the food items on the menu but also how the food is prepared in the galley, and improvements in the appearance of the areas where sailors sit down to eat their meals. The navy's long standing tradition of preparing the best food in the military continues to be a strong tradition that has been nurtured by research and implementation of positive changes.

In 2000, looking into the twenty-first century, Commander Frank Lindell, director of the Navy Food Service, Naval Supply Systems Command (NSSC), lines out initiatives in place to move the navy food service forward with the goal of "optimization of the use of the best commercial business practices available to improve Quality of Life (QOL) and reduce work load."[143] The initiatives are bringing positive changes to the galley and mess decks. Pre-prepared foods such as frozen lasagna, frozen chicken patties, and frozen bread dough save preparation time. Coated cooking pans allow easier and quicker clean up. Self serve chow lines with several stations cut down on long mess lines. Additionally new up to date galley equipment includes combination ovens, clamshell griddles, skittles, powdered condiment dispensers, induction plates, blast chillers and deep fat fryers with filters. Galleys and mess decks are being re-designed and updated.

Information made available in a yearly update publication by Natick explains the Navy Standard Core Menu (NSCM) now used by culinary specialists in galleys. Its purpose is to "standardize food service throughout the Navy fleet while providing more variety and nutritious choices to Sailors." The menu includes a different menu, over a 21 day cycle, for each of the three daily meals. Special theme meals, ethnic choices, holiday meals, and healthy choice entrees are evident in the NSCM. Flexibility in the menu allows for such events as "'steel beach' picnics" and ice cream socials. The menu includes "more heat and serve items then in the past." Another positive feature of the NSCM is that even as it adds more variety, it cuts back on the line items that previously were available for meal planning—687 items instead of 2,500 items. According to this information provided by Natick, among other advantages, the NSCM reduces cargo requirements and streamlines catalogs.[144]

So what is next for the galley of the future as culinary specialists continue to dish up chow for the sailors? After creating a mock galley in the Combat Feeding Navy Lab at Natick, researchers and engineers continue to work on the Smart Galley project. Smart Galley uses a "computerized system to control kitchen processes." How does it work? "The Smart Galley uses off-the-shelf software on a main computer. The main computer would have a layout of the galley on the screen, which would identify the various appliances it's connected to. Through touch screens, a sailor or engineer would be able to control appliances, check maintenance schedules, plan meals, check on problems and more." Information delivered in the article explains how this approach would benefit the culinary specialist in meal planning. The system would have recipes in a database that the culinary specialist could access and enter into the automated system. Temperature monitoring and control with visual and audible alarms also appear to be positive features of the Smart Galley.[145]

10

"...and then there was POW food"

Talk turned to "a nice, juicy loin roast, and some mashed potatoes, fried spring chicken, and biscuits and butter ... as light and fluffy as a dandelion puff."
— John McElroy while incarcerated at Andersonville

Throughout America's military conflicts, American POWs have been faced with problems related to their food. In prisoner of war situations, historically, food or lack of food has been used to attempt to control and also to punish. In some instances the promise of food has been used to elicit information. Escape attempts have been met with food deprivation, and prisoners also went hungry because of food shortages in areas of imprisonment. Whether prisoners were paroled, exchanged, or kept in captivity certainly affected how much food they had to eat. POW first person accounts document challenging and dire conditions, many times food related, that they had to endure. Other accounts find POWs in less threatening situations with the issue of food less critical.

Revolutionary War Prisoner Food

American prisoners were held in a variety of locations during the Revolutionary War. In New York, the center of British operations during the war, American prisoners were packed in churches, public buildings, established prisons, sugar houses, and at Columbia College. As these accommodations became insufficient, prison ships were anchored off the coast of New York for holding prisoners. American prisoners were also held in prisons in England.

During the Revolutionary War the British and American military each had commissaries of prisoners. Washington in 1777 selected Elias Boudinot for this assignment. The commissary of prisoners administered British prisoners held by the American military as well as assumed the responsibility of determining and supplying, whenever possible, the needs of American prisoners held by the British. This plan wasn't always successful.

Even with these plans agreed upon, it becomes apparent in POW first person accounts and in communications during the war that American prisoners suffered from lack of food in unacceptable living conditions. On one occasion Boudinot writes of conflicts concerning provisions for prisoners in Philadelphia: "Provisions were accordingly attempted to be sent in, When Genl Howe pretending to ignorance in the business, forbid the provisions to be admitted."[1]

Danske Danbridge gives an account of food being carried to one of the prisoners at the Old Sugar House, designated as a prison: "The other prisoners would try to wrest away the foods, as they were driven mad by hunger. They were frequently fed with bread made from old, worm-eaten ship biscuits, reground into meal and offensive to the smell."[2] She shares an account written by Thomas Stone who mentions that there was "no fire but once in three days to cook our small allowance of provision." From the same account — "Old shoes were bought and eaten with as much relish as a pig or a turkey; a beef bone of four or five ounces, after it was picked clean, was sold by the British guard for as many coppers."[3]

Accounts of prisoners back up the opinion of the day that the *Jersey* was the most dreaded of the New York prison ships. Andrew Sherburne spent time on the *Jersey*. About it he writes, "The old Jersey had become notorious in consequence of the unparalleled mortality on board of her." He continues, "She was moored in the East river, at or near a place called the Wallabout, on Long Island shore."[4] Prisoners on the *Jersey* were to be given two-thirds allowance of provisions that were provided men in the British navy. The British provision: "On Sunday, 1 lb. of biscuit, 1 lb. of pork, and half a pint of peas. On Monday, 1 lb. of biscuit, 1 pint of oat meal, 2 ounces of butter. On Tuesday, 1 lb. of biscuit and two lbs. of beef. On Wednesday, 1½ lbs of flour, and two ounces of suet. On Thursday, The same as Sunday. On Friday, The same as Monday. On Saturday, The same as Tuesday."[5]

Ebenezer Fox comments, "All our food appeared to be damaged."[6] Sherburne says of his provisions that they were "ordinary and very scanty." He lists "worm eaten ship bread and salt beef" believing that "it was supposed that this bread and beef had been condemned in the British navy."[7] Fox declared that his pork "was so unsavory that it would have been rejected as unfit for the stuffing even of Balogna sausages."[8] He writes, "The peas were generally damaged" and "the flour and the oat-meal were often sour" and when mixed with suet "we should have considered it a blessing to have been destitute of the sense of smelling before we admitted it into our mouths: it might be nosed half the length of the ship."[9] Dring remembers craving vegetables while held as prisoners: "No vegetables of any description were ever afforded us by our inhuman keepers."[10]

Thomas Dring describes the cooking process on the *Jersey*: "The cooking for the great mass of the prisoners was done ... in a boiler or 'Great Copper' ... divided into two separate compartments, by a partition. In one side of the Copper, the peas and oatmeal for the prisoners were boiled, which was done in fresh water. In the other side, the meat was boiled. This side of the boiler was filled with salt water from alongside the ship."[11] Fox elaborates on the problem of cooking meat in this water: "The Jersey, from her size and lying near the shore, was imbedded in the mud; and I do not recollect seeing her afloat during the whole time I was a prisoner. All the filth that accumulated among upwards of a thousand men was daily thrown overboard, and would remain there till carried away by the tide. The impurity of the water may be easily conceived; and in this water our meat was boiled."[12]

Matthews and Wecter believe that British prisons in England, Mill Prison near Plymouth and Forton Prison near Portsmouth, and the other naval prisons in England and Ireland "were more endurable than the improvised prisons in America."[13] Francis D. Cogliano explains why these prisons might be preferred to those in the New York area: "While those sent to England would endure prolonged captivity and isolation, they were likely to survive their ordeal." He explains that in England, "There was a great deal of public curiosity about the captured rebels." This curiosity led locals to make Sunday visits with the hope of taking a look at the prisoners. "The prisoners took advantage of these Sunday visits to sell souvenirs to the curious tourists." He notes that these same visitors also donated money, food, and drink. Also prisoners could take advantage of markets located at the prisons.[14]

Charles Herbert writes of his food experiences while in Old Mill Prison in England: "Our allowance here in prison is a pound of bread, a quarter of a pound of beef, a pound of greens, a quart of beer and a little pot-liquor that the beef and greens are boiled in, without any thickening — per day." At the prisons in England, some of the prisoners took advantage of opportunities to make money so that they could supplement their daily food issue. As his hunger increases, Herbert devises a method to obtain money by using his carpentry skills and decides to make boxes to sell at the prison gate. He first makes a box for Sunday afternoon visitors in which they could place donations, and then makes boxes to sell at the prison gate. He mentions items sold by prisoners, "punch ladles, spoons, chairs, and the like; for which they, now and then, get a shilling." His business of selling boxes becomes so successful that, he explains, "I can afford to buy myself a breakfast every morning; commonly bread and milk, which is brought to prison every morning for sale."[15]

Others don't seem to fare as well. Herbert notes that "a great part of those in prison, eat at one meal what they draw for twenty long hours, and then go without until the next day." Trying to appease their hunger, "Many are strongly tempted to pick up the grass in the yard, and eat it, and some pick up old bones in the yard, that have been laying in the dirt a week or ten days, and pound them to pieces and suck them." He adds, "Some will pick up snails out of the holes in the wall, and from among the grass and weeds in the yard, boil them and eat them, and drink the broth." Even though those who make items for sale make only a little money they seem to be better off than those who "are obliged to live upon their allowance." He estimates that about two-thirds of the prisoners do not supplement their food allowance.[16]

Sherburne, like Charles Herbert, also includes an example of how some prisoners, who were fortunate enough to arrive at the prison with money, earned money to buy extra food: "There were individuals who would furnish themselves with a kettle, a few pounds of coffee, and a small quantity of fuel, (bones were carefully collected for fuel,) and make some coffee and sell for half a penny a pint, and if they could realize the gain of three or four pence, or even one penny a day, it was an inducement to continue the business."[17]

War of 1812 Prisoner Food

During the War of 1812, American prisoners were once again held in British prisons and on prison ships. Prisoners on both sides of the ocean faced problems of quantity and quality of food when they were captured.

Samuel White served as a captain under the command of Colonels Fenton and Campbell. After success in the Battle of Chippewa in Canada, unfortunately, White, Colonel Bull and Major Galloway were captured by Indians and delivered to the British. It was several days after the capture before they were given rations. He remembers, "Late in the afternoon of the forth day ... we were furnished with rations—we ate our beef as it came out of the pickle, as we could not think of waiting to cook it."[18]

During his imprisonment, White records that he had to eat in a variety of situations, including a parole situation. Once he arrived in Quebec, he was paroled to Baufort with a group of other officers who were paroled from a prison in Quebec. He gives a detailed description of how the paroled officers managed their food: "At Beaufort the officers formed themselves into messes, and rented a room or two.... The Colonel and Major Galloway had each a man to wait on them, who cooked for us. We paid three dollars a week for the room, and the privilege of cooking at the kitchen fire; a cart load of wood cost two dollars, a turkey one dollar, a chicken twenty-five cents, and beef was twenty cents a pound, and by marketing for ourselves, and messing together we fared better at less cost, than if we were at a boarding house."[19]

When being transported to Halifax, White and the other prisoners were informed that it wasn't necessary to take sea rations. Unfortunately, after some of the prisoners executed an escape, the captain informed the remaining prisoners that they were being moved to the hold of the ship. There, they did not fare so well: "We were kept for twenty-one days, three days and nights of which we had nothing to eat." When they were finally supplied provision, "They consisted of old sea bread or biscuit ... so completely eaten up by the worms ... the outside part being only left, and that was so hard that I would require a hammer to break it." He explains that their allowance, "one forth of a common soldier's ... was shoveled up into a sack and with a bone of beef thrown into the hold as if to so many dogs." They boiled the bread and meat together making lobscouce. "While it was in preparation, we made each of us a spoon" and then "it was poured out upon a large wooden dish, and standing round, we played away, until the hollow rattle of our spoons upon the dish reminded us that it was empty." Once they reached Halifax, they were paroled to Prescott, a village across the bay from Halifax.[20]

Benjamin Waterhouse edited the journal of Dr. Amos G. Babcock who, during the war, was captured and transported to Halifax and was placed in Melville Prison on Melville Island. The journal lists the daily allowance of the British for American prisoners there as one pound of bread, one pound of beef, and one gill of peas. "Over and above this we received from the American agent a sufficiency of coffee, sugar, potatoes and tobacco. The first may be called the bare necessaries of life, but the latter contribute much to its comfortable enjoyment."[21]

Babcock is then transferred to an English prison. When he arrives at England, he observes thirteen prison ships. He later identifies the location of the ships as the Medway River. While he is on a prison ship in that area, he becomes aware of market boats which bring items of food to be purchased by prisoners who have money. He believes that repeated attempts by prisoners to escape from the "fleet of prison ships" caused the British to transfer prisoners to a more isolate placed of incarceration, the Dartmoor Prison.[22] Dartmoor Prison was built by the British as an alternative to using prison ships to confine thousands of French prisoners. Taking three years to complete, "In 1809 the first French prisoners arrived, and were joined by the American POWs taken in the War of 1812."[23]

Charles Andrews, an American prisoner at Dartmoor, includes the ration allowed prisoners. According to the rules and regulations made by the English Transport Board, prisoners should receive the following ration: "For five days in the week, one and a half pounds of coarse brown bread; one-half pound of beef including the bone; one-third of an ounce of barley; the same quantity of salt; One-third of an ounce of onions; one pound of turnips. The residue of the week the usual allowance of bread; one pound of pickled fish, and just a sufficient quantity of coals to cook the same. These to be served out daily by the contractors."[24]

He also is happy with news in February 1814 coming from Mr. Beasley, the American agent living in England. The United States government planned to start paying American prisoners "one penny halfpenny per day, for the purpose of procuring tobacco and soap." Andrews, looking at the money in a bit of a different light, calculates that "the day's allowance of cash would purchase two pounds of potatoes, or three chews of tobacco."[25]

Like the prisons in England during the Revolutionary War, Dartmoor also had a market system. Prisoners who record time spent there frequently write about the benefit of the market to them if they had money to purchase food items. Andrews describes how the market was managed: "The Transport Board directed that a market should be held every day, in front of each prison yard. [Dartmoor was a complex of seven prisons.] This market was supplied with provisions by the inhabitants of the adjacent country; twenty or thirty of whom came every day, and furnished it with every kind of country produce." One problem with the market that prisoners mention is that as punishment sometimes they were not allowed to use the market. During these times, the only way they were able to obtain market items was through the French prisoners who had, over their years of incarceration, earned market privileges. When privileges were taken away, the French "obliged us to pay twenty-five per cent. above the market."[26]

American prisoners used the market to sell items in order to make purchases. Josiah Cobb comments on the ingenuity of prisoners that he had observed. Beef bones retrieved from the cook-house were used to carve trinkets for sale. Other enterprising prisoners "employed beating beef bones to a powder, between stones." He explains their purpose: "As dry as these bones ... appear, after being reduced to a powder and boiled, a palatable, sweet, unctuous marrow is extracted, which is far more rich as a shortening for pastry, or any other culinary purpose, than either butter or lard. It readily commands a shilling per pound, and is bought up with avidity by all who know its worth." He also details how his mess earned money: "The mess that I had joined, was decidedly of a business turn, having for months been catering to the public's taste, by preparing a palatable mixture of potatoes, meat, onions, pepper and salt, stewed to a half-mush, half-soup consistency, dealt out to cash customers, at a penny a pint."[27]

Cobb comments on the cooks and preparation of food for the prisoners. As he remembers, the cooks prepared food for the prisoners in "two copper boilers, each capable of holding more than a large sized bullock, a cart load of turnips and cabbages, and two or three bushels of barley" prepared daily. He notes, "This mass of flesh and vegetable in the copper kettles" was boiled for six hours.[28]

Mexican War POW Food

Accounts of American prisoners of war during the war with Mexico are sparse, in part because of the reality that few American prisoners were taken by Mexico during the conflict. American soldiers were captured in January 1847 at Hacienda Encarnacion where two scouting parties totaling about seventy-two men had taken shelter. They were surrounded by a force of three thousand Mexicans. Captain Cassius M. Clay was among the seventy-two who surrendered. He later wrote in his memoirs about the ordeal. The soldiers were first taken to San Luis Potosi. On the way they received little food. Clay wrote they were "half starved for water and food — at time, no doubt, eating mule meat. They continued on toward Mexico City with Clay commenting again about their lack of food: "We had a hard time of it, often wanting food, and were then supplied, as we thought, with dog or mule-meat." Passing an occasional ranch, women "would run out with eggs and the staple beans and tortillas, and relieve our hunger."[29]

In towns, however, the prisoners had to be protected from angry mobs of Mexican citizens. Once in prison in Mexico City, Clay notes that "we had poor fare in prison." While they were paroled while in Mexico City and were free to go into town, Clay and the other prisoners seldom did so, "on account of the enmity of the populace." They borrowed money from an American living in Mexico City to supplement the meager food provided.[30]

Civil War POW Food

Historian Holland Thompson explores the prisoner of war situation during the Civil War: "From first to last, omitting the armies surrendered during April and May, 1865, more than four hundred thousand prisoners were confined for periods ranging from days to years." Unfortunately, "At the beginning of the war no suitable provision for prisoners was made on either side" because the South "did not believe that there would be a war" and the North "believed that the South would be subjugated within ninety days." Therefore, according to Thompson, "When the war began in earnest, the task of organizing and equipping the fighting men so engrossed the attention of the authorities that no time to think of possible prisoners was found." However, before the war was over, prisoners in the north and the south were placed in a variety of "already constructed" buildings, at forts, and later in the war in prison camps specifically designed and constructed for holding prisoners. "More than one hundred and fifty prisons, widely separated in space, served to confine these men."[31]

Much has been written on the living conditions in Civil War prisons with each side sharing controversy related to the treatment of prisoners including adverse food supplies. These living conditions created in and subject to a wartime environment certainly had an effect on how much the men on both sides had to eat. Thompson comments on the basic treatment of prisoners: "According to the rules and regulations, first set forth by both Departments of War, prisoners were to be fed precisely as regular troops, and humane regulations were announced. All rules, laws, and regulations must be carried out by men, and in the enforcement and administration of regulations there was much variance on both sides. He adds, "Prisoners in the North got more to eat than in the South, after 1862, at least, yet they often got less than the amount to which they were entitled by the army regulations. In the South during the last year of the war, prisoners starved, while their guards fared little better."[32]

The decision by General Grant to suspend exchanges of soldiers in May 1863 led to a significant increase in prisoners on both sides. This dramatic increase in numbers found both sides dealing with the expense of feeding so many more prisoners. Southern prisoners in northern prisons had already experienced a cutback in their rations in July 1862. At this time the Commissary General of Prisoners announced that there could be ration "reduction at the discretion of the commandants." Two additional reductions in rations were made in April and June 1864. These reductions, Thompson believes, were influenced by "reports of suffering in Southern prisons" that those in the North felt were "intentionally inflicted."[33] The following accounts give a personal point of view of daily food issues that prisoners had to deal with in prisons in the North and in the South.

Food for Confederate Prisoners in the North

The reduced ration as of 1864 for prisoners in the North is as follows: "Pork or bacon 10 ounces, in lieu of fresh beef; Fresh beef 14 ounces; Flour or soft bread 16 ounces; Hard bread 14 ounces, in lieu of flour or soft bread; Cornmeal 16 ounces, in lieu of flour or soft bread; And Per 100 rations— Beans or peas 12½ pounds Or rice or hominy 8 pounds; Soap 4 pounds; Vinegar 3 quarts; Salt 3¾ pounds"[34]

Marcus B. Toney shares his food experiences while he was held at the new Elmira prison built in New York to house Southern prisoners. At the prison there was "one large cook house where the light bread was baked and soup and meat cooked. Adjoining the cook house was a large shed with tables that would accommodate three hundred men, and there were in the shed about twenty tables which were higher than my waist when standing." He explains that they were not allowed to sit and eat. "The men were marched in two ranks, and separated at the head of the table, making one rank face each other. Each man had a plate and spoon; in their plate were his bean soup and beans, by the side of his plate was a small piece of light bread, and on the bread a thin portion of salt pork." He writes that a baker "who lived outside" was responsible for baking bread at the prison.[35]

Toney shares food details about fresh meat. He comments on the rather large population of rodents in the prison, indicating that prisoners were able to quite easily knock "them over with sticks and there was quite a traffic in them." Apparently "tobacco, rats, pickles, pork and light bread" became "the mediums of exchange since the prisoners had very little money. The exchange worked like this: "Five chews of tobacco would buy a rat, a rat would buy five chews of tobacco, a loaf of bread would buy a rat, a rat would buy a loaf of bread, and so on." He acknowledges, "I am glad that I did not have to go on this diet; but I have tasted a piece of rat, and it is much like squirrel. I bought one for one of my men who was sick."[36]

Curtis R. Burke, from Kentucky, was imprisoned at Camp Douglas in Chicago, Illinois, for almost eighteen months. He writes, frequently including his food experiences, as he also records a challenging and frustrating prison life for soldiers incarcerated there. It appears that he tries to make the best of a bad situation. He describes where the pris-

Elmira Prison in New York, opened in May 1864. Photograph from Francis Trevelyan Miller, ed. *The Photographic History of the Civil War.*

oners stay. Four long one story buildings form a square "with a cook house on the out-side of the square to each barrack and the length of the barrack."[37]

His mess of four joins three soldiers from another company to bunk in one of the rooms in the barracks. They immediately take steps to fix up the room to suit their needs. "We nailed up a cracker box and three shelves to put our rations and other tricks on." He made a bench to go with a table that was there. They receive their first rations: "crackers, bread, bacon, pickled pork, coffee, sugar, potatoes, hominy, salt, soap, and candles." He says, "Of course, a man only got a handful of each when it was divided." He adds, "I got Sergeant [William] Millers coffee pot and we made a little chip fire in the square, and we had some coffee, crackers and broiled bacon for supper."[38]

He and some of the mess, having received no cooking utensils, decide to "visit an empty hospital, that they had noticed." They brought back "four tin cups, three tin plates, two spoons, four knives, one fork, one stew pan, and one half gallon tin bucket, and a small camp kettle." Once they returned to their quarters, they "scoured them all up while the other boys got supper."[39]

It becomes apparent that Burke likes to cook. His mess decides to pool their money and order a cooking stove for their room from a woman in Chicago. He writes about their daily meals and special occasion meals: "We draw fresh beef every other day, but it it's not a number one article being mostly neck, flank, bones and shanks." Those who have money are able to buy extra food items from the sutler. If prisoners had money when they arrived or when money was mailed to them, it was taken by prison officials and they were given credit at the sutler's store. Letters were opened, the money removed and the amount marked on the envelope: "Then we had to take sutler's checks for it and pay whatever the sutler choose to ask for his goods, which made the profit very large."[40]

When he has money, Burke plans special holiday meals. On his first Christmas there in 1863, he purchases several items to make the meal possible — "one bottle of pepper sauce, two lbs of coffee, 7 lbs. sugar, 1 paper of black pepper, 1 paper of allspice, 1 lb butter, and one lb. lard at a total cost of $2.45." He cooked this meal on one of the stoves in the cook house that "was crowded with other messes." He writes, "My bill of fare was, biscuits, tea, beans and bacon, buttered bakers bread, toasted, molasses, boiled onions laid in butter, cheese, peach pie, apple pie, onion pie, plain doughnuts, and sweet doughnuts." A week later on New Year's Day, he "put a pot of dried peaches to cooking on the stove to bake a big peach roll for dinner."[41]

In contrast, Burke tells about lean meal times. He writes about men killing rats to eat: "Two of the men gathered them up to clean them up to eat them. I understand that rat eating is very extensively carried on in the other squares, but my curiosity had never made me taste any rats yet." He tells how they are prepared for cooking. They "clean them like squirrels and then let them soak in salt water."[42]

Changes are made that Burke doesn't like. Hoffman, the commissary of prisoners in the north, issued an order to take the stoves from the barrack kitchens and instead switch to the use of large boilers, eliminating individual cooking in open fireplaces and in camp-kettles. He also learns that "no supplies of any kind will be allowed to prisoners of way by their relatives or friends, except in cases of illness." Items deemed acceptable had to be addressed to the surgeon of the hospital. He, at this time, had to rely on his typical issued rations: "We are getting boiled beef and sour light bread six days out of ten, and boiled pickle pork and sour light bread the other four and coarse hominy for dinner extra."[43]

He writes, "The sutler has sold out or removed all the eatables and other things that the regulations do not allow him to sell." Evidently the sutler's stock changed significantly when the U.S. inspector came for a visit.

The large population of rats in Elmira led to their being used by prisoners to supplement meager rations either by eating them or by trading them for other items. Photograph from Marcus B. Toney, *The Privations of a Private.*

Confederate prisoners at Camp Douglas, Chicago. Photograph from Francis Trevelyan Miller, ed. *The Photographic History of the Civil War.*

Burke writes, "The U.S. Inspectors are expected here to inspect the camp for the next two or three days. When they are gone the Sutler will commence filling up the store again. As it is now it looks like a Yankee peddler stand. *Stock light and easily moved.*"[44]

Food for Northern Prisoners in Confederate Prisons

Alva C. Roach spent time in southern prisons. His first stop was Libby Prison in Richmond. Libby Prison, an old warehouse, had a concentration of officers in an area of the building that included six rooms. He writes, "In the narrow limits of these six rooms were confined for many months nearly eleven hundred United States officers, prisoners of war. This included all our room for cooking, eating, washing, bathing and sleeping." The officers were allowed to "send out and make a few purchases of bread, meat and vegetables."[45]

On the other hand, the enlisted men who were held on the floors below the officers saw very little variation in the quantity or quality of their food, according to Roach. They received "a small slice of bread and about a pint of broth, in which rusty, decayed and spoiled bacon had been boiled, thickened sometimes with a small quantity of rice or beans, twice each day, and this is all."[46] He explains what he had observed.

Libby prison located in Richmond, Virginia. Photograph from Francis Trevelyan Miller, ed. *The Photographic History of the Civil War.*

I have witnessed the issue of those articles to our men, perhaps a hundred times, and solemnly affirm that I have never seen any variation in the quantity or quality above stated. The soup was brought in to the prisoners in wooden buckets, and I have frequently noticed it when the top was covered with white maggots that the process of cooking had forced from the meat and beans. These prisoners, when not too hungry to wait for their respective allowance, would skim off with an old tin cup, or wooden spoon of their own manufacture, for, be it remembered, that they were robbed of knives, forks, spoons, plates and cups, as well of their blankets, clothing, hats and boots.[47]

The cooking procedure at Libby follows: "After morning roll call, the next business ... if for those whose turn it is to act as cooks of their respective messes, to commence their culinary labors, which consisted in boiling a little rice, which was served up with salt.... Each mess of twenty enjoyed its privilege of the mess kettles and tables in regular order, and one succeeds another in the greatest rapidity practicable."[48]

After arrangements were made for the prisoners to receive provisions from the North, the services of good cooks were in great demand. "And among those who were living, or rather *starving* on Confederate rations, there were always enough who would willingly become the servants of their brother officers for the sake of something good to eat." He also points out that officers, "brigadier as well as Lieutenant, was at length compelled to do his own cooking. The avidity with which they would pour over the household department of old magazines and newspapers in search of receipts for preparing various dishes, was no less astonishing than the rapidity with which they became adepts [sic] in this branch of house keeping."[49]

After Roach was moved from Libby prison, he spent time at the Charleston jail. No mess pans were provided and "cornmeal was issued to us all the time there." After they had been eating boiled rice and mush for some time, they bought cast iron spittoons from the turnkey and made Dutch ovens out of them. They very much enjoyed their first batch of corn dodgers made with their new cooking equipment.[50]

John L. Ransom details the food situation when he had been held at Belle Isle, a tent prison holding Northern prisoners. He writes, "A large portion of the prisoners who have been in confinement any length of time are reduced to almost skeletons from continued hunger, exposure and filth." He adds, "We received for today's food half a pint of rice soup and one-quarter of a pound loaf of corn bread. The bread is made from the very poorest meal, coarse, sour and musty; would make poor feed for swine at home." About how the food is prepared, "The rice is nothing more than boiled in river water with no seasoning whatever, not even salt, but for all that it tasted nice." He mentions that "the prisoners are blue, downcast and talk continually of home and something good to eat." Appearing to have money to supplement his government rations, he, however, explains that he has "enough to eat myself, but am one of a thousand." He has become aware of scurvy in the prison.[51]

Michael Dougherty spent time in several Southern prisons. At Pemberton Building not far from Libby, he "got one-fourth pound bread and one-fourth pound of beef" to last for 24 hours. When moved to Libby, he recalls seeing "men draw their bean soup in their shoes for want of a cup or plate of any kind to put it in." His entries log food details: "Rations very small to-day; a mixture of corn meal and flour and only get about four ounces of that, and about three ounces of raw half rotten bacon for the next twenty-four hours." His rations continue to dwindle when he is moved back to Pemberton to make room for additional captured officers at Libby. "Ration half a loaf of corn bread, to last till tomorrow" and the same a couple of days later with "a spoonful of molasses." Thankfully, he receives a box from home that includes cake, tea, coffee, sugar, salt and pepper. He also mentions "a ham and two dried beef tongues."[52]

Likewise, when he is moved to Belle Isle, he finds rations scarce: "Rations half a loaf of some kind of stuff, Don't know what to call it. It is cobs all ground up and raw, also half a pint of rice." Fortunately, he falls back on his box and also receives half a loaf of bread and two small raw turnips. An entry indicates, "Three men found dead this morning; dying of starvation; no rations at all to-day; many taken to the hospital."[53]

John McElroy tells his prisoner of war story that happened while he was incarcerated at Andersonville. One of his frustrations was that the prisoners did not have "a tin cup or a bucket issued to a prisoner." Consequently, "Pantaloons or coats were pulled off and their sleeves or legs used to draw a mess's meal in. Boots were common vessels for carrying water, and when the feet of these gave way the legs were ingeniously closed up with pine pegs, so as form rude leathern buckets."[54]

He records food experiences remembering that "the loathsome maggot flies swarmed about the bakery, and dropped into the trough where the dough was being mixed, so that it was rare to get a ratio of bread not contaminated with a few of them." As well, their supply of bread dwindled when the bakery was unable to keep up with the demand of added prisoners. Therefore, "The great iron kettles were set, and mush was issued to a number of detachments, instead of bread." He is concerned that "not so much cleanliness and care" was used in the preparation process: "A deep wagon-bed would be shoveled full of the smoking paste, which was then hauled inside and issued out to the

Union prisoners at Andersonville receiving rations. Photograph from Francis Trevelyan Miller, ed., *The Photographic History of the Civil War.*

detachments, the latter receiving it on blankets, pieces of shelter tents, or, lacking even these, upon the bare sand." As numbers continued to increase, some prisoners, instead of being provided bread or mush, simply were issued meal for their ration. His detachment chose the meal option because this allowed them each day to decide how they would prepare it — as bread, mush or dumplings. He mentions trading buttons to the guards for hot peppers in hopes of seasoning their food but found that peppers were not an adequate substitute for salt. "One pinch of salt was worth all the pepper pods in the Southern Confederacy."[55]

Like fellow prisoners, his thoughts frequently turned to food: "We thought of food all day, and were visited with torturing dreams of it at night." He adds, "Naturally the boys — and especially the country boys and new prisoners — talked much of victuals — what they had had, and what they would have again, when they got out." Talk turned to "a nice, juicy loin roast, and some mashed potatoes," "fried Spring chicken," and "biscuits and butter ... as light and fluffy as a dandelion puff."[56]

Spanish-American War POW Food

Patrick McSherry, Spanish-American War historian and editor of the Spanish-American War Centennial website, writes that "one of the most dramatic events of the Spanish American War and one which caught the public imagination, was that of the deliberate sinking of the collier MERRIMAC."[57] Richard Hobson, a naval constructor, and a small group of navy men under his command were chosen from a host of volunteers for the job of sinking the *Merrimac* in the channel which led into Santiago Harbor with the hope of blocking it. Unfortunately, the mission was not as successful as they had planned and Hobson and his crew were taken by the Spanish as prisoners of war. In his account of this prisoner experience, he details how he and his crew were fed during the time they were held, first in the cell of Morro Castle and later at Santiago. It becomes apparent in his account of the mission that he and his crew were given plenty of food at both locations. Once they were retrieved from the water following the event, they were taken to the Spanish vessel *Reina Mercedes*.[58] Hobson indicates that his men were sent to one area of the ship and then the executive officer, after providing dry clothing for him, "invited me to come into the ward-room, when ready, and join him at breakfast." Hobson notes, "Evidently we were to be treated kindly as prisoners of war." Later Hobson is informed that they are to be taken to Morro Castle instead of remaining on the *Reina Mercedes*.[59]

Hobson explains that at Morro Castle their rations consisted of "frijoles, rice, and bread, and, except the bread, continued to be served in full quantity till the end of our captivity. As a rule, a piece of sausage came with the frijoles. The cooking did not vary, both staples being invariably boiled without seasoning, and exactly the same food was served at every meal, until the system somewhat rebelled and after a while called strongly for variety; yet on the whole the food was nourishing. After the transfer to Santiago a ration of beef was added, and it was clear that the authorities were giving me the same food that was issued to the Spanish officers." His men received the same ration with "a reduced ration of beef, while no beef at all was included in the ration of the Spanish soldier."[60]

It would seem that their cordial treatment and acceptable supply of food was reflected in a comment made by the captain of the *Reina Mercedes*. Hobson recalls, "Captain Acosta gallantly opened the conversation by saying that there was no reason why officers engaged in honorable warfare, though opposing to their utmost in battle, might not be the best of friends."[61]

World War I POW Food

In his book, *Prisoners of the Great War*, Carl P. Dennett discusses the conditions of the prisoners of war during World War I and the steps that the Red Cross took to help provide needed food and other supplies for American prisoners of war from the beginning of American involvement to the end of the war. A storeroom at Bumpliz, a suburb of Berne, was leased for American Red Cross supplies and in November 1917 the first food parcel was shipped to the American military prisoners in Germany. "Dennett was sent by the American Red Cross to Switzerland to take charge of supplies sent by the organization." As they began their work with the prisoners, Dennett indicates that "at that time the German Government was giving the prisoners a very small quantity, two hundred grammes per day, of dark, soggy bread, coffee made of toasted acorns, thin, watery soups, very few vegetables, and practically no meat."[62]

After being informed in July 1918 that there were a million American soldiers in France and that an additional million were on the way, he beefed up his plan: "Steps were immediately taken to provide for a total of 50,000 prisoners. Arrangements were made with General Rogers, the Chief Quartermaster of the A.E.F. in France, to furnish all the food and clothing necessary for his stocks there, the American Red Cross to furnish certain luxuries for the military prisoners and everything required for the civilian prisoners." The Red Cross then developed a system for locating POWs and then started delivering packages.[63]

Dennett lists the contents of the first package delivered to each prisoner via the Camp Help Committee prisoners elected by prisoners at each prison camp. (These committees, allowed by the prison officials, managed the distribution of Red Cross parcels to fellow prisoners.) Food items in the package included "1 lb corned beef, 1 lb. roast beef, 1 lb. salmon, 2 lbs. hash, 1 lb. jam, 2 cans pork and beans, 1 can tomatoes, 1 can corn, 1 can peas, 2 lbs. hard bread, 2 pt. evap. Milk, 1 lb. sugar, and ½ lb. coffee." To offer some variety, four weekly menus were prepared from a monthly menu that allowed substitution or addition of "butter, corned beef hash, prunes, raisins, fig, vinegar, rice, cocoa, and chocolate bars."[64]

Dennett comments on problems relating to the Red Cross packages: "It was not unusual, especially during the last three months of the war, for the German population in certain districts where they were very short of food at that time, to loot the individual packages sent to the prisoners." He indicates that as time went on the problem became more severe: "At first such articles as soap and grease (butter or bacon) would be stolen and the rest of the package left intact, but in September and October, 1918, food conditions became so bad in Germany that the packages would frequently be looted of sugar, coffee, canned meats, or canned vegetables." Eventually, "In some cases the packages would arrive with only the bread in them. In such instances the camp committee would immediately deliver to the prisoner whose package had been robbed, sufficient supplies form the reserve stores to make up his weekly ration." According to Dennett, officials allowed a space for reserve packages to be stored under the direction of the Camp Committees. Dennett reports that "this overcame any actual suffering for lack of food by the American prisoners, and was a safe-guard against the individual stealing from the parcels while in transit."[65]

He discusses how food was prepared in German prison camps: "Cooking facilities varied greatly in different camps. In some there were fairly well-equipped kitchens; in others each prisoner did his own cooking on rough portable stoves." A lack of fuel presented cooking problems in some camps. "In some camps great difficulty was experienced in getting any fuel with which to cook, and in a great many there was constant complaint about the totally inadequate cooking facilities and lack of fuel." Prisoners were allowed to receive any number of letters or packages, some of which contained food from home. About the treatment of officers, he indicates that they were "quartered in many instances in hotels, schools, barracks, and chataux taken over for the purpose," and were "allowed cooks and orderlies to look after their comfort."[66]

Dennett makes concluding observations about the food supply of the prisoners during World War I: "The German population had been systematically educated to believe that an American army of any size could not possibly be sent to France, and then even if such an army was sent, it would be physically impossible to transport the necessary food, clothing and other supplies. And yet there were the American prisoners, scattered all over Germany, receiving from America twenty pounds per week of better food than the German population had seen for two years, and better clothing." He adds, "Starvation and suffering were prevented solely by the relief supplies sent to the prisoners from the outside." Finally, "The Germans simply let them eat the food and wear the clothing which was sent in and which was some economic advantage to Germany."[67]

POW Food for World War II Prisoners

The U.S. Department of Veterans Affairs places the number of prisoners of war at 130,201.[68] POW historian Harry Spiller discusses the distribution of the prisoners during World War II: "About 25 percent of them were held by the Japanese Imperial Army and the remaining 75 percent were held by Hitler's Third Reich." He adds, "Although all of these men were POWs in World War II, there were marked differences in the captives' experiences."[69]

The first Red Cross parcel sent to American World War I prisoners of war contained food and clothing. Photograph from Carl P. Bennett, *Prisoners of the Great War.*

Spiller addressed the treatment of POWs in the Pacific: "With the Japanese not adhering to the Geneva Convention, this resulted in a cold blooded plan on the part of the Japanese of brutality and extermination." According to Spiller, "Those lucky enough to survive the inhumane treatment ... were rewarded with hard labor, starvation and disease." In the Japanese camps, "The food was not enough for the prisoners to maintain their health and many developed diseases from the diet as well as the unsanitary conditions." Spiller then turns "to the other side of the globe" where Nazi Germany held American prisoners. Unlike the Japanese, "the Nazis' adherence to the Geneva Convention was generally correct." Food accounts vary greatly depending upon where and when they were held and who was in charge of them in Germany."[70]

Food in German Prison Camps

Much to his surprise, David Ferris, U.S. Air Force, when he parachuted down and was captured and taken to Brussels to a German Air Force hospital, he was "operated on by the head German doctor who had trained at Johns Hopkins and ... interned in Boston." Another surprise came in the form of "Schwester Linda, Sister Linda" who "kinda took care of me. She'd bring me fresh eggs. What I had to do is put a hole in that egg and suck it out." He had problems with eating his egg in this manner saying, "No way." However, she persisted in her encouragement: "You must eat." And he did.[71]

Ferris was moved by train to Stalag Luft 1. He discusses the benefits of Red Cross parcels received there and some of his food experiences: "When we first got there, we got a Red Cross parcel every week." He remembers the parcel containing cigarettes, chocolate D-Bars, Spam, and corned beef. "It was a supplement to whatever the Germans gave you. And we got that for, oh, maybe, the first six months maybe. But then it started getting sporadic. And the last three months, we didn't see any of 'em. 'Cause the Germans needed the food themselves, and so they didn't get 'em to us."[72]

In Stalag 11-B at Fallingbostel, Glen Maddy, Army 347th Infantry Regiment, 87th Infantry Division, tells what foods they were allowed and how food was divided: "There our bread—our food ration consisted of a seventh of a German military loaf of bread. And the way we determined whether you got the heel is we had seven playing cards and there were seven men in squad, and you draw a playing card every day to see how your chances were." Three small boiled potatoes, two to three inches in diameter, and a cup of rutabaga soup completed the daily ration. They weren't as fortunate about receiving Red Cross packages. They were so hungry that they traded with the Germans for food — "Some fellows would trade wedding bands, fountain pens, anything with gold on them."[73]

Staff Sergeant Edwin Douglass, Jr., U.S. Army, was captured in Nance, France. He comments on the food at Stalag XIIA indicating that it was "inadequate ... bread and soup." As far as receiving Red Cross boxes, he notes that one box had to be shared by four men. "It was what kept us alive." Since the other men sharing the box did not smoke, Douglass got all of the cigarettes which "he later traded for food." He remembers a special Red Cross box — the one delivered during Christmas of 1944. It included "boned turkey and the trimmings." The richer food in the box didn't set well, making some of them sick.[74]

Ned Handy, U.S. Air Force, spent 13 months in Stalag 17. In his book, *Flame Keepers*, written with Kemp Battle, Handy shares food experiences. One is of special interest. Shortly after his arrival at Stalag 17, he is invited by a POW, who obviously by his appearance had been in Stalag 17 for some time, to pay a visit to where he and fellow POWs had been staying in the camp. This experience demonstrates how some dealt with their hunger and with their frequent food thoughts driven by their short supply of food. Handy experiences an imaginary breakfast prepared by Axel Jack, apparently known as "the greatest griddle man the Army Air Corps has ever known." As Handy arrives, the men are gathered in a group, anxiously waiting for something to take place. He hears one of the men, the leader, say, "We are gonna have ourselves a feast.... So now, you know the drill. Let's just close our eyes and set right up to my griddle. She's good and hot. Ready as she can be for this morning's special. An omelet, boys, a big, beautiful, fluffy omelet." Handy explains that Axel Jack then details a lengthy set of culinary instructions for the perfect preparation of the dish of the morning, sharing his secret skills for its preparation. After several minutes of detailed sensory description and acting out the necessary culinary steps to prepare the omelet, he concludes his drama: "Smell that beauty. Now let's crease ... fold it over ... turn it out on a warm plate and you got it. The perfect omelet, boys." One man from the quiet circle reacts: "Best goddamed omelet I ever ate."[75]

Food in Japanese Prison Camps

First person accounts in Spiller's book feature men captured by the Japanese who were immediately faced with food problems when they were marched from their place of capture to a prison camp, many of them marching days with very little food or water. Gunnery Sergeant Edward Sturgeon, U.S. Marine Corps, captured on Wake Island, said it was on the second day of the march before they were given food: dry bread and water. "They used empty gas barrels to carry water to us. The water tasted like gasoline."[76]

Sergeant Charles Branum, U.S. Army, was captured during the fall of Bataan and survived the Bataan Death March. He remembers walking nine days covering 90 miles, some days being given water and other days not: "It was nine days of Hell." After the march, he was held in the Bilibid Prison Camp where he was given "poor quality rice … with an occasional rotten vegetable." While working on a concrete runway for the Japanese, he was allowed a "straight rice diet" that was "full of worms." He also mentions that there were days when the only food they received was "shell corn" which they had to cook. Even after they cooked it, "The skin wouldn't come off and it was hard to eat."[77]

Joseph Rust Brown, captured after his plane went down, was held in the Zentsuji War Prison: "At first in 1942, the average meal was about two cups of boiled rice and a cup or so apiece of vegetable soup with a little oil, fish, or rabbit meat sometimes added. The rice was often wormy, but most of us ate it as it was—worms and all; others fastidiously picked out every worm." Some handled the situation differently: "A few jokers would carefully pile the worms beside their dish and after eating everything else, gobble them down for dessert." Brown indicates this was "a perverted piece of humor even by Zentsuji standards."[78]

Gregory F. Michno in *Death on the Hellships: Prisoners at Sea in the Pacific War* documents the horrific conditions that developed aboard ships when captured prisoners were transferred to prisons by the Japanese during World War II. Food on the ships was sparse and unhealthy. On the *Argentina Maru* prisoners packed in areas "four decks down" were served "buckets of slop, lowered on lines from the boat deck above." Michno gives an account shared by Lt. Tom Henling Wade who, with other prisoners, was placed onboard a cargo ship and was "fed rice twice a day, with a thin soup made of flour and water." Wade remembers an ice box full of "rotten pork, bright with emerald patches." He indicates that "the cooks sliced off the worst parts and the rest went into the prisoners' soup." As a result "all eleven hundred [prisoners] developed diarrhea." The author gives another account of "Japanese justice" when "a prisoner suffering from malaria and dysentery screamed that he had to be let topside for some air." Finally allowed up the ladder, "The guard shoved a bayonet into his neck," and "because one man had disobeyed the rules, the rest would only get one ration of rice that day."[79]

POW Food during the Korean War

According to the U.S. Department of Veterans Affairs, 7,140 American military were captured and interned in Korea during the Korean War.[80] In his book, *American POWs in Korea*, Harry Spiller discusses three different "time periods of captivity" in which American prisoners found themselves and what their food situations were like at these times. "The first started with capture and ended in the first permanent camp. During this period the prisoners were denied food and shelter and forced to participate in long marches, often lasting for weeks. These were later to become known as the death marches." The second period of captivity "began at the first permanent camp and ended about

"ARMY A" FOOD PARCEL (FIRST WEEK)

Subsequent parcels sent to American POWs contained primarily food. Photograph from Carl. P. Bennett, *Prisoners of the Great War.*

October 1951." At these locations, "The food was grossly inadequate." After the October date, "There were gradual increases in food ... but the diet remained inadequate in protein and vitamin content."[81]

Spiller indicates that the policy of Communist indoctrination of the prisoners affected their food supply. The first step in indoctrination was to break down the normal resistance by keeping the prisoners cold, hungry, and in a state of confusion." In the second stage of indoctrination the Communists compared their concept of America as "imperialist, with a few rich people running the country" with the communist government "that reflected the aims of all the people." During this second stage "food was improved."[82]

Private First Class Donald M. Elliot, U.S. Army, was held in the Bean Camp, the Mining Camp, and Camp One. After surviving a march after capture lasting three weeks, his group arrived at the Bean Camp. He explains that at this camp prisoners were fed "almost exclusively ... soybeans." Unfortunately time was not taken to cook the soybeans long enough to break down the outer shell. By 1952 he had been moved to Camp One. He notes that in the spring, with the situation improving with peace talks continuing, the prisoners asked for vegetables: "The Chinese got a truckload of turnips. We had 101 meals of boiled turnips, two meals a day for 50 days."[83]

Staff Sergeant Thomas B. Gaylets remembers a two week march to Camp One in 1951 "filled with sickness, hunger, and fatigue" and also his bill of fare at the camp—"four ounces of bean milk" for breakfast, "three ounces of white rice at noon and in the evening." Much to his surprise one day, he discovered meat in his rice. After enjoying the delicious addition, he later became aware that "a rat had gotten in the rice" and had not been removed. He also adds that they didn't see any more meat until 1953 when "the Chinese occasionally started feeding us dog meat."[84]

First Lieutenant William H. Funchess, U.S. Army, details some of his food memories at Death Valley, Camp Two, and at Camp Five. The march to Death Valley took four weeks. On the third day they received their first food, a bucket of shelled soaked corn. The starvation diet continued when he was later moved to the officer's compound at camp 5: "millet seed" and "cracked corn and dried soy on occasion." He also recalls that once, after they were allowed to do their own cooking, they "received a couple of boxes of fatback and pork livers" and some time later boxes of fish that were more maggots than fish" which they made into soup.[85]

Captain Henry Humphries Osborne, U.S. Navy, explains what the officers were supplied to eat. He was held in a schoolhouse while at Camp Two with airmen, senior non-commissioned officers and pilots, doctors, and senior officers: "For 200 plus, we received rations of about one small pig a week, along with very small portions of rice and sugar."[86]

Author Lewis H. Carlson, in *Remembered Prisoners of a Forgotten War*, includes a food memory shared by POW Richard Basset. Basset explains how the POWs cooked their meals in Camp Five when the Chinese took over the camp: "Each company had its own kitchens ... a long shed with a series of fireplaces over which hung a huge black pot" in which everything was boiled. He remembers a special occasion when the cooks were able to "get enough bean oil to fry the chow, which was something special." Each kitchen POW cook and kitchen crew "were supervised by one Chinese officer and two Chinese soldiers."[87]

Vietnam War POW Food
(Based on interviews with Elmo "Mo" Baker and Paul Galanti)

Between the two of them, Elmo C. "Mo" Baker and Paul Galanti spent well over 4,000 days in captivity in Vietnam. Baker spent 2,030 days and Galanti 2,432 days, surviving primarily on a soup, bread, and rice diet served to prisoners there. Galanti indicates that the diet there has been estimated, by the Mitchell Center for POW Studies, as averaging about 700 calories per day.

He remembers eating "pumpkin soup and a small crust of bread and what the V[iet-namese] considered 'bad' rice, i.e., husks/chaff still on it which was probably better for us since it contained the vitamins. Also rocks which broke many teeth. The pumpkin soup in the warmer months and the greens (like kale) in the cooler months. Evidently, once in a while, a rat would fall into the soup and a few lucky guys would get some protein (or a tiny jawbone to chew on)."

He remembers an "occasional holiday meal" and "sometimes we'd get a half a beer." He adds, "I weighed myself one time when I saw a scale in an interrogation room." After three months of solitary of confinement he "had gone from 165 lbs to 110 pounds."

Baker describes the second soup mentioned by Galanti as "Sewer Green Soup" prepared with "an edible morning glory type plant that grew on a nearby ditch. It was chopped up and put in the soup that also contained a bit of fat back and salt." He remembers having "140 bowls of pumpkin soup in a row with 4 or 5 tablespoons of solid chunks of pumpkin in the pumpkin soup ... also a cabbage soup following the same formula ... 4 or 5 tablespoons of cabbage in a watery soup." The bread he compared to a "hard dinner roll sometimes with sand on it because it was baked in an earthen oven." He also recalls a "banana soup made of whole chopped immature bananas " which reminded him "a bit of potato soup." Ever to be remembered was a "sickening sweet rice served on Sunday" instead of the soup. He believed it was prepared on Saturday for use on Sunday.

Baker elaborates on the small amount of protein in their diet and on the four yearly "holiday meals." What little meat they had came from "a scrap barrel." Evidently the cook would throw in whatever was left in the barrel: "pieces of dog ... a monkey hand ... fat back with hair on it." Holiday meals showed up 4 times each year: "Our Thanksgiving, Ho Chi Minh's birthday, Christmas, and Tet (their New Year in the spring)." He remembers " a chunk of baked turkey, probably chopped up with a machete, green beans (with pig fat) and a boiled potato for Thanksgiving." The cook shared a holiday food, Ban Chung on Tet. This he describes as a "sticky steamed rice wrapped around beans and suet which was then wrapped in banana leaf and steamed." They were given a piece of fruit (sometime green) once a month. He said they ate the whole thing, skin and all.

Both men indicated they had slight improvement in their diet when it appeared that there was a chance that they were to be released and also during the months after Ho Chi Minh's death. This improvement amounted to "a small side dish of solids (4 to 5 tablespoons) of whatever the soup was made of." Baker indicates during the last year, especially the last six months, the cook added additional protein, "powdered fish made with trash fish." They also added cracked corn to the rice that was served. Baker remembers a "rare occasion when they received, for several days in a row, small chunks of an injured water buffalo that had been cooked.

Galanti shares the memory of his first meal at Clark Air Force Base in the Philippines a few hours after release: "The Air Force doc wanted me on a bland diet. I refused. I ate six eggs (over easy) with ham and sausage for course #1. Followed by a huge steak, medium rare, smothered in mushrooms and nearly ½ gallon of vanilla ice cream. No bad consequences that I recall.... So I didn't feel badly for being rude to the doctor...."

Galanti sums up his POW food experience: "Bottom line. The food in Hanoi was truly awful. But it kept us alive. Not sure that the weight loss was totally due to the lack of food or some huge tape worms. But all's well that ends well. Now, I'm trying to lose weight."[88]

Elmo C. Baker, Colonel 0–6, U.S. Air Force
POW 1967–1973
Paul Edward Galanti, Lieutenant Comander, U.S. Navy
POW 1966–1973

Appendix: Military Recipes

Recipes from Army Cookbooks

Mexican War Period (from Army Regulations 1841)

The publication of cooking manuals was still several years away. However, the regulations for 1841 provide these directions: "Bread and soup being the principal items of the soldiers' diet, care must be taken to have them well prepared. The bread must be thoroughly baked, and not eaten until it is cold. The soup must be boiled at least five hours, and the vegetables always cooked sufficiently to be perfectly soft and digestible."

Civil War Period (from *Camp Fires and Camp Cooking*, 1862)

• BEANS FOR BREAKFAST

The beans left from the soup of the day before should be put in pans and warmed over the fire, care being taken to prevent them from scorching. In the meanwhile a few onions — say three or four — should be chopped fine and slightly fried, and then strewed over the beans, with pepper and salt, and a tablespoonful of vinegar. In this way they make a first-rate dish for breakfast or supper with bread and coffee.

• BUBBLE-AND-SQUEAK

This is an old and favorite mode of getting rid of bits of corned beef among good house-wives at home, and can be advantageously introduced into camp. Any pieces of cold corned or salt beef that may be on hand should be cut into slices and sprinkled with pepper then put them in a pan, with a little grease or fat, and fry them slightly. Boil some cabbage, and squeeze it quite dry; then cut it up very fine, and serve a piece of beef with a spoonful of cabbage, first seasoning it with pepper, salt, and vinegar.

Spanish-American War Period (from the 1896 *Manual for Army Cooks*)

• LITTLE PIGS IN BLANKETS

Season large oysters with salt and pepper. Cut fat bacon in very thin slices, wrap an oys-

243

ter in each slice, and skewer (toothpicks are the best things). Heat a frying pan and cook just long enough to crisp the bacon — about two minutes. Place on slices of toast, and serve immediately. Do not remove the skewers. The pan must be very hot before the "pigs" are put in, and then great care taken that they do not burn.

World War I Period (from the 1916 *Manual for Army Cooks*)

• CHICKEN STEW WITH DUMPLINGS   (for 60 men)

Ingredients used:

    25 pounds of chicken
    15 pounds potatoes, diced
    5 pounds flour for dumplings

Cut each chicken into 10 or 12 pieces and place in sufficient hot water to cover; boil until nearly done. Then thicken the stew slightly with a flour batter; season with salt and pepper; add dough for the dumplings and allow to cook for 10 or 15 minutes; depending on the size of the dumplings. If desired, the amount of dumplings may be increased and the amount of chicken correspondingly reduced. Time to prepare, about two and one-half hours.

World War II Period (from the 1942 *The Army Cook*)

• BEEF, DRIED, CHIPPED OR SLICED ON TOAST

7 pounds chipped or sliced dried beef	2 bunches parsley, chopped fine
2 pounds fat, butter preferred	½ ounce pepper
1 pound flour, brown in fat	4 gallons beef stock
4 cans milk, evaporated	130 slices bread (about 12 pounds)

Melt the fat in the pan and add the flour. Cook a few minutes to brown the flour. Add the milk and beef stock, stirring constantly to prevent lumping. Add the dried beef and cook 5 minutes. Add the parsley and pepper. Serve hot on toast.

Post World War II Period
(from *Pastry Baking*, 1962, used by both army and air force)

• BAKING POWDER BISCUITS   Yield: 200 2½-inch diameter biscuits.

Ingredients

Flour, hard 12 pounds	10 ounces baking powder
Salt 3 ounces	Shortening 4 pounds
Milk, evaporated 3 pounds 8 ounces	Water 4 pounds 12 ounces

STEP 1. Sift all dry ingredients together twice

STEP 2. Add to above and blend by rubbing together by had until mixture resembles coarse crumbs. Do not mix to a paste.

STEP 3. Mix milk and water together. Add to above mix only enough to combine dry and liquid ingredients. Do not overmix or biscuits will be tough.

1. Place dough on flour-dusted bench.

2. Divide dough into four equal size pieces.

3. Knead one piece by folding and flattening it several times.

4. Cut with sharp cutter and place in sheet pan in rows of 6 by 9.

5. Add leftover pieces of dough to the next piece of dough, and repeat steps 1 through 4.

6. Dough may be cut into 2 or 2½ inch squares to eliminate the handling of leftover pieces each time.

7. Bake in a hot (450° F.) oven for about 15 minutes.

8. Biscuits may be brushed with melted butter or shortening before and after baking.

Recipes from Navy Cookbooks

(from the 1902 *General Mess Manual and Cookbook for us on board vessels of the United States Navy*)

• PLUM DUFF

Soak 25 pounds of stale bread in cold water and drain dry. Add 25 pounds of sifted flour, 5 pounds of suet chopped fine, 3 pounds of raisins, 5 pounds of sugar, 4 pounds of currants, 2 pounds of prunes, 3 tablespoonfuls of salt, 1 teaspoonful of ground cloves, 1 tablespoonful of ground cinnamon, and 1 wineglassful of vinegar, and mix all thoroughly with cold water. Turn the bags inside out, drop then in boiling water, render out slightly, and drop into dry flour, dredging them thoroughly. Turn the bags flour side in and fill them with the pudding, securing the opening firmly, drop into the copper in which water is boiling and cook for at least two hours. If there is sufficient time, the pudding will be improved by boiling three or four hours.

(from the 1904 U.S. Navy *General Mess Manual and Cookbook*)

• BEAN SOUP WITH SALT PORK

Soak 5 gallons of beans in fresh water and 80 pounds of salt pork in fresh or salt water overnight. Put the beans in a copper and let them come to a boil, then add 15 pounds of the pork. Continue boiling until the pork is tender, then remove. In a separate copper boil the rest of the pork until tender. When bean soup is done, season with pepper. Cut up 6 pounds of stale bread, brown it on a pan in the oven and add to the soup, stirring it in.

(*Note*— One gallon of the stock from the copper in which pork is boiled may be added to the soup.)

• SALT BEEF

Soak 80 pounds of beef in fresh or salt water overnight. Place in cold water in the copper. Boil for one hour, then draw off water and fill copper again with boiling water. Allow beef to boil until tender and serve with boiled carrots, turnips, and onion.

From the 1908 *U.S. Navy Cook-Book*

• MINCED BEEF NO. 1

Take 30 lbs. of **lean beef** and cook, or left over meats can be used. Put through meat chopper with 5 lbs. of onions. Place in scouse kettle with a little butter. Add two cans of tomatoes and place on back of range to simmer. Add 8 oz. of salt, 2 oz. of pepper, 1 oz. of mace, 4 oz. of chopped parsley. Add stock enough to cover, and thicken with flour. Serve on toast.

• MINCED BEEF NO. 2

Prepare **meat** same as recipe No. 1. Place 2 lbs. of butter in scouse kettle, when melted, add 2 lbs. of flour. Stir continuously. When smooth add 3 gallons of stock, ¼ oz. cayenne pepper, 8 oz. of salt. Divide roux into 2 scouse kettles or receptacle holding 8 gallons. Take 5 lbs. of onions, parboil for 30 minutes then run through chopper. Add onions to chopped meat, then add to the roux and simmer 20 minutes and serve on toast, or serve in border of mashed potatoes. This can be improved by adding parsley and cream. If Spanish minced beef is desired, add Spanish peppers and lemon juice.

From the 1920 *U.S. Navy Cook Book*

• ROAST BEEF HEARTS

40 pounds of beef hearts, salt and pepper, bay-leaves, beef drippings and flour. Wash the hearts in cold water, removing all the blood from the cavities; have some water boiling in the copper, drop the hearts and bay-leaves in and boil for 30 minutes, remove from the copper, prepare a bread dressing, place a layer in a black pan, then place the hearts on top, dredge with flour, season with salt and pepper and a little beef droppings, bake in a moderate oven, baste with stock and serve very hot with a brown sauce.

• FRIED SALT PORK

After the pork has soaked all night and has been parboiled, it may be cut in slices and fried on the range, in this case it is advisable to allow a little more fat to remain. A brown gravy may be made by frying some onions in a pan after the pork has cooked, then add flour and reduce with water.

From 1927 *The Cook Book of the United States Navy*

• BAKED PORK AND BEANS   (Cooked in a Steam Kettle)

20 pounds beans	¼ ounce mustard
2 pounds salt pork, bacon, or ham fat, diced	2 quarts sirup
2 pounds tomatoes	½ pound mince onions
Salt and pepper to taste	

Prepare the beans the same as for "Baked beans." Bring to a boil and let cook at a simmering temperature until about half done. Then add tomatoes, strained mustard, sirup, minced onions, seasoning and diced salt pork, bacon or ham fat. Let cook at a simmering temperature with just enough stock to barely cover the beans for about three hours.

This method for cooking beans requires six hours to soak and them and four hours to cook.

From 1932 *The Cook book of the United States Navy*

• CREAMED DRIED BEEF

12 pounds dried beef sliced	1 pound butter
½ ounce soda	2 pounds flour
3 pounds milk, evaporated	Salt and pepper
2 gallons water	

Rinse the beef well in warm water. Put in a copper or kettle and cover with cold water. Add the soda (this counteracts the sour in the dried blood). Let it soak over night; then drain off the water. Add enough clean fresh water to cover the meat and bring to a boil and let simmer for 10 minutes. Make a roux with flour, butter, and stock from the dried beef the thickness of cream sauce. Drain the remainder of the stock form the dried beef and add the roux. Stir in the milk before serving. This requires about 5 minutes for boiling and 15 minutes to make the roux separately. Serve on dry toast.

• COFFEE

Put 12½ gallons of clean fresh water into a clean kettle or coffee urn. Then put 4 pounds of ground coffee into a clean coffee sack. Bring the water to a boil 30 minutes before the meal is served. Drop the coffee in and boil slowly for 10 minutes. Shut off the steam from the copper and dilute 3 pounds of evaporated milk in 1 quart of water. Add 4 pounds of sugar; pour some of the hot coffee over this, stirring it until thoroughly mixed. Pour this into the coffee urn and stir until well mixed.

From 1944 *The Cook Book of the United States Navy*

• SCRAMBLED EGGS   (Using powdered eggs)   100 portions

Ingredients	Weights	Amounts
Eggs, whole, powdered	6 lbs.	2 gallons
Water, cool	2½ gallons	
Salt	3 oz.	6 tablespoons
Pepper	1 tablespoon	
Fat, melted	3 lb.	1½ quarts

Stir powdered eggs into 1½ gallons of water. Stir vigorously with whip to prevent lumping until a perfectly smooth mixture is obtained. Add remaining water, salt and pepper. Stir until mixture is smooth. Let stand about 20 minutes. Pout fat into frying pans or roasting pans. Add eggs. Cook, slowly, over low heat until eggs are properly coagulated, stirring occasionally. Remove from heat while eggs are still soft. Eggs will continue to cook slightly after removal from heat.

Note—1. It is desirable to prepare 25 portions of Scrambled Eggs at one time. However, if care is taken and directions carefully followed, 100 portions can be prepared satisfactorily at one time.

2. Do not prepare Scrambled Eggs more than 10 minutes before serving. Eggs toughen upon standing.

3. Powdered eggs need to be carefully reconstituted. Always use *cool* water for reconstituting.

4. Powdered eggs are highly perishable after water has been added and should not stand longer than 1 hour after reconstitution.

5. The flavor of Scrambled Eggs made from powdered eggs can be greatly improved by the addition of diced, cooked bacon or ham, sausage, luncheon meat or cheese.

• BUTTERED CARROTS   (Using dehydrated carrots)   100 portions

Ingredients	Weights	Amounts
Carrots, diced, dehydrated	3 lb.	1 gallon
Water		2½ gallons
Butter, melted	12 oz.	1½ cups
Salt	2½ oz.	5 tablespoons
Pepper	½ oz.	1¾ tablespoons

Soak carrots in water 45 minutes. Cover. Heat, slowly, to boiling temperature, about 45 minutes. Let simmer 10 minutes or until tender. Remove from heat. Add butter, salt, and pepper. Stir until thoroughly mixed.

Note—1. 1 pound dehydrated carrots is approximately equivalent to 12½ pounds fresh, unpeeled carrots or to 6 pounds drained, cooked carrots, or to 7½ pounds canned carrots with liquor.

2. Cook carrots with minimum amount of water.

• MOCK CHERRY PIE
    (Using dehydrated apple nuggets and dehydrated cranberries)   100 portions

Ingredients	Weights	Amounts	Mixing Method
Apple Nuggets,	3 lb.	4½ qt.	Combine first three ingredi-
Cranberries,			minutes. Let soak 45 to 60
Sliced, dehydrated,		3½ qt.	minutes. Heat to boiling
Water, cool		4½ gallons	temperature. Let simmer
Sugar	12 lb.		20 minutes. Add sugar and
Pie pastry	14		simmer 10 minutes.
			Roll to a thickness of ⅛ inch.
			Line pie tins.

Makeup: Use approximately 2 pounds (1 quart) filling per pie. Fill. Brush edge of bottom crust with cold water. Add top crust. Perforate. Press edges together firmly.

Baking: bake at 435° F to 450° F about 45 minutes.

From 1945 *The Cook Book of the United States Navy*

• BAKED LUNCHEON MEAT   (100 portions)

Ingredients	Weights	Amounts
Pork luncheon meat	35 lb.	

Sugar, brown	1 lb. 4 oz.	3¾ cups
Orange juice	1 quart	
Water	¾ gallon	

Score surface of luncheon meat with knife. Place meat in roasting pans. Mix together sugar and orange juice. Cover loaves with mixture. Add water. Bake in a moderate oven (350° F.) 45 to 60 minutes.

Note— Luncheon meat may be baked with barbecue Sauce or Tomato Sauce.

From the U.S. Naval Training Center, Commissary Department, Great Lakes, Illinois

• FRIED CHICKEN MARYLAND   (1000 Rations)

650 lb. chickens, dressed	3 dozen eggs
15 lb. flour	3 quarts milk
1½ lb. salt	5 quarts *fine* bread crumbs
¼ lb. pepper	

1. Prepare chickens for serving. If they weigh 4½ lb. or over, cut into 6 servings; if they weigh less than 4½ lb., cut into 4 servings.

2. Combine flour, salt, and pepper. Combine beaten eggs and milk.

3. Dredge chicken with flour mixture, dip in milk, then roll in crumbs, coating thoroughly.

4. Place in greased roasting pans, add some fat, and bake at 350 degrees until tender and brown — approx. 1–1½ hrs.

Note: Suggest serving with giblet gravy.

23 August 1945   Ration: 1 piece chicken.

• BEEF LOAF   (1000 Rations)

300 lb. beef, bone-out, or	1½ lb. salt
boneless ground	¼ lb. pepper
10 lb. onions, chopped	30 eggs
10 lb. celery, chopped	Beef stock to moisten
10 lb. bread cubed	

1. Combine all ingredients, and mix lightly. Scale 5 lbs. per loaf and place in greased black pans, allowing 5 loaves to a pan.

2. Bake, uncovered, at 325 degrees for 2 hrs. or until done.

3. Remove from oven, and slice.

4. Keep hot in 150 degree oven, or stack in pans in heated coppers.

1 August 1945   Ration: Approximately 5 oz. cooked meat.

Chapter Notes

Chapter 1

1. *Journals of the Continental Congress, 1774–1789,* Worthington C. Ford et al., eds. 2: 91. (Hereafter JCC).
2. JCC, 2: 94.
3. JCC, 2: 101.
4. JCC, 3: 257.
5. JCC, 3: 322.
6. "A History of Rations Conference Notes, January 1949," U.S. Army Quartermaster Foundation, http://www.qmfound.com/history_of_rations.htm.
7. Ibid.
8. Ibid.
9. Ibid.
10. Ibid.
11. William Matthews and Dixon Wecter, *Our Soldiers Speak,* 55.
12. Erna Risch, *Supplying Washington's Army,* 191.
13. George Washington, *The Writings of George Washington,* John C. Fitzpatrick, ed., 5: 320 (hereafter Fitzpatrick).
14. Ibid., 19: 437–438.
15. Kenneth Roberts, *March to Quebec: Journals of the Members of Arnold's Expedition,* 261.
16. John C. Dann, ed., *The Revolution Remembered Eyewitness Accounts of the War for Independence,* 366–367.
17. Dann, 371.
18. Joseph Lee Boyle, ed., *The Ephraim Blaine Letterbook, 1777–1778,* 203.
19. Boyle, 14.
20. Fitzpatrick, 6: 218.
21. Risch, 198.
22. Boyle, 49.
23. Ibid., 16.
24. Ibid., 164.
25. Joseph Plumb Martin, *Private Yankee Doodle,* 192.
26. Risch, 194.
27. JCC, 7: 323.
28. Risch, 195–196.
29. Jeremiah Greenman, *Diary of a Common Soldier in the American Revolution, 1775–1783,* 17.
30. Fitzpatrick, 6: 7.
31. Martin, 77.
32. Matthews and Wecter, 54.
33. Fitzpatrick, 8: 351.
34. Boyle, intro., vi.
35. Risch, 197.
36. Fitzpatrick, 6: 409.
37. Ibid., 9: 474–475.
38. Ibid., 8: 107.
39. Ibid., 8: 55.
40. Ibid., 8: 210.
41. Ibid., 12: 54.
42. Ibid., 8: 350–351.
43. Boyle, 142.
44. Ibid., 129–130.
45. Charles Knowles Bolton, *The Private Soldier Under Washington,* 81–82.
46. JCC, 6: 989.
47. Fitzpatrick, 12: 361.
48. Ibid., 12: 242.
49. Risch, 385, 392.
50. Boyle, 142.
51. Martin, 175.
52. Fitzpatrick, 8: 142.
53. Ibid., 9: 19–20.
54. John U. Rees, "Finding Water and Carrying Food During the War for Independence and the American Civil War." *Food History News* 10, no. 1, p 2.
55. "History of Rations."
56. Fitzpatrick, 11: 265.
57. Ibid., 25: 411.
58. Ibid., 16: 149.
59. Ibid., 25: 375.
60. Ibid., 24: 397.
61. Ibid., 5: 436.
62. Matthews and Wecter, 57.
63. Fitzpatrick, 8: 375.
64. Boyle, 10.
65. John U. Rees, "Less Commonly Used Utensils, Eating Implements, and Officers' Cooking Equipment, *The Brigade Dispatch* 4, no. 2 (Summer 2001): 2–4.
66. John U. Rees, "Earthen Camp Kitchens," *Food History News* 9, no. 2, 2.
67. John U. Rees, http://www.revwar75.com/library/rees/kitchen.htm.
68. Martin, 97.
69. Ibid., 103.
70. Fitzpatrick, 3: 449–450.
71. Ibid., 10: 466.
72. Roberts, p. 202–203.
73. Holly Mayer, *Belonging to the Army,* 1, 5.
74. John C. Dann, *The Revolution Remembered: Eyewitness Accounts of the War for Independence,* 240.
75. Ibid., 240–244.
76. Ibid., 244–245.
77. Matthews and Wecter, 22.
78. Ebenezer Fox, *The Adventures of Ebenezer Fox in the Revolutionary War,* 50–51.
79. Roberts, 322.
80. Ibid., 342.
81. Ibid., 210.
82. Ibid., 139, 478.
83. John Joseph Henry, *Account of Arnold's Campaign Against Quebec,* 20–21.
84. Samuel Harvard Barboo, "A Historical Review of the Hygiene of Shipboard Food Service in the

United States Navy, 1775–1965"
(Ph.D. diss., University of California, 1967), 1–2.

85. "Low-Down on Chow-Down." *All Hands*, no. 375 (May 1948): 3.

86. J.H. Skillman, "Eating Through the Years," *U.S. Naval Institute Proceedings*, March 1941, 362.

87. Boyle, 190.

88. Naval Historical Center, "Navy Birthday Information — 13 October 1775," http://www.history.navy.mil/birthday.htm.

89. JCC, 3: 293–294.

90. "Navy Birthday Information."

91. JCC, 3: 380.

92. Ibid., 380, 383.

93. Ibid., 380–381.

94. Ibid., 383.

95. Samuel Eliot Morison, *John Paul Jones: A Sailor's Biography*, 78.

96. Barboo, 14.

97. Morison, 107.

98. Ibid., 133, 264.

99. Barboo, 18.

Chapter 2

1. JCC, 27: 53: 530–531.

2. "History of Rations."

3. American State Papers: Military Affairs 1: 284.

4. Ibid., 1: 285.

5. Erna Risch, *Quartermaster Support of the Army, 1775–1939*, 76, 135, 136.

6. Ibid., 142.

7. Annals of Congress, 13th Cong., 3rd sess., 550–551.

8. Ibid., 599–600.

9. American State Papers: Military Affairs 1: 600.

10. Ibid.

11. Ibid., 600–601.

12. Ibid.

13. Robert Fantina, *Desertion and the American Soldier, 1776–2006*, 33.

14. Donald Graves, ed., *Soldiers of 1814: American Enlisted Men's Memoirs of the Niagara Campaign*, 5, 7, 12.

15. Ibid., 12.

16. Harlow Lindley, ed., *Fort Meigs and the War of 1812, Orderly Book of Cushing's Company and Personal Diary of Captain Daniel Cushing*, 11–12.

17. Graves, 23, 25, 46.

18. Ibid., 58–59.

19. Ibid., 63.

20. Lindley, preface.

21. "Fort Meigs," Ohio's War of 1812 Battlefield Museum, http://fortmeigs.org/history.htm.

22. Lindley, 20, 32.

23. Ibid., 71.

24. Ibid., 90, 94, 103.

25. Ibid., 121.

26. Ibid., 123, 126.

27. "Navy Birthday."

28. Naval Historical Center, "Reestablishment of the Marine Corps," http://www.history.navy.mil/faqs/faq59-16.htm.

29. Act of March 27, 1794, ch. 2, Stat, 350.

30. Ibid., ch. 12, 1 Stat, 351.

31. J.H. Skillman, "Eating Through the Years," *U.S. Naval Institute Proceedings*, March 1941, 363.

32. "A History of the Navy Supply Corps," *Navy Supply Corps Newsletter* 33, no. 2 (February 1970): 13.

33. "Constellation — A Stellar History," U.S.S Constellation CVA/CA-64 Association, http://www.ussconstellation.org/constellation_history.html.

34. Thomas Truxtun, "A Short Account of the Several General Duties of Officers, of Ships of War," Naval Historical Center, http://www.history.navy.mil/faqs/faq59-2.htm.

35. Ibid.

36. "A History of the Navy Supply Corps," 12.

37. Naval Historical Center, "Navy Regulation, 1814," http://www.history.navy.mil/faqs/faq59-19.htm.

38. Mark Hilliard, "Biscuits, Bugs, & Broadsides," 1812 U.S. Marines & Navy Progressive Campaign Oriented Living Historians, 4, http://www.1812usmarines.org/Home.htm.

39. Ibid., 5.

40. American State Papers: Naval Affairs 1: 252.

41. Charles A. Malin, "Rating and the Evolution of Jobs in the U.S. Navy," Naval Historical Center, http://www.history.navy.mil/faqs/faq78-1.htm.

42. Skillman, 363.

43. David Porter, Betty Shepherd, ed., *Bound for Battle*, dust jacket, 27.

44. Ibid., 28–29, 31, 35–36.

45. Ibid., 31–32, 35.

46. Ibid., 32.

47. Ibid., 37.

48. Ibid., 42, 56.

49. Ibid., 46–47, 64–65.

50. Ibid., 49.

51. Ibid., 55–56, 60.

52. Ibid., 83.

53. Ibid., 81–84, 112.

54. Naval Historical Center, "Navy Regulations, 1814," http://www.history.navy.mil/faqs/faq59-19.htm.

55. Donald L. Canney, *Lincoln's Navy*, 8.

Chapter 3

1. John W. Barriger, *Legislative History of the Subsistence Department of the United States Army*, 75.

2. Act of April 14, 1818, ch. 61, 7 Stat. 427.

3. American State Papers: Military Affairs 1: 807.

4. Ibid., 807.

5. Ibid.

6. Ibid., 781.

7. Erna Risch, *Quartermaster Support of the Army: A History of the Corps, 1775–1939*, 203.

8. American State Papers: Military Affairs 1: 781.

9. Act of July 5, 1838, ch. 162, 17 Stat. 258.

10. Act of May 13, 1846, ch. 16, 1 Stat. 9.

11. Naval Historical Center, "American War and Military Operations Casualties: Lists and Statistics," http://www.history.navy.mil/Library/online/american%20war%20casualty.htm.

12. Alvin P. Stauffer, "The Quartermaster's Department and the Mexican War." *Quartermaster Review*, May-June 1950, U.S. Quartermaster Foundation, http://www.qmfound.com/quartermaster_department_mexican_war.htm.

13. Risch, 258.

14. Ibid., 260–262.

15. Stauffer, 4.

16. John R Kenly, *Memoirs of a Maryland Volunteer*, 33–34.

17. Ibid., 33.

18. Ibid., 35.

19. Risch, 248.

20. Benjamin Franklin Scribner, *Camp Life of a Volunteer: A Campaign in Mexico; or, A Glimpse at Life in Camp by "One Who Has Seen the Elephant,"* 22, 50.

21. William H. Richardson, *Journal of William H. Richardson, A Private Soldier in the Campaign of New and Old Mexico*, 5.

22. Richard Smith Elliott, *The Mexican War Correspondence of Richard Smith Elliott*, 78.

23. Frank S.A. Edwards, *Campaign in New Mexico with Colonel Doniphan*, 17.

24. George C. Furber, *The Twelve Month Volunteer; or, Journal of a Private in the Tennessee Regiment of Cavalry, in the Campaign in Mexico, 1846–1847*, 53.

25. Elliott, 78.

26. Richardson, 10.

27. Ibid., 12.

28. Ibid., 13.

29. Ibid., 15.

30. Ibid.

31. Richardson, 28.

32. Ibid., 35.

33. Edwards, 12.

34. Scribner, 23.

35. Richardson, 11.

36. Kenly, 62–63.

37. Risch, 248.

38. Edwards, 45–46.

39. Elliott, 92.

40. Richardson, 29.

41. Ibid., 30.

42. Ibid., 31.

43. James M. McCaffrey, *The Mexican War Letters of Lieutenant Theodore Laidley*, 75.

44. Elliott, 87.

45. Richard Bruce Winders, *Polk's Army: The American Military Experience in the Mexican War*, 18.

46. Richardson, 55.

47. Elliott, 88.

48. Richardson, 24.

49. Ibid., 34.

50. Risch, 248.

51. Donald L. Canney, *Lincoln's Navy*, 9–10.

52. Ibid., 11.

53. American State Papers: Naval Affairs 1: 518.

54. Ibid., 1: 527.

55. Ibid., 1: 528.

56. Ibid.

57. Act of August 26, 1842, ch. 206, 1 Stat. 535.

58. "History of the Navy Supply Corps," *Navy Supply Corps Newsletter* 33, no. 2 (February 1970): 14.

59. Act of August 29, 1842, ch. 267, 1–3 Stat. 546–547.

60. Act of August 29, 1842, ch. 267, 5 Stat. 547.

61. Act of August 31, 1842, ch. 286, 1–2 Stat. 579.

62. "History of the Navy Supply Corps," *Navy Supply Corps Newsletter* 33, no. 2 (February 1970): 14.

63. George Jones, *Sketches of a Naval Life with Notices of Men, Manners, and Scenery on the Shores of the Mediterranean*, 99–100.

64. Ibid., 101–102.

65. Ibid., 192.

66. Ibid.

67. Ibid., 192–193.

68. Ibid., 194.

69. E. E. Wines, *Two Years and a Half in the Navy: or, Journal of a Cruise in the Mediterranean and Levant on Board of the U.S. Frigate Constellation*, 17, 48–49.

70. Ibid., 49.

71. Ibid., 152–153.

72. Herman Melville, *White Jacket, or the World on a Man-of-War*, 409.

73. Ibid., 410–411.

74. Ibid., 486.

75. Charles Nordoff, *Man-of-War Life*, 29–30.

76. Ibid., 36.

77. Ibid., 45, 46.

78. Ibid., 47.

79. Ibid., 47–48.

80. Ibid., 69.

81. Ibid., 111.

82. Ibid., 111–113, 199, 187.

83. Ibid., 113.

84. Ibid., 114, 116.

85. Ibid., 119.

86. Ibid.

87. Ibid., 155.

88. Melville, 647–648.

89. Ibid., 648.

Chapter 4

1. United States Army, *American Military History*, 195–196.

2. War Department, *Revised Regulations for the Army of the United States 1861*, 243.

3. Ibid.

4. Eban Horsford, *The Army Ration of 1864*, 10–11.

5. Ibid.

6. Henry G. Sharpe, "The Art of Supplying Armies in the Field as Exemplified during the Civil War," *Journal of the Military Science Institute*, January 1896, 72, 48.

7. Ibid., 51–53.

8. War Department, *How to Feed an Army*, 24, 38–39.

9. H.G. Sharpe, 57–58, 63, 65.

10. Ibid., 79.

11. *How to Feed*, 8–9, 61, 82.

12. Henry Pippitt, Schoff Civil War Collections, Clements Library, University of Michigan, 10-31-64.

13. George W. Barr, George W. Barr Papers, Schoff Civil War Collections, Clements Library, University of Michigan. 6-21-62.

14. Solomon Starbird, Schoff Civil War Collections, Clements Library, University of Michigan. 8-30-63.

15. John D. Billings, *Hard Tack and Coffee, or the Unwritten Story of Army Life*, 134–135.

16. Revised Reg. Army 1861, 37.

17. Bell Irvin Wiley, *The Life of Billy Yank*, 232.

18. Billings, 224–226.

19. Philip Hacker, Hacker Brother Papers, Schoff Civil War Collections, Clements Library, University of Michigan, 3-13-62.

20. Henry Grimes Marshall, Schoff Civil War Collections, Clements Library, University of Michigan, 10-11-62.

21. Pippitt, 2-3-64.

22. Edwin C. Burbank, Schoff Civil War Collections, Clements Library, University of Michigan, 11-14-62.

23. V.H. Moats, Virgil Henry Moats Papers, Schoff Civil War Collections, Clements Library, University of Michigan, 9-25-62.

24. J.L. Smith, comp., *History of the 118th Pennsylvania Volunteers Corn Exchange Regiment*, 34.

25. Edward P. Bridgeman, Schoff Civil War Collections, Clements Library, University of Michigan, July 1863.

26. Marshall, 9-14-62.

27. George Starbird, Schoff Civil War Collections, Clements Library, University of Michigan, 8-31-62.

28. David McKinney, David McKinney Papers, Schoff Civil War Collections, Clements Library, University of Michigan, 10-27-65, 11-24-65.

29. Marshall J. Pixley," The Adams Express Company," http://www.floridareenactorsonline.com/adamsexpress.htm.

30. William C. Jones, William C. Jones Papers. Schoff Civil War Collections, Clements Library, University of Michigan, 10-10-62.

31. Pippitt, 5-16-64, 5-19-64, 5-24-64.

32. William C. Davis, *A Taste for War: The Culinary History of the Blue and the Gray*, 7–9.

33. Davis, 8–9.

34. James M. Sanderson, *Camp Fires and Camp Cooking: or Culinary Hints for the Soldier*, 4.

35. Ibid., 5.

36. Billings, 134, 136.

37. Bridgeman, September 1862.

38. Moats, 2-11-62.

39. Billings, 135.

40. Soloman Starbird, 9-13-62.

41. Mary A. Livermore, *My Story of the War*, 131.

42. Ibid., 132.

43. Charles J. Stillé, *History of the United States Sanitary Commission*, 326–327, 330–331, 339.

44. Lemuel Moss, *Annals of the United States Christian Commission*, 654, 547.

45. Ibid., 547.

46. Ibid., 663, 665, 670.

47. Annie Wittenmyer, *Special Diet Kitchens in Military Hospitals*, intr.

48. "Annie Wittenmyer, "Annie Wittenmyer," Quad City Memory-Local History, Davenport Public Library, http://www.qcmemory.org/page/AnnieWittenmyer.aspx?nt=231.

49. Moss, 445–446.

50. L.P. Brockett and Mary C.

Vaughan, *Woman's Work in the Civil War*, 111, 115.

51. Ibid., 117, 118–119, 120, 128.

52. Pilgrim Hall Museum, "Thanksgiving Proclamations" http://www.pilgrimhall.org/thankpro.htm.

53. Frank B. Goodrich, *The Tribute Book*, 431–432.

54. Ibid., 434, 438–439.

55. Robert O. Zinnen, "City Point: The Tool That Gave General Grant Victory," *Quartermaster Professional Bulletin*, Spring 1991, 7, www.qmfound.com/citypt.htm.

56. Frank J. Allston, *Ready for Sea*, 79–80.

57. Editors of Time-Life Books, *The Blockade: Runners and Raiders*, 10, 20.

58. Norvelle W. Sharpe, "Salt Horse to Sirloin," *U.S. Naval Institute Proceedings* 80, no. 5, whole no. 615 (May 1954): 515.

59. Act of July 18, 1861, Ch. 7, 1 Stat. 264–265.

60. Ibid., 2–4 Stat. 265.

61. Ibid., 5 Stat. 265.

62. Ibid., 7 Stat. 265.

63. J.H. Skillman, "Eating Through the Years," 365.

64. Act of July 14, 1862, Ch. 164, 4 Stat., 565.

65. Norvelle Sharp, "Salt Horse to Sirloin," 515.

66. James Merrill, *The Rebel Shore: The Story of Union Sea Power in the Civil War*, 56, 57.

67. Dennis Ringle, personal phone communication, February 20, 2009.

68. Allston, 81.

69. Dennis Ringle, *Life in Mr. Lincoln's Navy*, 64, 66.

70. Ibid., 70, 73, 74, 76.

71. Frederick Keeler, *Letters of Paymaster William Frederick Keeler, U.S. Navy*, 41.

72. Alva Folsom Hunter, *A Year on a Monitor and the Destruction of Fort Sumter*, 11.

73. Ibid., 36.

74. Ibid., 42–43.

75. Henry R. Browne and Symmes E. Brown, *From the Fresh-Water Navy: 1861–64, The Letters of Acting Master's Mate Henry R. Browne and Acting Ensign Symmes E. Browne*, 215, 218, 219.

76. Bell Irvin Wiley, *The Plain People of the Confederacy*, 4–5.

77. Carlton McCarthy, *Detailed Minutiae of Soldier Life in the Army of the Northern Virginia*, 57.

78. Ibid., 63.

79. J.F.J. Caldwell, *The History of a Brigade of South Carolinians First Known as "Gregg's" and Subsequently as "McGowan's Brigade,"* 52–53.

80. Randolph H. McKim, *A Soldier's Recollections: Leaves from the Diary of a Young Confederate*, 42.

81. Marcus B. Toney, *The Privations of a Private*, 20.

82. McKim, 42–43.

83. Ibid., 43.

84. Dorothy Denneen and James M. Volo, *Daily Life in Civil War America*, 116.

85. Caldwell, 202.

86. Volo and Volo, 128.

87. McCarthy, 59.

88. The Law Offices of Mark B. Tackitt and Eviction Services.com, "Flying Dutchman, Confederate Coffee Substitutes," http://44tennessee.tripod.com/dutchman/jan0002.html.

89. Solomon Starbird, 9-30-63.

90. Toney, 70–71.

91. McCarthy, 63–64.

92. Ibid., 62.

93. McCarthy, 71, 67.

94. Caldwell, 254–255.

95. Pippett, 7-11-64.

96. William Speed, Schoff Civil War Collections, Clements Library, University of Michigan, 6-16-63.

97. J.L. Underwood, *The Women of the Confederacy*, 70.

98. Mrs. A.T. Smythe, et al., eds., *South Carolina Women in the Confederacy*, intr.

99. Ibid., 86, 88.

100. Ibid., 137.

101. Ibid., 151.

102. Ibid., 218.

103. Phoebe Pember, *A Southern Woman's Story*.

104. Jan Longone, personal e-mail communication, May 18, 2009.

105. Reynolds Historical Library, University of Alabama at Birmingham, "Major Figures in Civil War Medicine: Julian John Chisolm," http://www.uab.edu/reynolds/CivilWarMedFigs/Chisolm.htm.

106. Julian John Chisolm, *A Manual of Military Surgery*, preface.

107. Ibid., 35.

108. Tom Henderson Wells, "The Confederate Navy, A Study in Organization" (Ph.D. diss., Emory University, 1963), 91–93.

109. Ibid., 92.

110. ORN, Series II, vol. 2, August 25, 1863, Navy Agent W.F. Howell to Paymaster John DeBree, 557, courtesy of Cornell University Library, Making of America Digital Collection.

111. Ibid.

112. Ibid., 557–558.

113. Ibid., 558.

114. ORN, Series II, vol. 2, November 14, 1863, Paymaster De Bree to Mallory, 553, courtesy of Cornell

University Library, Making of America Digital Collection.

115. ORN, Series II, vol. 2, October 18, 1864, Paymaster James A. Semple to Mallory, 762.

116. Wells, 96.

Chapter 5

1. Erna Risch, *Quartermaster Support of the Army: A History of the Corps, 1775–1939*, 468; Richard W. Stewart, ed., *American Military History*, vol. 1, *The United States Army and Forging a Nation, 1775–1917*, 324.

2. Risch, 468.

3. Stewart, 324.

4. Risch, 301.

5. Stewart, 322–323.

6. Risch, 306.

7. Ibid., 309–310.

8. Elizabeth B. Custer, *Tenting on the Plains*, 222.

9. Richard E. Killbane, *Circle the Wagons: The History of US Army Convoy Security*, 4–5.

10. Percival G. Lowe, *Five Years a Dragoon*, 234.

11. *General Regulations for the Army of the United States, 1841*, Article XXIII, paragraph 1102.

12. Ibid., Article XXIII, paragraph 96.

13. United States War Department, *Revised Regulations for the Army of the United States, 1861*, Article 43, section 1101, 1191, 213, 241, 243.

14. Ibid., section 1181, 211.

15. Martha Summerhayes, *Vanished Arizona*, 90–91.

16. Ibid., 97.

17. Custer, 518.

18. Francis M.A. Roe, *Army Letters From an Officer's Wife*, 28.

19. Barbara K. Luecke, *Feeding the Frontier Army*, 41.

20. Ibid., 115–116.

21. Ibid., 41.

22. Francis Paul Prucha, ed., *Army Life on the Western Frontier: Selections from the Official Reports Made Between 1826 and 1845 by Colonel George Croghan*, 65.

23. Ibid., 66.

24. Risch, 315.

25. Prucha, 67.

26. Ibid., 68.

27. United States War Dept., Quarter Master General's Office. *Outline Description of U.S. Military Posts and Stations in the Year 1871*.

28. Roe, 73.

29. Don Rickey, Jr., *Forty Miles a Day on Beans and Hay*, 98.

30. E.A. Bode, *A Dose of Frontier Soldiering: the Memoirs of Corporal E.A. Bode, Frontier Regular Infantry,*

1877–1882, Thomas T. Smith, ed., www.questia.com, 66.

31. Ibid., 65.

32. Ibid., 49; Fort Scott National Historic Site, "Cooking Overview," http://www.nps.gov/archive/fosc/cooking3.htm.

33. Bode, 42.

34. Rickey, 121.

35. Frances C. Carrington, *My Army Life*, 105–106.

36. Ami Frank Mulford, *Fighting Indians in the 7th United States Cavalry*, 43.

37. Risch, 587.

38. Rickey, 82.

39. Sally Johnson Ketchum, *The Bake House, Fort Scott, Kansas: Furnishing Plan*, 2.

40. Ketchum, 5.

41. Rickey, 79.

42. Ibid., 118–119.

43. Ibid. 119.

44. Mulford, 97.

45. Ibid.

46. Summerhayes, 92.

47. Elizabeth B. Custer, *Following the Guidon*, 16.

48. Mulford, 69.

49. George A. Forsyth, *The Story of a Soldier*, 165.

50. Mulford, 62.

51. Ibid., 72–73.

52. Ibid., 75, 109.

53. Ibid., 79.

54. Ibid., 116.

55. Augustus Meyers, *Ten Years in the Ranks of the U.S. Army*, 95.

56. Ibid., 97.

57. Ibid., 100.

58. Ibid.

59. Philippe Regis Denis de Keredern de Trobriand, *Army Life in Dakota, Selection form the Journal of Philippe Regis Denis de Keredern de Trobriand*, www.questia.com/reader/printPaginator/111, 226.

60. William Murphy, "Winning the West for the Nation," http://www.rootsweb.ancestry.com/~wysherid/forts/murhpy-6-7-28.htm.

61. War Department, *Outline Description of U.S. Military Posts and Stations in the Year 1871*, 221, 231.

62. Mulford, 116–117.

63. Meyers, 95–96.

64. Ibid., 96.

65. Stewart, 339.

66. Risch, 506.

67. Ibid.

68. Ibid.

69. War Department, *General Orders 1890*, GO 78, 25 July, 1890.

70. Stewart, 339.

Chapter 6

1. Richard W. Stewart, ed. *American Military History*, vol. 1, *The United States Army and Forging a Nation, 1775–1917*, 343.

2. Ibid., 342.

3. Erna Risch, *Quartermaster Support of the Army: A History of the Corps, 1775–1939*, 535.

4. Charles Johnson Post, *The Little War of Private Post: The Spanish-American War Seen up Close*, 239.

5. Charles F. Gauvreau, *Reminiscences of the Spanish-American War in Cuba and the Philippines*, 29, 35.

6. United States War Department, *Manual for Army Cooks, 1896*, 47–48.

7. Ibid., 216–217.

8. N.N. Freeman, *A Soldier in the Philippines*, 12.

9. Post, 48.

10. Stewart, 349.

11. Risch, 548.

12. Herbert Omando Kohr, *Around the World with Uncle Sam; or, Six Years in the United States Army*, 56.

13. Post, 87.

14. Freeman, 21.

15. Gauvreau, 36.

16. Ibid., 37.

17. Ibid.

18. Trumbull White, *Pictorial History of Our War with Spain for Cuba's Freedom*, 538.

19. Gauvreau, 46.

20. White, 540.

21. Gauvreau, 48.

22. White, 551.

23. Post, 15–16.

24. Gauvreau, 110.

25. Ibid., 114.

26. Ibid., 137.

27. Freeman, 40.

28. Ibid., 48.

29. Ibid., 54.

30. Kohr, 102–103.

31. Ibid., 120.

32. Ibid.

33. Gauvreau, 110.

34. Risch, 567.

35. *Annual Report of the War Department, 1903*, Vol. I, 491.

36. White, 554.

37. American Red Cross, "The American Red Cross in the Spanish-American War." http://www.redcross.org/museum/spanishAmWar.asp.

38. Freeman, 16.

39. Ibid., 19.

40. R.A. Alger, *The Spanish-American War*, 406.

41. Risch, 531.

42. Grenville M. Dodge, James A. Sexton, and Charles Denby, *Report of the Commission Appointed by the President to Investigate the Conduct of the War Department in the War with Spain*, 51.

43. Alger, 383–384.

44. Ibid., 382–383.

45. United States War Department, *Food Furnished by Subsistence Department to Troops during the Spanish-American War — Record of a Court of Inquiry*, 1885.

46. Ibid., 1886.

47. Ibid., 1889.

48. Ibid., 1865.

49. Ibid., 1889.

50. Ibid.

51. Ibid., 1885.

52. Ibid., 1889–1893.

53. "A History of the Navy Supply Corps," *Navy Supply Corps Newsletter* 33, no. 2 (February 1970): 14.

54. Ibid., 14–15.

55. Skillman, 365.

56. Allston, 102, 105, 116–117.

57. Ibid., 118.

58. Benton C. Decker, "The Consolidated Mess of the Crew of the U.S.S. Indiana," *U.S. Naval Institute Proceedings* 23, no. 3 whole no. 83 (1897): 566–567.

59. Allston, 124–125.

60. Decker, 463.

61. Ibid., 464.

62. "History of the Navy Supply Corps," 15.

63. Decker, 465.

64. Ibid., 466.

65. Ibid.

66. Ibid., 571.

67. George Oscar Paullin, *Paullin's History of Naval Administration 1775–1911*, 445, 452.

68. Ibid., 450.

69. Ibid.

70. Allston, 125.

71. George W. Robinson, "The Diary of George W. Robinson," contributed by Sean Cox, Spanish American War Centennial Website. http://www.spanamwar.com/Oregondiary1.htm.

72. Ibid.

73. Ibid.

74. Ibid.

75. Ibid.

76. Bertram Willard Edwards, "The Diary of Bertram Willard Edwards, Contributed by Susan Abbe, transcribed by Jack L. McSherry, Spanish American War Centennial Website, http://www.spanamwar.com/Oregonedwardsdiary1.htm.

77. Ibid.

78. Ibid.

79. Ibid.

80. Frederick T. Wilson, *A Sailor's Log: Frederick T. Wilson, USN, on*

Asiatic Station, 1899–1901, introduction.

81. Wilson, 23.
82. Ibid., 26.
83. Ibid., 30.
84. Ibid., 42.
85. Ibid., 43, 31.
86. Ibid., 46.
87. Ibid., 66.
88. Ibid., 113–114.
89. Ibid., 123–124.
90. Ibid., 341–342.

Chapter 7

1. Richard W. Stewart, ed., *American Military History*, vol. 2, *The United States Army in a Global Era, 1917–2003*, 18.
2. Ibid., 20.
3. Erna Risch, *Quartermaster Support of the Army: A History of the Corps, 1775–1939*, 613.
4. Ibid., 614.
5. Ibid.; United States Food Administration, *Food and the War*, 54–220.
6. Risch, 614.
7. *War Department Annual Reports, 1918*, vol. 1, "Report of the Quartermaster General," 303.
8. Henry G. Sharpe, *The Quartermaster Corps in the Year 1917 in the World War*, 96.
9. U.S. Army Quartermaster Foundation, *Rations*, Conference Notes prepared by the Quartermaster School for the Quartermaster General, 5. http://www.qmfound.com/history_of_rations.htm.
10. United States War Department, *Regulations for the Army of the United States*, 1901, 188.
11. Ibid., 189.
12. Ibid., 187.
13. Ibid., 189–190.
14. Risch, 586.
15. Ibid.; *Rations*, 5; Sharpe, 306.
16. Benedict Crowell, *America's Munitions, 1917–1918*, 439.
17. L.L. Deitrick, *Manual for Army Cooks, 1916*, 24.
18. Franz A. Kohler, *Special Rations for the Armed Forces, 1946–53*, 12–13.
19. Crowell, 445.
20. Kohler, 12.
21. Crowell, 450.
22. *Stars and Stripes*, September 6, 1918, 1.
23. United States War Department, *War Department Annual Reports, 1902*, vol. 1, "Report of the Commissary General," 554.
24. L.L. Deitrick, *Manual for Army Bakers, 1916*, 80–83.
25. Ibid., 64, 103–104.

26. Sharpe, 113.
27. Ibid., 114.
28. Ibid., 121.
29. Ibid., 118–120.
30. Wayne O. Kester, "Army Food Inspection," *Canadian Journal of Comparative Medicine* 2, no. 12, 301–306, http://www.ncbi.nlm.nih.gov/pmc/articles/PMC1702054/.
31. Shipley Thomas, *The History of the A.E.F.*, 411.
32. Risch, 655.
33. Ibid., 656–660.
34. War Department, *Historical Report of the Chief Engineer, American Expeditionary Forces*, 297.
35. Risch, 663.
36. Ibid.
37. War Department, *Historical Report*, 362.
38. Risch, 666.
39. Crowell, 443.
40. Ibid., 487–489.
41. Ibid., 480.
42. Ibid., 481.
43. Sharpe, 314.
44. Risch, 685.
45. Risch, 686.
46. *Stars and Stripes*, June 28, 1918, 2.
47. Ibid.
48. Ibid.
49. Ibid.
50. Ibid.
51. Risch, 672.
52. *Stars and Stripes*, August 23, 1918, 8.
53. Ibid.
54. Crowell, 447.
55. Risch, 671.
56. Franz A. Koehler, *Coffee for the Armed Forces: Military Development and Conversion to Industry Supply*, 16.
57. The Doughboy Center, "History of the Salvation Army in World War I." The Great War Society. http://www.worldwar1.com/dbc/salvhist.htm.
58. American Red Cross, "World War I Accomplishments of the American Red Cross," 3 http://www.redcross.org/museum.history/wwla.asp.
59. National World War I Museum, "Candy, Coffee, and a Smile," 3, http://www.theworldwar.org/s/110/new/index.aspx?sid=110&gid=1&pgid=1063.
60. Joe Mitchell Chapple, *"We'll Stick to the Finish!"* 151.
61. *Stars and Stripes*, July 19, 1918, 3.
62. Anthony D. Cone, "Battery 'E' Goes to War: Extracts from the War Time Diary of First Sergeant Anthony D. Cone," *The Field Artillery Journal* 21, no. 1, 43.

63. The Doughboy Center, "History of the Salvation Army in World War I," 4.
64. Evangeline Booth and Grace Livingston Hill, *The War Romance of the Salvation Army*, 194.
65. The Doughboy Center, "History of the Salvation Army in World War I," 4.
66. *Stars and Stripes*, October 25, 1918, 4.
67. William Howard Taft and Frederick Harris, et. al., eds., *Service with the Fighting Men*, vol. 1, 564.
68. Ibid., 529.
69. Ibid., 530–531.
70. The Doughboy Center, "The History of the Knights of Columbus in World War I," http://www.worldwar1.com/dbc/knightsc.htm.
71. Edwin H. Simmons and Joseph H. Alexander, *Through the Wheat*, 123.
72. Kemper F. Cowing, *Dear Folks at Home—*, 152.
73. William Matthews and Dixon Wecter, *Our Soldiers Speak*, 296.
74. Robert K. Brady Papers, Western Historical Manuscript Collection—Columbia, University of Missouri.
75. John G. Westover Papers, Western Historical Manuscript Collection—Columbia, University of Missouri.
76. Brady Papers.
77. *Stars and Stripes*, November 22, 1918, 4.
78. Edward Van Winkle Collection, William L. Clements Library, The University of Michigan.
79. Ibid.
80. Westover Papers.
81. Matthews and Wecter, 300.
82. G. F. Doriot, "Subsistence Research Laboratory," http://www.qmfound.com/sublab.htm.
83. Kohler, *Special Rations*, 14.
84. Ibid., 14–15.
85. Ibid.
86. J.H. Skillman, "Eating Through the Years," 365.
87. J.W. Crumpacker, "Supplying the Fleet for 150 Years," *U.S. Naval Institute Proceedings* 71, no. 6, whole no. 508 (June 1945): 707.
88. Ibid.
89. George P. Dyer, "The Modern General Mess," *U.S. Naval Institute Proceedings* 32, no. 2, whole no. 118 (June 1906): 621.
90. Ibid., 624–630.
91. Ibid., 633.
92. Ibid., 635.
93. Crumpacker, 709.
94. Allston, *Ready for Sea*, 138–139.

95. Sharpe, "Salt Horse to Sirloin," 516.
96. Paymaster General, *General Mess Manual and Cookbook* (1902), 6.
97. Ibid., 15–16.
98. Josephus Daniels, *Our Navy at War*, 354, 355.
99. Ibid., 77.
100. Ibid., 351.
101. Allston, 159–160.
102. Allston, 162, 163, 174.
103. Michael C. Besch, *A Navy Second to None: The History of U.S. Naval Training in World War I*, 54, 90.
104. Ibid., 67.
105. Ibid., 144–145.
106. Ibid., 184.
107. Philadelphia War History Committee, *Philadelphia in the World War, 1914–1919*, 329–330.
108. Ibid., 331.
109. Besch, 127.
110. *New York Times*, December 30, 1917.
111. Joseph Husband, *A Year in the Navy*, 19–20, 41–42.
112. Ibid., 79.
113. Ibid., 91.
114. Ibid., 131.
115. Ibid., 144–145, 152.
116. Reginald J. Johnson Papers, John L. Clements Library, University of Michigan, June 18, 1917, July 1, 1917, July 4, 1917.
117. Ibid., March 8, 1918, July 29, 1918, November 28, 1918.
118. Lloyd Brown, Veterans History Project, Library of Congress.
119. Daniels, 249.
120. National Archives and Records Administration, "U.S. Food Administrator," Hoover Online! http://www.ecommcode.com/hoover/hooveronline/hoover_bio/food.htm.
121. Ida Clyde Clark, *American Women and the World War*, 17, 24–25.
122. United States Food Administration, *War Economy in Food with Suggestions and Recipes for Substitutions in the Planning of Meals*, 7–9.
123. Ibid., 9–10.
124. United States Food Administration, "Victory Breads," np.
125. United States Food Administration, *War Economy*, 11.
126. Charles Lathrop Pack, *The War Garden Victorious*, 2–5.
127. Ibid., 8–9.
128. Ibid., 23.
129. Ibid., 24, 30, 31.
130. Skillman, 366–367.
131. Crumpacker, 709.
132. "Low Down on Chow Down," 5.

133. Barboo, 94.
134. E.D. Foster, *Cafeteria Afloat*, 19.
135. Ibid., 20, 19, 21–23.

Chapter 8

1. Richard W. Stewart, ed. *American Military History*, vol. 2, *The United States Army in a Global Era, 1917–2003*, 71.
2. Franz A. Koehler, *Special Rations for the Armed Forces, 1946–1953*, 16.
3. Hershey Community Archives, "Ration D Bars," 1, http://www.hersheyarchives.org/essay/printable.aspx?EssayId=26.
4. Koehler, 16.
5. Hershey Community Archives, "Ration D Bars," 2.
6. Koehler, 17–18; Erna Risch, *The United States Army in World War II — The Technical Services: The Quartermaster Corps: Organization, Supply, and Services*, vol. 1, 180–181.
7. Risch, 184.
8. Renita Foster, "The Best Army Invention Ever," Army Public Affairs, U.S. Army, http://www.army.mil/-news/2009/08/11/25736-the-best-army-invention-ever/.
9. Risch, 182.
10. Ibid., 181.
11. Ibid., 184–185.
12. William Hoffman, "Meet Monsieur Cholesterol," http://www.mbbnet.umn.edu/hoff_ak.html.
13. Ibid.
14. Risch, 185.
15. Koehler, 26.
16. Ibid.
17. Koehler, 25, note 39.
18. Hoffman.
19. Koehler, 27.
20. Ibid., 29.
21. William F. Ross and Charles R. Romanus, *The Quartermaster Corps: Operations in the War Against Germany*, 131.
22. Koehler, 32.
23. Risch, 191–192.
24. Koehler, 32–33.
25. Ibid., 34–37.
26. Ibid., 39.
27. Ibid., 40–42.
28. United States War Department, *The Army Cook*, 103–105.
29. Hormel Foods, "Fact Sheet: SPAM Family of Products—World War II," http://www.hormelfoods.com/newsroom/brandinfo/SPAMFamilyOfProductsWWWIIFS.aspx.
30. Bruce Heydt, "Spam Again," *America in World War II*, http://www.americawwii.com/stories/spamagain.html.

31. Herbert R. Rifkind, *Fresh Foods for the Armed Forces*, 23.
32. Ibid.
33. Ibid., 31; Risch, 39.
34. Rifkind, 31, 43.
35. Ibid., 54–55.
36. Ibid., 61.
37. Risch, 194.
38. Ibid., 201.
39. Ibid., 39–40.
40. Ward B. Cleaves, "Food Service Program," *Quartermaster Review*, July-August 1945, http://www.qmmuseum.lee.army.mil/WWII/food_service_program.htm.
41. United States Merchant Marines, "War Shipping Administration," http://www.usmm.org/ww2.html.
42. Erna Risch, *United States Army in World War II — The Technical Services: The Quartermaster Corps: Organization, Supply, and Services*, vol. 2, 322.
43. Scott D. Trostel, *Angels at the Station*, iv.
44. Bob Greene, *Once Upon a Town*, 6–8.
45. Risch, vol. 2, 270.
46. Ibid., 271.
47. Franz A. Koehler, *Coffee for the Armed Forces: Military Development and Conversion to Industry Supply*, 19.
48. Ibid., 19, 53.
49. Ibid., 31.
50. United States War Department, *Cooking Dehydrated Foods*, TM 10-406, III.
51. Risch, vol. I, 145–149.
52. Ibid., 149–450.
53. Kansas Historical Society, "Coleman Portable Stove," http://www.kshs.org/cool2/colemanstove.htm.
54. Alvin P. Stauffer, *The Quartermaster Corps: Operations in the War Against Japan*, 227.
55. Risch, vol. 1, 151.
56. Ibid., 153.
57. Stauffer, 231.
58. War Department, *Mess Management and Training*, 36.
59. Ross and Romanus, 527.
60. Ibid., 522.
61. Stauffer, 302.
62. Steven Anders, "Bundles from the Sky," *Quartermaster Professional Bulletin*, Autumn-Winter, 1994, 43.
63. Ross and Romanus, 141.
64. Ibid., 142–143.
65. Ibid., 512–513, 514–515.
66. Stauffer, 103–104.
67. Ibid., 120.
68. Ibid., 127–128.
69. Ross and Romanus, 294.
70. Stauffer, 130–132.
71. Risch vol. 1, 157–159.

72. Terrence H. Witkowski, "World War II Poster Campaigns," *Journal of Advertising* 32, no. 1 (Spring 2003): 79.

73. Wessels Living History Farm, York, NE, "Farming in the 1940s: Victory Gardens," http://www.livinghistoryfarm.org/farminginthe40s/crops_02.html.

74. George Korson, *At His Side: The Story of the American Red Cross Overseas in World War II*, 278.

75. Ibid., 219.

76. Ibid., 165.

77. USO, "History of the USO" http://www.uso.org/whoweare/our proudhistory/historyoftheuso/.

78. Jim Boan, *Rising Sun Sinking*, 7.

79. Everett Farmer, personal interview, November 2, 2009.

80. Ibid.

81. Boan, 28.

82. Farmer interview.

83. Frederick Lafferty Papers, William L. Clements Library, The University of Michigan.

84. Paul Alexa Collection (AFC/2001/001/1025), Veterans History Project, American Folklife Center, Library of Congress.

85. Farmer interview.

86. Wilbert Amos Collection (AFC/2001/001/52840), Veterans History Project, American Folklife Center, Library of Congress.

87. Boan, 86.

88. Farmer interview.

89. Benjamin Armour Collection (AFC/2001/001/38025), Veterans History Project, American Folklife Center, Library of Congress.

90. Keith Burlingan Hook Papers, William L. Clements Library, The University of Michigan.

91. Paul Alexa Collection.

92. Lyndell Thomasson Highley Papers, Western Historical Manuscript Collection-Columbia, University of Missouri.

93. Farmer interview.

94. Paul Alexa Collection.

95. Gordon L. Hansen Papers, William L. Clements Library, The University of Michigan.

96. Jake Alabaster Collection (AFC/2001/001/38024), Veterans History Project, American Folklife Center, Library of Congress.

97. Robert L. Huber Papers, Western Historical Manuscript Collection — Columbia, University of Missouri.

98. Ernest, J. King, *U.S Navy at War 1941–45: Official Reports to the Secretary of the Navy*, 4, 20, 152.

99. Ibid., 155, 157.

100. Worrall Reed Carter, *Beans, Bullets, and Black Oil: The Story of Fleet Logistics Afloat in the Pacific During World War II*, 2–4.

101. Ibid., 8, 9.

102. Ibid., 46.

103. Ibid., 50–53.

104. Ibid., 60.

105. Ibid., 80.

106. Ibid., 81.

107. Ibid., 98, 102.

108. Ibid., 99–100.

109. Ibid., 100–101.

110. Julius Augustus Furer, 452.

111. Ibid., 452–453.

112. Ibid., 454–455.

113. Worrall Reed Carter and Elmer Ellsworth Duval, *Ships, Salvage, and Sinews of War*, preface.

114. Ibid., 91, 95–96.

115. Ibid., 96, 98.

116. Ibid., 96, 98.

117. Ibid., 295.

118. Ibid., 295.

119. Ibid., 296.

120. HyperWar: U.S. Navy in World War II, "U.S. Naval Activities, World War II, by State," http://ibiblio.org/hyperwar/USN/ref?USN-Act/index.html.

121. *War Training Programs World War II: Naval Training Schools*. Vol. A8. Ames: Iowa State College, 1945, 100.

122. Ibid., 101.

123. Ibid.

124. Ibid., 100.

125. Bureau of Supplies and Accounts, *The Cook Book of the United States Navy* (1945), foreword.

126. Ibid., 19.

127. Bureau of Supplies and Accounts, *The Cook Book of the United States Navy* (1944), 52.

128. Norbert Wooley Collection AFC/2001/001/760, Veterans History Project, American Folklife Center, Library of Congress.

129. Jack Haberstroh, *Swabby: World War II Enlisted Sailors Tell It Like It Was!*, 344.

130. Ibid., 440.

131. Ibid., 622.

132. Ibid., 692.

133. Ibid., 247.

134. Ibid., 592.

135. Naval History & Heritage Command, "Enlisted Rating and Jobs in the U.S. Navy," http://www.history.navy.mil/faqs/faq78-1.htm.

136. Seabee Museum and Memorial Park, "Seabee History," http://www.seabeesmuseum.com/History.html.

137. William Bradford Huie, *Can Do! The Story of the Seabees*, 30–33, 41–42.

138. Ibid., 160–161.

139. Ibid.

140. Ibid., 198–199.

141. Ibid., 121–122.

Chapter 9

1. Franz A. Koehler, *Special Rations for the Armed Forces, 1946–53*, 49.

2. Ibid., 53–57.

3. This is the term used by Natick to refer to all members of the military services.

4. Koehler, 60–73.

5. Ibid., 74–75.

6. United States Department of Defense, *Operational Rations Current and Future*, 1963, U.S. Army Natick Laboratories, 8.

7. United States Department of Defense, *Operational Rations of the Department of Defense*, 8th ed., 7–16.

8. Koehler, 89.

9. Ibid., 92.

10. Ibid., 102–104.

11. Ibid., 117.

12. United States Department of Defense. *Operational Rations Current and Future of the Department of Defense*, January 1983.

13. United States Department of Defense, *Operational Rations of the Department of Defense*, Natick Pam 30–25, 8th ed., 17.

14. Ibid., 18.

15. Ibid., 23.

16. Koehler, 125–127.

17. Ibid., 129.

18. United States Department of Defense, *Operational Rations of the Department of Defense*, Natick Pam 30–25, 4th ed., 21–22.

19. United States Department of Defense, *Operational Rations of the Department of Defense*, Natick Pam 30–25, 5th ed., 29.

20. Koehler, 163.

21. Ibid., 168–169.

22. Ibid., 174.

23. United States Department of Defense, *Operational Rations* (1983), 18.

24. United States Department of Defense, *Operational Rations*, 5th ed., 29.

25. United States Department of Defense, *Operational Rations*, 8th ed., 39, 48.

26. Koehler, 184–188.

27. Armed Forces Food and Container Institute, *Operational Rations, Ration Supplements, and Food Packets Used by the Armed Forces* (1950), 29.

28. Koehler, 303.

29. Ibid., 306.

30. Ibid., 319.

31. Ibid., 323–324.

32. United States Department of Defense, *Operational Rations*, 8th ed., 51.

33. Defense Logistics Agency, Defense Supply Center Philadelphia, "DSCP Subsistence History," http://www.dscp.dla.mil/subs/aboutsubs/history.asp.

34. Patricia A. Sigle, "BRAC and Quartermaster Reorganization," *Army Sustainment*, November-December 2009, 45–46.

35. Brian C. Keller, "Supporting the 21st Century Warrior," *Army Logistician*, January-February 2001, 134, 135.

36. Carlos N. Keith, "Field Feeding in the 21st Century," *Army Logistician*, September-October 2001, 19.

37. Irwin A. Dahl, "QM Distribution System in Korea," *The Quartermaster Review*, January-February 1954, U.S. Quartermaster Foundation, http://www.qmmuseum.lee.army.mil/korea/Distro_Korea.htm.

38. Alex N. Williams, "Subsistence Supply in Korea," *The Quartermaster Review*, January-February 1953, reprinted in *Quartermaster Professional Bulletin*, Spring 2000, 34.

39. Ibid., 36; "Logistics: Vegetable Run," *Time*, June 4, 1951, http://www.time.com/time/magazine/article/0,9171,858069,00.html.

40. Williams, 36.

41. John G. Westover, *Combat Support in Korea*, 165.

42. Ibid., 167.

43. Ibid., 168.

44. Ibid.

45. James Hays Collection (AFC/2001/001/21698), Veterans History Project, American Folklife Center, Library of Congress.

46. Richard A. Peters and Xiabing Li, *Voices of the Korean War*, 57.

47. Ibid., 58.

48. Ibid., 101.

49. Joseph M. Heiser, Jr., *Vietnam Studies, Logistic Support*, 197–199.

50. Ibid., 200.

51. Ibid., 199.

52. Robert Kattness Collection (AFC/2001/001/6500), Veterans History Project, American Folklife Center, Library of Congress.

53. Douglas Kathary Collection (AFC/2001/001/1605), Veterans History Project, American Folklife Center, Library of Congress.

54. Dave Augustyn Collection (AFC/2001/001/25923), Veterans History Project, American Folklife Center, Library of Congress.

55. Phillip Kaiser Collection (AFC/2001/001/18776), Veterans History Project, American Folklife Center, Library of Congress.

56. Edward Allen Collection (AFC/2001/001/1613), Veterans History Project, American Folklife Center, Library of Congress.

57. Ibid.

58. Richard W Stewart., ed. *American Military History*, vol. 2, *The United States Army in a Global Era, 1917–2003*, 371.

59. Frank N. Schubert and Theresa L. Kraus, eds., *The Whirlwind War: The United States Army in Operations Desert Shield and Desert Storm*, 55–56.

60. Ibid., 56.

61. Ibid., 59.

62. Ibid., 65.

63. Ibid., 66.

64. Michael Harris Collection (AFC/2001/001/18862), Veterans History Project, American Folklife Center, Library of Congress.

65. Mary K. Blanchfield, "Transportation Challenges in Afghanistan," *Army Logistician*, March-April 2005, 24.

66. James J. McDonnell and J. Ronald Novack, *Logistics Challenges in Support of Operation Enduring Freedom*, 10–11.

67. Eric Peltz, et al., "Sustainment of Army Forces in Operation Iraqi Freedom," 44–45.

68. Michael K. Pavek, "Feeding the Soldiers in Iraq," *Army Logistician*, 17–19.

69. Eric Lathrop Collection (AFC/2001/001/21748), Veterans History Project, American Folklife Center, Library of Congress.

70. Todd Walton Collection (AFC/2001/001/38931), Veterans History Project, American Folklife Center, Library of Congress.

71. Marissa Pelke Collection (AFC/2001/001/47478),Veterans History Project, American Folklife Center, Library of Congress.

72. Ibid.

73. Shannon Wilde Collection (AFC/2001/001/43989), Veterans History Project, American Folklife Center, Library of Congress.

74. James Monk Collection (AFC 2001/001/52429), Veterans History Project, American Folklife Center, Library of Congress.

75. Mark Cancian, "Contractors: The New Element of Military Force Structure," *Parameters*, 61–62.

76. Ibid., 64.

77. Ibid., 66.

78. Ibid., 70.

79. Ibid., 75.

80. Ibid., 72.

81. Defense Logistics Agency, http://www.dscp.dla.mil/sbo/subsistence.asp.

82. Ibid.; James A. Blanco, "Subsistence Prime Vendor," *Quartermaster Professional Bulletin*, Autumn 1996, 32.

83. Susan Declercq Brown and Phyllis Rhodes, "DLA: Logistics Backbone of Iraqi Freedom," *Army Logistician*, July-August 2003, 7.

84. Defense Commissary Agency, "History of U.S. Military Commissaries," http://www.commissaries.com/history.cfm.

85. Sharpe, "Salt Horse to Sirloin," 516.

86. Ibid., 516.

87. Ibid., 517.

88. Naval Historical Center, Department of the Navy, "Korean War Underway Replenishment, July–December 1950," http://www.history.navy.mil/photos/events/kowar/log-sup/unrp50-1.htm.

89. Naval Historical Center, Department of the Navy, "Trans-Pacific Logistics-Overview," http://www.history.navy.mil/photos/events/kowar/log-sup/pac-tran.htm.

90. Frank Mireless Collection AFC/2001/001/1826), Veterans History Project, American Folklife Center, Library of Congress.

91. Dale McKinley Collection AFC/2001/001/1107, Veterans History Project, American Folklife Center, Library of Congress.

92. Eldon Morrison Collection AFC/2001/001/2672, Veterans History Project, American Folklife Center, Library of Congress.

93. Wayne Rudisill Collection AFC/2001/001/311, Veterans History Project, American Folklife Center, Library of Congress.

94. Barboo, 147, 155, 135.

95. Ibid., 175–176.

96. Bob Carter, telephone interview, January 18, 2010.

97. Bill Orr, telephone interview, January 17, 2010.

98. Naval Historical Center, Department of the Navy, "Vietnam Service 1962–1973," http://www.history.navy.mil/faqs/stream/faq45-25.htm.

99. Edward J. Marolda, *The U.S. Navy in the Vietnam War: An Illustrated History*, 233, 239–240.

100. Ray Nabors, written interview, September 14, 2008.

101. Ibid.

102. Ibid.

103. Ibid.

104. Ibid.

105. Bill Monroe, e-mail interview, November 10, 2009.

106. Ibid.

107. Ibid.

108. Michael Marmon, e-mail interview October 30, 2009.
109. Ibid.
110. Ibid.
111. Naval Historical Center, Department of the Navy, "U.S. Navy in Desert Shield/Desert Storm — Bullets, Bandages and Beans," Logistics Operations, Report of Chief of Naval Operations, http://www.history.navy.mil/wars/dstorm/ds4.htm.
112. Ibid.
113. Military Sealift Command, "Overview MSC History," http://www.msc.navy.mil/N00P/overview.asp?page=history.
114. Military Sealift Command, "Naval Fleet Auxiliary Force," http://www.msc.navy.mil/pm1/.
115. Military Sealift Command, "Fact Sheet Fast Combat Support Ships-T-AOE," http://www.msc.navy.mil/factsheet/t-aoe.asp.
116. Military Sealift Command, "Naval Fleet Auxiliary Force."
117. Robert Burrell Collection AFC/2001/991/4848, Veterans History Project, American Folklife Center, Library of Congress.
118. Arkansas Inland Maritime Museum, promotional brochure.
119. Arkansas Inland Maritime Museum, "Maurice Barksdale — Ship's Cook, 1960–63. Oral History Interview," http://www.aimm.museum/oral.asp.
120. Ibid.
121. Ibid.
122. Maurice Barksdale, e-mail interview, October 29, 2009.
123. Ibid., October 26, 2009.
124. Ibid.
125. Ibid.
126. Michael Marmon, e-mail interview, January 18, 2010.
127. Ibid., October 30, 2009.
128. Ibid.
129. Ibid.
130. Ibid.
131. Joseph Mathis, e-mail interview, November 7, 2009.
132. Ibid.
133. Ibid.
134. Ibid.
135. Ibid.
136. Ibid.
137. Submarine Research Center, Submarine Cuisine, 17.
138. Ibid., 19–20, 23.
139. Jeff Baquer, "Name Change of the Mess Management Specialist (S) Rating to Culinary Specialist (CS)," The Navy Supply Corps Newsletter, March-April, 2004, 32–33.
140. Patricia A. Sigle, "BRAC and Quartermaster Reorganiza-

tion," Army Sustainment, November-December 2009, 45–46.
141. Debbie Dortch, "Finalists Identified for Best Navy Mess Award," United States Navy, http://www.navy.mil/search/display.asp?story_id=48884.
142. Marcel Barbeau, "Chef at Sea," Navy Supply Corps Newsletter, March-April 2008, 27.
143. Frank Lindell, "Navy Food Service — Improving the Quality of Life for Our Sailors," The Navy Supply Corps Newsletter, March-April 2000, 23.
144. United States Department of Defense, Operational Rations of the Department of Defense, Natick Pam 30–35, 8th edition, 37–38.
145. "Smart Galley Steams Along," The Warrior, http://www.natick.army.mil/about/pao/pubs/warrior/05/septoct/index.htm#a2.

Chapter 10

1. Elias Boudinot, Journal of Historical Recollections of American Events During the Revolutionary War, p 58.
2. Danske Dandridge, American Prisoners of the Revolution, 110–111.
3. Ibid., 113.
4. Andrew Sherburne, Memoirs of Andrew Sherburne: A Pensioner of the Navy of the Revolution, 109, http://www.archive.org/details/sherburnememoirs00sherrich.
5. Thomas Dring and Albert G. Greene, Recollections of the Jersey Prison-ship, 26, http://www.archive.org/details/jerseyprisonship00drinrich.
6. Ebenezer Fox, The Adventures of Ebenezer Fox, 102.
7. Sherburne, 111.
8. Fox, 103.
9. Ibid., 103, 104.
10. Dring, 35.
11. Ibid., 29.
12. Fox, 106.
13. Matthews and Wecter, 39.
14. Francis D. Cogliano, American Maritime Prisoners in the Revolutionary War: The Captivity of William Russell, 40, 61–62.
15. Charles, Herbert, Relic of the Revolution, 44–47.
16. Ibid., 59–60, 76.
17. Sherburne, 87.
18. Samuel White, History of the American Troops, During the Late War, 28, http://www.archive.org/details/amertroopslate00whitrich.
19. Ibid., 50.
20. Ibid., 51–53.

21. Benjamin Waterhouse and Amos G. Babcock, A Journal, of a Young Man of Massachusetts, 18 http://www.archive.org/details/journalofyoungma00waterich.
22. Ibid., 48–49, 110–111.
23. Prison Museum and Visitor Centre, "Dartmoor Prison History," http://www.dartmoor-prison.co.uk/history_of_dartmoor_prison.html.
24. Charles Andrews, The Prisoners' Memoirs, or Dartmoor Prison, 21, http://www.archive.org/details/cihm_22302.
25. Ibid., 37.
26. Ibid., 13, 14–15, 17.
27. Josiah Cobb, A Green Hand's First Cruise. 40–41, 132–133.
28. Ibid., 41–42.
29. Cassius Marcellus Clay, The Life of Cassius Marcellus Clay, 144, 150, http://book.google.com.
30. Ibid., 154, 155.
31. Francis Trevelyan Miller and Holland Thompson, eds., The Photographic History of the Civil War in Ten Volumes: Prisons and Hospitals, 24, 36, 156.
32. Ibid., 46, 48.
33. Ibid., 166, 168.
34. Ibid., 168.
35. Marcus B. Toney, The Privations of a Private, 98.
36. Ibid., p. 100–101.
37. Curtis R. Burke, "Curtis R. Burke's Civil War Journal," Indiana Magazine of History 66, no. 2 (June 1970): 121.
38. Ibid., 121.
39. Ibid., 122.
40. Ibid., 131, 128, 124.
41. Ibid., 134–135.
42. Ibid., 137.
43. Curtis R. Burke, Indiana Magazine of History 66, no. 3 (December 1970): 325, 327, 329.
44. Ibid., 360–361.
45. Alva C. Roach, The Prisoner of War, and How Treated, 47, 58, http://www.archive.org/details/prisonerofwar00roacrich.
46. Ibid.
47. Ibid., 58.
48. Ibid., 73.
49. Ibid., 73–74.
50. Ibid., 138.
51. John L. Ransom, Andersonville Diary, 14, 24. http://www.archive.org/details/andersonvilledi00ransgoog.
52. Michael Dougherty, Prison Diary of Michael Dougherty, 2, 4, 6, 10, http://www.archive.org/details/prisondiaryofmic00doug.
53. Ibid., 25.
54. John McElroy, Andersonville: A Story of Rebel Military Prisons, 130.

55. Ibid., 198–199.

56. Ibid. 341–343.

57. Patrick McSherry, "The Sinking of U.S. Navy Collier Merrimack," The Spanish American War Centennial Website, http://www.spanamwar.com/merrimac.htm.

58. Richmond Pearson Hobson, *The Sinking of the "Merrimac,"* 126, http://www.archive.org/details/sinkingmerrimac00hobsrich.

59. Ibid., 128, 138, 140.

60. Ibid., 167–168.

61. Ibid., 131.

62. Carl P. Dennett, *Prisoners of the Great War,* 15–16, 19.

63. Ibid., 20.

64. Ibid., 28.

65. Ibid., 32–33.

66. Ibid., 48–49, 53.

67. Ibid., 229–230, 231–232.

68. U.S. Department of Veterans Affairs, "Former American Prisoners of War," http://www1.va.gov/vetdata/docs/POWCY054-12-06jsmwrFINAL2.doc.

69. Harry Spiller, *American POWs in World War II,* 1.

70. Ibid., 1–4.

71. David Ferris Collection AFC-2001/001/20724, Veterans History Project, American Folklife Center, Library of Congress.

72. Ibid.

73. Glen Maddy Collection AFC/2001/001/5136, Veterans History Project, American Folklife Center, Library of Congress.

74. Spiller, 135–137.

75. Ned Handy and Kemp Battle, *The Flame Keepers,* 64–66.

76. Spiller, *American POWs in World War II,* 15.

77. Ibid., 101, 104, 106.

78. Joseph Rust Brown, *We Stole to Live,* 44.

79. Gregory F. Michno, *Death on the Hellships: Prisoners at Sea in the Pacific War,* 3, 25, 38.

80. U.S. Department of Veterans Affairs, "Former Prisoners of War."

81. Harry Spiller, *American POWs in Korea,* 1, 2.

82. Ibid., 2.

83. Ibid., 8, 11.

84. Ibid., 21.

85. Ibid., 47, 54, 55.

86. Ibid., 69.

87. Lewis H. Carlson, *Remembered Prisoners of a Forgotten War,* 125–126.

88. Paul Galanti e-mail interview, March 1, 2010; Elmo "Mo" Baker, telephone interview, March 7, 2010.

Bibliography

Books

Adams, James. *Dartmoor Prison*. Pittsburgh: Engles, 1816. http://www.archive.org/details/dartmoor prisonor00adam.

Alger, R.A. *The Spanish-American War*. New York: Harper & Brothers, 1901. http://www.books.google. com.

Allston, Frank J. *Ready for Sea*. Annapolis, MD: Naval Institute Press, 1995.

American Can Company. *Canned Food Manual*. New York: American Can, 1942.

Andrews, Charles. *The Prisoners Memoirs, or Dartmoor Prison*. New York: published by author, 1815 (1852) http://www.archive.org/details/cihm_22302.

Andros, Thomas. *The Old Jersey Captive: or, A Narrative of the Captivity of Thomas Andros*. Boston: William Peirce, 1833. Reprint, Tarrytown, NY: W. Abbatt, 1916. http://www.archive.org/details/old jerseycaptive00andrrich.

Barriger, John W. *Legislative History of the Subsistence Department of the United States Army*. Washington, DC: United States Army, 1877.

Bernhardt, Joshua. *Government Control of the Sugar Industry in the United States*. New York: Macmillan, 1920.

Besch, Michael. *A Navy Second to None: The History of the U.S. Naval Training in World War I*. Westport, CT: Greenwood Press, 2002.

Billings, John D. *Hard Tack and Coffee, or the Unwritten Story of Army Life*. Boston: Smith, 1887. Reprint, William L. Shea, ed., Lincoln: University of Nebraska Press, 1993.

Blaine, Ephraim, and Joseph Lee Boyle, eds. *My Last Shift Betwixt Us & Death: The Ephraim Blaine Letterbook*. Bowie, MD: Heritage Books, 2001.

Blake, Christopher. *Charlie Ration Cookbook*. Avery Island, LA: McIlhenny, 1966.

Boan, Jim. *Rising Sun Sinking: The Battle for Okinawa*. Austin, TX: Eakin Press, 2000.

Bode, E.A. *A Dose of Frontier Soldiering: The Memoirs of Corporal E.A. Bode, Frontier Regular Infantry, 1877–1882*. Thomas T. Smith, ed. Lincoln: University of Nebraska Press, 1994. www.questia.com.

Bolton, Charles Knowles. *The Private Soldier Under Washington*. Williamstown, MA: Corner House, 1976.

Booth, Evangeline, and Grace Livingston Hill. *The War Romance of the Salvation Army*. New York: Lippincott, 1919.

Boudinot, Elias. *Journal or Historical Recollections of American Events during the Revolutionary War*. Philadelphia: Bourquin, 1894. Reprint, LaVergne, TN: Kessinger, 2009.

Brockett, L.P., and Mary C. Vaughan. *Woman's Work in the Civil War*. Philadelphia: Zeigler, McCurdy, 1867.

Brown, Joseph Rust. *We Stole to Live*. Cape Girardeau, MO: Missouri Litho and Printing Company, 1982.

Browne, Henry R., and Symmes E. Brown. *From Fresh-Water Navy: 1831–1864, The Letters of Acting Master's Mate Henry R. Browne and Acting Ensign Symmes E. Browne*. John D. Milligan, ed. Annapolis, MD: United States Naval Institute, 1970.

Bureau of Navigation. *U.S. Navy Cook-Book: Prepared at the School for Cooks and Bakers U.S. Naval Training Station Newport, Rhode Island*. Annapolis: U.S. Naval Institute, 1908.

Bureau of Supplies and Accounts. *The Cook Book of the United States Navy*. Washington, DC: Government Printing Office, 1944.

_____. *The Cook Book of the United States Navy*. Washington, DC: Government Printing Office, 1945.

Caldwell, J.F.J. *The History of a Brigade of South Carolinians First Known as "Gregg's" and Subsequently as "McGowan's Brigade."* Lee Wallace Jr., ed. Philadelphia: King and Baird, 1866. Facsimile revised and edited, Dayton, OH: Morningside Press, 1992.

Canney, Donald L. *Lincoln's Navy*. Annapolis, MD: Naval Institute Press, 1998.

Carlson, Lewis H. *Remembered Prisoners of a Forgotten War*. New York: St. Martin's, 2002.

Carrington, Frances C. *My Army Life*. Philadelphia: Lippincott, 1910. http://www.books.google.com.

Carter, Worrall Reed. *Beans, Bullets, and Black Oil: The Story of Fleet Logistics Afloat in the Pacific during World War II*. Washington, DC: Government Printing Office, 1953.

_____, and Elmer Ellsworth Duval. *Ships, Salvage, and Sinews of War*. Washington, DC: Government Printing Office, 1954

Chapple, Joe Mitchell. *"We'll Stick to the Finish!"* Boston: Chapple, 1918.

Chisolm, Julian John. *A Manual of Military Surgery for the Surgeons in the Confederate States Army*. Richmond, VA: West & Johnston, 1862. 2nd ed. microform, Hatcher Library, University of Michigan.

Clarke, Ida Clyde. *American Women and the World War*. New York: Appleton, 1918.

Clay, Cassius Marcellus. *The Life of Cassius Marcellus Clay*. Cincinatti: J. Fletcher Brennan & Co., 1886. http://www.books.google.com.

Cobb, Josiah. *A Green Hand's First Cruise*. Boston: Otis, Broaders, 1841. http://www.archive.org/details/greenhandsfirstc02cobb.

Cogliano, Francis D. *American Maritime Prisoners in the Revolutionary War: The Captivity of William Russell*. Annapolis, MD: Naval Institute Press, 2001.

Commissary School U.S. Naval Training Station. *U.S. Navy Cook-Book*, 2nd ed. Annapolis: U.S. Naval Institute, 1920.

Cooke, James J. *Chewing Gum, Candy Bars, and Beer: The Army PX in World War II*. Columbia: University of Missouri Press, 2009.

Cowing, Kemper F. *Dear Folks at Home—*. Courtney Ryley Cooper, ed. New York: Houghton Mifflin, 1919.

Crocker, Betty. *Your Share*. Minneapolis: General Mills, 1943.

Crowell, Benedict. *America's Munitions 1917–1918*. Washington, DC: Government Printing Office, 1919. http://www.books.google.com.

Custer, Elizabeth B. *Following the Guidon*. New York: Harper & Brothers, 1890. http://www.books.google.com.

_____. *Tenting on the Plains*. New York: Webster, 1893. http://www.archive.org/details/tentingonplainso00cust.

Cutbush, Edward. *Observations of the Means of Preserving the Health of Soldiers and Sailors*. Philadelphia: Dobson, 1808.

Dandridge, Danske. *American Prisoners of the Revolution*. 1910. Reprint, Charleston, SC: BiblioBazaar, 2006.

Daniels, Josephus. *Our Navy at War*. New York: Doran, 1922.

Dann, John C. ed., *The Revolution Remembered: Eye-witness Accounts of the War for Independence*. Chicago: University of Chicago Press, 1980.

Davis, William C. *A Taste for War: A Culinary History of the Blue and the Gray*. Mechanicsburg, PA: Stackpole Books, 2003.

Deitrick, L.L., et al. *Manual for Army Bakers*. Washington, DC: Government Printing Office, 1916.

_____. *Manual for Army Cooks*. Washington, DC: Government Printing Office, 1916.

Dennett, Carl P. *Prisoners of the Great War*. Boston: Houghton Mifflin, 1919.

Department of the Navy. *The Cook Book of the United States Navy*. Washington, DC: Government Printing Office, 1927.

de Trobriand, Philippe Regis Denis de Keredern. *Army Life in Dakota: Selection from the Journal of Philippe Regis Denis de Keredern de Trobriand*. Milton Quaife, ed. George Francis Will, trans. Chicago: Lakeside Press, 1941. http://www.questia.com/reader/printPaginator/111.

Dougherty, Michael. *Prison Diary of Michael Dougherty, Late Co. B, 13th., Pa., Cavalry*. Bristol, PA: Dougherty, 1908.

Dring, Thomas. *Recollections of the Jersey Prison-ship*. Albert G. Greene, ed. Providence, RI: H.H. Brown, 1829. http://www.archive.org/details/jerseyprisonship00drinrich.

Editors of Time-Life Books. *The Blockade: Runners and Raiders*. Alexandria, VA: Time-Life Books, 1983.

Edwards, Frank S. *A Campaign in New Mexico with Colonel Doniphan*. Albuquerque: University of New Mexico Press, 1996.

Elliott, Richard Smith. *The Mexican War Correspondence of Richard Smith Elliott*. Mark L. Gardner and Marc Simmons, eds. Norman: University of Oklahoma Press, 1997.

Fantina, Robert. *Desertions and the American Soldier, 1776–2006*. New York: Algora, 2006.

Forsyth, George A. *The Story of a Soldier*. New York: Appleton, 1900. http://www.books.google.com.

Fowler, H.C. *Recipes out of Bilibid*. Dorothy Wagner, comp. New York: Cornwall Press, 1946.

Fox, Ebenezer. *The Adventures of Ebenezer Fox in the Revolutionary War*. Boston: Fox, 1847. Reprint, Whitefish, MT: Kessinger, 2008.

Frazer, Robert W. *Forts and Supplies: The Role of the Army in the Economy of the Southwest, 1846–1861*. Albuquerque: University of New Mexico Press, 1983.

Freeman, N.N. *A Soldier in the Philippines*. New York: Neely, 1901. http://www.archive.org/details/soldierinphilipp00freerich.

Frigidaire Division. *Wartime Suggestions*. Dayton, OH: General Motors, 1943.

Frost, John. *Pictorial History of Mexico and the Mexican War*. William Croome, illus. Philadelphia: Charles DeSilver; Claxton, Remsen and Haffelfinger; J.B. Lippincott, 1871.

Furber, George C. *The Twelve Month Volunteer; or, Journal of a Private in the Tennessee Regiment of*

Cavalry, in the Campaign in Mexico, 1846–1847. Cincinnati: James, 1850. http://www.books.google.com.

Furer, Julius Augustus. *Administration of the Navy Department in World War II.* Washington, DC: Government Printing Office, 1959. HyperWar Foundation. www.ibiblio.org/hyperwar.

Gauvreau, Charles F. *Reminiscences of the Spanish-American War in Cuba and the Philippines.* Rouses Point, NY: Authors, 1915. http://www.archive.org/details/reminiscencesofs00gauviala.

Gibson, Josephine. *Wartime Canning and Cooking Book.* New York: Bedford, 1943.

Goodrich, Frank B. *The Tribute Book.* New York: Derby and Miller, 1865.

Graves, Donald, ed. *Soldiers of 1814: American Enlisted Men's Memoirs of the Niagara Campaign.* Youngstown, NY: Old Fort Niagara Association, 1995.

Greene, Bob. *Once Upon a Town.* New York: Morrow, 2002.

Greenman, Jeremiah. *Diary of a Common Soldier in the American Revolution, 1775–1783.* Robert C. Bray and Paul E. Bushnell, eds. DeKalb: Northern Illinois University Press, 1986.

Haberstroh, Jack. *Swabby: World War II Enlisted Sailors Tell It Like It Was!* Bowie, MD: Heritage Books, 2003.

Handy, Ned, and Kemp Battle. *The Flame Keepers.* New York: Hyperion, 2004.

Hayes, Thomas, ed. A. B. Feuer. *Bilibid Diary.* Hamden, CT: Archon Books, 1987.

Heiser, Joseph M., Jr. *Vietnam Studies: Logistic Support.* Washington, DC: Department of the Army, 1991.

Henry, John Joseph. *Account of Arnold's Campaign Against Quebec.* Albany: Joel Munsell, 1877. Reprint, New York: Arno Press, 1968.

Henry, Robert Selph. *The Story of the Mexican War.* New York: Ungar, 1950.

Herbert, Charles. *A Relic of the Revolution.* Boston: Peirce, 1847. Reprint, New York: Arno Press, 1968.

Hobson, Richmond Pearson. *The Sinking of the Merrimac.* New York: Century, 1899. http://www.archive.org/details/sinkingmerrimac00hobsrich.

Holbrook, L.R. *Straight Army Ration and Baking Bread.* Kansas City: Hudson, 1905.

_____. *The Army Baker.* Fort Riley, KS: Mounted Service School Press, 1908.

Horsford, E.N. *Horsford's The Army Ration of 1864.* New York: Van Nostrand, 1864. Reprint, Quartermaster Food & Container Institute for the Armed Forces, U.S. Army, Chicago, 1964.

Huie, William Bradford. *Can Do! The Story of the Seabees.* New York: Dutton, 1944. Annapolis, MD: Naval Institute Press, 1997.

Hunter, Alva Folsom. *A Year on a Monitor and the Destruction of Fort Sumter.* Craig L. Symonds, ed. Columbia: University of South Carolina Press, 1987.

Husband, Joseph. *A Year in the Navy.* Boston: Houghton Mifflin, 1919.

Jones, George. *Sketches of a Naval Life with Notices of Men, Manners, and Scenery on the Shores of the Mediterranean.* New Haven, CT: Hezekiah Howe, 1829. Reprint, Whitefish, MT: Kessinger, 2007.

Keeler, William. *Letters of Paymaster William Frederick Keeler, U.S. Navy.* Robert W. Daly, ed. Annapolis, MD: United States Naval Institute, 1968.

Kenly, John R. *Memoirs of a Maryland Volunteer.* Philadelphia: Lippincott, 1873. http://www.archive.org/details/memoirsamarylan00kenlgoog.

Kilburn, C.L. *Notes on Preparing Stores for the United States Army.* Cincinnati: Webb, 1863.

Killbane, Richard E. *Circle the Wagons: The History of U.S. Army Convoy Security,* Fort Leavenworth, KS: Combat Studies Institute Press, 2005.

King, Ernest J. *U.S. Navy at War 1941–45 Official Reports to the Secretary of the Navy.* Washington: Unites States Navy Department, 1946.

Koehler, Franz A. *Coffee for the Armed Forces: Military Development and Conversion to Industry Supply.* Quartermaster Historical Studies, Series II, No. 5, Historical Branch Office of the Quartermaster General. Washington, DC: 1958.

_____. *Special Rations for the Armed Forces, 1946–53.* Quartermaster Historical Studies, Series II, No. 6, Historical Branch Office of the Quartermaster General. Washington, DC, 1958.

Kohr, Herbert Omando. *Around the World with Uncle Sam; or, Six Years in the United States Army.* Akron, OH: Commercial, 1907. http://www.archive.org/details/aroundtheworld00kohriala.

Korson, George. *At His Side: The Story of the American Red Cross Overseas in World War II.* New York: Coward-McCann, 1945.

Lawton, Eba Anderson. *An Artillery Officer in the Mexican War: Letters of Robert Anderson.* New York: G.P. Putnam's Sons, 1911.

Lindley, Harlow, ed. *Fort Meigs and the War of 1812.* Columbus: Ohio Historical Society, 1975.

Livermore, Mary A. *My Story of the War.* Hartford: Worthington, 1889.

Lowe, Percival G. *Five Years a Dragoon.* Norman: University of Oklahoma Press, 1991.

Luecke, Barbara K. *Feeding the Frontier Army.* Eagan, MN: Grenadier, 1990.

Marolda, Edward J. *The U.S. Navy in the Korean War.* Annapolis, MD: Naval Institute Press, 2007.

_____. *The U.S. Navy in the Vietnam War: An Illustrated History.* Washington, DC: Brassey's, 2002.

Marshall, C.G. *Baking Manual for the Army Cook.* Chicago: National Live Stock and Meat Board, 1943.

Martin, Joseph Plumb. *Private Yankee Doodle.* George E. Scheer, ed. Boston: Little, Brown, 1962. Reprint, Fort Washington, PA: Eastern National, 2006.

Matthews, William, and Dixon Wecter. *Our Soldiers Speak.* Boston: Little, Brown, 1943.

Mayer, Holly A. *Belonging to the Army.* Columbia: University of South Carolina Press, 1999.

McCaffrey, James M. *The Mexican War Letters of Lieutenant Theodore Laidley.* Denton: University of North Texas Press, 1997.

McCarthy, Carlton. *Detailed Minutiae of Soldier Life in the Army of Northern Virginia, 1861–1865*. Richmond: McCarthy, 1882. Reprint, Alexandria, VA: Time-Life Books, 1982.

McConnell, H.H. *Five Years a Cavalryman: or Sketches of Regular Army Life on the Texas Frontier*. Jacksboro, TX: Rogers, 1880. http://www.archive.org/details/fiveyearsacaval100mccogoog.

McElroy, John. *Andersonville: A Story of Rebel Military Prisons*. Washington, DC: National Tribune, 1899.

McIlhenny Company. *The Unofficial MRE Recipe Booklet*. Mort Walker, illus. Avery Island, LA: McIlhenny, 1984.

McKim, Randolph H. *A Soldier's Recollections: Leaves from the Diary of a Young Confederate*. New York: Longmans, Green, 1910.

Mead, Gary. *The Doughboys: America and the First World War*. Woodstock, NY: Overlook Press, 2000.

Melville, Herman. *White-Jacket, or The World in a Man-of-War*. New York: Library of America, 1983.

Merrill, James. *The Rebel Shore: The Story of Union Sea Power in the Civil War*. Boston: Little, Brown, 1957.

Meyers, Augustus. *Ten Years in the Ranks of the United States Army*. New York: Stirling Press, 1914. http://archive.org/details/tenyearsinranksu00meyerich.

Michno, Gregory F. *Death on the Hellships: Prisoners at Sea in the Pacific War*. Annapolis, MD: Naval Institute Press, 2001.

Miley, John D. *In Cuba with Shafter*. New York: Charles Scribner's Sons, 1899. http://books.google.com.

Miller, Francis Trevelyan, ed. *The Photographic History of the Civil War*. Vols. 7 and 8. New York: Review of Reviews, 1912.

Moore, William E., and James C. Russell. *U.S. Official Pictures of the World War Showing America's Participation*. Washington, DC: Pictorial Bureau, 1920.

Morison, Samuel Eliot. *John Paul Jones: A Sailor's Biography*. Boston: Northeastern University Press, 1985.

Moss, Lemuel. *Annals of the United States Christian Commission*. Lippincott, 1868.

Mulford, Ami Frank. *Fighting Indians in the 7th United States Cavalry*. Corning, NY: Mulford, 1879. http://www.archive.org/details/custersfavregime00mulfrich.

Nightingale, Florence. *Directions for Cooking by Troops, in Camp and Hospital; Prepared for the Army of Virginia, and Published by Order of the Surgeon General, with Essays on "Taking Food." And "What Food" by Florence Nightingale. Recipe Collection by Alex Soyer*. Richmond, VA: Randolph, 1861. Hatcher Library, University of Michigan, microform.

Nordhoff, Chas. *Man-of-War Life: A Boy's Experience in the United States Navy, During a Voyage Around the Word, in a Ship of the Line*. New York: Dodd, Mead, 1855. Reprint, Annapolis, MD: Naval Institute Press, 1985.

120 Wartime Meat Recipes. American Meat Institute.

Pack, Charles Lathrop. *The War Garden Victorious*. Philadelphia: Lippincott, 1919.

Paullin, Charles Oscar. *Paullin's History of Naval Administration, 1775–1911*. Annapolis, MD: U.S. Naval Institute, 1968.

Paymaster General. *General Mess Manual and Cookbook*. Washington, DC: Government Printing Office, 1902. Naval Historical Center, Navy Department Library http://www.history.navy.mil/library/online/genmessmanual.htm.

_____. *General Mess Manual and Cookbook*. Washington, DC: Government Printing Office, 1904. Reprint, Whitefish, MT: Kessinger, 2009.

Pember, Phoebe Yates. *A Southern Woman's Story*. Bell Irvin Wiley, ed. Jackson, TN: McCowat-Mercer Press, 1959.

Pendergast, Mark. *Uncommon Ground: The History of Coffee and How It Transformed Our World*. New York: Basic Books, 1999.

Peters, Richard A., and Xiabing Li. *Voices from the Korean War: Personal Stories of American, Korean, and Chinese Soldiers*. Lexington: University of Kentucky Press, 2004.

Philadelphia War History Committee. *Philadelphia in the World War, 1914–1919*. New York: Wynkoop-Hallenbeck, 1922.

Porter, David. *Bound for Battle: The Cruise of the United States Frigate* Essex *in the War of 1812 as told by Captain David Porter*. Betty Shepherd, ed. New York: Harcourt, Brace & World, 1967.

Post, Charles Johnson. *The Little War of Private Post: The Spanish-American War Seen up Close*. Lincoln: University of Nebraska Press, 1999. http://www.questia.com.

Prucha, Francis Paul, ed. *Army Life on the Western Frontier: Selections from the Official Reports Made Between 1826 and 1845 by Colonel George Croghan*. Norman: University of Oklahoma Press, 1958

Ransom, John L. *Andersonville Diary*. Philadelphia: Douglass Brothers, 1883. http://www.archive.org/details/andersonvilledi00ransgoog.

Richardson, William H. *Journal of William H. Richardson, A Private Soldier in the Campaign of New and Old Mexico*. Baltimore: Woods, 1848. http://www.archive.org/details/newandoldmexico00richrich.

Rickey, Don, Jr. *Forty Miles a Day on Beans and Hay*. Norman: University of Oklahoma Press, 1963.

Rifkind, Herbert R. *Fresh Foods for the Armed Forces*. Quartermaster Corps Historical Studies No. 20. Washington, DC: Government Printing Office, 1951.

Ringle, Dennis J. *Life in Mr. Lincoln's Navy*. Annapolis, MD: Naval Institute Press, 1998.

Risch, Erna. *Quartermaster Support of the Army, 1775–1939*. Washington, DC: Center of Military History, United States Army, 1989.

_____. *Supplying Washington's Army*. Washington, DC: Center for Military History United States Army, 1981.

_____, and Chester L. Kieffer. *United States Army in World War II — The Technical Services: The Quartermaster Corps: Organization, Supply, and Serv-*

ices. Vols. 1 and 2. Washington, DC: Office of the Chief of Military History, Department of the Army, 1955.

Roach, Alva C. *The Prisoner of War, and How Treated.* Indianapolis: Railroad City Publishing House, 1865. http://www.archive.org/details/prisonerof war00roacrich.

Roberts, Kenneth L. *March to Quebec: Journals of the Members of Arnold's Expedition.* New York: Doubleday, Doran, 1938.

Roe, Frances M. A. *Army Letters From an Officer's Wife.* New York: Appleton, 1909. http://www. archive.org/details/armylettersfrom00roegoog.

Ross, William F., and Charles R. Romanus. *The Quartermaster Corps: Operations in the War Against Germany.* Washington, DC: Center of Military History, United States Army, 2004.

Sanderson, James M. *Camp Fires and Camp Cooking: or, Culinary Hints for the Soldier.* Washington, DC: Government Printing Office, 1862.

School for Cooks and Bakers, Newport, RI. *U.S. Navy Cook-Book.* Annapolis, MD: U.S. Naval Institute, 1908.

Schubert, Frank N., and Theresa L. Kraus, eds. *The Whirlwind War: The United States Army in Operations Desert Shield and Desert Storm.* Washington, DC: Center of Military History, 1995.

Scribner, Benjamin Franklin. *Camp Life of a Volunteer: A Campaign in Mexico; or, A Glimpse at Life in Camp by "One Who Has Seen the Elephant."* Philadelphia: Grigg, Elliot, 1847. http://www. books.google.com.

Settle, Raymond, W., ed. *The March of the Mounted Riflemen: The Journals of Major Osborne Cross and George Gibbs.* Lincoln: University of Nebraska Press, 1989.

Sharpe, Henry G. *The Quartermaster Corps in the Year 1917 in the World War.* New York: Century, 1921.

Simmons, Edwin Howard, and Joseph H. Alexander. *Through the Wheat: The U.S. Marines in World War I.* Annapolis, MD: Naval Institute Press, 2008.

Sherburne, Andrew. *Memoirs of Andrew Sherburne: A Pensioner of the Navy of the Revolution.* Providence, RI: Brown, 1831. http://www.archive.org/details/ sherburnememoirs00sherrich.

Sherman, W.T. *William Tecumseh Sherman: Memoirs of General W.T. Sherman.* New York: Library of America, 1990.

Smith, J.L., comp. *History of the 118th Pennsylvania Volunteers Corn Exchange Regiment.* Philadelphia: Smith, 1905.

Smythe, Mrs. A.T., Miss M.B. Poppenheim, and Mrs. Thomas Taylor, eds. *South Carolina Women in the Confederacy.* Columbia, SC: State, 1903.

Spiller, Harry. *American POWs in Korea.* Jefferson, NC: McFarland, 1998.

_____. *American POWs in World War II.* Jefferson, NC: McFarland, 2009.

Stauffer, Alvin P. *The Quartermaster Corps: Operations in the War Against Japan.* Washington, DC: Center of Military History, United States Army, 2004.

Stewart, Richard W., ed. *American Military History.* Vol. 1. *The United States Army and Forging of a Nation, 1775–1917.* Washington, DC: Center of Military History, United States Army, 2005.

_____, ed. *American Military History.* Vol. 2. *The United States Army in a Global Era, 1917–2003.* Washington, DC: Center of Military History, United States Army, 2005.

Submarine Research Center. *Submarine Cuisine.* Bangor, WA: Submarine Research Center, 2004.

Stiles, Henry Reed. *Letters from the Prisons and Prison-ships of the Revolution.* New York: Beadstreet & Son, 1854. http://www.archive.org/details/ lettersfrompriso00stil.

Stillé, Charles J. *History of the United States Sanitary Commission.* Philadelphia: Lippincott, 1866.

Summerhayes, Martha. *Vanished Arizona.* 2nd ed. Salem, MA: Salem Press, 1911, http://books.google. com.

Supply Corps. *The Cook Book of the United States Navy.* Washington, DC: Government Printing Office, 1932, 1940.

Survivor's Association. *History of the 118th Pennsylvania Volunteers Corn Exchange Regiment.* Philadelphia: Smith, 1905.

Taft, William Howard, Frederick Harris, et al., ed. *Service with Fighting Men.* Vols. 1 and 2. New York: Association Press, 1922.

Thomas, Shipley. *The History of the A.E.F.* New York: Doran, 1920. http://www.googlebooks.com.

Toney, Marcus B. *The Privations of a Private.* Nashville: Publishing House of the M.E. Church, South, 1907.

Trostel, Scott D. *Angels at the Station.* Fletcher, OH: Cam-Tech, 2008.

Ukers, William H. *All About Coffee.* New York: Tea and Coffee Trade Journal, 1922.

Underwood, J.L. *The Women of the Confederacy.* New York: Neale, 1906.

United States Army. *Recipes Used in the Cooking Schools, U.S. Army.* Washington, DC: Government Printing Office, 1906. http://www.archive.org/ details/recipesusedincoo00wash.

_____. *American Military History 1607–1958.* 3rd ed. ROTC. Washington, DC: Government Printing Office, 1997.

United States Food Administration. *Food and the War: A Textbook for College Classes.* New York: Houghton Mifflin, 1918.

_____. *Food Guide for War Service at Home.* New York: Charles Scribner's Sons, 1918.

_____. *United States Food Leaflet* (multiple volumes) Washington, DC: U.S. Food Administration, 1917.

_____. *War Economy in Food, with Suggestions and Recipes for Substitutions in the Planning of Meals.* Washington, DC: Government Printing Office, 1918. www.internetarchives.com.

_____, Division of Home Conservation. "Victory Breads." Washington, DC: Government Printing Office, 1918.

United States Navy. *U.S. Navy Cook-Book.* Annapo-

lis, MD, Commissary School, U.S. Naval Training
Station, Newport, RI: U.S. Naval Institute, 1920.
United States War Department. *The Army Cook*. TM
10-405. Washington, DC: United States Govern-
ment Printing Office, April 24, 1942.
_____. *Cooking Dehydrated Foods*. TM 10-406. Wash-
ington, DC: United States Government Printing
Office, 1943.
_____. *How to Feed an Army*. Washington, DC: Gov-
ernment Printing Office, 1901.
_____. *Inspection of Subsistence Supplies*. TM 10-210.
Washington, DC: United States Government Print-
ing Office, 1940.
_____. *Manual for Army Cooks*. Washington, DC:
Government Printing Office, 1896.
_____. *Mess Management and Training*. TM 10-205.
Washington, DC: United States Government
Printing Office, 1944.
Volo, Dorothy Denneen, and James M. Volo. *Daily
Life in Civil War America*. Santa Barbara, CA:
Greenwood Press, 1998.
*War Training Programs World War II: Naval Train-
ing Schools*. Vol. A8. Ames: Iowa State College,
1945.
Washington, George. *The Writings of George Washing-
ton*. 30 vols. John C. Fitzpatrick, ed. Washington,
DC: Government Printing Office, 1930–1939.
Waterhouse, Benjamin, and Amos G. Babcock. *A
Journal, of a Young Man of Massachusetts*. Boston:
Rowe & Hooper, 1816. http://www.archive.org/
details/journalofyoungma00waterich.
Welch, Spencer Glasgow. *A Confederate Surgeon's Let-
ters to his Wife*. Marietta, GA: Continental Book,
1954.
Westinghouse. *Meal Planning Guide*. Mansfield, OH:
Home Economics Institute, Westinghouse Electric
& Manufacturing, November 1943.
Westover, John G. *Combat Support in Korea*. "Ra-
tions in Korea," from an oral report Major
Lawrence Dobson, observer for the Quartermaster
General. CMH Publication 22-1, Facsimile Re-
print, 1990. Washington, DC: Center of Military
History, United States Army.
White, S.W. *History of the American Troops During
the Late War*. Rochester, NY: Humphrey, 1896.
http://www.archive.org/details/amertroopslate00
whitrich.
White, Trumbull. *Pictorial History of Our War with
Spain for Cuba's Freedom*. Chicago: Freedom, 1898.
Wiley, Bell Irvin. *The Life of Billy Yank*. Baton Rouge:
Louisiana State University Press, 1994.
_____. *The Life of Johnny Reb*. Baton Rouge: Louisi-
ana State University Press, 1993.
_____. *The Plain People of the Confederacy*. Colum-
bia: University of South Carolina Press, 2000.
Wilson, Frederick T. *A Sailor's Log, Water-Tender*.
James R. Reckner, ed. Kent, OH: Kent State Uni-
versity Press, 2004.
Wilson, Mary A. *Mrs. Wilson's Cook Book*, Philadel-
phia: Lippincott, 1918.
Winders, Richard Bruce. *Polk's Army: The American*

Military Experience in the Mexican War. College
Station: Texas A & M University Press, 1997.
Wines, E.C. *Two Years and a Half in the Navy: or,
Journal of a Cruise in the Mediterranean and Lev-
ant on Board of the U.S. Frigate Constellation*.
Philadelphia: Carey & Lea, 1832. Reprint, White-
fish, MT: Kessinger, 2007.
Winkler, Allan M. *Home Front U.S.A.: America dur-
ing World War II*. Wheeling, IL: Harlan Davidson,
2000.
Wittenmyer, Annie. *Special Diet Kitchens in Military
Hospitals*. Mattituck, NY: United States Christian
Commission, 1864. Reprint, Bryan, TX: Carrol,
1983.

Government Documents

American State Papers. http://memory.loc.gov/
ammem/amlaw/lwsp.html.
Annals of Congress. http://memory.loc.gov/ammem/
amlaw/lwac.html.
Armed Forces Food and Container Institute. *Operational Rations, Rations Supplements, and Food Packets Used by the Armed Forces*. Chicago: Armed
Forces Food and Container Institute, November
1950.
Dodge, Grenville M., James A. Sexton, and Charles
Denby. *Report of the Commission Appointed by the
President to Investigate the Conduct of the War Department in the War with Spain*. Washington: Government Printing Office, 1899. http://www.books.
google.com.
Journals of the Continental Congress, 1774–1789. Edited by Worthington C. Ford, et al. Washington,
DC: Government Printing Office, 1904–37.
http://memory.loc.gov/ammem/amlaw/lwjc.
html.
Ketcham, Sally Johnson. *The Bake House, Fort Scott,
Kansas: Furnishing Plan*. Unpublished manuscript
for National Park Service, 1979.
"Navy Regulations, 1814." Naval Historical Center.
http://www.history.navy.mil/faqs/faq59-1.htm.
Official Records of the Union and Confederate
Navies. http://digital.library.cornell.edu/m/moa
war/ofre.html.
Peltz, Eric, et al. "Sustainment of Army Forces in Op-
eration Iraqi Freedom." Rand, 2005.
Quartermaster Corps School. *Operations of the Quar-
termaster Corps, U.S. Army during the World War*.
Monograph no. 9. Philadelphia: Quartermaster
Corps School, Schuylkill Arsenal, 1929. www.
carlisle.army.mil/ahec/index.cfm.
Statutes at Large. http://memory.loc.gov/ammem/
amlaw/lwsl.html.
United States Department of Defense. *Operational
Rations Current and Future*. Natick, MA: U.S.
Army Natick Laboratories, 1963.
_____. *Operational Rations Current and Future of the
Department of Defense*. Natick, MA: U.S. Army
Natick Laboratories, June 1970.
_____. *Operational Rations Current and Future of the*

Department of Defense. Natick, MA: U.S. Army Natick Research and Development Laboratories, January 1983.

_____. *Operational Rations Current and Future of the Department of Defense,* Natick Pam 30-25, 3rd ed, Natick, MA: U.S. Army Soldier Systems Command Natick Research, Development and Engineering Center, 1997.

_____. *Operational Rations of the Department of Defense,* Natick Pam. 30-25, 4th ed. Natick, MA: U.S. Army Natick Research and Development Laboratories, 2000.

_____. *Operational Rations of the Department of Defense,* Natick Pam. 30-25, 5th ed. Natick, MA: U.S. Army Soldier Center, April 2002.

_____. *Operational Rations of the Department of Defense,* Natick Pam. 30-25, 6th ed. Natick, MA: U.S. Army Soldier Center, April 2004.

_____. *Operational Rations of the Department of Defense,* Natick Pam 30-25, 8th ed. Natick, MA: U.S. Army Natick Research, Development, and Engineering Center, April 2009.

United States War Department. *Annual Reports, 1899.* Vol. 1. "Annual Report of the Surgeon General." Washington: Government Printing Office, 1899.

_____. *Annual Reports, 1902,* vol. 1 "Report of the Commissary General." Washington: Government Printing Office, 1903.

_____. *Annual Reports, 1918,* vol. 1. "Report of Quartermaster General." Washington: Government Printing Office, 1919.

_____. *Annual Reports, 1920.* Vol. 1, "Report of the Quartermaster General." Washington: Government Printing Office, 1920.

_____. *Annual Reports of the War Department.* Washington, DC: Government Printing Office, 1900.

_____. *Food Furnished by Subsistence Department to Troops During Spanish-American War: Record of a Court of Inquiry.* Washington, DC: Government Printing Office, 1900. http://www.google.books.com.

_____. *General Orders, 1890.* GO 78, 25 July 1890.

_____. *General Regulations for Army of the United States, 1841.* Washington: Gideon, 1841.

_____. *Historical Report of the Chief Engineer, American Expeditionary Forces.* Washington, DC: Government Printing Office, 1919.

_____. *Regulations for the Army of the United States, 1901.* Washington: Government Printing Office, 1901.

_____. *Revised Regulations for the Army of the United States, 1861.* Philadelphia: Brown, 1861.

_____. *The Soldier and His Food,* Washington: United States Government Printing Office, 1942.

_____, Quartermaster General's Office. *Outline Description of U.S. Military Posts and Stations in the Year 1871.* Washington: Government Printing Office, 1872.

U.S. Serial Set. http://memory.loc.gov/ammem/amlaw/lwss.html.

Collections

Brady, Robert K. Papers. Western Historical Manuscript Collection — Columbia. University of Missouri, Columbia.

Hansen, Gordon L. Papers. William L. Clements Library, University of Michigan, Ann Arbor.

Highley, Lyndell Thomasson Papers. Western Historical Manuscript Collection — Columbia. University of Missouri, Columbia.

Hook, Keith Burlingan Papers. William L. Clements Library, University of Michigan, Ann Arbor.

Huber, Robert L. Papers. Western Historical Manuscript Collection — Columbia. University of Missouri, Columbia.

Johnson, Reginald J. Collection, William L. Clements Library. University of Michigan, Ann Arbor.

Lafferty, Frederick Papers, William L. Clements Library, University of Michigan, Ann Arbor.

Schoff Civil War Collection. William L. Clements Library. University of Michigan, Ann Arbor.

Veterans History Project, American Folklife Center, Library of Congress.

Westover, John G. Papers. Western Historical Manuscript Collection-Columbia. University of Missouri, Columbia.

Van Winkle, Edward Collection. William L. Clements Library. University of Michigan, Ann Arbor.

Web Sites

American Red Cross. "The American Red Cross in the Spanish-American War." http://www.redcross.org/museum/history/spanishAmWar.asp.

_____. "World War 1 Accomplishments of the American Red Cross." http://www.redcross.org/museum/history/wwla.asp.

Arkansas Inland Maritime Museum. "Maurice Barksdale — Ship's Cook, 1960–1963. Oral History Interview." http://www.aimm.museum/oral.asp.

Civil War Guide Project. Ohio Historical Society. Letter. September 3, 1861. http://www.ohiohistory.org/onlinedoc/civilwar/sa0147/06_07.cfm.

Cleaves, Ward B. "Food Service Program." *Quartermaster Review,* July-August 1945. http://www.qmmuseum.lee.army.mil/WWII/food_service_program.htm.

Dahl, Irwin A. "QM Distribution System in Korea." *The Quartermaster Review,* January-February 1954. U.S. Quartermaster Foundation. http://www.qmmuseum.lee.army.mil/korea/Distro_Korea.htm.

Dartmoor Prison Museum and Visitor Centre. "Dartmoor Prison History." http://www.dartmoorprison.co.uk/history_of_dartmoor_prison.html.

Defense Commissary Agency. "History of U.S. Military Commissaries." http://www.commissaries.com/history.cfm.

Defense Logistics Agency. Defense Supply Center Philadelphia. "DSCP Subsistence History." http://www.dscp.dla.mil/subs/aboutsubs/history.asp.

_____. "Subsistence Supply Chain." http://www.dscp. dla.mil/sbo/subsistence.asp.

Doriot, Colonel G.F., "Subsistence Research Laboratory." U.S. Army Quartermaster Foundation. *The Quartermaster Review*, March-April 1944. http:// www.qmfound.com/sublab.htm.

Dortch, Debbie. "Finalists Identified for Best Navy Mess Award." U.S. Navy. http://www.navy.mil/ search/display.asp?story_id=48884.

Doughboy Center, The Great War Society. "Doughnut! The Official Story." http://www.worldwar1. com/dbc/doughnut.htm.

_____. "The History of the Knights of Columbus in World War I." http://www.worldwar1.com/dbc/ knightsc.htm.

_____. "The History of the Salvation Army in World War I." http://www.worldwar1.com/dbc/salvhist. htm.

_____. "The History of the YMCA in World War I." http://www.worldwar1.com/dbc/ymca.htm.

Ferris State University Library. "An Anonymous War of 1812 Diary." http://library.ferris.edu/~cochranr/ 1812/nov12.htm.

Fort Scott National Historic Site. National Park Service. "Cooking Overview." http://www.nps.gov/ fosc/forteachers/cookhistory.htm.

Foster, Renita. "The Best Army Invention Ever." U.S. Army Public Affairs. http://www.army.mil/-news/ 2009/08/11/25736-the-best-army-invention-ever.

Hershey Community Archives. "Ration D Bars." http://www.hersheyarchives.org/essay/printable. aspx?EssayId=26.

Heydt, Bruce. "Spam Again." America in World War II. http://www.americainwwii.com/stories/spam again.html.

Hilliard, Mark. "Biscuits, Bugs, & Broadsides." 1812 U.S. Marines & Navy Progressive Campaign Oriented Living Historians. http://www.1812usmarines. org/Biscuits, %20Bugs, %20&%20Broadside.doc.

Hoffman, William. "Meet Monsieur Cholesterol." *Update*, Winter 1979, University of Minnesota. http://www.mbbnet.umn.edu/hoff/hoff_ak.html.

Hormel Foods. "Fact Sheet: SPAM Family of Products—World War II." http://www.hormelfoods. com/newsroom/brandinfo/SPAMFamilyOfProd uctsWWIIFS.aspx.

HyperWar: The U.S. Navy in World War II. "U.S. Naval Activities, World War II, by State." http:// www.ibiblio.org/hyperwar/U.S.N/ref/?U.S.N-Act/index.html.

Kansas Historical Society. "Cool Things: Coleman Portable Stove." http://www.kshs.org/cool2/cole manstove.htm.

Kowalski, Eva. "Navy's Culinary Specialist 'A' School Relocates to Great Lakes" http://www.navy.mil/search/print.asp?story_id=2315 6&imagetype=1&page=1.

Law Offices of Mark B. Tackitt and Eviction Services.com. "Flying Dutchman,

Malin, Charles A. "Ratings and the Evolution of Jobs in the U.S. Military." Naval History & Heritage Command. http://www.history.navy.mil/faqs/faq 78-1.htm.

McCarley, J. Britt. "Feeding Billy Yank: Union Rations between 1861 and 1865."

Quartermaster Professional Bulletin. December 1988. U.S. Army Quartermaster Foundation. http:// www.qmfound.com/feeding_billy_yank.htm.

McSherry, Patrick. "The Sinking of U.S. Navy Collier Merrimac." The Spanish-American War Centennial Website http://www.spanamwar.com/merri mac.htm.

Military Sealift Command. "Fact Sheet Fast Combat Support Ships-T-A0E." http://www.msc.navy.mil/ factsheet/t-aoe.asp.

_____. "Naval Fleet Auxiliary Force." http://www. msc.navy.mil/pml.

_____. "Overview MSC History" http://www.msc. navy.mil/N00P/overview.asp?page=history.

Murphy, William. "Winning the West for the Nation." *National Tribune*, June 7, 1928. http://www. rootsweb.ancestry.com/~wysherid/forts/murhpy-6-7-28.htm.

National Archives and Records Administration. "Hoover Online! U.S. Food Administrator." http:// www.ecommcode.com/hoover/hooveronline/ hoover_bio/food.htm

National World War I Museum. "Candy, Coffee, and a Smile." http://www.theworldwar.org/s/110/new/ index.aspx?sid=110&gid=1&pgid=1063.

Naval Historical Center, Department of the Navy. "Korean War Underway Replenishment, July–December 1950." http://www.history.navy.mil/pho tos/events/kowar/log-sup/unrp50-1.htm.

_____. "Korean War Underway Replenishment." http://www.history.navy.mil/photos/events/kowar/ log-sup/unrp50-1.htm.

Naval History & Heritage Command. "American War and Military Operations Casualties: Lists and Statistics." http://www.history.navy.mil/Library/on line/american%20war%20casualty.htm.

_____. "Enlisted Ratings and Jobs in the U.S. Navy." http://www.history.navy.mil/faqs/faq78-1.htm.

_____. "Mars." http://www.history.navy.mil/danfs/ m5/mars-iii.htm.

_____. "Navy Birthday Information-13 October 1775." http://www.history.navy.mil/birthday. htm.

_____. "Niagara Falls." http://www.history.navy.mil/ danfs/n4/niagara_falls.htm.

_____. "Reestablishment of the Marine Corps." http://www.history.navy.mil/faqs/faq59-16.htm.

_____. "*Sacramento*." http://www.history.navy.mil/ danfs/s2/sacramento-iii.htm.

_____. "Trans-Pacific Logistics-Overview." http:// www.history.navy.mil/photos/events/kowar/ log-sup/pac-tran.htm.

_____. "U.S. Navy in Desert Shield/Desert Storm — Bullets, Bandages and Beans." http://www.history. navy.mil/wars/dstorm/ds4.htm.

_____. "Vietnam Service 1962–1973." http://www. history.navy.mil/faqs/stream/faq45-25.htm.

Ohio's War of 1812 Battlefield Museum. "Fort Meigs." http://www.fortmeigs.org/history.htm.

Pilgrim Hall Museum. "Thanksgiving Proclamations." http://www.pilgrimhall.org/thankpro.htm.

Pixley, Marshall J. "The Adams Express Company." Florida Reenactors Online. http://www.florida reenactorsonline.com/adamsexpress.htm.

Quad City Memory, Davenport Public Library Local History. "Annie Wittenmyer." http://www.qcmem ory.org/page/AnnieWittenmyer.aspx?nt=231.

Rees, John R. "'As many fireplaces as you have tents...' Earthen Camp Kitchens." http://www.revwar75. com/library/rees/kitchen.htm.

Reynolds Historical Library, University of Alabama. Birmingham. "Major Figures in Civil War Medicine: Julian John Chisholm." http://www.uab.edu/ reynolds/CivilWarMedFigs/Chisolm.htm.

Seabee Museum and Memorial Park. "Seabee History." http://www.seabeesmuseum.com/History.html.

Spanish-American War Centennial Website. "The Diary of Bertram Willard Edwards." http://www. spanamwar.com/Oregonedwardsdiary1.htm.

_____. "The Diary of George W. Robinson." http:// www.spanamwar.com/Oregondiary1.htm

Stauffer, Alvin P. "The Quartermaster's Department and the Mexican War." *Quartermaster Review*, May-June 1950, U.S. Quartermaster Foundation. http://www.qmfound.com/quartermaster_depart ment_mexican_war.htm.

Truxtun, Thomas. "A Short Account of the Several General Duties of Officers, of Ships of War." http://www.history.navy.mil/faqs/faq59-2.html.

U.S. Army Quartermaster Foundation. "A History of Rations Conference Notes, January 1949" http:// www.qmfound.com/history_of_rations.htm.

_____. "Rations." Conference Notes prepared by the Quartermaster School for the Quartermaster General, January 1949. http://www.qmfound.com/ history_of_rations.htm.

U.S. Army Veterinary Service. "U.S. Army Veterinary Corps History." http://www.veterinaryservice. army.mil/history.html.

U.S. Department of Veterans Affairs. "Former American Prisoners of War." http://www1.va.gov/vet data/docs/POWCY054-12-06jsmwrFINAL2.doc.

United States Merchant Marines. "War Shipping Administration." http://www.usmm.org/ww2.html.

U.S.O. "History of the U.S.O." http://www.uso.org/ whoweare/ourproudhistory.

U.S.S. Constellation CVA/CV-64 Association. "Constellation — A Stellar History." http://www.usscon stellation.org/constellation_history.html.

Wessels Living History Farm, York, NE. "Farming in the 1940s: Victory Gardens." http://www.livinghis toryfarm.org/farminginthe40s/crops_02.html.

Zinnen, Robert O. "City Point: The Tool That Gave General Grant Victory." U.S. Quartermaster Foundation, *Quartermaster Professional Bulletin*, Spring 1991. www.qmfound.com/citypt.htm.

Periodical Articles

Alspach, Rita, Susan D. Gagne, and Alice Meyer. "New and Improved: T-Ration and MRE Development." *Quartermaster Professional Bulletin*, December 1988, 8–9.

Anders, Steven. "Bundles from the Sky." *Quartermaster Professional Bulletin*, Autumn-Winter 1994, 42–45.

Baquer, Jeff. "Name Change of the Mess Management Specialist (S) Rating to Culinary Specialist (CS)." *The Navy Supply Corps Newsletter*, March-April 2004, 32.

Barbeau, Marcel. "Chef at Sea." *The Navy Supply Corps Newsletter*, March-April 2008, 27.

Barrett, Judy, and David C. Smith. "U.S. Women on the Home Front in World War II." *The Historian* 57, no. 2 (1994): 349+. http://www.questia.com/reader/ action/readchecked?docId=5000294832.

Bibbs, Derell M., et al. "Mercenary Logistics and Today's Military Operations." *Quartermaster Professional Bulletin*, Summer 1997, 33–35.

Blanchfield, Mary K. "Transportation Challenges in Afghanistan." *Army Logistician*, March-April 2005, 24–27.

Blanco, James A. "Subsistence Prime Vendor." *Quartermaster Professional Bulletin*, Autumn 1996, 32–33.

Brown, Susan Declercq, and Phyllis Rhodes. "DLA: Logistics Backbone of Iraqi Freedom." *Army Logistician*, July-August 2003, 6–7.

Burke, Curtis R. "Curtis R. Burke's Civil War Journal." Pamela J. Bennett, ed. *Indiana Magazine of History* 66, no. 2 (June 1970): 110–172.

_____. "Curtis R. Burke's Civil War Journal." Pamela J. Bennett, ed. *Indiana Magazine of History* 66, no. 4 (December 1970): 318–361.

_____. "Curtis R. Burke's Civil War Journal." Pamela J. Bennett, ed. *Indiana Magazine of History* 67, no. 2 (June 1971): 129–170.

Cancian, Mark. "Contractors: The New Element of Military Force Structure." *Parameters*, Autumn 2008, 61–77.

Cone, Anthony D. "Battery 'E' Goes to War: Extracts from the War Time Diary of First Sergeant Anthony D. Cone." *The Field Artillery Journal* 20, no. 6 (November-December 1930): 603–691.

_____. "Battery 'E' Goes to War: Extracts from the Wartime Diary of First Sergeant Anthony D. Cone." *The Field Artillery Journal* 21, no. 1 (January-February 1931): 34–49.

Cook, Corey A. "U.S.S Gonzales Mess Setting the Standard." *The Navy Supply Corps Newsletter*, January-February 2001, 27.

Crumpacker, J.W. "Supplying the Fleet for 150 Years." *U.S. Naval Institute Proceedings* 71, no. 6, whole no. 508, June 1945, 705–713.

Decker, Benton C., "The Consolidated Mess of the Crew of the U.S.S. Indiana." *U.S. Naval Institute Proceedings* 23, no. 3. whole no. 83 (1897): 463–573.

Dyer, George P. "The Modern General Mess." *U.S. Naval Institute Proceedings* 32, no. 2, whole no. 113 (June, 1906): 621–643.

Dyer, George. "The Ship's General Mess." *U.S. Naval Institute Proceedings* 39, no. 4, whole no. 148 (December 1913): 1589–1606.

"FISC Puget Sound's Navy Food Management Team Hosts Iron Chef Competition." *Navy Supply Corps Newsletter*, January-February 2006, 11–12.

Foster, E.D. "Cafeteria Afloat." *U.S. Naval Institute Proceedings* 63, no. 407 (January 1937): 19–27.

"History of the Navy Supply Corps." *Navy Supply Corps Newsletter* 33, no. 2 (February 1970): 12–17.

Jarvela, Benjamin. "Mess Decks Open — Ike Dishes Up First Meal on Board in Three Years." *Navy Supply Corps Newsletter*, July-August 2004, 19–20.

Keith, Carlos N. "Field Feeding in the 21st Century." *Army Logistician*, September-October 2001, 18–21.

Keller, Brian C. "Supporting the 21st Century Warrior." *Army Logistician*, January-February 1999, 133–137.

Kester, Wayne O. "Army Food Inspection." *Canadian Journal of Comparative Medicine* 2, no. 12 (December 1938): 301–305. http://www.ncbi.nlm.nih.gov/pmc/articles/PMC1702054.

Lindell, Frank. "Navy Food Service — Improving Quality of Life for Our Sailors." *The Navy Supply Corps Newsletter*, March-April 2000, 23–29.

"Logistics: Vegetable Run." *Time*. June 4, 1951. http://www.time.com/time/magazine/article/0,9171,858069,00.html.

"Low-Down on Chow-Down." *All Hands*, no. 375 (May 1948): 2–5.

Merrill, James M. "Men, Monotony, and Mouldy Beans—Life on Board Civil War Blockaders." *The American Neptune: A Quarterly Journal of Maritime History* 16, 49–59.

McDonnell, James J., and J. Ronald Novack. "Logistics Challenges in Support of Operation Enduring Freedom." *Army Logistician*, September-October 2004, 9–13.

New York Times. "Training Cooks for the Navy." December 30, 1917.

Pavek, Michael K. "Feeding the Soldiers in Iraq." *Army Logistician*, January-February 2005, 17–19.

Prescott, Samuel C. "Dried Vegetables for Army Use." From the Section of Food and Nutrition, Division of Sanitation, Medial Department, United States Army, June 3, 1919. Reprint, American Physiological Society, http://ajplegacy.physiology.org/cgi/reprint/49/4/573.

Rees, John U. "Finding Water and Carrying Food During the War for Independence and the American Civil War." *Food History News* 10, no. 1, 2, 8–9.

_____. "Less Commonly Used Utensils, Eating Implements, and Officers' Cooking Equipment." *The Brigade Dispatch* 31, no. 2 (Summer 2001): 2–4.

http://www.revwar75.com/library/rees/biblio.htm.

_____. "Earthen Camp Kitchens, " *Food History News* 9, no. 2, 2, 8–9.

Seaman, Louis Livingston. "Observations in China and the Tropics on the Army Ration and the Post Exchange or Canteen." *Medical Record* 60, no. 1 (July 6, 1901): 1–4. http://books.google.com.

Sharpe, Henry G. "The Art of Supplying Armies in the Field as Exemplified during the Civil War." *Journal of the Military Science Institute*, January 1896, 45–95.

Sharpe, Norvelle W. "Salt Horse to Sirloin." *U.S. Naval Institute Proceedings* 80, no. 5, whole no. 615 (May 1954): 514–521.

Sigle, Patricia A. "BRAC and Quartermaster Reorganization." *Army Sustainment*, November-December 2009, 44–46.

Smart, Charles. "The Army Ration." *The New York Times*, December 10, 1899, p. 25.

"Smart Galley Steams Along." *The Warrior*, September-October 2005. http://www.natick.army.mil/about/pao/pubs/warrior/05/septoct/index.htm.

Skillman, J.H. "Eating Through the Years." *U.S. Naval Institute Proceedings*, March 1941, 361–367.

"U.S.S Taylor Takes DESRON 24 Bake Off." *Navy Supply Corps Newsletter*, November-December, 11.

Von Brinken, Friedrich A. "The Tokyo QM Depot." *The Quartermaster Review*, May-June 1954, reprinted in *Quartermaster Professional Bulletin*, Spring 2000, 10–13.

Wassilieff, Lisa. "Mobile Bay Sailors Get a New Taste of Navy Chow." *Navy Supply Corps Newsletter*, November-December 2004, 17–18.

Williams, Alex N. "Subsistence Supply in Korea." *The Quartermaster Review*, January-February 1953, reprinted in *Quartermaster Professional Bulletin*, Spring 2000, 32–37.

Witkowski, Terrence H. "World War II Poster Campaigns." *Journal of Advertising* 32, no. 1 (Spring 2003): 69–82. http://www.csulb.edu/~witko/ja.ww2postercampaigns.pdf.

Dissertations

Barboo, Samuel Harvard. "A Historical Review of the Hygiene of Shipboard Food Service in the United States Navy, 1775–1965." Ph.D. diss. University of California, Los Angeles.

Wells, Tom Henderson. "The Confederate Navy, A Study in Organization." Ph.D. diss. Emory University, 1963.

Interviews

Baker, Elmo (Mo), telephone interview, March 2, 2010.

Barksdale, Maurice, email interviews, October 29, 2009, October 26, 2009.

Carter, Bob, telephone interview, January 18, 2009.

Farmer, Everett, personal interview, January 15, 2010.

Galanti, Paul, e-mail interview, March 1, 2010.

Longone, Jan, e-mail communication, May 18, 2009.

Marmon, Michael S., e-mail interviews, October 30, 2009, January 8, 2010.

Mathis, Joseph S. e-mail interview, November 7, 2009.

Monroe, Bill, e-mail interview, January 17, 2010.

Nabors, Ray, written and personal interviews, September 14, 2008.

Orr, Bill, telephone interview, January 17, 2010.

Ringle, Dennis, phone and email communication, February 20, 2009.

Index

P-38 can opener 149, 150, 183
Pacific Ocean 30, 32, 44,168
Pacific, South and Southwest 159, 161, 167, 170
Pacific Theater 161, 163
Pack, Charles Lathrop 144, 145, 147
packages from home 57, 58, 141, 164, 168, 206
Pagonis, Lt. General William 198
Parachute Emergency Ration (bailout ration) 153
Parker, Colonel Alexander 22
parsnips 85
Pastores 173
Patrol Boat, River 207
Patterson, Nicholas 7
Paullin, Charles Oscar 108, 109
Pay Corps 105
Pay Department 43
paymasters 105, 110
Payne, Frederick R. 138
peaches 57, 62, 75, 77, 115, 141, 230
peanut butter 205
Pearl Harbor 179
pears 180
peas 15, 19, 21, 26, 29, 31, 36, 38, 44, 45, 55, 68, 69, 76, 79, 82, 85, 95, 96, 115, 132, 141, 165, 174, 223, 225, 228; field 75; English garden 75
Pelke, Marissa 199
pemmican 91, 150, 151
Pennsylvania 7
peppers 161
Pershing, General John J. 122
persimmons 56, 75
Petaluma, CA 190
USS *Petrof Bay* 178
Philadelphia 49, 64, 138, 157, 223
Philadelphia in the World War 137
Philadelphia War History Committee 137
Philippines 95, 96, 97, 98, 99, 100, 102, 103, 105, 108, 140, 161, 242
pickles 26, 36, 45, 58, 61, 69, 77, 115, 119, 165, 228
pies 57, 129, 135, 141, 166, 205, 207, 214, 230
pigeons 47, 57
pigs 30, 46, 47, 48, 167, 241; *see also* hogs
pineapple 42, 99, 113, 205
Pippett, Henry 58, 76
Pippin, Henry 55
Pittsburgh 61
Pixley, Marshall J. 58
plantain 30, 31, 42, 50, 99
Plantano 170
USS *Point Defiance* 205
Point Isabel 37
Polk, James K. 37
Polaris 173
Pontiac 173
pork 6, 18, 24, 26, 32, 36, 38, 39, 40, 41, 44, 49, 55, 60, 80 82, 83,

91, 95, 99, 143, 203, 223, 228, 239; salt 13, 17, 19, 20, 22, 25, 28, 29, 35, 36, 45, 47, 48, 49, 60, 68, 69, 87, 89, 92, 229, 230; ham 233; pork and beans 133
Porter, Captain David 26, 29, 30, 31, 32
Portugal 30, 161
Post, Charles 95, 97
post exchange 101, 129, 164
post fund 101
post gardens 84, 85
post trader 101
pot liquor 224
potato masher 134
potatoes 19, 20, 24, 25, 38, 47, 61, 77, 87, 88, 90, 92, 93, 95, 96, 98, 108, 113, 115, 117, 126, 131, 132, 141, 166, 174, 180, 207, 225, 226, 229, 234, 238, 242
poultry 154
Practical Instructions in Bread Making 87
Prairie du Chien 85
Preble, Commodore Edward 27, 28
Prescott 225
prison ships 222, 223, 225
Prisoners of the Great War 235
prisons 222
Procurement programs, joint Army-Navy 172
provision ships 170, 173, 174
provisions 12, 22, 30, 31, 32, 40, 45, 47, 49, 72, 79, 111, 113, 169, 170, 171, 205, 232
prunes 97, 115, 118
pudding 19, 20, 26, 27, 47, 65, 135, 205
Puerto Rico 97, 98, 102, 103, 105
Pullman Company 156
pulque 43, 100
pumpkin 13, 50, 241
punk 139
Pure Food and Drug Act 120
purser 33, 45, 47, 49
Purveyor of Public Supplies 27

Quaisi War 21, 27
Qualifications and General Instructions for Ships's Cook 175
Quantity Cookery 175
Quartermaster Corps 120, 125, 130, 193
Quartermaster Corps Subsistence School 132, 133, 148
Quartermaster Department 22, 35, 37, 41, 43, 82, 94, 99, 105
Quartermaster Food and Container Institute 181, 182, 184, 185, 187, 188
Quartermaster Museum 1, 4, 22, 36, 54, 57, 59, 95, 119, 165, 166
Quartermaster Research Facility 182
Quartermaster Subsistence

Research Laboratory 133, 149, 151, 152, 154, 155, 156, 181
Quebec 5, 15, 225
Quebec Campaign 7, 17
Qui Nhon 195
quinces 73

rabbits 40, 47, 194, 239
raccoons 57
radishes 85, 108, 133, 161
raisins 10, 45, 88
USS *Ranger* 146, 147, 206, 208, 210, 215
Ransom, John L. 233
ration cart 124
Ration, Cold Weather 185
ration supplements 189; Carbopack 189; Hooah Bar 189
rationing 162
rats 31, 32, 228, 241
rattlesnakes 91
USS *Razorback* 214, 215
Ready for Sea 67
The Rebel Shore: The Story of Union Sea Power in the Civil War 70
receiving ship 49
recipe cards 202; *see also* Armed Forces Recipe Card Service
Recipes Used in the Cooking Schools 119
Reckner, James R. 112
Red Cross packages 236, 237, 238
Reed's New Hampshire Regiment 11
Rees, John U. 10, 12, 13
refrigerated beef 103, 104, 105
refrigeration 162, 180
refrigeration plants 122
refrigerator ships 110, 169, 170, 173
Reina Mercedes 235
Remembered Prisoners of a Forgotten War 241
Rendels, Peter 166
reserve ration 118, 132
restaurant style messing 216
Revolutionary War 4
rice 4, 10, 19, 21, 26, 29, 36, 38, 40, 44, 45, 52, 69, 82, 83, 95, 96, 99, 101, 111, 115, 117, 228, 231, 232, 233, 235, 239, 241, 242
Richardson, William H. 38, 40, 41, 42, 43
Rickey, Don 86
Rifkind, Herbert 154
Ringle, Dennis 67, 71
Rio de Janeiro 50
Rio Grande 37, 38
Risch, Erna 5, 6, 7, 22
Roach, Alva C. 231, 232
Robinson, George W. 110, 111, 112
Roe, Francis M.A. 84, 86
Rogers, General 236
rolling field kitchen 123, 124, 126
Romanus, Charles F. 152, 159, 161
Roosevelt, Franklin 155, 164